Fifty years of communism in Russia

FIFTY YEARS OF COMMUNISM IN RUSSIA

HOOVER INSTITUTION PUBLICATION 77

A PUBLICATION OF THE HOOVER INSTITUTION
ON WAR, REVOLUTION AND PEACE

FIFTY YEARS OF COMMUNISM IN RUSSIA

---

edited with an introduction by

MILORAD M. DRACHKOVITCH

The Pennsylvania State University Press
University Park and London

Library of Congress Catalogue Card 68–8178
Printed in the United States of America

PREFACE

To mark the fiftieth anniversary of the Bolshevik coup d'état in Russia, the Hoover Institution on War, Revolution and Peace sponsored an international conference at Stanford University. For five days, October 9–13, 1967, thirty distinguished American and European scholars discussed the most important aspects of "Fifty Years of Communism in Russia"—the official theme of the conference. This volume contains the ten main papers read and discussed and the text of the closing address delivered by Professor Sidney Hook at a luncheon of the Commonwealth Club in San Francisco. Because of technical difficulties it was not possible to include the critical remarks made at the conference, but several of the contributors have modified their papers to take them into account. The editor wishes to express his gratitude to Mr. James McSherry of The Pennsylvania State University Press for his help in giving this volume its final form.

M. M. D.

April 25, 1968

CONTRIBUTORS

LEWIS S. FEUER is Professor of Sociology at the University of Toronto. From 1957 to 1966 he was Professor of Philosophy and Social Science at the University of California at Berkeley, and from 1957 to 1964 Chairman of the Social Science Integrated Course. An Exchange Scholar at the Institute of Philosophy of the Soviet Academy of Science in Moscow during the spring semester of 1963, he is the author of *Spinoza and the Rise of Liberalism* and *The Scientific Intellectual.*

RAYMOND L. GARTHOFF is currently Counselor for Political-Military Affairs in the United States Mission to N.A.T.O. He has recently been serving in the Department of State as Special Assistant for Communist Politico-Military Affairs, and concurrently on the faculty of the School for Advanced International Studies of The Johns Hopkins University. He is author of a number of works including *Soviet Military Policy* (1967), *Soviet Strategy in the Nuclear Age* (1958, revised ed. 1962), and *Soviet Military Doctrine* (1953).

MAX HAYWARD is a Fellow of St. Antony's College, Oxford. His recent publications include an edition of the poetry of Andrei Voznesensky, *Anti-Worlds,* and *On Trial, The Soviet State versus Abram Tertz and Nikolai Arzhak.*

JOHN N. HAZARD has been Professor of Public Law and a member of the staff of the Russian Institute at Columbia University since 1946. At the age of twenty-five he was sent to the Moscow Juridical Institute by the Institute of Current World Affairs in New York to begin a study of Soviet law. For thirty-four years he has continued this study, serving during the war as Deputy Director of the U.S.S.R. Branch of the Foreign Economic Administration and for a time as adviser on Soviet Law to the United States prosecutor preparing the indictment for the Nuremberg trials. His books include *Law and Social Change in the U.S.S.R., The Soviet System of Government, Settling Disputes in Soviet Society,* and, with Isaac Shapiro, *The Soviet Legal System.*

SIDNEY HOOK is Professor of Philosophy at New York University, a Fellow of the American Academy of Arts and Sciences, and a former President of the American Philosophical Association (Eastern Division). For many years he has been a close student of Marxism and communism and other philosophical movements. The first of his numerous works, *The Metaphysics of Pragmatism,* was published in 1927, and the most recent, *The Place of Religion in a Free Society,* in 1967.

JEAN LALOY, after working for a number of years for the French Ministry of Foreign Affairs, is presently Professor at the Institutes of Political Studies in Paris and Grenoble as well as at the National School of Administration (International Relations and History of the U.S.S.R.). Among his recent publications are *Entre Guerres et Paix, 1945–1965* (1966) and *Le socialisme de Lénine* (1967).

IVO J. LEDERER is Professor of History and Chairman of the Committee on Russian, East European, and Communist Studies at Stanford University. His publications include: (editor) *Russian Foreign Policy: Essays in Historical Perspective* (1962), and *Yugoslavia at the Paris Peace Conference: A Study in Frontier Making* (1963).

G. WARREN NUTTER is Paul Goodloe McIntire Professor of Economics and Chairman of the Department of Economics at the University of Virginia. Associated with the National Bureau of Economic Research and formerly on the faculty at Yale University, he is the author of *The Extent of Enterprise Monopoly in the United States* (1951), *Growth of Industrial Production in the Soviet Union* (1962), and various articles in professional journals.

LEONARD SCHAPIRO is Professor of Political Science with special reference to Russian studies at the London School of Economics, a Foreign Honorary Member of the American Academy of Arts and Sciences, and Chairman of the Editorial Board of *Government and Opposition.* Until 1955 he practiced at the bar. His works include *The Origin of the Communist Autocracy* (1955), *The Communist Party of the Soviet Union* (1960), and *Rationalism and Nationalism in Russian Nineteenth-Century Political Thought* (1967).

JOHN TURKEVICH has been a member of the Princeton faculty since 1936, holding at present the Eugene Higgins Chair in Chemistry. He was Acting Science Attache of the U. S. Embassy in Moscow in 1961 and Science Attache in 1962, with the rank of Counselor of Embassy. He has lectured at Moscow University, Leningrad University, and a number of institutes of the U.S.S.R. Academy of Sciences. He has written *Soviet Men of Science, Chemistry in the Soviet Union* and articles in the *Atlantic Monthly, Foreign Affairs,* and *The Saturday Review.* In organizing the study of scientific Russian, he published with his wife, Ludmilla Turkevich, a textbook on *Russian for the Scientist.*

BERTRAM D. WOLFE is a Research Fellow at the Hoover Institution on War, Revolution and Peace at Stanford University. His most recent academic appointment was as Distinguished Visiting Professor of Russian History at the University of California (Davis). Among his books are *Three Who Made a Revolution* (4th revised ed. 1964), *Marxism: One Hundred Years in the Life of a Doctrine* (1965), and *The Bridge and the Abyss: The Troubled Friendship of Maxim Gorky and V. I. Lenin* (1967). His works have been translated into sixteen languages.

MILORAD M. DRACHKOVITCH is a Senior Staff Member of the Hoover Institution and Lecturer in the Department of Political Science at Stanford University. He is the editor of three volumes of essays stemming from the Hoover Institution's 1964 conference on "One Hundred Years of Revolutionary Internationals" (*Marxism in the Modern World, The Revolutionary Internationals,* and *Marxist Ideology in the Contemporary World*) and the 1966 *Yearbook on International Communist Affairs.*

CONTENTS

FIFTY YEARS OF COMMUNISM IN RUSSIA

INTRODUCTION

Milorad M. Drachkovitch

Half-a-century of a political regime is a short period of time *sub specie aeternitatis;* measured, however, in historical terms it allows a scrutiny which if necessarily nondefinitive is nonetheless meaningful. In the Soviet Union during the autumn of 1967, the October Revolution was hailed as "the beginning for delivering mankind from the exploiting system and implementing the ideas of scientific communism" (as stated in the theses of the Central Committee of the Communist Party of the Soviet Union). But the organizers of the conference at Stanford have viewed the event from a different angle. For them the most significant problem in evaluating the Bolshevik Revolution and the subsequent reign of the Communist Party was the relationship between the original promise or message of the revolution and the performance of the new regime in the most important fields of Soviet life over the relatively long period of five decades.

This relationship between promise and performance represents a legitimate analytical approach for historians and political scientists who must relate the origins of political systems to their later functioning. In the case of the Soviet Union, this is not only a methodologically indispensable approach but also a fascinating intellectual venture and a rewarding undertaking for anyone interested in the experiences of the past and the prospects of the future. For the Soviet Union was not conceived and established simply as a new political entity but as *the* new society, qualitatively different from everything previously existing. As the founding fathers of Bolshevism saw it, their revolution fulfilled the Babouvist *Manifeste des Egaux* of 1796 which envisioned "another, more magnificent revolution, which will be the last"; it also carried out the prescription of Marx and Engels in the 1848 *Manifesto*—the "forcible overthrow of all existing social conditions" ushering in a free human association "in which the free development of each is the condition for the free development of all."

The uniqueness of the revolutionary mission in Russia was perceived by Lenin as early as 1902 when he wrote that "the national tasks of Russian Social Democracy are such as have never confronted any other socialist party in the world" (*What Is To Be Done?*). Fifteen years later, in his last writing—*State and Revolution*—that separated his oppositional dreams from his governmental action, Lenin depicted socialism as a revival of "primitive" democracy in the sense that "for the first time in the history of civilized society, the mass of the population rises to independent participation, not only in voting and elections, but also in the everyday administration of affairs. . . . The whole of society will have become one office and one factory, with equal work and equal pay."

The "never before" and the "for the first time" in these quotations found their expression in the initial legislative flurry of the Bolshevik regime (Decree on Peace and Decree on Land of November 8, 1917; Declaration of the Rights of the People of Russia of November 15; Decree Abolishing Classes and Civil Ranks of November 23; Decrees on the Workers' Control and the People's Courts of November 27 and December 7, respectively; Abolition of Military Ranks and Titles of December 29; Revolutionary Divorce Law of December 31, etc., etc.). Although these measures were enacted partly to confute political rivals and gain popular acceptance, they also aimed at something far beyond the realm of political games. Viewed from that angle they resembled less the acts establishing a new political, social, and economic order than the proclamation of a new phase in human destiny, the liberation of mankind from the fetters of the past, the breaking of Prometheus' chains. The dawn of the new society in Russia was simultaneously considered the beginning of a regeneration of the international movement of the proletariat betrayed in 1914 by the "social patriotic" leaders of the Second International. As a consequence, in March 1919 Moscow became the world center of a new, Third International, and on the very evening of its foundation Lenin prophesied: "The comrades who are in this hall have seen how the Soviet Republic was established; they see now how the Communist International is being established; and they will see how the Soviet Universal Federal Republic will be established."

In their respective fields, the essays in this volume analyze why and how these initial promises were not and could not have been kept. Lenin himself died full of doubts and possibly even despair—observing the rudeness of his heir apparent, the growth of bureaucracy which shattered his earlier bucolic vision of "simple, fundamental rules of every-day social life in common," the inability of the Bolshevik regime to get rid of "chauvinism" in domestic inter-nationality relations, and the propensity of the Comintern to dictate to foreign

Communists the typically Russian solutions. He left, moreover, the rigid legacy of a monolithic Party, source of subsequent Soviet totalitarian controls, and an ambiguous legacy—through the New Economic Policy—of experimentation with the national economy. His highly individual interpretation of Marxism, his iron will and absolute authority over the Bolshevik faction, and the total state power at his disposal were not adequate for his self-imposed task of remolding not only Russia's destiny but also human nature. He was and remained a prophet, but he did not lead his people to the promised land.

Lenin's failure to make reality conform to his utopian schemes and the unlimited power he bequeathed to less scrupulous hands made Stalin's rule over the Soviet Union crucially important. Rejecting Trotsky's cosmopolitanism, Stalin realized that the survival of communism in Russia depended not on a mythical proletarian revolution in other countries, but on harnessing national energies to build "socialism in one country." He became thus the first "national communist," and by putting nationalism in the service of a Communist party provided a model for subsequent Communist "isms" (Titoism, Maoism, Castroism). Many other goals and promises of Lenin's times were also sacrificed or lost in the process. The basic tenet of *State and Revolution*—the withering away of the state—was discarded in favor of the mutually competing bureaucracies of Party, state, and police, manipulated each and all by the omnipotent leader. Other concepts, such as equality of work and pay and workers' control of factories, were sacrificed to the imperatives of strictest working discipline and the economic incentives necessary to the crash program for industrialization of the country. The letter and the spirit of the 1917 Decree on Land and the 1922 N.E.P. Land Decree were completely erased by the total collectivization of agriculture. A complex military hierarchy was rebuilt, replacing the original egalitarian army of "revolutionary people."

In foreign affairs events also altered the original perspectives. At the outset, all the trappings of the new Soviet state, including its diplomacy, were considered merely as weapons serving the world revolution believed to be the most immediate item on the agenda of history. When it became obvious that Communist Russia remained the isolated "citadel of socialism," a dualism emerged which still characterizes Soviet foreign policy. The search for security remained uppermost on the minds of the Kremlin's rulers, but they never discarded the claim that the Soviet Union had an internationalist role and mission, that it differed in nature from all conventional "bourgeois" states and was fundamentally antagonistic to them. Stalin tried to profit to the fullest extent from that duality. His diplomacy was always geared to benefit from or exacerbate rivalries in the "imperialist" camp, while his "cult of personality" was designed to enforce Communist discipline both at home and abroad. Probably the main paradox of Stalinism was that while the Soviet police were physically exterminating the elite of the Old Bolsheviks in the late 1930's, Stalin was worshiped as "infallible and sinless" (in Milovan Djilas's words) by Communist neophytes around the world. Then, in a crucial moment of overconfidence, he acted on the dogma of a fundamental antagonism between capitalist states and the one socialist state. The pact with Hitler helped plunge the capitalist "camp" into war, but the collapse of France meant almost inevitable disaster for Russia. Saved, however, from his treacherous Nazi ally by the patriotism of the Russian people and the military involvement and aid of his Western capitalist partners, Stalin left his heirs a seemingly unshakable imperial domain in East Central Europe and the unchallenged leadership of the Communist world. But both achievements barely survived his death.

On this ground of the Leninist myth of classless society, restratified and politically congealed by Stalin, his heirs had to confront the changing realities in and outside of the Soviet Union. This process of experimentation and adjustment is still unfinished, but many of its aspects continue to dazzle the world. To that flamboyant personality, Nikita Khrushchev, fell the stupendous (impossible?) task of conserving and even strengthening the exclusive authority of the Party while adjusting its rule to a maturing industrial society whose members were desperately seeking an escape from the material drabness and spiritual stultification of Stalinism. Khrushchev demolished what had been sacrosanct for two and a half decades—Stalin's "cult of personality"—and opened the two-edged process of de-Stalinization with its obvious advantages and potential threats to Party dictatorship. He came to terms with and offered multiple facilities to the scientific community and lived probably his finest hour when the first Sputnik whirled into space—the highest tribute to Soviet technological talents and to the regime sustaining the project. On the other hand, Khrushchev lacked both understanding and sympathy for new artistic aspirations, and despite some pragmatic concessions he remained faithful to the dogma of "socialist realism" and the "partiinost" in literature and intellectual life. He wanted to be a genuine reformer of Soviet society, but lacked patience, consistency, and even luck in many of his endeavors.

The new, 1961, party program was the expression of his optimism and self-confidence, even bravado. It promised that in the current decade, 1961–70 (whose end Khrushchev certainly envisioned with himself at the helm of the state), the Soviet Union would "surpass the strongest and richest capitalist country, the U.S.A., in production per head of population." Soon afterwards, however, a decline in the Soviet industrial growth rate and a sharp fall in agricultural output (1962–63), tarnished these glowing predictions and dealt a heavy blow to Khrushchev's own political career. He was not served any better by his periodic and hasty reorganizations of the state and Party machineries, and in the process offended many vested interests. He fell ingloriously, the victim of a palace intrigue by his former protégés, and was condemned to ruminate in political oblivion on his former power and prestige as the third Soviet tsar.

Khrushchev's record in foreign policy was also a mixture of daring, achievement, and failure. By a more flexible approach in international affairs, Khrushchev extended Soviet prestige and influence to many parts of the world where they were practically nonexistent or minimal under Stalin. He retreated in the nuclear confrontation with the United States over Cuba in 1962, but in turn claimed he had preserved the first Communist outpost in the Western Hemisphere. He pursued a complex foreign policy, concluded limited agreements with the United States, and advocated "peaceful coexistence" in inter-state relations while rejecting the same principle in the realm of ideology; he preached against nuclear and even conventional warfare among the great powers, but gave his blessings to the formula of "national liberation wars." In the balance, Khrushchev enhanced the role of the Soviet Union in world affairs, though his diplomatic maneuverings cost his Party prestige and influence in the international Communist movement.

Closer to home, in the Soviet "imperial" domain, he displayed both naked force and subtle calculation in coping with the potentially explosive post-Stalin situation. He restored "order" in Hungary when reverberations of his attacks on Stalin threatened to collapse the entire satellite-states structure. He then launched his grand design of bloc-wide economic integration through a socialist division of labor and long-term supranational planning. At the Twenty-First Party Congress, in 1959, Khrushchev expounded a "theory of simultaneity," stating that "by successfully employing the potentialities inherent in socialism, the socialist countries will enter the higher phase of communist society more or less simultaneously." On another occasion he asserted that the common economic base of world socialism would eventually make the question of borders a pointless one; he advocated economic planning on the scale of the socialist world system, and favored common enterprises among the member states of the Comecon (Council of Mutual Economic Assistance) as well as the creation of a central executive committee to determine the bloc-wide specialization of production. He failed to achieve these goals, however, and in 1963 had to put aside the concepts of supranational planning, integration, and specialization, in favor of voluntary coordination of national economic plans and bilateral consultations between Comecon members. Probably the most painful aspect of this retreat was that most of the blocs on the road to integration were erected by one of the formerly most subservient satellites—Rumania. The failure of Khrushchev's grand design did not deprive the Soviet Union of all control over the region, but it indicated that if it was impossible to rule Stalinistically without Stalin, it was also difficult to find imaginative *and* workable solutions to replace the previous order of things.

The most spectacular of Khrushchev's problems and complications, which must have contributed to his fall in October 1964, was the escalation of the Sino-Soviet conflict, which reached a climax of mutual hostility and vituperation at the close of his rule. It is a particular irony of history that many of the arguments and much of the Maoist style in attacking Khrushchev's "revisionism" resembled those Lenin used in his campaigns against the Social Democratic "traitors" to Marxism. The dispute between Khrushchev and Mao Tse-tung illustrated vividly the global fragmentation of the once almost monolithic Stalinist bloc.

Denouncer of Stalin's rule, Khrushchev in turn was denounced by his successors. *Pravda* of October 17, 1964, without mentioning his name, attacked his "harebrained schemes, half-baked conclusions and hasty decisions and actions divorced from reality, bragging and bluster, attraction to rule by fiat, unwillingness to take into account what science and practical experience have already discovered." But the new "collective leadership" was also unable to find answers to problems which Khrushchev had failed to solve. It discarded for all practical purposes the 1961 Party Program, and the targets of the new Five-Year Plan (1965–70) remained well below the overambitious goals set forth in the program. In the same vein, the new leadership indicated clearly at the Twenty-Third Party Congress (March–April 1966) that it would proceed very cautiously in its domestic policies, a fact that prompted Isaac Deutscher to write about "a swing from reform and de-Stalinization to more rigid and authoritarian policies which may be described, for the lack of a better term, as crypto- or neo-Stalinist." It is perhaps more appropriate to remark that by going back verbally to the haven of Leninism (as the rock bottom of the regime's legitimacy), the new leadership implicitly admits that it will not experiment in coping with domestic situations. Whether such *immobilisme* represents an adequate answer to the problems of a complex society remains, of course, to be seen. There certainly exists one ominous course whose elemental force was perceived by Stalin, namely a "brutal nationalism, kept in line only by the regime's adherence to an international doctrine" (in the words of Professor Richard Pipes) as a way out in case of deeper domestic and foreign complications. And the present harsh policy toward nonconformist intellectuals points to the mood of the people in the seats of power.

Significantly enough, however, the domestic de-Khrushchevization did not affect signally the realm of foreign affairs. The new "collective leadership" pursues a sort of early Khrushchevian foreign policy, less his personal style. It tries to carry on a skillful above and below the board policy of avoiding a direct confrontation with the United States (and even achieving accommodation on some specific questions), while profiting from the disarray in the Western camp, and building a sort of "anti-imperialist" front with the more militant members of the "nonaligned" bloc. On the other hand, like Khrushchev, the new leaders of the Soviet Union are still seeking a new approach that will allow them to reassert Soviet authority and leadership in both East-Central Europe and the international Communist movement. And despite their erstwhile hopes of accommodation with Communist China, they are compelled to wage their own "cold war" with Mao's China—even with added bitterness because their removal of Khrushchev has not changed Peking's attitude toward Moscow.

Here we are then at the end of the first half-century of Communist rule in Russia. The essays in this book tell its many-faceted story. It is an extraordinary story of human passions, strivings, and sufferings, of dizzying promises, spectacular achievements, and dismal, often paradoxical, failures. It is also a modern version of a very old story of man's dissatisfaction with his condition and his attempts to make a *tabula rasa* of the past in order to build a completely new society. In this sense, early Bolshevism was a modernized version of the millenarian groups which flourished around the close of the Middle Ages, with Lenin descending directly from Thomas Müntzer and his "League of the Elect" in the German peasants' revolt of 1525. Norman Cohn in his work, *The Pursuit of Millenium,* found a common description for both Müntzer and Lenin: "As social tensions mounted and the revolt became nation-wide, there would appear, somewhere on the radical fringe, a *propheta* with his following of paupers, intent on turning this one particular upheaval into the apocalyptic battle, the final purification of the world."

Lenin's eschatological vision, moreover, was nurtured by his selective interpretation of Marx's teaching, what Nicolas Berdyaev appropriately called "a Russification and orientalizing of Marxism." Leninism, as it emerged both in 1902 and 1917, diverged from the mainstream of Marxist thought, above all because its elitism and revolutionary voluntarism were at odds with the postulates of Marxist economic determinism and with those ingredients of democracy which Marx himself had absorbed from the Western political tradition. This may have been one factor in the success Lenin did achieve. But just because his original aims were of such extraordinary magnitude, they could not be transformed into an objective, worldly, reality. The Bolshevik Revolution did not purify the world, but it did transform the destiny of Russia and did send its shock waves around the earth.

Lenin's heirs up to the present day have thus had to labor on two levels: the sacral, immutable level of fidelity to Lenin's intentions and the profane, flexible level of nation making. Both must be taken into account when analyzing Soviet idiosyncrasies and behavior. It is arguable that today the Soviet leaders are much more preoccupied with this second level of operations: strengthening the already powerful state they dominate, extending its influence abroad through skillful diplomacy, and checking all domestic aspirations going in opposite directions. On the other hand, the first level continues to play a crucial role though in an ambiguous sense. Because of the debunking of Stalin's myth, and the denunciation of Khrushchev's harebrained schemes, the incantation of the pristine purity of the early Bolshevik rule and goals gives the present regime some legitimacy and justifies it to a certain extent to Soviet citizens. Still, Lenin's own stateless and anti-bureaucratic visions, clashing with his own Machiavellianism and nascent totalitarian controls, find an echo in Soviet minds, an echo that contradicts much of Soviet reality. Thus while today's Communist *prophetae* bear Chinese and Cuban names, and the very complexity of the maturing Soviet society as well as the "return of the repressed" (as Professor Lewis Feuer argues in his essay in this volume) challenge the *immobilisme* of the ruling class, the Soviet Union enters a second half-century inscribed with many large interrogation marks.

The contributors to this book do not indulge in crystal gazing, but in a sense they all suggest that a country composed of an immensely talented people will not remain indefinitely bound to the promise of a bygone era, when "a chemist working in his laboratory on living material" (as Maxim Gorky wrote reproachfully about Lenin in November 1917) projected a future which he himself finally realized had gone askew and which his successors have conducted in their own disparate and mutually incompatible ways.

MARXISM AND THE RUSSIAN REVOLUTION

Bertram D. Wolfe

Historically, Marxism is an offshoot of the idea of Revolution, an idea comparatively new in history. The idea was born in the last quarter of the eighteenth century and has dominated much of the thinking of the nineteenth and twentieth. Contrary to what Marxism in all its varieties holds, the idea of Revolution arose unexpectedly, unplanned, unthought of, taking its leading actors by surprise, creating for itself an explanation and an ideology or a complex of conflicting ideological fragments only after the fact.

Some would locate the starting point of the idea in North America in 1776. But the inherited English freedoms and physical sources of liberty in America were already the matter of European utopian dreams long before Franklin arrived in Paris or Lafayette came to the rebellious colonies, or before the celebrated "self-evident truths" of the Declaration of Independence were proclaimed to mankind. The freedoms of the English colonies from the outset, and the social conditions of a continent where unoccupied land seemed limitless, poverty no longer a God-ordained state, and careers were open to talents without limitations of estate or caste—these, and not national independence, were what made the New World seem *new* to Europe.[1]

Moreover, ours was never a proper revolution to capture the imagination by scenes of unforgettable drama. At best it was a revolution *manqué*. It had no fascinating engine in the public square that by mere force of gravity could make men shorter by a head; no emotion-choked reign of terror to chew up rich and poor, men and women, young and old, and finally devour the revolution's own children; no dramatic extermination of generals and factions during the revolution; no sequel of purge and Thermidor and Bonapartism. It did not dream of starting the world afresh with a new calendar and history with *the year one*. At its end, impenitent Loyalists went off freely to Halifax; our leaders of "factions," Jefferson, Hamilton,

Adams, Daniel Shays, lived out their lives to die a natural death, a death most unnatural for French or Russian revolutionaries.

Even the War Between the States, the bloodiest in military history up to its time, was not a proper civil war for, as the stillness descended upon Appomattox, the voice of General Grant could be heard saying to the Confederate cavalry "Keep your horses, boys, you'll need them for the spring planting," while the leaders of the rebellion, Jefferson Davis and Robert E. Lee, were to live out the remainder of their lives in peace and die in bed.

Yet, not in the Marxian but in a narrow and literal sense there was an economic connection between the American War for Independence and the Revolution in France. The French monarch had been so generous in his aid to the American colonists that at our Revolution's end his treasury was empty and the monarchy bankrupt. Not the rise of a new social class nor dire poverty in France, but a bankrupt treasury in a prospering land, opened, unexpectedly to all, a period of revolutions.

In 1787 the King of this powerful, prospering country called together an Assembly of Notables to listen to a shocking report of royal bankruptcy and to approve suggested reforms whose main purpose would be to tax the notables who had not been taxed before, in order to replenish the empty coffers of their King. The nobles had no more far-reaching intention than that of defending their privileges against these incursions, and of finding fault with Calonne for permitting the greatest treasury on the continent to go bankrupt. Yet their year-long resistance to the finance minister's plans was the first in a series of revolutions which, in retrospect, are lumped together as the Great French Revolution. It was this *révolte nobiliaire* and not some action of the petty, insignificant, and un-self-confident industrial bourgeoisie of France that opened what Marxists and Marxist-Leninists, and many historians along with them, persist in calling "the bourgeois revolution." If by bourgeoisie is meant a "rising social class" begotten by industrial capitalism, its wealth largely invested in industry and the employment of industrial labor, with its values derived from "capitalism," with a special and distinct "relationship to the forces of production," and a distinct more or less uniform psychology and will, such a class appears nowhere upon the scene throughout the great drama. Neither initiator nor actor nor chorus, it did not "come to power" nor displace another "ruling class" nor substitute its values for the prevailing ones, either during the revolution or at its end, nor gain substantial benefits from it, nor win from it free room for industrial development.

The chief beneficiaries of the Revolution were the new and expanded bureaucracy, the landed proprietary groups that got the *biens nationaux* at bargain prices, and the peasants. Then Napoleon, Jacobin child of the Revolution, established a new nobility, requiring a landed endowment of any one he raised to the peerage and forbidding him or his heirs to alienate the land except in exchange for other lands. The old values that gave more prestige to land than to trade and industry continued to prevail in France after the Revolution was over and after Napoleon's fall from power. The enormously expanded bureaucracy continued to be the real ruler of France all through the nineteenth century and into the second half of the twentieth, through volatile periods of French political life when ministries and governments changed so frequently that, were it not for the stable rule of the bureaucracy, France would have been in a state of perpetual chaos. As to the third beneficiary of the Revolution, the peasant, his acquisition of a family farm left him without the need or urge to crowd into the cities, so that French industrialization was delayed by the lack of a free-floating labor reserve.

Beyond that, I must leave it to the Marxists of various stripes to torture the image of the independent peasant, owner of his land and implements and the product of his toil, into some semblance of a "bourgeoisie." I leave, too, to the self-appointed spokesmen of the proletariat the task of falsely flattering the bourgeoisie by calling the Rights of Man and the all too slow widening of democratic suffrage and parliamentarism "bourgeois freedoms." I can only think that their purpose is not so much to exalt the bourgeoisie as to belittle the freedoms.

Far from opening up a period of rapid industrialization, the French Revolution left French industry feeble, backward, and confined by all sorts of limitations inherited from the Empire. French industry remained stagnant, and French banking investment remained limited to loans to governments and speculation in currencies for well over a half century after the "bourgeois" revolution. The long period of economic stagnation was broken only in the sixties when Isaac Pereire introduced the first industrial investment bank, the Credit Mobilier. Then an upsurge of industrialization began, not under "bourgeois" auspices but under the auspices of a group of bankers and entrepreneurs who were ideological followers of the utopian socialist Saint-Simon. Thus it took fervent adherents of a socialist creed to weaken somewhat, and then only partially, the power of the aristocratic proprietary and *rentier* tradition which felt that to invest in commerce —and still more so in industry—was to lose one's ease and dignity.

"THE DREAM OF REASON"

The year-long resistance of the nobles compelled the monarch to convoke an Estates-General, a time-honored device of bankrupt monarchs, but one which had not had to be used since 1610. Naively, the King made the democratic gesture of asking the people of France for advice on how the Estates-General should be constituted. It was this, and not the growth of a new rising class with a new ideology, that opened the floodgates to a spate of ever more sweeping proposals.

Inditers of addresses to the King and of proclamations and editorials in new provincial and urban journals; orators in a flowering of clubs and meetings, assemblies, *communes, parlements,* and accidental mobs; new baked pamphleteers; authors of resolutions and *cahiers de doléances;* obscure provincial lawyers and journalists who had never had an audience or a voice in political life—all of them might have taken as their common device: "I know nothing about it, therefore I can speak freely." One has only to hearken to this confusion of voices, and ponder these shiny new proposals for making the world afresh, to realize that they were anything but the voice of political experience or the expression of the interests of any estate or "social class," least of all of the careful calculations of a *bon bourgeois.*

The stream of suggestions grew in number and fury like a spring flood. The *révolte nobiliaire* "taught the Third Estate the language, tactics, and gallantry of opposition." And, once the floodgates were open, each suggestion overreached its predecessor. "What this interpretation restores," as the historian George Taylor observes, "is the sense of an unplanned, unpremeditated revolution that in many and startling ways exceeded the aims expressed in the *cahiers de doléances.*" [2]

Thus an essential feature of a revolution is that it gains in unplanned momentum and constantly overreaches itself until it takes the form of the idea that the world can be swept clean of all that exists, all that time, experience, tradition, custom, habit, law, and the slow organic growth of society have engendered, and "history can begin anew." Nothing is to be examined for the purposes of improving or reforming it, correcting some specific abuse or some obsolescent feature. That is not revolution but "reformism," and there are no more abusive epithets in a Lenin's vocabulary than the words *reformist* or *reformism.* What a revolution needs, Marx wrote on the eve of the upheavals of 1848, was "destruction and dissolution" and "the forcible overthrow of all existing conditions." In the space made clean and empty by the iron broom of revolution, a totally new world would be created. Thus the day comes, as it did on September 22, 1792, when the very calendar is scrapped and time itself begins anew with the First Day of the Year One of the New World in creation. At this point man becomes as God, and replaces the old God in the temple by enshrining there his own Reason to be worshiped. And, as the Devil reminded Ivan Karamazov, "There is no law for God. . . . all things are permitted, and that's the end of it." With that "all things are permitted," the history of contemporary nihilism begins. It is fulfilled in the terror of the French Revolution; in the attempt to exterminate whole classes of the population and the blood-purges of the Russian Revolution; and in the crematoriums of Hitler's German and projected European revolution. Said Talleyrand of the French Revolution, "it was made by builders of theories for an imaginary world." According to Robespierre, it was accomplished "by putting into laws the moral truths culled from the philosophers." To these striking formulae we need only add the wry summary of the artist Goya: "The dream of reason produces monsters."

THE LEGEND OF THE BOURGEOIS REVOLUTION

In historical terms, then, Marxism may be defined as an elaborate misunderstanding of the French Revolution, of the role of "classes," and of the very nature of revolution. Marx took as his initial axioms —self-evident truths that seemed to him in need of no proof—first, that a revolution begins as a consequence of a social transformation of society and takes on overt political form only when a new class has grown ripe enough to challenge an old "ruling class," take power itself, and make over the world in its image. But we have seen how unexpectedly revolutions come, how they take their initiators and principal actors by surprise, how they create their ideologies in torrents only after the fact, and how these ideologies compete, displace each other, overreach themselves, until society, which cannot live forever at fever heat and under perpetual tension, disorder, and confusion, welcomes a subsidence of excitement and a relapse into quiet, even if order is brought about by the same guillotine that symbolized the culmination of disorder, even if order is brought about by a Bonaparte or a Stalin, even if the new despot continues and enlarges disorder from above but no longer demands or permits that it arise from below.

Marx took it for granted that the French Revolution could be meaningfully defined as a *bourgeois revolution,* its ideological dreams and nightmares described as *bourgeois ideologies,* and its driving force and victor could be termed *the revolutionary bourgeoisie*. Each of these "axioms" dissolves in the face of empirical examination of the events, the leaders, the roles, the ideas, and the actions of the revolution.

The same dogmas were taken for granted and given yet cruder formulation by the Marxist epigoni, and notably by Russian Marxists of all schools. Russian worshipers of the poetry of the machine and technology might look to Germany as the model to follow, as Germany had looked to England, and as later many lands, including Bolshevik Russia, would look to America. But however far behind the French economy might limp, when it came to revolution France was the land to follow. In the workshop of French history there was a mode for every taste: 1789, 1793 and 94, 1799, 1804, 1830, 1848, 1870, and 1871. The France they dreamed of and lived by was a France seen through the prism of the writings of Marx, more real to them than the France of history. Almost every figure on the Russian political stage wore a costume tailored in Paris.

Tsarism was the *ancien régime*. Vyshnegradskii, Witte, and Stolypin, were the Turgot, Calonne, and Necker. Lenin was a Jacobin—his opponents said this to denounce him, and he repeated it after them with pride. He was a Russian Robespierre—both he and his opponents agreed. And he was as well a Russian Blanqui. In a gentler mood, he called his rivals Girondins or the Swamp; when harsher, he called them Cavaignacs.[3] Trotsky dramatized himself as the Marat of the Revolution, later as its Carnot. To the sailors of Kronstadt, whose hands were stained with the blood of their officers, he said in the summer of 1917 that they were "the flower of the Revolution" and their deeds would be copied all over Russia until every public square would be adorned by a replica of that famous French invention "which makes the enemies of the people shorter by a head." Trotsky and Stalin in their debates hurled at each other the epithet "Bonapartist." Stalin's regime was branded by Trotsky as "Thermidor." When Tsereteli in 1917 proposed to disarm the Bolshevik Red Guard lest they overthrow the Provisional Government, and Lieber supported him (Mensheviks both), from his seat another Menshevik leader, Martov, hurled the epithet *versalets* (Versaillist).[4]

As the French revolutionaries had donned imaginary togas and fancied themselves ancient Romans, so Russian revolutionaries sought to reenact the scenes and roles of revolutionary France. Much ink would be spilled, and in the end much blood, to determine Russia's place on the French revolutionary calendar (was she on the eve of her 1789 or 1793, her 1848, or her 1870?). The soviets were pictured by Lenin as enlarged replicas of the "Paris Commune type of state." [5] After the Bolsheviks took power, the ink and blood would be poured out in combat with the ghosts of "Bonapartism" and "Thermidor," while the real problems were those arising out of an entirely new formation, totalitarianism, which had no exemplar in French revolutionary history.

In justice to the Marxists it should be said that they were not alone in their use of the formulae, "bourgeois revolution" and "revolutionary bourgeoisie." Whole generations of historians, most of them non-Marxist or only tenuously Marxist in outlook, took the same terms for granted. But recently, particularly in the last decade, the French Revolution has been undergoing a far-reaching re-examination. In France itself, and in England and the United States, historians have been questioning the vocabulary of social history and interpretation, and with devoted scholarship and freedom from preconceptions, have been examining the tax rolls, the banking records, provincial and municipal archives, the composition of committees, of delegations to assemblies, the actual records of investment in land, in annuities, in venal offices, the records of ownership of land, the histories of great families, the texts of *cahiers de doléances,* and a host of similar materials. Their work has reopened questions long considered settled, questions that are economic, social, political, and intellectual. Recently a battle has been raging in the usually somnolent pages of the *American Historical Review* between historians engaged in this work of empirical re-examination and those who would cling to the old terms "bourgeois revolution" and "revolutionary bourgeoisie" even if they have to stretch the terms to the point where *bourgeoisie* no longer means a definite class with a definite relation to the forces of production and a definite degree of participation in the starting of the revolution, in the inspiring of its ideological fantasies and programs, and the guiding of its results.

A brilliant summary of the labor of re-examination that has been accomplished thus far appears in the article by George V. Taylor cited above on which I have leaned for some of the statements and direct quotations in the present paper. Those who would follow this discussion further can find a rich bibliographical guide in his footnotes, and in the same issue of the journal other contenders crossing swords with each other. Professor Taylor, like Alfred Cobban in his *Social Interpretation of the French Revolution* (Cambridge, England, 1964) finds that "the phrase, *bourgeois revolution,* incorporates a self-confirming system of deception [and] acts as a standard for selecting, interpreting, and arranging evidence, and because of this the research usually ends by confirming assumptions that creep in with the terminology." After reviewing the entire re-examination and much of the argument of the opposing school, Professor Taylor concludes his many-faceted, closely reasoned study with these words: "The phrases, *bourgeois revolution* and *revolutionary bourgeoisie,* with their inherent deceptions, will have to go, and others must be found to convey with precision and veracity the realities of social history."

The conclusions of these historians who have thus been reopening a long "closed" question will come as no surprise to those of us who, having questioned the dogma that the Russian Revolution was a proletarian revolution, have earlier been driven to re-examine the French Revolution as to its supposed bourgeois character. But the devotion, thoroughness, and precision with which they have been going about their task of re-examination merits the gratitude of all who take seriously the field of social history.

FROM ABBÉ SIEYÈS TO KARL MARX

When the King of France asked for suggestions on the composition of the Estates-General, Abbé Sieyès was ready with an answer which, if it clarified nothing, had a ring to it that echoed down the corridors of time and, over half a century later, evoked in the mind of Karl Marx one of the core ideas of his own doctrine: "What is the Third Estate?" asked Sieyès, and answered, "Everything. What has it been hitherto? Nothing. What does it desire to be? Something."

The misunderstanding concerning the Third Estate began with the Third itself. The First Estate represented the clergy, the Second the nobility, the Third the towns. Since a walled town is a *bourg,* all the inhabitants thereof, whether noblemen, clergy, *noblesse de robe* and other purchasers of high office, *rentiers,* owners of urban property, merchants, bankers, industrialists, artisans, lumpenproletariat, unemployed, or beggars, all may be denominated *bourgeois.* Immediately it came together the Third Estate passed a decree claiming to represent "96% of the nation" and constituted themselves as a "national assembly" qualified to represent the "will of the people." They demanded double representation and a vote by head in place of the traditional vote by estates, which would give them a majority in any vote, and then invited clergy and nobility to join their Assembly. When the King ordered them to meet separately, the other two estates left the hall, but the Third sat tight. "You have heard His Majesty's orders," admonished the Master of Ceremonies. "Know you," answered a thunderous voice, "that nothing but the bayonet will avail to disperse the commoners of France." The mild King said, "Well, let them stay," and he directed the other two estates to join the "National Assembly." Ironically, the first champion of the Third Estate was an Abbé, the voice that rang out on their behalf was the voice of le Comte de Mirabeau, while the group of *propriétaires* as a whole "furnished 87% of the Third Estate's deputies to the Estates-General" and provided it with its leadership.[6]

Thus the second stage of the French Revolution began, along with the legend of "the bourgeois revolution" and the "revolutionary bourgeoisie." The legend that the Third Estate represented the people of France was a convenient political fiction, like Lenin's fiction that whenever the Party speaks, it is the proletariat that is speaking. Moreover, for a people who for several centuries had been juridically distinguished as to privileges and duties by membership in juridical estates, it was natural to imagine that men think, act, and feel, as "classes." (I should like to give it as my own opinion that the concept of class and the notion that men think, feel, act and react as social classes distinguishable by their relationship to the process of production is a concept that also needs to be called in question and re-examined.)

In 1843 when Karl Marx went with his new bride to Paris to become co-editor of a journal, he was still anti-Communist. But the smell of revolution in the Paris air transformed him completely. Within six months, he had lost his job, been thrust thereby into the "intellectual proletariat," fallen in love with Paris redolent with revolutionary memories and socialist theories, and he had found his true vocation. He became possessed by the idea that a new Great French Revolution impended that would somehow fulfill the large ideological fantasies which the first had left unfulfilled. When next the Gallic cock should crow, sleepy Germany too would awaken and take its place, not merely in the revolutionary procession but at its head.

If the "revolutionary" bourgeoisie had left its promises unfulfilled in the "bourgeois" revolution, where, Marx asked, was the class that would fulfill them? And where the nation best fitted to lead beyond the political revolution to the social revolution? He found his answers in two logically untenable but psychologically understandable *non-sequiturs*. With the words of the Abbé Sieyès echoing in his ears, he asked: "Where is the class bold enough to cry out the defiant challenge: *I am nothing, I must become everything?*"[7] And he answered:

> One must admit that the German proletariat is the *theoretician* of Europe, as the English proletariat is its *national economist* and the French proletariat its *politician*. One must admit that Germany has

> just as much a classical vocation for the *social* revolution as it has *political* incapacity. . . . Only in socialism can a philosophical people find its corresponding practice, hence only in the proletariat the active element in its liberation.

Two *non-sequiturs,* but in them was contained the central core of Marxian doctrine. It would become Marxism-Leninism when in the place of the German proletariat Lenin put the Russian.

LENIN'S INTERPRETATION OF MARX

The term "Marxism-Leninism" was never used by Lenin himself, but is the hallmark of the successor ideology. Only upon his death did his orphaned lieutenants design it as a cloak to cover the fact that there was no Lenin among them, and as a way of claiming continuity with him through the collective possession of his doctrine, thus establishing the basis for an apostolic succession: Marx, Engels, Lenin, Stalin, Khrushchev, Brezhnev . . . *X*.

The struggle for the mantle of the apostolic succession between Leon Trotsky, masterly organizer of the seizure of power and of the Red Army, and Joseph Stalin, made by Lenin the master of the Leninist political machine, was a struggle to the death. Trotsky was organically incapable of using his power lever, the army; Stalin made skillful use of his, the party machine. Except for Zinoviev, the other lieutenants did not dream of taking Lenin's place nor count as serious contenders, but all of them perished in the struggle for the succession. As differences grew on matters for which Lenin had had or had left no clear solution, his leading lieutenants disputed with each other as to which of their proposed solutions was the most truly Leninist, but all the contenders agreed on the same general definition of Leninism as "the only Marxism of the period of imperialism, proletarian revolution, and the construction of socialism." To this they added Lenin's own claim that in the Bolshevik faction he had built "a party of a new type"—as indeed it was insofar as it could be considered a party. Though the problems Lenin's successors faced have changed constantly and their attempted solutions and very outlook have departed from Lenin's views, their definition of Leninism has survived unaltered.

In the *Theses of the Central Committee on the Fiftieth Anniversary of the October Revolution* the nature of Leninism and the relation of Lenin to Marx are defined as follows:

> The Bolshevik Party, a proletarian party of a new type, emerged and gained strength in the course of the class struggle on the firm founda-

> tion of Marxism-Leninism. . . . Under the new conditions brought into being by the epoch of imperialism, Lenin creatively developed Marxism, raising it to a new higher stage. His theory of the socialist revolution was one of the greatest contributions to scientific communism. . . . Drawing upon the teachings of Marx and Engels, he produced solutions to key theoretical and practical problems of the building of socialism and communism. . . . Leninism is the eternal source of revolutionary thinking and revolutionary action. The name of Lenin has become the symbol of the new world.

In the eyes of orthodox Marxists, the great heresy of the closing decade of the nineteenth century was the heresy of "Revisionism," a heresy born of the pronouncement of Eduard Bernstein, Engels' literary executor, to the effect that Marxism was a brilliant analysis of the political and economic structure of capitalist society in Marx's own day, but since his death in 1883 new conditions had developed not foreseen or experienced by him, so that a fresh look at society and the tactics of the socialist movement was needed. Though Lenin was one of the angriest denouncers of Bernstein's "revisionism," it is clear that Lenin's "creative development of Marxism under the new conditions of the epoch of imperialism" is itself such a "revision." Let me add lest I appear to be siding with Mao Tse-tung in a current controversy, that Mao's revision of Marxism leaves even less of the richness and complexity of the original doctrine intact than does Lenin's or Stalin's or Khrushchev's. Indeed, Lenin, Trotsky, Stalin, and their epigoni all belong to that order of "terrible simplifiers" that Burckhardt foresaw for our century, while Mao and his disciples, from Lin Piao to Mao's wife and public voice, are more terrible simplifiers still.

In any case it is clear from the Fiftieth Anniversary Theses as it is from everything published nowadays in Russian "theoretical organs" that while Lenin is cited endlessly, and as a rule irrelevantly, and in China Mao Tse-tung is cited *ad nauseam,* in both lands Marx is hardly quoted at all. His name is receding into the distance along with the comparatively peaceful and stable days of the world he knew. When it is invoked it is as a warrant for the "scientific certitude" of victory, as an act of residual piety, or as the sonorous opening for the litany of the apostolic succession.

But this was not always so, for Lenin accounted himself an orthodox Marxist, at times the only orthodox Marxist on the face of the earth. In his *Philosophical Notebooks,* written during the First World War only for his own eyes, he gravely set it down that "after a half century, not a single Marxist has understood Marx!" It is clear that he allowed for one exception, else how could he judge that the others had misunderstood? He read and reread the works of Marx and Engels, treating the two as a single sacred person every utterance of whom was equally "scientific," i.e. infallible, and of equal probative value. At every turn and in every controversy, "Ilyich consulted Marx," looking for helpful suggestions and for quotations with which to crush his opponents. In so vast a body of writing set down for changing situations and in varying moods, one could find a quotation for almost anything, so that his opponents had their authoritative quotations, too. Yet Lenin devoutly believed that the whole body of writing of his two-headed oracle made up a single, monolithic structure. In *Materialism and Emperio-Criticism* Lenin wrote: "In this philosophy of Marxism cast from a single block of steel, you cannot eliminate a single substantial premise, a single essential part, without deviating from objective truth, without falling into the hands of bourgeois-reactionary falsehood." [8]

An actual count reveals that Lenin quotes Engels far more often than Marx, and that the quotations from Marx come almost entirely from a single period that begins as the storms of 1848 are brewing and ends when Marx belatedly became aware of their subsiding, in the late summer of 1850. This is the most violent period of Marx's writing. The ebbing of the storm should have been obvious by 1849, but for a year and a half Marx kept trying to bring back the lightning by making a noise like thunder. This is the period of his exaltation of Blanqui, and the latter's "class dictatorship of the proletariat" and "the revolution in permanence," the period of Marx's hymns to terror and "the fist," of his praise of "so-called popular excesses, the people's revenge against hated individuals or public buildings," and his urging that the Communists should not discourage but encourage and seek to take leadership over such acts of mob violence. This was the Marx Lenin loved to quote, for belief in the efficacy of voluntarism, revolutionary violence, terror, and "street justice," along with belief in Blanqui's elitist conspiratorial attempts to seize power and from the heights of power to try to win the approval and stir the revolutionary activity of the masses—these were to become constituent parts of Lenin's Marxism, and of Marxism-Leninism.

But in September 1850, Marx and Engels broke with the Communist League whose *Manifesto* and *Circular Letters* Marx and Engels (actually Marx) had been drafting. Instead of acknowledging error and correcting it, Marx broke with his followers for remaining faithful to his tactics and outlook of the three years preceding the break. He wrote off "naked will as the driving force of revolution, instead of the real facts of the situation." Thereupon Marx began his major lifelong task: to study "the real facts of the situation" in order to prove that a social revolution would flow inevitably not from the impassioned will and superhuman energy of revolutionary voluntarists, but from the "law of motion" inherent in the nature of capitalism. At this point the schizoid rift between the sense of fatalism and the exaltation of the revolutionary will became complete—as complete as the irreducible revolutionary passion in Marx's temperament could permit it to become.

From this "riper" or later Marx-the-inevitabilist, burrowing his mole's way through the tomes and statistical reports in the British Museum, and devising "objective proofs" and "objective measurements" to determine when the "crisis of capitalism" would "mature" and bring about the "expropriation of the expropriators," Lenin found little to use. His quotations from Marx pick up in volume again when, after the fall of the Paris Commune in 1871, Marx glorified the Commune he had opposed in 1870. But when ten years later Marx reviewed and rejected this interpretation of the Commune, as we have noted, Lenin looked at this Marx with wilfully unseeing eyes.[9]

Marx's increasing recourse to determinism and inevitabilism Lenin simply translated into the "scientific" guarantee of the inevitable victory of socialism. But to use Marxism as a computer for calculating the ripeness of a given country for social revolution went against Lenin's spirit, for the "given country" in his case was backward Russia which at best seemed to promise by this method of calculation only a "bourgeois revolution." Still less did Lenin permit himself to recognize that Engels, freed at Marx's death from the titanic will that characterized Karl Marx, proceeded to develop the determinist, measure-of-ripeness side of Marxism to its logical extreme, as he did in the last half decade of his life in the articles collectively intended as a political testament.[10]

That Lenin's uncritical admiration of Engels was not a mere tactical maneuver in his feuds with other socialists is proved by passages in his letters to Inessa Armand never intended for other eyes. Because of the intimate nature of their relationship, he could not silence her with abusive epithets when she disagreed with him, but had to explain himself. Inessa, it seems, noted important differences between Engels' pacifism and defensism for Germany in the event of a two-front war with Russia and France and Lenin's defeatism for his own country, and between Engels' growing determinism and passive waiting until the time should be "ripe" and the socialists have a majority in the Reichstag and in the army before his party should take power, and Lenin's ardent and impatient voluntarism. I have not seen her letters which the Marx-Engels Institute keeps under seal, but in a number of letters written by Lenin to Inessa Armand in the last three months of 1916 and the first three of 1917, he defends Engels against her strictures: "Engels was right," he says in one of them. "In my time I have been pained to see many accusations charging Engels with opportunism, and my attitude is sceptical in the extreme. . . . Try, say I, just once to prove that Engels was wrong!! You will never be able to." In another letter he writes: "I am still 'in love' with Marx and Engels, and will not tolerate in silence any slander against them. No, these are real people! From them we must learn. From *this* ground we must not depart." And in yet another: "Engels the father of passive radicalism? Not true! Not at all. This you will never be able to show." [11]

Inessa Armand seems to have done her homework on Engels, and her unpublished letters were apparently well founded. Moreover, from the very outset, Engels had brought to the famous partnership a far less stormy temperament and a much greater inclination to "science rather than utopia" and to inevitabilist determinism rather than voluntarism than were natural to Marx. As early as the autumn of 1850, that is, as soon as Marx and he had sobered up from their apocalyptic illusions of 1848, Engels published a warning on the "premature" seizure of power in a backward country not "ripe" for socialism, a warning that reads as if it might have been addressed to the Lenin of 1917. At any rate, his socialist opponents were constantly quoting this to Lenin while his rage was the greater since he was incapable of repudiating Engels.

The reproach of Engels as echoed by Lenin's contemporaries during his rule would trouble him to the end. The last theoretical article he ever wrote, published in January, 1923, just before paralysis silenced forever his tongue and pen, was a final attempt to answer the reproach that he had seized power in a country unripe for socialism in the name of a class insufficiently advanced in culture and organization to exercise power.[12] Ostensibly he was answering the semi-Bolshevik Sukhanov, but Sukhanov was only enlarging upon the words of Engels written almost three-quarters of a century before:

> The worst thing that can befall a leader of an extreme party is to be forced to take power in an epoch when the movement is not yet ripe for the rule of the class he represents, nor for the carrying out of the measures which the rule of that class would demand. What he *is able* to do does not depend upon his will but upon the level that the conflict between the various classes has reached, and upon the degree of development of the material conditions of existence, on which at any given moment the level of development of class antagonisms rests.

> What he *ought* to do and his party expects of him, doesn't depend upon his will either, nor upon the then degree of development of the class struggle. He is bound by the doctrines and demands that he has been advancing. . . . Thus necessarily he finds himself facing an insoluble dilemma: what he is *able* to do contradicts his entire previous activity, his principles, and the direct interests of his party; and what he *ought* to do he cannot realize. In a word, he is forced to represent not his party nor his class, but the class for whose rule the movement is ripe. In the interests of the movement itself he must realize the interests of a class that is alien to him, and put off his own class with phrases and promises and the assertion that the interests [he is actually realizing] are their interests. Whoever gets himself into this twisted position is irretrievably lost.[13]

Since this was written more than a century ago, Engels could have no presentiment that the "class" whose interests Lenin would come to represent would be Djilas's "new class," the Party-state bureaucracy.[14]

THE INNOVATIONS OF V. I. LENIN

The problem of dating the Russian revolution on the French revolutionary calendar caused no end of controversy, and for Lenin an intense internal struggle, until he contrived to reconcile his strong will to power with the "orthodox" dictum of his masters, Plekhanov and Axelrod, that Russia was too backward for a proletarian-socialist and ripe only for a bourgeois-democratic revolution. This required an alliance with and support to the "revolutionary bourgeoisie" in their struggle to take power and establish a "bourgeois democracy." Lenin propagated his view with his usual dogmatic energy, yet in his heart he could not reconcile himself to it. The bourgeoisie, he held with contempt, was not a consistently revolutionary class (and one must agree with him). They were no fighters, not bold enough nor courageous enough, nor ruthless enough to see "their own" revolution through to the end. They would be ready to compromise, to strike a miserable bargain and sell out their proletarian supporters.

Of course Lenin did not trust the proletariat either to be consistently revolutionary. (And again we must agree with him.) This leaves as "consistently revolutionary" only self-chosen individuals like Lenin, and special groups and detachments of extremists that at one time or another cooperated with him. Indeed, he measured their revolutionary consistency by the extent to which they did cooperate with him, and to all of them he applied his formula that the central question of all alliances and confrontations was *kto kogo?* (who whom?). Miraculously, the formula translates to perfection. Lenin bade his followers put now one verb now another between the two pronouns, to wit: Who *uses* whom? Who *gets the better of* whom? Who *vanquishes* whom? Who *destroys* whom?—or any other suitable verb that the reader may wish to supply.

Thus there is the case of the Kronstadt sailors, anarcho-Bolsheviks, impatient, turbulent men. They began their epic deeds in February 1917 by thrusting some of their officers under the ice. They marched in Lenin's demonstrations fully armed, bearing banners with any slogan Lenin thought up; they were the trigger happy men in trucks and armored cars who shot at shop windows and passers-by during the abortive July uprising; provided some detachments and two destroyers and the battleship Aurora that fired the terrifying blank shell during the October coup; were used by Lenin as a bludgeon when he threatened his Central Committee that he "would resign and go to the sailors" if they outvoted him; and supplied some shock troops for the ensuing civil war. But when the war was won and the sailors of Kronstadt demanded that he implement some of the promises he had made to the Russian people, then he and his lieutenants outlawed their meeting, took their fortress by storm over the ice, and executed their leaders both Communist and Anarchist, giving a tragic answer to the question of *Kto kogo?*

Other such alliances in which extremist groups marched together with Lenin were the Maximalists and Social-Revolutionary terrorists in the *exes* (revolutionary holdups) of 1906 and 1907; and the Left Social Revolutionaries who entered his Council of Commissars on December 1, 1917. There the Commissar of Justice Steinberg tried in vain to dilute Lenin's dictatorship with some considerations of ethics and justice. Early in March 1918 the S. R.'s walked out on the issue of Brest Litovsk, then were provoked into an uprising, and crushed by the Cheka.

The temporary alliance with the anarchists in 1917 unfolds a similar story. Anarchists of various varieties marched together with the Bolsheviks, attracted by Lenin's emphasis on those parts of his program for subverting the Provisional Government that seemed to be borrowed from their arsenal. The Bakuninist-Kropotkinist school found encouragement in his picture of the Soviets as a federation of communes modelled on the Paris Commune; the anarcho-syndicalists were won by his calls for workers' control and union management of industry and peasant seizure of the land; while all shadings found sustenance in his attacks on the war and the government, his slogan of *All Power to the Soviets* when he meant *All Power to the Bolshevik*

Party, and his declared intention to set up a government that would begin to wither away on the first day of its existence.[15] But Lenin's first acts in power were disillusioning, now that anarchic impulses were not useful but troublesome to his new government. The setting up of the Council of Peoples Commissars, and the Cheka, the abolition of freedom of the press, the attack on the right to strike, the setting up of the Supreme Economic Council to run industry, the proclamation that anarcho-syndicalism was a bourgeois and counter-revolutionary deviation—all these developments made it only too clear that the man who seemed almost an anarchist while overthrowing a government was at the opposite pole where his own power was concerned, more ruthless, more efficient, more ambitious to embrace every aspect of life than any tsar. The anarchists fought rear-guard actions side by side with the Kronstadt sailors, with Makhno in the Ukraine, with the green peasants in Tambov. Thereafter they were silenced by the Bolshevik government's ownership and monopoly of all newspapers, meeting halls, and printing plants, and their voices were stifled in isolator cells and concentration camps, by firing squad or pistol shot in the base of the brain in the cellar of the Lubyanka.

If this was Lenin's attitude towards organized detachments that had fought by his side, his attitude towards accidental street gatherings, mobs, and the unorganized masses generally was to encourage their outbursts of violence and vengeance, but he found their wrath too short-lived to be dependable. On October 10, two weeks before his coup, he acknowledged that the masses had become weary and apathetic. Four months after he seized power he complained that "the revolutionary enthusiasm of the masses which sustains their state of tension and gives them the strength to apply merciless terror to the suppression of demoralizing elements doesn't last long enough. . . . Dictatorship is iron rule, boldly revolutionary, swift and merciless in the suppression alike of exploiters and hooligans. But our rule . . . is often more like jelly than like iron." He was through with reliance on the masses for merciless, systematic terror, and turned the task over to the newly created Cheka, the Extraordinary Commission for the Suppression of Counter-Revolution, Speculation and Sabotage.

The question of Russia's ripeness only for a "bourgeois democratic revolution" was more complicated for Lenin than the inconstancy of the masses or the impermanence of the various alliances he entered into. If the central question of alliances was *who uses whom?* the central question of revolution was *who gets power?* If it was to be a bourgeois revolution, the bourgeoisie would get power: Thus they would be using him, not he them. From 1898 to 1905 his lips and pen repeated the formula of orthodoxy, but his spirit wrestled with the problem of who then would be using whom. When he went abroad in 1900 for a pilgrimage to Plekhanov and Axelrod, both sensed this conflict. "We turn our face to the liberals," Plekhanov said, "You turn your behind." [16] Yet so dutiful was Lenin in retailing their formula to opponents and followers that he uttered a prophetic warning: "Whoever attempts to achieve socialism by any other route than that of political democracy will inevitably arrive at the most absurd and reactionary conclusions both political and economic." [17] It must be said that history has borne out the truth of this prophecy, as it has a matching prophecy made about the same time by Leon Trotsky concerning Lenin's centralized and dictatorial party machine: "The organization of the party will take the place of the party itself; the central committee will take the place of the organization and finally the dictator will take the place of the central committee."

Both forebodings were fulfilled to the letter. In 1917 when they joined forces for the seizure of power, the two men amnestied each other's errors. Trotsky accepted Lenin's party machine, Lenin Trotsky's impatient formula for skipping the "bourgeois" democratic revolution in favor of a proletarian dictatorship in permanence. An undemocratic party machine to make an undemocratic revolution—from such a mating what progeny could spring except a permanent single-party dictatorship?

During the upheavals of 1905 Lenin was still wrestling with the prescription that the revolution had to be bourgeois and democratic. At the same time he was issuing such horrendous slogans, that his opponents told him he would "frighten off" the bourgeoisie. That gave him a unique idea for reconciling the appearance of orthodoxy with the impatience of his will to power. The bourgeoisie, he answered his critics, could not be trusted to carry out their own revolution. They would compromise, make deals with the throne, settle for a limited monarchy, desert when the going got rough. Well then, good riddance!

> Those who really understand the role of the peasantry in the victorious Russian revolution would not dream of saying that the sweep of the revolution would be diminished if the bourgeoisie deserted it. For, as a matter of fact, the Russian revolution will assume its real sweep, will really assume the widest revolutionary sweep possible in the epoch of bourgeois-democratic revolution, only when the bourgeoisie deserts it and when the masses of the peasantry come out as active revolutionaries side by side with the proletariat. The proletariat must carry out to the end the democratic revolution, and in this unite

> to itself the mass of the peasantry in order to crush the autocracy by force and paralyze the instability of the bourgeoisie.[18]

In short, a bourgeois revolution without the bourgeoisie! Who but Lenin could have thought up that? The peasantry would serve as an *ersatz* "bourgeoisie," and "the democratic dictatorship of the proletariat and the peasantry" would serve as a substitute for "bourgeois democracy." Who but Lenin could have thought that one up, either?

Having invented a bourgeois revolution without the bourgeoisie and a democratic revolution without democracy, there was one more innovation for Lenin to make: a proletarian revolution without the proletariat. Actually, he had been working on that since 1902. "Cut off from the influence of Social Democracy," Lenin wrote in his first signed article for *Iskra,* "the workingmen's movement becomes petty and inevitably bourgeois." That single sentence was enough to finish off the entire existentialist class theory of Marx. With his usual methodical hammering home of his views, Lenin expanded it in article after article, then into that classic formulation of Leninism, *What's to be Done?* If "consciousness" comes not from the instincts and experience of the working class but only "from outside," if its bearers and formulators are "by their social position educated representatives of the possessing classes, the intelligentsia," then such a classless elite of "professional revolutionaries" might seize power, not as Marx thought, where the economy was most advanced and the working class most numerous, organized and cultured, but just as easily, nay more easily, where the economy was backward and the workingmen neither a majority nor mature nor conscious nor organized, and where the political organization of all parties was rudimentary. Not ripeness is all as Marx had thought, but readiness is all. This line of thought runs back not to Marx but to Babeuf, Buonarroti, Blanqui, Pestel, Bakunin, Nechaev, Tkachov, and Chernyshevsky.

Such a classless elite as Lenin contemplated, since it was "the vanguard of the proletariat" by self-selection and definition, could seize power through nationalist uprisings in colonial lands or at the head of peasant armies. It would be possible for restless students, ambitious officers, politicians out of power, and nondescript guerrilla bands to seize power in the name of the proletariat in lands where the proletariat was in its infancy, or represented only in the rudimentary form of artisans and craftsmen, or plantation workers and serfs, and modern industry was virtually nonexistent. Such proletarian power could come out of the mouth of the guns of peasant armies. Thus Ho Chi-minh and Mao Tse-tung could found their "proletarian regimes" in lands not yet "ripe for capitalism" but by definition ripe for socialist or communist power or, more precisely, for single party dictatorships where the single party, though it speaks of socialism, may be nothing more than a dictator's praetorian guard.

When it became apparent to Lenin that the workingmen of Western Europe were rejecting communism, at the Third Congress of the Comintern he turned his face to the East and spelled out the implications of his elitist doctrine for the nationalist revolutionaries of Asia and Africa. Indeed, it is only Hitler and Mussolini in Europe, and nationalists become heads of states in Asia and Africa, who imitated certain aspects of Bolshevism. What they imitated was not soviets' or workers' rule, but one-party government, an elitist ruling caste, and personal dictatorship. Thus was completed the transformation of Marxism into Marxism-Leninism, and Lenin's successors from Stalin to Brezhnev have in varying ways applied this doctrine to Nasser, Nkrumah, Sekou Touré, Ben Bella, Sukarno, Ho Chi-minh and Mao Tse-tung. Support for "wars of liberation" is the Siamese twin of the slogan of "peaceful coexistence," particularly if the leader of the war proclaims himself dictator in the name of socialism or communism, backs Russia's proposals in the United Nations, and plays the dangerous game of *kto kogo* by seeking arms and "technicians" in Moscow.[19]

However far this may be from Marx's conceptions, there is a kind of *valenki* (homespun) wisdom in Lenin's paradoxical bourgeois revolution without the bourgeoisie and his substitution of an elite one-party dictatorship for proletarian rule. How else could he strive for his own revolution and his own power in a backward and overwhelmingly peasant land, where even demography spoke against proletarian dictatorship?

In 1917, when the tsarist regime collapsed unexpectedly to the surprise of Lenin and of the demoralized, "slothful, and unfit for combat" (Trotsky's words) [20] garrison of the capital, when a company of soldiers impulsively disobeyed a command to fire on a demonstration, and a few "well-aimed stray bullets" felled some officers, it was fear of punishment for their unexpected violation of army discipline that made the peasants in uniform fear to return to their barracks, caused them to try to call out other regiments or seek to mingle with the crowds and give up their arms. The same fear made them turn to the Duma, the spokesman of unfamiliar parties, and the Soviet, in a search for justifications, protection from punishment, and larger meanings for their impulsive act of mutiny. All these things they got in full measure. After a moment of fear and hesitation, society gave them celebration and glorification, and gave them to understand that they were the victorious heroes of a century-long, forlorn struggle that tiny bands of intellectuals had waged for freedom.[21]

It was Lenin, irreconcilable enemy of the spontaneous and elemental *stikhia,* who understood most clearly that in this gray mass, with its fear of punishment for indiscipline, its desire to avoid transfer to the front, its disorderly use of its weapons, its new-found glorification, its unrest, uncertainty, inexperience, and vulnerability to plausible demagogic slogans, he had the dynamite to blow up the infirm foundations of the Provisional Government. Lenin wrote of the *dvoevlastie,* the dual power of Provisional Government and Soviet, but actually, in 1917 and 1918, both before and after Lenin's minuscule party seized the telephone and telegraph office, the bank, the Winter Palace, and other symbols of centralized rule, the real power lay in this third and only real force, the gray mass of the *stikhia* with guns in their hands and a profound uncertainty as to what use to put them to. Unlike the soviets of 1905, the Soviet of 1917, along with delegates from the factories, was made up of soldiers' deputies. In that lay its superiority over the Duma and the Provisional Government.

"A revolution," wrote Mussolini, "is an idea with bayonets." Or as Mao put it more nakedly: "Power comes out of the barrel of a gun." Both of them had learned from Lenin, who knew instantly that if he could link up even for a brief moment of history those guns with his ideas, or at least alienate these peasants-in-uniform from their superiors and their habit of obedience long enough to neutralize them on the day of his coup, then the coveted power might be his. After that there would be time enough for the renewal of his battle with the *stikhia* to "transform it from a revolutionary mass into a captive mass," a transformation that Merle Fainsod was to call "one of the most poignant of totalitarian achievements." Lenin was not abandoning his war to "organize everything," merely furthering it by first disorganizing everything in order to open for himself the road to power. Out of this dual process he might not be able to make a proletarian revolution or a socialist revolution, but it would not be a bourgeois revolution either.

What then would it be? Out of the past seems to come once more the voice of Friedrich Engels, this time telling Vera Zasulich how tricky a revolution can be when the "conditions work against" those who are making it: "The people who boasted that they had *made* the revolution always found out the next day that they did not know what they were doing, that the revolution *made* by them was not at all like the revolution they wanted to make." [22]

"When we get power," Lenin wrote in 1916, "we will establish a dictatorship of the proletariat. . . . Dictatorship is the rule of a part of society over the whole of society, and, moreover, a rule basing itself directly on force." After two years in power, he summed up his rule in one grim sentence: "Dictatorship is a harsh, heavy, and even bloody word." And on October 10, 1920, rounding out his third year as dictator, he bade his opponents remember: "The scientific concept of dictatorship means neither more nor less than unlimited power, resting directly on force, not limited by anything, not restricted by any laws nor any absolute rules. Nothing else but that."

This formulation is beautiful in its pedantic clarity, for the first giant step in the establishment of a totalitarian power is the destruction of all the restraints that, even in a nonrevolutionary autocracy, tend to limit power: the restraints of religion, morals, traditions, institutions, constitutions written or unwritten, laws, customs, private conscience, public opinion—in short, anything and everything that may place any limits on power and any restrictions upon an attempt to atomize and remake a people. The history of all totalitarian regimes [23] has proved the rightness of Lenin's "scientific" definition.

Lenin moved naturally from his prior dictatorial regime inside the Bolshevik party to dictatorship over the land in which his party ruled. Except for his strange utopian dreams of the period when he was writing *State and Revolution,* there is nothing in Lenin's basic writings to suggest that he ever thought the proletariat itself capable of dictating or ruling. From the outset he showed distrust of all the social orders of society. To his distrust of court and gentry natural in a revolutionist of his temper, his distrust of the "bourgeoisie" and of liberals and democrats, which tended to distinguish him from the Mensheviks, and his distrust of the peasantry as property-minded because they wanted to own the land they tilled and dispose of the product of their own labor, Lenin alone among socialists added and forcefully expressed distrust of the working class and of the rank and file and the local and district organs of his party. His dictatorship was correspondingly wide and deep in its scope.

> The spontaneous development of the workers' movement [he had written at the beginning of his career as a "Leninist"] leads to . . . the ideological enslavement of the workers to the bourgeoisie . . . Therefore, the question: what is to be done to bring to the workers political knowledge? cannot be answered by "go to the workers," . . . The Social Democrats must *go into all classes of the population* . . . direct all manifestations of this all-sided struggle, to be able "to dictate a positive program of action" alike to rebellious students, to dissatisfied zemstvo figures, discontented members of the dissenting religious sects, indignant schoolteachers, and so on.[24]

Thus, what Lenin was aiming at in 1917 was nothing less than a dictatorship over the proletariat through its self-appointed vanguard, and, through the proletariat as "the most advanced and revolutionary class in society," over the entire population. Quite literally he proposed to do in 1917 what he had first outlined in 1902: "go into all classes of the population . . . direct all manifestations of this all-sided struggle, dictate a positive program of action alike to rebellious students, dissatisfied zemstvo figures, discontented members of the dissenting religious sects, indignant schoolteachers, and so on." *Dictate a positive program of action to every class of society*—that is what he and his successors have been doing for fifty years. In this sense, too, their dictatorship has been totalitarian.

That "dictate" was never merely metaphorical, Lenin made clear quite early while still an editor of *Iskra.* To his colleagues he wrote a memorandum saying: "We should show every kindness to the peasantry but not yield an inch in our maximum program. . . . If the peasants don't accept socialism when the dictatorship comes, we should say to them, *It's no use wasting words when you've got to use force.*" On the margin of his memorandum Vera Zasulich wrote: "Upon millions of people? Just you try!" When Lenin came to power, that is just what he tried. For more than three years of his four-year rule he tried force, until the disappearance of agricultural goods and the uprising in Kronstadt forced him to retreat. But his "best disciple" returned to the attack: With fire and sword, force and famine and concentration camp against millions of peasants, he drove them minus their hastily slaughtered livestock into the new serfdom of the collective farms. And Stalin's successors seem determined to continue the system of collectivized agriculture though their agricultural statistics proclaim that on 3.3 per cent of the arable land of Russia (their private parcels) the self-same peasants produce 34 per cent of the meat, milk, butter, eggs, fruit, and vegetables—with nothing but a hoe, a spade, a watering can, a bent back, and the joy of knowing that they are working for themselves.

For all Lenin's distrust of the "petty-bourgeois spontaneity" of the masses, it was they and not his little band of professional revolutionaries who in 1905 shook the foundations of autocracy and in 1917 overthrew the Tsar. Lenin then saw that the role of his professional revolutionaries was not to prepare a revolution but to prepare to take advantage of an upheaval which, like the French Revolution, took all the principal actors by surprise, astonishing the victors no less than the vanquished. His *apparat* proved to be a machine not for making revolution but for seizing power once the revolution had been made and power lay in the barracks and the street. So unexpected to Lenin was the fall of the Tsar that as late as January 20, 1917, he told a youth audience in Zurich that he did not expect his generation to live to see the revolution, a privilege reserved for theirs. And no less unexpected was the freedom accorded him by the Provisional Government. He expected to be arrested when his train pulled into the Finland Station on April 3, but was greeted instead by brass bands, honor guards, searchlights sweeping the midnight sky, a bouquet of flowers, and an armored car to take him to Kseshinskaya's Palace.

"Mir schwindelt—my head spins!" he said to Trotsky as they waited in the wings in the early morning of October 25. And in 1918, to console his followers for the "delay" in the revolution in the West, he confided in a moment of frankness:

> To foretell when a revolution will ripen, to promise that it will come tomorrow, is to deceive. You remember, particularly those of you who have lived through both Russian Revolutions, which of you could have asserted in 1904 that in two months a hundred thousand Petersburg workers would go to the Winter Palace and open a great revolution? And remember, how could we in December 1916 assert that in two months, within a few days, the tsarist monarchy would be overthrown? [25]

When the Tsar fell and power was nominally in the hands of the Council of Ministers of "the freest war-time government in the world," when the masses, worn out by the babel of conflicting voices, unfulfilled expectations, and unsolved problems, were relapsing into apathy,[26] and the government had lost its reliable support in the army after the Kornilov fiasco, then Lenin's party and its scratched together armed detachments were sufficient, under Lenin's unremitting pressure, to forestall both the Soviet Congress that was to meet on the morrow of their coup, and the Constituent Assembly. Lenin had his way even against the judgment of the majority of his Central Committee, and his so-called "Soviet Government" not only faced the Constitutional Convention, but the soviets as well, with a *fait accompli.* Thus did Lenin seize power not in a land "ripe for socialism" but in a land ripe for seizing power. Afterwards he said in astonishment, "it was as easy as lifting up a feather." [27]

LENIN'S VISION OF UTOPIA

A few months before he made his bid for power, a strange thing happened to Lenin in a succession of hideouts during July 1917. The Bolshevik-Anarchist attempt to probe the ground with the bayonet in early July had ended in failure, and the government had gotten wind of the fact that he was receiving money from the German General

Staff. "Won't they shoot us now?" he asked Trotsky, who apparently knew nothing of the German help.[28] Uncertain how much the government had learned, Lenin thought it best to go into hiding, while Trotsky courted arrest and trial.

Enforced leisure in scenes remote from the day-to-day struggle, gave Lenin time to meditate on the world he would bring into being on taking power. He was secure in his hideouts, in the home of Alliluev, hidden in a haystack on the marshy shore of a lake, then in the cozy safety of the home of the Police Chief of Helsinki in Finland; a long suppressed side of his nature came to the surface as he dreamed of the cloud-cuckoo land he would create when he could sweep away the old and build the world anew.

Since 1916 he had been under the spell of something Bukharin had written. Bukharin had spoken of "a general attack [of the proletariat] on the ruling bandits in which they destroy the state organization of the bourgeoisie," and free society from the crushing weight of the modern super-state Leviathan; then "production will be directed by *society* and not by the state." Lenin had been as much taken by Bukharin's fierce image of the smashing of the state as by his gentle dream of the beginning of stateless freedom. It was not like Lenin to think thus, yet now the vision of a stateless society took possession of him. In his hideout, buttressed by a handful of quotations from Marx and a much greater number from Engels, he wrote his own version of the dream. He spoke of "a magic means of getting the toilers, the poor, to share in the day-to-day work of governing," of "setting up a state apparatus of ten or twenty million people," of making that administration so simple that "every laborer or kitchen cook [kukharka]" could master it.[29]

His imagination continued to soar as he proclaimed an unwonted and unlimited faith in the spontaneous creative power of the masses, and outlined unlimited promises in a little book to be known as *State and Revolution.* There had always been in Lenin a recessive strain of an insurrectionary anarchist, until then held firmly in check by the authoritarian, centralist, dictatorial strain that had dominated his spirit since 1902. But now, in the sheltered remoteness of his hideouts, he meditated on Bukharin's little book,[30] recalled the hitherto repressed but no less sacred quotations from Marx and Engels, and built his daydream utopia. If he deceived the masses with his simplified slogans and sweeping promises, if he took in Anarchists, Left Social-Revolutionaries, and many of his own intellectual followers by this dream, I cannot help but think that for a brief moment he persuaded himself as well.

Nothing in the resultant *State and Revolution* fits into the pattern of the orthodox Leninism that runs from *What's To Be Done?,* begun in the autumn of 1901, to the *April Theses* begun on the train headed for the Finland Station, nor into the pattern of the steps he would take beginning on the morning of October 25, 1917 to consolidate the power he had seized during the night. But there had been a young Lenin once who dreamed of freedom and who "bore a passionate love" for his master, Plekhanov. He had stifled the dream as he had the great love and sought to remake his spirit according to his blueprint of what a revolutionary should be. The model for his blueprint was the "rigorist," Rakhmetov, from Chernyshevsky's novel, the title of which he had borrowed for his own key work, *What's To Be Done?* Like Rakhmetov he would harden his spirit by sleeping on nails, stifle the love within his breast, school himself "to regard all persons without sentiment and keep a stone in one's sling," stop listening "too often" to his favorite music ("It makes you want to stroke people's heads, but you mustn't stroke any one's head, you might get your hand bitten off, you have to hit people over the head").[31]

In *State and Revolution* there is no party to command and centralize all direction and control, no submissive mass to carry out the party's orders. Indeed, in all the hundred odd pages there is only one scant mention of the word "party" and then in a context which makes it not a "general staff" but the performer of an ancillary task. In this utopia it is the masses who are in command. An unwonted Lenin expressed complete faith in the soundness of their spontaneous reactions, their elemental moods and instincts. There is no need of *edinonachalie* or one-man rule, such as he was to advocate after a year or so of attempting to rule over mass chaos.

> The workers, having conquered political power, will break up the old bureaucratic apparatus, shatter it to its very foundations until not one stone is left standing upon another; and they will replace it with a new one consisting of these same workingmen and employees, *against* whose transformation into bureaucrats measures will be taken at once . . . 1) not only electivity but also subjection to recall at any time; 2) wages no higher than that of a workingman; 3) immediate going over to a situation in which *all* in turn will become "bureaucrats" and for that reason *no one* can become a "bureaucrat." [32]

There was to be no standing army, no police, no bureaucracy, no hierarchy; justice would be dispensed on the spot by the revolutionary instinct of any accidental crowd that gathered at the scene of a crime.

(Lenin called it "trial by the street," in America we call it lynch law.) The affairs of state would be so simplified that from the beginning they could be handled by any one who knew how to read and write and perform simple operations in arithmetic, and later would become so simple that affairs of state might be mastered by any female cook. Such is Utopia in this un-Leninist Leninist classic.

DREAM INTO NIGHTMARE

Once in power, the dream of a utopia where the masses were free and managed everything on their own initiative, was converted overnight from bright dream to nightmare. On November 18 Lenin called upon the people to "show initiative" by "arresting and handing over to revolutionary tribunals" all who were guilty of sabotage, opposition, or concealing of supplies. The street would be the judge. Then, in a draft article, with unconscious irony entitled "How to Organize Competition," Lenin called upon each village, town, and commune to show "initiative and inventiveness" in devising ways of "cleansing the Russian land of all noxious insects, scoundrel fleas, bedbug rich." (Such epithets deprive men of their humanity and make inhumanity more "natural.")

> In one place they will put into prison a dozen rich men, a dozen scoundrels, a half dozen workers who shirk on the job. . . . In another, set them to cleaning outside toilets. In a third give them yellow tickets [prostitutes' identity cards] after a term in prison . . . so that the entire people can act as overseers over them. . . . In a fourth, they will shoot on the spot one out of every ten guilty of sloth. . . . The more varied, the better . . . for only practice can work out the best measures and means of struggle.

Within another three weeks, Lenin's faith in the masses even for vengeance had ebbed away and he invented the Extraordinary Commission or Cheka. On January 27, 1918 he demanded that the entire working class be conscripted for the terror. Workers who did not want to join in the hunt against "speculators" must be "forced to under threat of deprivation of their bread cards." "Regiments and workshops that do not accurately set up the required number of detachments [*accurately* is a typical word for this pedantry of terror] will be deprived of bread cards and subject to revolutionary measures of persuasion and punishment." "Speculators caught with the goods . . . will be shot on the spot." "The same punishment for members of the detachments convicted of bad faith."

Capital punishment for crimes against property had been abolished in tsarist Russia. As a socialist, Lenin himself had voted for the abolition of capital punishment for all crimes in 1910 at the Copenhagen Congress of the Socialist International. But now he restored the death penalty even for "bagmen," peasants who brought grain or vegetables in bags on their backs to trade for things made in the city. "As long as we don't apply terror, shooting on the spot," he said on January 14, 1918, "we won't get anywhere."

When the Civil War ended, in January 1920, the death penalty was abolished, but it was restored in May. It was not abolished again until 1947, then once more restored in 1950. Under Khrushchev the death penalty was imposed with great publicity for "exceptionally serious economic crimes," including looting and embezzling of state and public property (private property is not that sacred), counterfeiting, speculating in foreign goods and currencies, cheating on a large scale, and for "repeated" crimes against state property. Under Brezhnev capital punishment for crimes against property seems not to be enforced, but it has not been repealed. As the philosopher George Kline observed: "To take a man's life because he has taken the state's property is a practice that cannot be morally justified in terms of *any* ethical position that recognizes the non-instrumental worth or intrinsic dignity of the human person." [33] When the twentieth century opened, men were sure that capital punishment for crimes against property, and torture to extract confessions, had been abolished for good in all civilized lands. What then shall we think of the regime Lenin set up and his successors continue?

Il n'y a que le provisoire qui dure—It is only the provisional which lasts. Doubtless Lenin did not intend his application of terror to chaos to be more than temporary. But the terror outlasted him and his successors have guarded this part of their heritage. The *che* in Cheka signifies "extraordinary" or "temporary," but with ever changing names and initials, G.P.U., O.G.P.U., N.K.V.D., M.V.D., M.G.B., K.G.B., the secret police has swelled up and become ubiquitous, spying on Communists no less than on non-Communists, spying on each other and on the army, planting agents in every embassy, getting reports from *dvorniki* in every apartment house, seeking to ferret out economic crimes, thought crimes, and all the galaxy of crimes that "socialist legality" can think of. A recent informed estimate puts the number of the secret police at approximately a million. They themselves and the people of Russia recognize the continuity in all the changing initials by still using for their members the term *chekist*.

LENIN'S BELATED DOUBTS

As he lay dying, Lenin began to have second thoughts on his proud "scientific" definition of dictatorship as unlimited power, resting directly on force and unrestrained by any limits, ethical, legal, or traditional. Surely force should not be used by Communists in their discussions with each other. Anxiously, he said to Bukharin in one of the latter's last visits to him, "Let no blood flow among us." And the peasants? Did he remember the words of Vera Zasulich as he dictated now in the scant four to fifteen minutes per day allowed to him by his doctors? One cannot use force to bring the peasants to socialism, he decided, nor did the N.E.P. need to be reversed. What was needed was more industrial goods for the peasants in exchange for their own products, better equipment, general literacy, and genuine cooperatives that would attract the entire peasantry, and indeed the entire population. The N.E.P., plus cooperatives, plus culture [34]—would carry the peasant, and carry Russia, from state capitalism to socialism.

On January 4 and 6, 1923, he dictated in two fifteen minute sessions his "On Cooperation." He recognized that he was shifting from the use of power ("we don't need more power, we have enough of it") and "political struggle" to "cultural work" and "civilized, i.e. European cooperatives." "We are forced," he dictated in words that must have taken much travail to come to, *"We are forced to admit a radical change in our entire view of socialism."*

> In introducing the N.E.P., we forgot to think about cooperatives. . . . the only task that really remains for us (in connection with the N.E.P. and because of the N.E.P.) is to organize the population in cooperative societies. When the greatest possible part of the population is organized in cooperatives, socialism automatically achieves its aim. . . . Now we have the right to say that the simple growth of cooperation is identical with the growth of socialism. . . . Before us remain two main tasks. The one is to completely transform our apparatus which is worthless. . . . the other is cultural work among the peasants . . . with the economic aim of their learning cooperation.

Not force, Lenin sought to explain to those in whom earlier he had so often inculcated the idea of force as the sovereign means, not force but patience and simplicity and generosity were needed. The means must be *"the simplest, easiest, most acceptable to the peasant."* It had cost hundreds of millions of rubles to bring capitalism into being. In the same way "we too must give extraordinary support to the system we are trying to bring into being, the system of cooperatives." He spoke of financial aid, help to cooperative marketing in which "the really great masses of the population take part," tax aid, bank loans, subsidies, bonuses, more culture on the part of the Communists to fit them to foster more culture in the peasantry, financial assistance against bad harvests and famines, and "a number of other economic, financial, and banking privileges."

> N.E.P. is adjustable to the level of most ordinary peasants and does not make any excessive demands of him. But it will take a whole historical epoch, in the best case one or two decades, to get the entire population through the N.E.P. into the habit of reading books, the ability to be a cultured trader, which means a good cooperator . . . and to give the assistance that will produce a civilized cooperator.[35]

The work was published with proper fanfare in *Pravda*. But neither Trotsky, nor Kamenev, nor Zinoviev, nor Piatakov, nor Stalin accepted the solemn injunction. And when Bukharin sought to enjoin this attitude toward the peasantry upon Stalin, it cost him his good name and his life. What would have come of following Lenin's behest we cannot say. But one thing is clear: Forty years of Stalin's way of forced collectivization has produced an unending state of crisis in Russian agriculture, while the petty incentive remedies proposed from time to time do not touch the heart of the problem then created, nor give signs of solving it.

Lenin longed to be able to address one more congress of his party to communicate his belated doubts on the value of unrestricted and unlimited force as the great solver of all problems. It was not only about the peasantry that he wanted to speak, but on the way force was beginning to corrode the inner life of his party. He had just learned that Orjonikidze, a Georgian carrying with him plenary powers as representative of the Central Committee, had bullied the two leading Georgian Communists, Mdivani and Makharadze in a discussion on the problem of the extent of Georgian Communist autonomy, and had struck Mdivani a blow in his face. Then General Secretary Stalin and Cheka Chief Dzerzhinsky had investigated and sustained Orjonikidze. To Mdivani and Makharadze Lenin wrote, with a copy for Trotsky whom he begged to take up the case on his behalf: "I am heart and soul behind you. . . . Orjonikidze's brutalities and the connivance of Stalin and Dzerzhinsky have outraged me. On your behalf I am preparing notes and a speech."

The speech could never be delivered; Trotsky, for reasons he has never been able to make clear, refused to take the case. As for Stalin, whom Lenin in his last days sought to have removed from the dangerous power post of General Secretary, he went on to flesh out

Lenin's "scientific definition" with a nightmarish content, untrammelled by the moral impedimenta that Lenin carried with him from the more humane age and social layer into which he had been born. It was Joseph Stalin who showed what naked force not limited by anything could really amount to. Now indeed, "the dream of reason was to beget monsters," at the thought of which even the imagination of Stalin's closest accomplices still reels. Stalin went on to complete the atomization of society that Lenin had begun; to destroy the last vestiges of independence of such organizations as the trade unions and the various bodies of writers; to break up the silent solidarity of the village, wipe out the independent peasantry, and agglomerate the separate atoms into the new serfdom of the kolkhoz; to introduce speedup and piece work into the factory along with Stakhanovism, chaining workers to their jobs, and adding to the classic Russian body-soul-and-passport a new document, the workbook. It is not these measures that repel Stalin's successors, indeed, they regard this part of their heritage with pride and build upon it.

But many of Lenin's lieutenants of the generation of Stalin were shocked by the ruthless exploitation of worker and peasant for the "primitive accumulation" of capital funds for forced industrialization. As Stalin became aware of the disagreement inside the ruling party, the blood purge spread into the party that Lenin had built, until it too was completely atomized. With every purge of a leader came the purge of a retinue, those who admired him, those who had served under him, those whose fortunes had been advanced by him, those related to him by friendship or blood. More Communists were killed on the orders of Joseph Stalin in time of peace than all the anti-Communist governments, armies, police, and courts had executed during civil war, White terror, and the suppression of Communist uprisings. If Hitler could number his Communist dead in tens of thousands, Stalin could number them in hundreds of thousands.

The bloody stain spread through the army, disgracing it as no other army in history when seventy per cent of all its high officer staff from the rank of colonel up to general and marshal were declared to have been "traitors in the service of foreign enemy powers" and were executed. A social mobility of sorts was promoted by decimating whole strata of party secretaries, managers, technicians, engineers, planners, and even statisticians (all of which doesn't prevent some denizens of ivory towers from asking solemnly whether Stalin wasn't "necessary for the industrialization and defense of Russia?") The purge culminated in a purge of the purgers, prosecutors, judges, executioners, even chiefs of the secret police. And just before death claimed the despot, he was busy planning a new widespread purge beginning with the most reputable doctors in Russia, those serving the health of the top rulers in the Kremlin.

If one were to say that Stalin was necessary to the total atomization of the Russian people, there would be some truth in it, though how much of the nightmare arose from the vengeful and paranoid nature of an aging tyrant, and how much was "rational" from the standpoint of atomization for totalitarian rule, is impossible to say. What is certain is that at the time of his death, even the closest circle of his lieutenants and his own family had lost members in the purges while the rest feared for their lives.

A REGIME OF PERMANENT ILLEGITIMACY

As the survivors engaged in a muted struggle for the succession and did away with Beria in good Stalinist fashion, they gave pledges to each other that no secret police or praetorian guard would ever again be permitted to make a shambles of the Party. Yet such is the alluring nature of total power, and such their heritage from Lenin and Stalin, that they have done nothing to institutionalize their pledge so as to safeguard their country from the possible rise to leadership of another "mad dictator."

Since Stalin's death, his lieutenants have been wrestling with his ghost, de-Stalinizing, rehabilitating some of his victims, partially re-Stalinizing, as they strive to determine the proper size for the ghost, a problem that remains insoluble. They cannot write him too large lest they remind people of their own complicity in his crimes, and lest he continue to dwarf them all, rendering them too small to succeed him. Yet they cannot write him too small either, for from him they inherit their power, the atomized society over which they rule, the conquests he made during World War II, the totally subjugated peasantry, the monopoly of the means of communication, the legend of an infallible party possessing an infallible doctrine. Moreover, through him runs the apostolic succession and their very claim to rule over a great nation.

A strange infallibility this, for they themselves have testified that the infallible doctrine and Party-structure gave them five years of a Lenin so soft in the head that he surrounded himself with traitors, all of them able to fool the great genius. His death was followed by twenty-five years during which the Party and country were ruled by a dictator increasingly paranoid who unjustly and capriciously calumniated and killed countless loyal and wise comrades. Then came seven years of the rule of a lout who proved to be a feckless adventurer and a hair-brained schemer. What does that make of the first fifty years of Communist rule?

Elsewhere [36] I have ventured to formulate a "law of diminishing dictators," not merely because Stalin seemed to me to be of smaller stature than Lenin, and Khrushchev smaller than Stalin (as Brezhnev seems smaller than Khrushchev), but because there is something in the nature of Lenin's epigoni and their dictatorship that causes them to exclude from their entourage men of independent mind or original and critical intelligence in favor of unquestioning supporters, eager executors, courtiers and sycophants. To be sure, there is always the possibility of surprises. The man who seems smallish while dwarfed by the infallible-in-power, once he succeeds to unrestrained power himself over one-sixth of the earth, more than two hundred million people, the world's largest army, orbital bombs, and rockets that can hit Venus and the moon—may grow into his job in ways that may surprise his entourage. Absolute power, unrestrained by any institutional checks or moral code or any surrounding critical voices, tends to unhinge the mind. And always there is that sickness that affects all tyrants—they cannot trust their friends.

When, fifty years ago, the Tsar of All the Russias renounced his throne for himself and his son, the ancient monarchical hereditary legitimacy was ruptured. The Provisional Government that succeeded was of doubtful legitimacy but possessed the grace—the only significant grace in a government arising out of revolution—to regard itself as *provisional* or *pre-legitimate,* and to recognize as its highest political task that of founding a new legitimacy through a constitutional convention. When Lenin forestalled the Soviet Congress, presenting it with a dictatorship of his party as a *fait accompli,* and then dispersed the Constituent Assembly by force of arms, Russia remained without a legitimate government. Lenin formulated this view himself with admirable clarity when he described his dictatorship as "nothing more nor less than unrestricted power, not limited by anything, not restrained by any laws, nor by any absolute rules, resting directly on force, *that, and nothing else but that.*"

Having rejected all limitations, constitutional, legal, traditional, or moral, having taken power by force and held it by force, having deliberately forestalled or dispersed any possible source of a new legitimacy, Lenin had openly proclaimed a dictatorship that should last until the apocalypse, the coming of "complete communism." This consummation he devoutly believed before he took power, or so he wrote in the bemused pages of *State and Revolution,* was a blessed event that would come with astonishing celerity. The revolution would spread to the ends of the earth. The state would "begin to wither away" on the day he took power, and state affairs would become so simple that they would provide "a magic means of getting the toilers and the poor to share in the day-to-day work of governing," beginning with "a state apparatus of ten or twenty million people" in which none would be bureaucrats for all would be mastering the affairs formerly reserved for the bureaucracy. In time those affairs would become so simple that every *kukharka* could master them.

But what withered away on the grim morrow of power was not the state but the very idea of the withering away of the state. With the one-party state that Lenin founded, he strove and Stalin strove more successfully, to embrace every aspect of social and individual life, until the Party and its state became, or sought to become, co-extensive with society, thereby swelling to totality. In place of every cook becoming master of affairs of state, the state became master of the affairs of every cook. Gradually, the apocalypse of "complete communism" was pushed into an ever remoter future, becoming a part of eschatology, the "science of the last things." Until then, an unending succession of present generations are to be sacrificed to that ever receding future, which means that each present generation will continue to be discontented with its lot and in need of continued dictatorship.

For such a regime, even after half a century of continued existence, no legitimacy is possible. It may well continue to endure indefinitely, for it rules over an atomized society and possesses a total monopoly of the means of livelihood of its subjects, a total monopoly of power over them, and a total monopoly of the means of communication and public expression of thought.

To disarm its critics, Lenin early developed four devices of semantic confusion to supplement his honestly held belief that his party was entitled to absolute and total power because it possessed an infallible scientific doctrine which told men what history wanted them to do, be, and become. The first device is the confusing of the proletariat with the people. The second is the confusing of the Party with the proletariat. The third is the confusing of the *apparat* or Party machine with the Party. The fourth is the confusing of a tiny oligarchy, or a single *Vozhd'* or Leader or Boss, with the Party machine. Thus when the *Vozhd'* speaks, the Party leadership has spoken. When the Party leadership has spoken, the Party has spoken. When the Party, vanguard of the proletariat, has spoken, the proletariat has spoken. When the proletariat has spoken, the people have spoken. And insofar as the Russian Party manages to retain leadership of the International Communist Movement and "All Progressive Forces," the peoples of the world have spoken. As for the totalitarian state, it is merely the most all-embracing of the transmission belts of the Party.

All of these semantic inventions are to be credited to Lenin. As Pascal called hypocrisy the tribute that vice pays to virtue, so we may recognize these subterfuges as the tribute that dictatorship pays to democracy, man's will to be free and to control his rulers. These inventions have grown stale and unprofitable after fifty years of repetition, but Lenin's heirs do not dare dispense with them lest their world come tumbling down. As we probe these fictions they dissolve before our eyes. The Soviet Government is no government by soviets, for all decisions are made elsewhere, in Party councils. The Party is no party, for party means a part; where there are no contending parties and no groupings on principles allowed within the single party, life dies out in it.

Where then shall legitimacy lodge? There is no provision in statutes or constitutions for a personal leader, yet an infallible doctrine in the long run requires a single infallible interpreter. If there are a number of conflicting interpretations the doctrine itself loses its certainty and its "scientific" and infallible character. The people, being voiceless and denied independent organization, may look with sympathy on one of the contending factions, and pluralism will break out in the *monolith.* The word monolith is well chosen for it is the single block of granite that marks the spot where political life lies entombed under the weight of total dictatorship.

When a leader dies, who shall name his successor? Not the soviets, for they have been drained of life; not the people, for they have no voice; not the Central Committee for it has been replaced by the Politburo or Presidium, and that in turn by the Secretariat. Only "a handful of politicians, a clique," as Rosa Luxemburg put it, remains to proclaim its "collective leadership," concealing its rivalries and internal differences until a new Infallible emerges to proclaim his former collective associates to be anti-Party, or opponents of all the sound and wholesome policies that the Party in its wisdom is adopting.

From her cell in prison in the summer of 1918, fifty years ago, Rosa Luxemburg admonished Lenin with friendly intention in these words:

> Freedom for the supporters of the government alone, freedom only for members of one party—that is no freedom at all. Freedom is always and exclusively freedom for one who thinks differently. All that is wholesome and purifying in political freedom depends upon this essential characteristic, and its effectiveness vanishes when freedom becomes a special privilege.
>
> With the suppression of political life in the land as a whole, life in the Soviets must also grow more and more crippled. Without general elections, without unrestricted freedom of press and assembly, without a free struggle of opinion, life will die out in every institution. . . . A few dozen leaders will direct and rule. . . . an elite of the working class will be invited from time to time to meetings to applaud the speeches of the leaders and unanimously approve resolutions. . . . not a dictatorship of the proletariat but a dictatorship of a handful of politicians, a clique. . . . Such conditions must inevitably cause a brutalization of public life.[37]

How grimly history has confirmed her prophecy! What she could not foresee was that it would be Lenin himself who would destroy the internal life of his party by prohibiting under pain of expulsion serious groupings for the discussion of differences. Or that his General Secretary would kill more members of his Party than all its enemies put together.

The vision of purpose that once inspired this dictatorial structure began to erode the moment Lenin found himself in possession of the levers of power. But the basic ideology of Marxism-Leninism was structural in character. Organization, centralization, the monopoly of economic power, political power and spiritual power, permanent dictatorship, force unrestrained by anything, these were the substance of Lenin's dreams from 1902 onward. He completed the edifice of dictatorship not under the impact of civil war but after the civil war was safely over when, at the Tenth Congress of his Party, he pushed through the provision prohibiting groupings for internal party discussion.

Like despotic structures in general this totalitarian structure has built-in staying powers. Given the "law of diminishing dictatorships," given too the muted discontents and weariness and boredom with fifty years of ever less vivid repetition of the semantic fictions we have noted, there is no way of telling how long this system will endure. But at the end of fifty years it is clear that within it inheres no independent public life, no true legitimacy, nor any intention of seeking it by a free discussion and free vote of the people subject to its rule, or a free functioning of the "public bodies" imposed by the Party and state upon an atomized, yet over-organized people.

"Yes, the dictatorship of a single party!" said Lenin in 1919. "We stand on this, and from this ground we cannot move." [38] "The Communist Party has been, is, and will be, the only master of the minds, the only expresser of the thoughts and hopes, the only leader and organizer of the people," said *Pravda* on the fortieth anniversary of the seizure of power by Lenin. And the First Secretary of the Armenian Central Committee added the fitting commentary: "Only ignoramuses (for I do not speak now of outright enemies) could maintain that there might exist some other force besides the party . . . some other force than the party leadership, that could express the will of the Soviet people." [39] All through the self-congratulatory editorials of the fiftieth jubilee year, *Pravda* rang the monotonous changes on the same theme in such formulae as "The Communist Party is the mind, the conscience, and the will of the Soviet people."

In this formula is expressed the durable core of what has been misnamed the "Soviet" system. What I said of it ten years ago at Oxford, I am afraid must still be said today:

> As long as collective leadership does not determinedly broaden itself instead of narrowing; as long as it does not openly treat itself as pre-legitimate in the sense of aiming to replace itself by a broader, non-dictatorial organization of power; as long as power itself does not flow down into the basic units of the Party (where it did not inhere even in Lenin's day); and as long as it does not then overflow the party dikes and spill over into self-organizing corporate bodies, independent of Party, police, and state; as long as there do not develop organs and arenas of organization and expression free of party controls; as long, finally, as there develop no organized, independent, institutionalized checks upon the flow of power to the top, not a mere slowing but an actual reversal of the whole trend of totalitarianism—there is no reason to regard any directory or collective leadership as more than an interregnum between dictators, [and at every dictator's death] there will be no legitimacy to provide a lawful succession.[40]

And at the moment of this writing I cannot imagine any faction in the Communist Party that would make as its program and purpose the devolution of power to the limbs and parts of the body politic, or a genuine attempt to establish a new democratic legitimacy. Nor can I presently imagine a set of circumstances that might engender such a faction or tendency.

THE BASIS AND DEVELOPMENT OF THE SOVIET POLITY

Leonard Schapiro

The Soviet state came into existence in November 1917 as the result of a revolutionary seizure of power. The Bolsheviks claimed then, as their successors still maintain, that they were creating a society of an entirely new kind, the like of which has never been known before, and that the result in no way resembled anything that had ever existed before. It is not necessary at this point to comment on this traditional view. The uncommitted historian will perhaps be more concerned to look for the main elements which went into the composition of the new state, and these can, I think, be summarized under three headings.

There is first the theoretical element, since no one can deny that the Bolsheviks were, at any rate in part, motivated by strongly ideological considerations. There was secondly the traditional element. Whatever the Bolsheviks may have said about themselves, their revolutionary seizure of power took place within Russian history and within the orbit of Russian traditions and it was inevitable that some specifically Russian features should have left their mark on what emerged. And then, thirdly, as in every revolution there were the fortuitous and unpredictable happenings, and these form the necessary third element in our analysis of the origins of the Soviet polity.

Under the heading of the theoretical element, one might list three components: There is first of all Marxism; and within Marxism in particular the broad identification of state and society, the view that society and the state must become co-extensive to such a degree that the state ceases to be something independent of society, and society in turn absorbs all the functions and activities of the state. I should also list as one of the fundamental features of Marxist doctrine, though perhaps associated more with Engels than with Marx, the belief that society, until it has been transformed into a socialist society, cannot provide real freedom for the individual; the individual will always be subject to exploitation by the dominant bourgeois class which will prevent his exercise of real freedom and will leave him only formal freedom. There is also the component of Marxism which takes the dynamic, forward looking view of human society. Society is moving toward a goal and therefore the individual or the present generation must, if necessary, be sacrificed to the benefit of all, or to the benefit of the future, in order to achieve that great destiny which history has in store for mankind.

Next, there is the Bolshevik adaptation of Marxism. This consists mainly of the two essential elements which Lenin added to the theories of Marx—no doubt with the Russian situation in mind. There is first of all, of course, the elitism, the reliance on the Party, on organization, the realization that without a determined organization nothing can be achieved, and so forth. But I think there is something else as well. There is a kind of hard "Bazarovism" about Lenin, a kind of assertion of the need to put an end to the sentimentality, the vacillations, the intellectual cerebrations, which characterized the Russian intelligentsia. In Lenin's terms it would be "anti-Oblomovism." One could argue that in making the Russian intellectual more tough, more fit for his revolutionary task, more ruthless, Lenin at the same time destroyed the features which had made his nobility and self-sacrifice the center of so much admiration. But I think this transformation of the Russian *intelligent* was as essential an addition to Leninism as Lenin's insistence on Party leadership and Party organization.

There is also a third feature of this general element. However much Bolshevism may have neglected or may have transformed the Social Democratic tradition, however much Lenin may have scoffed at and derided the Social Democratic tradition of freedom of speech for the working class, nevertheless something of this tradition of freedom remained which even Lenin could not destroy. In the early years, after all, the Party was a very mixed company. The first serious purge took place only in 1921. Until then the Party remained a conglomeration of socialists of many colors who had hastily joined the victorious Bolshevik group. Something of the old libertarian tradition lingered on until rooted out by Stalin.

So much for the theoretical element. Let us look at the traditional element. Now of course it is a commonplace to argue that in a country in which there had been so long a tradition of autocracy the chances of one dictatorship replacing another were always very high. I should go rather farther than that. I think the habit of autocracy had persisted in Russia in spite of the interlude of the constitutional period and the even shorter interlude of the Provisional Government. On the one hand Lenin was probably the only Social Democrat to recognize the need in Russian conditions to capture and use the central autocratic power. He was, as is known, relatively indifferent to the soviets, which he was prepared to support or discard as opportunity required, and much of his talk of democracy and mass support has to be taken with a very large grain of salt. In this respect Lenin was very different not only from the Mensheviks but from many of his followers—as events very soon after the Bolshevik coming to power were to show. Conversely, the one institution which might have replaced the autocracy as a viable center of legitimate authority, the Duma, had signally failed. The whole of its existence was not a failure, on the contrary it had some very remarkable achievements to its credit. But at the crucial time, when the unexpected revolution broke out in March, the Duma failed to take over and to become the center of authority and very soon lost the position which it might conceivably have been able to win in the imagination of the population. The Provisional Government, as it were, operated in a vacuum, with the Petrograd Soviet increasingly occupying the place in popular imagination that might legitimately have been won by the Duma had circumstances been otherwise. Whatever the reason, within this vacuum the Bolshevik restoration of the one institution which had a traditional and accepted reason for its existence, the monarchy, in the new guise of Lenin and his Council of People's Commissars, was a fairly easy step.

Another tradition, however, was equally decisive in shaping the nature of the new state. This was the traditional revolutionary fear of counterrevolution. This was based on the experience of Europe, the defeat, as the revolutionaries saw it, of the French Revolution and more recently in revolutionary imagination the defeat of the revolutions of 1848 and the suppression of the Paris Commune. We need not consider the rights and wrongs of this tradition, nor indeed how far the traditional fear, even if valid for West European conditions, had very much application in Russian conditions. But it was very strongly felt indeed by revolutionaries from the extreme right to the extreme left. It colored all Bolshevik policy from the start. But what was more important, during the rule of the Provisional Government it had strongly colored the policy of that government. The Provisional Government lived in the belief that the revolution was in danger and had to be safeguarded. That these fears were grossly exaggerated may very well have been the case, but they did much to hamper the Provisional Government in its attempts to establish the kind of authority which might have given it a chance to survive. Notable of course was the episode of Kornilov's rising, when the reaction of the

Provisional Government to a threat of which the magnitude was enormously inflamed by their own imagination led directly to the rise and triumph of the Bolsheviks. I should also add that the emergence within the Bolshevik faction, at the very earliest stages, of a powerful terror organization to deal with its enemies was also a part of this tradition.

And lastly what might be called the fortuitous, the accidental element, the concatenation of circumstances which do not appear to have been foreseen or planned, but which nevertheless closely affected the course of events. One could list many such circumstances connected with the foundation of the Soviet state, but two in particular seem to have been of outstanding importance. The first was the divergence, quarrel even, between Lenin and Trotsky on the course which the revolution should take during the last days before the seizure of power by the Bolsheviks. Lenin was primarily insistent on speed. To wait, for example, for the meeting of the Second Congress of Soviets was according to Lenin nothing short of madness. Trotsky on the other hand, who unlike Lenin was on the spot in Petrograd, saw the importance of linking what was essentially a military coup d'état to the democratic façade of the soviets. He was therefore insistent that the seizure of power should coincide with the meeting of the Second Congress of Soviets which in fact took place on November 7, 1917 (October 25, Old Style). The actual seizure of power by the Red Guards took place shortly before the opening of the congress, but in the result, either by accident or by design, the seizure of power could be portrayed as a seizure of power by the soviets in the name of the people. The whole future democratic façade was therefore made possible by this brilliant tactical move of Trotsky's.

The second fortuitous circumstance was the mistake of the Mensheviks and the Social Revolutionaries in leaving the Second Congress of Soviets. The majority of them stumped out in protest against the military coup d'état by the Bolsheviks. Now protests are all very well in democratic societies where they can affect an electorate, but they were totally useless in the conditions then prevailing. The Bolsheviks voted themselves into power with the almost unanimous support of those who stayed behind. This was probably not a decisive factor, but it made it easier for Lenin to begin to build up the kind of monopoly of power which had been his aim from the first. The importance of this tactical victory may have been quite considerable, if one recollects that at that time the general view, even among rank-and-file Bolsheviks, was that the proper course was rule by the soviets, which meant rule by all the left-wing parties and not only by the Bolsheviks.

THE FOUNDATIONS LAID

During the period from November 1917 until April 1921 the Bolsheviks, having established themselves in sole power after a short and unsuccessful coalition with the Left Social-Revolutionaries, consolidated their precarious hold over the country. A policy of terror toward political opponents was a foregone conclusion, as some of Lenin's critics inside the Bolshevik faction had foreseen. It is indeed obvious that a minority party can establish itself in sole power only by methods of terror. The machinery of terror already existed in rudimentary form before the October Revolution, in the shape of the security organization within the Military Revolutionary Council, which the Bolsheviks of the Petrograd Soviet dominated on the eve of their seizure of power. There was, however, no fully consistent or worked out policy toward political opponents, so far as can be discovered, when the Bolsheviks came to power. The result was a policy which was never fully consistent and which took shape empirically largely under the impact of events.

So far as bourgeois opponents were concerned, that is to say center and right-wing opponents, there was never any question that these would be treated as enemies and rendered harmless. This was a matter on which there was no dissension in the Party, and Lenin's policy won almost unchallenged support from his colleagues. This was indeed an essential part of the revolutionary tradition which all Social Democrats, both Bolshevik and Menshevik, were prepared to accept. The position was quite different as regards the repression of socialist opponents, the Mensheviks and the Social Revolutionaries. Here the attitude of the Bolsheviks was ambivalent. That is not to say that Lenin himself had any serious qualms in the matter, but in the early years of power even Lenin could not go against the revolutionary tradition which accepted the right of all left-wing parties to a voice in the affairs of the new revolutionary state. The great majority of Bolshevik deputies to the Second Congress of Soviets in November 1917 had expressed, in answer to questionnaires submitted to them, their conviction that government should be shared by all left-wing parties. The notion of a complete monopoly of power still lay ahead.

The period up to the end of 1920 illustrates this ambivalent attitude. Both Mensheviks and Social Revolutionaries were continuously harried, arrested, released, rearrested on trumped up charges, forcibly expelled from soviets to which they were elected, and the like. But, except for a short period in 1918, they were not officially outlawed. Of course, the trend toward the establishment of a Bolshevik monopoly was already pretty obvious after the dispersal of the Constituent

Assembly and after the violent break up of the coalition with the Left Social-Revolutionaries in July 1918. But advice by Lenin to the Communists of the city of Yelets offered shortly after the July revolt illustrates the way in which even Lenin had to take account of the tradition of tolerance toward socialist opponents in the Social Democratic movement. The Communists of Yelets had pursued the usual practice of hounding and persecuting the Left Social-Revolutionaries who were still entitled to sit in the local soviet to which they had been elected. The Yelets Communists sought Lenin's advice on the matter, and he replied as follows: "It is a pity that you have not arrested them [the Left Social-Revolutionaries] as is being done everywhere. It is essential to oust all Social Revolutionaries from responsible posts . . . we cannot of course, give you written authorization to arrest Social Revolutionaries, but if you drive them out of Soviet organs, if you arrest them and expose them before the workers and peasants and if you destroy their influence before the peasantry (if they have any) you will be doing good revolutionary work, and we in the center . . . will only praise you for it."

There was one matter in which there was full agreement in the Party. This was the question of dissent inside the Party by Party members. Subsequent events suggest that this tradition may not have been entirely welcome to Lenin, but there are no indications until 1920 or 1921 that he was able to do very much about it. It must be remembered that the Party had grown very rapidly and was no longer the small band of carefully disciplined and purged followers which Lenin had built up before the revolution. Throughout the period until 1921, dissent in the Party was free, criticism was unrestrained, and debate was fast and furious. The subsequent opponents of Stalin were to look back on this period with nostalgia and to claim, somewhat inaccurately in view of Lenin's policy before the revolution, that this represented the true Bolshevik tradition. It was however a fact that during these years Lenin retained his authority in the Party not by forcible measures against his colleagues nor by repression of criticism, but by his powers of persuasion and by the logic of his case. It was in this way that he succeeded in winning over the party in 1918 against the views of the Left Communists, and in establishing the main outlines of his policy in the succeeding years.

The real break in policy came at the end of 1920 and the beginning of 1921, and took place in response to certain definite trends within the Party. The elimination of other socialists and the suppression of dissent in the Party is explained by Bolshevik and pro-Bolshevik historians as having been due to the emergency of the situation and the need to deal with enemies of the revolution. This is a very much oversimplified explanation, which is improbable if only for the reason that Socialist opponents, and in particular the Mensheviks, were tolerated throughout the Civil War when one might have expected, had there been any truth in the official explanation, their elimination as a threat to security; they were only finally suppressed after the virtual end of the Civil War in November 1920. One of the main reasons for the decision to eliminate the Mensheviks and Social Revolutionaries from the political scene, and to put an end to the very limited tolerance which had been extended to them hitherto, was the growing effectiveness of their criticism and the increase of their popularity. Menshevik criticism of Bolshevik repressive measures and of the growing intolerance of dissent was beginning to find considerable response in the trade unions and among workers generally. This was very much in contrast to the very low ebb of Menshevik popularity in 1917 and 1918. The Social Revolutionaries were in turn becoming the spokesmen of the wave of peasant discontent with the repressive policy of procurement and with communism generally, which was beginning to break out into violence on a big scale. Moreover, the Mensheviks had for some time before 1921 been advocating the essential features of what was to become Lenin's New Economic Policy. Once Lenin decided to make this break, it was essential for him to begin by eliminating his critics—unless he was prepared to take them into a coalition government.

Similarly, the virtual end of dissent inside the Communist Party, which was imposed at the Tenth Party Congress in March of 1921, has often been explained in terms of the emergency of the situation. The outbreak of the Kronstadt revolt and the wave of strikes in Petrograd certainly lend some justification to the view that this was a panic measure dictated by fear. But again it is doubtful if this is the whole story. By 1920 Lenin was facing a considerable crisis in the party in the form of syndicalist demands by the trade-union Communists who wanted more freedom of action and more extensive control over industry than the Bolshevik authoritarian and centralistic tradition could conceivably have tolerated. Again, it was in 1920 and early in 1921 that the disciplined central machinery of the party was forged. This was in part an improvisation resulting from a number of fortuitous circumstances. But the revival of what was so essential a feature of Lenin's political faith had a more immediate and practical cause: the threat of localism, the demand of Communists in the local soviets for greater initiative, even leading at times to questioning the need for Party leadership at all, except in the ideological sphere. One can imagine Lenin's reaction to this!

It is obvious that the policy established at the Tenth Party Congress, of central control and the virtual elimination of all dissent within the Party, was in tune with the whole of Lenin's pre-revolutionary thought as it developed in the last months of his exile in 1899. It is also true that there is a certain ambivalence in Lenin's views at this period which suggests that he may have wavered before deciding to create a monolithic party. Assertions were frequently made after 1921 that this was only a temporary solution which never represented Lenin's permanent policy. It is impossible to give a final answer on this, because Lenin only had about a year's work ahead of him and was not even in full control of affairs during this year. Moreover it can be said that if the measures of March 1921 were dictated by the emergency, then the emergency remained in full force so long as Lenin stayed at the helm. On the other hand, there is no doubt that there are elements of a totalitarian attitude in all Lenin's thought, beginning with *What Is to be Done*. There is further the strong element of utopianism in Lenin, as expressed in *State and Revolution,* which envisages a return to a kind of primitive city-state ideal, in which cooperation on a voluntary basis by all will take the place of government. Obviously, the realization of such utopian dreams can only be attempted by means of considerable force. There is moreover Lenin's consistent refusal to recognize the supremacy of the law or the separation of powers; also his faith in the predominance of the Party in all spheres of activity. Finally, one must recognize the progressive retrenchment by Lenin of the hope of the withering away of the state which was so boldly proclaimed in *State and Revolution* as about to begin immediately after the revolution. By 1921 Lenin was envisaging forty to fifty years of dictatorship, even if, as he believed, this dictatorship would take place in relaxed economic conditions, under which voluntary cooperation, especially by the peasants, in socialist schemes would take place progressively as evidence accumulated that socialism offered the best way of life. The question of Lenin's intentions must remain one of the unsolved problems of Soviet history. Of his policy as it developed in the hands of his successors, however, there is no doubt.

THE RISE OF STALIN: 1922–36

Two main aspects of the first period of Stalin's rise to power, after he became General Secretary in 1922, affected the nature of the Soviet state. First of all, the consolidation of the dominance over the country of the monopolistic Party in its monolithic form. This Stalin had inherited from Lenin: the Party which brooked no rivals, and the Party which had set up iron discipline in its own ranks.

The first clear assertion of Party supremacy was the role which the highly centralized Party was destined to play in the ostensibly federal structure embodied in the first Constitution of the Soviet Union. This constitution provided for a federal structure of union republics with wide autonomy, including the quite exceptional and quite unrealistic right of secession. But the debates at the Party congress in 1923 showed quite clearly, as indeed some of the Communist critics who were still bold enough to challenge Stalin were able to point out, that any autonomy granted by the constitution in the sphere of the state machinery was going to be totally unrealistic so long as the highly centralized Party predominated. This feature of Soviet federalism remains as prominent today as it was in 1923. True, at different periods, and particularly during the first phase of Khrushchev's rule, the union republics attained greater autonomy in certain spheres than they had ever enjoyed before. But then as today, republican autonomy was tolerated autonomy which the centralized "All Union" Party can always withdraw or circumvent.

The second aspect of this consolidation of the Party stranglehold during the first period of Stalin's rise to power was the elaborate development of the Party apparatus. Building on the foundations which had been evolved in 1920 and 1921, Stalin enlarged the apparatus and perfected its hold and control over individual Party members. The instruments of discipline were considerably strengthened, and by 1925 if not before the whole process of election of Party officials and of deputies to Party meetings was completely controlled by the Secretariat. It is, of course, common knowledge that this enabled Stalin with relative ease to defeat Trotsky and his other political opponents.

The third feature of this period was the rise of the police—the G.P.U. and later the O.G.P.U. The security organs dated from November 1917, but their use against the Party was generally avoided in the early years. The first prominent case of the direct intervention of the police in a Party affair was the trial in 1923 of Sultan-Galiev, the national Tartar communist leader. By the time the struggle with Trotsky and his supporters was reaching its height in 1926 and 1927, the police had become a normal instrument of action against opponents.

It is plain that in all these instances the debt Stalin owed to Lenin was great, even though the manner in which Stalin used the apparatus with which Lenin had provided him was very different from the way in which Lenin might have used it. No doubt also a large element in the development of Stalin's power was personal ambition. Lenin was ambitious in the sense that he was confident in his own rightness and therefore intolerant of all opposition to his views, but unlike Stalin Lenin did not seek his own personal aggrandizement. However, it would be wrong, in my view, to attribute Stalin's method of achieving control over the country solely to personal ambition. Stalin did not enjoy moral authority in the Party or the respect or even legitimacy which Lenin enjoyed as revolutionary leader. Therefore, insofar as the Soviet system demanded the presence of one authoritative leader, as I think was the case, there was no way other than violence open to Stalin to assert that authority. With the experience of fifty years of this type of rule we can confidently assert that the whole idea of a monolithic party is nonsense. Indeed, voices are being heard even in the ranks of the Party apparatus in the Soviet Union today to the effect that dissent and difference of opinion are healthy phenomena and that unanimity cannot be expected in any assembly of thinking human beings. It is not unreasonable to suppose that Lenin would at any rate have tempered violence with some attempt to conciliate the pluralistic forces which survived within the Communist Party for many years. But this path was not open to Stalin, and was indeed totally alien to his character.

Stalin's second main contribution to the nature of the Soviet state was his "third revolution": the enforced collectivization and rapid industrialization following upon the elimination of the right opposition headed by Bukharin. Of course, this momentous turn in Soviet policy can be explained, no doubt ought to be explained in part, in terms of economic necessity. It can again be argued that for a man like Stalin, who had already made so many enemies as General Secretary, there was no way other than terror to accomplish this economic revolution. But we must remember that the economic policy had a very definite political objective. This consisted mainly in the desire to eliminate possible opponents, who belonged to the earlier period of revolutionary history and who were therefore not prepared to accept Stalin as their undisputed leader. It is also possible, as often asserted by Soviet and pro-Soviet historians, that there was a genuine fear in 1928 or 1929 of peasant sabotage. I have never been strongly convinced by the evidence of this, but it is possible that Stalin was.

It is notable that throughout this period Stalin was unable to assert the kind of total control which appears to have been his object when he launched the terror in mid-1936. From the mysterious murder of Kirov on December 1, 1934 until mid-1936, much still remains obscure. But it seems a fair inference that Stalin was faced with the possibility of a revolt within the Party centered around Kirov, and that he was playing a very careful political game in order to deal with potential enemies. While playing for time, he skillfully exploited the fear within the Party that a violent change of leadership could precipitate the downfall of the whole regime. He was also very skillful in appearing to conciliate the more moderate elements, the former right-wing leaders who were allowed to return to some position of tolerated existence after the Seventeenth Party Congress in 1934. The whole farce of the ostensibly democratic constitution of 1936, drafted by a group of oppositionists headed by Bukharin and promulgated in the very midst of the terror, is one illustration of this conciliatory policy. Another was the toleration in 1936 of a discussion which took place in the Legal Institute, headed by Pashukanis, which aimed at liberalizing and humanizing the draconic Soviet criminal system. Here again Pashukanis was allowed to conduct his debate almost up to the moment in 1937 when the police swooped down upon him.

There was a certain inexorable logic about the use of Stalin's terror machine. True, his enemies were of his own creation. But, having created them, he was faced with the prospect that if he did not eliminate them they would eliminate him. These enemies were both the Old Bolsheviks who did not recognize his authority and the moderates of the N.E.P. period, the Leninists, as they saw themselves, headed by Bukharin, who believed that Lenin's policy of a long period of cooperation and relaxation of the class struggle was the right one.

The imposition of totalitarian control by Lenin and Stalin, in their different ways, required nearly twenty years, from 1917 until 1936. Throughout that time resistance in one form or another, both within the Party, and outside it, was never absent from the Soviet scene. If the accounts that have reached us are correct, then the last opposition within the Central Committee was only broken at the end of 1936 or the beginning of 1937. It is often asserted that the Soviet regime found ready acceptance among a population which had no sense of democracy and little ability to defend its freedom. It is probably true that the opposition displayed little skill in defending itself. But the suggestion that the Russian people suffered from some peculiar fatality which destined them for despotism will not stand up. It is only necessary to recall that the much more politically developed Germans were subjugated by Hitler in fourteen months in contrast to the nineteen or twenty years required by the Communists to achieve the same result in Russia.

PERSONAL DESPOTISM: 1936–53

The period of terror from 1936 to 1938 entirely transformed the Soviet system. Before the terror Stalin ruled through his monopolistic and monolithic party, after the terror the despotism was much more personal. I have never been convinced that Stalin's policy of terror was the policy of a madman or that it lacked a basic, inherent logic of its own. It can of course be argued that anyone who is prepared to sacrifice millions of lives in order to achieve his ends can scarcely be regarded as fully sane. But there is a pattern about Stalin's policy during the terror and a certain inherent logic in the whole process which does not suggest the action of a madman. In the first place, the elimination of those fantastic percentages of Party members and members of the bureaucracy seemed to serve a very definite plan, which was indeed recognized by Stalin himself at the Eighteenth Party Congress in 1939. What he achieved was a total social transformation of the ruling apparatus, and the replacement of Party and government officials, whose dependence on Stalin was not total in the sense that they had revolutionary records of their own, by henchmen whose sole loyalty was to Stalin, to whom they owed everything. Moreover the process by which tens if not hundreds of thousands rose to prominence on the corpses of their superiors whom they had denounced bound these men to Stalin in a link of common guilt. This common guilt made them more inclined to be circumspect in their actions and speech and created, in the phrase of Professor Fainsod, "a system of institutionalized suspicion," or to use a phrase which was current during and after the period of terror, and indeed still is, "the generation of those who had been frightened once and for all."

But there was also an inherent logic in the extent of the terror. Once you start on a policy of this kind, it must extend to all sections of society. No republic and no branch of the service, be it police, Party, state apparatus, or army, could be allowed to survive unscathed. Terror had to be extended to all so that dreams of revenge might be stilled, as Stalin hoped, forever. It may be that after the war he felt that memories of the thirties no longer inspired fear in the new generation which was beginning to knock at the door. Theories that toward the end of his life Stalin was contemplating another mammoth purge thus acquire a certain degree of conviction. It may indeed be that if you govern by terror you have to be prepared to repeat the dose at intervals.

The most notable feature of Stalin's second period of rule was the setting up of a much more elaborate democratic façade than had hitherto been the case. For example, the Party as part of the Soviet system of government had not even been mentioned in the constitution of the R.S.F.S.R. of 1918 or the first All-Union Constitution. In the Stalin Constitution of 1936 the Party is openly acclaimed as the leading core of all institutions. The whole machinery of government was also transformed in the sense that the unwieldy All-Union Congress of Soviets which was totally unsuited to be a legislature was replaced by the more compact Supreme Soviet with its Presidium and its two chambers. True, this Supreme Soviet has never played any part as a real legislative body. But it was part of Stalin's style of government to create the appearance of normal, democratic governmental institutions. Moreover, the new Soviet no longer harked back to the traditional soviets of Lenin's day which were specifically designed to unite executive and legislature and proclaimed with pride their novel and ostensibly totally democratic and popular nature. The Soviet Union was now endowed with an orthodox bicameral legislature, with secret elections based on universal and equal franchise. The cabinet, the Council of People's Commissars, later the Council of Ministers, was nominally responsible to the Supreme Soviet. This highly centralized executive and policy-making ministerial body was designed to run the entire nationalized industry of the country, and its scope of operation was very much extended.

In addition the constitution proclaimed fundamental civil rights. True, analysis of this constitution shows that in many instances the civil rights are not guaranteed even on paper in a way which would be of very much use if the relevant paragraphs should ever be tested in the courts. For example, freedom of speech, assembly, and the like are only guaranteed, even on paper, in the interests of strengthening the socialist system, and it was obvious that the Party alone, or Stalin himself, was going to be the final arbiter as to what did and did not "strengthen the socialist system." In any case, the question was academic because the one thing that the Soviet Constitution lacked was any provision for judicial review, or any other means by which the citizen could test the actions of the government before any independent tribunal. Nevertheless the constitution was quite sufficient to take in a great deal of quite enlightened opinion outside Russia, and may still take in some people today. No doubt, in the atmosphere of the Popular Front Era which then prevailed, the bemusing of foreign opinion, and particularly foreign Socialist opinion, was one of the main objects of the Stalin Constitution. But I do not think it was the sole object. It was part of the method of Stalin's rule to recognize the importance of a façade even if he had no intention of letting it become more than a façade. The constitution in force today is virtually identical with the one promulgated by Stalin. There is no more provision today for judicial review than there was in 1936. The nature of the guarantees is as limited as it was in 1936. Nevertheless, the very existence of the document is an important element in Soviet life in the sense that the inconsistency between constitution and daily practice is a constant stimulus to criticism and opposition. We repeatedly hear nowadays of protests to the Soviet authorities, from within the churches, particularly the Baptist movement, from intellectuals and so forth, in which violation of the constitution is criticized.

All this would suggest that Stalin intended to set up a democratic façade behind which the Party would in fact exercise the real power. Had this been the case it would have been little more than a continuation in rather more elaborate form of the principle of rule devised by Lenin in 1917. Paradoxically, however, this was very far from being the case. The Party under Stalin remained monolithic but not monopolistic. There was no longer a monopoly of rule by the Party, but a monopoly of rule by Stalin. In exercising this personal rule, Stalin naturally relied on the Party as one instrument of control. But however important, it was only one of several instruments. He relied additionally on the police, on the government apparatus, and even to some extent on the army. Each of these pillars of rule was used as required, and it cannot really be said of the second period of Stalin's reign that any one pillar was at all times clearly superior to another. Each was terrorized, streamlined, and thoroughly subordinated to the personal despotism which Stalin exercised over the whole country; but none could be singled out as supreme. This became particularly evident during the war, when Party and government apparatus became to a very large extent fused, and one or other was used interchangeably according to the needs of the moment. This was also evident after the war when at different periods in the later years of Stalin's rule it very often became impossible to determine whether the Party apparatus was more important or the government apparatus. At times the one appeared more influential and at different times the other. Indeed, some competent students of the Soviet scene have suggested that Malenkov, when presumably forced to choose between the two offices which he held after Stalin's death, Chairman of the Council of Ministers and Secretary of the Party, chose the former in the mistaken belief that the government apparatus was going to be the more influential in the future.

Of course Stalin's personal despotism was not exercised by one man alone. The hub of his rule lay in his private secretariat or Secret Department of the Central Committee, which was the center of authority, at any rate after 1936. It is very significant that this private secretariat has never been identified since his death and it is virtually certain that it no longer exists. Equally important were the personal agents who carried out Stalin's behests. Vyshinsky, the Chief Procurator, was one such agent and there were a number of others, all of whom met their death or at any rate disappeared very soon after Stalin's death. There is no reason to doubt Khrushchev's description in his speech in closed session to the Twentieth Party Congress in 1956 of how Stalin did not convene the Politburo, but operated through special meetings of two or three Party leaders. Plenary meetings of the Central Committee, let alone Party congresses, were likewise very infrequent. In short, Stalin created a personal despotism to which the entire bureaucratic machine both of the Party and of the government was in the last resort subordinate.

It was a notable feature of this regime of Stalin's that industry and agriculture, indeed the entire state bureaucracy, was controlled through a complex network of informers and police agents. But the police were not operating as an independent agency, and, as became evident in 1938, were themselves subject to purging and decimation as much as any of the other instruments of control. Stalin destroyed the whole polity, such as it was and such as it had been built up by Lenin, and replaced it by a system in which he held all the reins of power and in which there was no obstacle to his personal rule so long as he could control the few devoted agents whom he required to pass on his orders.

This seems of considerable relevance for our understanding of totalitarian systems in general. Insofar as "totalitarian system" implies control by a ruler or ruling elite of all institutions and the suppression of every conceivable kind of pluralism, no one could seriously dispute that Stalin's regime was totalitarian. But this totalitarian regime was maintained for years without the need for a monopolistic party. A number of authors have argued that the single party enjoying a monopoly of power is an essential feature of a totalitarian regime. The Soviet experience during the second phase of Stalin's rule certainly seems to throw considerable doubt on this particular hypothesis.

It was natural enough that this flouting of the Party—for it was little less than that—by Stalin should have created considerable resentment and anticipation in the minds of the members of the Party apparatus in particular, and indeed in the ranks of the Party as a whole. This must have been particularly true in view of the enormous growth from an elite to a mass Party during the war and the years immediately following the war. This had involved the influx of a new generation of younger men without much influence, but nevertheless men to whom an appeal to the traditions of the Party could still be made. It was therefore only to be expected that Stalin's death would be followed by an attempt to restore the Party to its former predominance, to its monopoly position in fact, and that the man who succeeded in doing so could get off to a good start in terms of support from that section of Soviet society where the biggest vested interest and the strongest tradition of rule was to be found. It was Khrushchev who understood the importance of this factor and introduced an entirely new relation between Party and state.

THE ERA OF KHRUSHCHEV: 1953–64

The rise and fall of Nikita Khrushchev appears as the drama of a flamboyant and ambitious personality who grew overconfident and allowed himself to be removed by his rivals. It would be wrong, however, to see this solely in terms of a personal struggle. When Stalin died in March 1953, certain objective factors determined the future course of Soviet politics and would probably have obtained irrespective of the personalities of his heirs. Having escaped from the terrorized atmosphere, and possibly from the imminent danger of another purge which, if Khrushchev was right, was to have been aimed at the highest levels of the Party leadership, Stalin's heirs must have been united on one thing: No one of them could be allowed to assume the position which Stalin had occupied. This became evident very shortly after Stalin's death in the clear determination of Stalin's heirs not to allow Malenkov to achieve a dominant position in the new leadership. The rise of the Party, in the person of its secretary Khrushchev, may have been facilitated by Malenkov's decision, if it was voluntary, to take the post of Chairman of the Council of Ministers rather than retain that of the senior Party secretary. But when once the position of senior secretary fell to Khrushchev, who was soon to assume the title of First Secretary, it became evident that his was the dominant machine. His rise to full power, which was achieved by November 1957, was more than the assertion by one man of his own position in the power struggle. It was also the putting through of a definite policy—the policy of re-establishing the authority of the Party which had been so severely damaged by Stalin.

If we ask ourselves why the division of the leadership lasted for so short a time, the answer must be sought not only in the superior tactical skill of Khrushchev—though that certainly played its part. The main reason was probably that Khrushchev was, as it were, on the better side. His policy of re-establishing the authority of the Party commanded considerable support; it enjoyed the full advantages of doctrine, of history, and indeed, in spite of Stalin's personal despotism, the advantage of long-established political habit. Moreover Khrushchev appeared to be the prime mover, or made himself appear to be the prime mover, in the policy of undoing the crimes of the past, in the policy of liberalization or de-Stalinization. In this he had the advantage that he was less associated in the public mind with the great purges in which Malenkov had played a very large part.

But the basic reason was, I think, that there is a natural tendency for the Soviet system to be dominated by one leader, and that a deliberate effort is required, of the kind which has apparently been made since 1964, to prevent one man from gaining ascendancy. Certainly Khrushchev had no intention of standing aside, and Malenkov was unable to resist his political skill. One further point should be noted. The dismantling or reduction of the whole policy of unbridled terror which was associated with Stalin was in a sense dictated by circumstances. You cannot exercise terror by committee. So long as Stalin's heirs were not prepared to allow any one man to assume the dominant role which Stalin had enjoyed, it followed that the only possible way of controlling the terror apparatus was through the Party apparatus. The rapid rallying of rivals to defeat what appears to have been an attempt by Beria to assume or assert control over the terror apparatus, showed how deeply the heirs of Stalin were concerned lest any one man usurp the role of Stalin in this respect. Khrushchev tried to avoid this mistake. Throughout his career the control of the police remained under the Party apparatus, though of course as First Secretary his share in that control was a very considerable one.

In examining the innovations which can be associated with the period of Khrushchev's rule, I think we can discount the so-called collective leadership period. He tolerated Malenkov as Prime Minister only for so long as he was unable to get rid of him; he replaced him by Bulganin, who was virtually a nonentity, and at the first opportunity, in March 1958, when he had defeated his rivals in the Party, assumed the post of Chairman of the Council of Ministers as well as that of First Secretary of the Party. In short, it is plain that the main plank of Khrushchev's policy was to reassert the complete domination of the Party over all aspects of Soviet life, including the machinery of government and the apparatus of administration.

Khrushchev's innovations were substantial, striking, and dramatic. Each of them helped to advance Party authority, and therefore his own, yet each of them also had some positive sides to it. It is therefore difficult in disentangling his policy to determine where personal ambition ends and statesmanship begins. The first innovation was the re-establishment of regular, institutionalized Party machinery. Congresses and the Central Committee began to meet once again regularly at all levels, and the Party assumed for the first time in many years the outward appearance of the main authority in the state. Although this was an aspect of Khrushchev's personal ambition in the power struggle, there was more to it. In a system of government based upon dual authority at all levels from top to bottom, interminable conflict is bound to arise. This conflict has bedevilled Soviet politics since the inception of the Soviet regime. Khrushchev's solution in making the Party beyond question the dominant element in the partnership, at all levels and in all aspects of public life, was at any rate one solution. As events were to show, it was not a solution which was acceptable to other powerful areas of influence in the Soviet regime or indeed one which was necessarily consonant with the requirements of a modern industrial state.

As many observers noted, one of the features of Khrushchev's reassertion of the dominance of the Party was an attempt to increase the technical education of members of the Party apparatus. This was designed to obviate friction between the expert and the nonexpert, between the political gadfly personified by the party *apparatchik* and the expertise personified by the director or planner. But giving the Party *apparatchik* a little technical education does not necessarily make him a more suitable person for telling the expert how to do his job, and this has been borne out by experience since the fall of Khrushchev. Still, this was one of the ways in which Khrushchev tried at any rate to tackle a perennial problem of Soviet government.

The second main reform was the great industrial rearrangement of 1957. It was much criticized and no doubt rightly, and has been abandoned by Khrushchev's successors. It was after all economically very much open to question; the economic regions as originally set up were quite unrelated to economic realities. Indeed, as Khrushchev himself was never tired of pointing out, the aim of the reform was not to weaken Party control but to strengthen it, and the adoption of the system, in the teeth of silent opposition from the planners, technicians, and managers, was plainly designed to please the existing hierarchy of first secretaries of Party regions, whose areas of control tended on the whole to coincide with the new Councils of National

Economy. Again the question arises: was this a genuine economic reform or merely playing for favor in the party? However mistakenly, it was probably intended as a genuine reform. When regional Party secretaries were inclined to follow the path of local patriotism rather than the national interest, they were ruthlessly removed. In the event, Khrushchev probably made more enemies by this reform than by any other move. Indeed the antagonism which he created was presumably one of the factors which made his fall in October 1964 much easier.

The next innovation was the reorganization of planning at the highest level which Khrushchev put through at the end of 1962. By this time the system of economic regions instituted in 1957 had largely broken down; the number of regions had been drastically reduced in the intervening years, and other signs of recentralization had become apparent. The new scheme involved a three pronged system of central control over planning and supervision in conjunction with the Councils of National Economy, but it also reintroduced a large measure of centralization. In all this process the Party was to play the dominant part, and there is some reason to suppose that this aroused considerable opposition among the planners, and particularly among those associated with the man who was later to become Prime Minister—Kosygin. This appears from the curious circumstance that when the plan outlined by Khrushchev to the Central Committee in November 1962 was embodied in legislation in January of 1963, a new super-planning organization had been added. This Supreme Council of National Economy had not been mentioned by Khrushchev in November 1962 and seems to have been set up against his wishes. Apparently it was designed as a counter-balance to the new top-level authorities which Khrushchev had set up and which he clearly planned to keep under Party control. The new and unheralded Supreme Council of National Economy, although of course technically subordinate to Khrushchev as Chairman of the Council of Ministers, was nevertheless under the more immediate control of Kosygin as First Deputy Prime Minister and of other persons associated with him who later predominated in the planning mechanism. We also know that Khrushchev referred disparagingly to the Supreme Council and its activities and to persons associated with it.

The refashioning of the planning apparatus was not the only innovation announced at this November 1962 meeting of the Central Committee. Many changes were made in the structure of the Party, of which the most notable was the introduction of two committees at the region level, an agricultural and an industrial committee. In the event not all regional committees were divided, and in any case the industrial one tended to remain the more important of the two. But again, this was a move by Khrushchev to increase Party control at the most significant level. The fact that he was prepared to antagonize an important section of the apparatus (regional first secretaries resented loss of authority) suggests that this curiously flamboyant character was motivated by idealism of a kind and not solely by considerations of personal power. The same can be said perhaps of most of the other innovations in the structure of the Party which were associated with Khrushchev, and none of which have survived him. One was an ephemeral and somewhat eccentric fusion of Party and state apparatus in the great Party-State Control Committee which disappeared soon after the fall of Khrushchev. Another was a new Party-state system of control of agriculture, which incidentally led to a drastic reduction in the number of *raion* (district) secretaries and likewise caused considerable dissatisfaction within the Party apparatus.

It is worth emphasizing once again the main doctrine behind all of Khrushchev's reforms. This was that the Party must become the dominant element in Soviet life. Associated with this was his theoretical innovation, his pronouncement in 1961 in connection with the new Party program adopted in that year, that the Party had now become not the vanguard of the proletariat, but the Party of the entire people. He also foresaw the withering away of the state, of which he claimed to see signs in the institutions of a so-called public nature in the field of law enforcement and in other areas. This was largely make-believe so far as the public organizations were concerned, but it was very real so far as the predominance of the Party was concerned. Soviet theorists were careful to explain that while the state would wither away with the advent of communism, which the program foresees for 1980, at any rate in its earliest stages, the Party would not wither away for a very long time, even under communism. Here then was a full theoretical assertion of the intention to make the Party apparatus the predominant element in Soviet government, and to force the soviets, the courts, the technical administrative machinery, and the like into a subordinate position. It is small wonder, looking back upon it now, that the planners and technocrats of a modern state should have been appalled by this prospect of a nationwide takeover by amateurs, and should have put their heads together to see how they could get rid of so dangerous an innovator. In this they had support from the Party apparatus which Khrushchev, in spite of the new life which he tried to infuse into the Party, had so carelessly antagonized, and no doubt the support of the police, who had suffered a diminution in status as a result of Khrushchev's denunciation of Stalin.

For all its eccentricity, Khrushchev's policy represented an attempt to return to Leninism. After all, it was Lenin for whom the supremacy of Party control at all levels was the ideal of government. Whether such an ideal makes any practical sense fifty years after a revolution, as distinct from the first hectic years immediately following a revolution, is another matter. In this respect Khrushchev may have been something of a throwback to an earlier era and a victim of his own romanticism. But Khrushchev was no Lenin. He antagonized many sections of the Party, he antagonized the planners, and he antagonized the police. In retrospect it is easy to see that when the opportunity came to dislodge him, he could look to no one for support; and in particular, in normal Soviet fashion, certainly not to those who owed their advancement and position solely to his influence.

COLLECTIVE LEADERSHIP

In the first three years after the fall of Khrushchev, virtually all of his innovations in the structure of the Soviet state and Party were dismantled. The Party committees have been reunited, the hybrid Party-state partnerships, with the Party as the senior partner, have been disbanded, and the whole economic regional network of Councils of National Economy has been scrapped. Once again as under Stalin, the ministries at the center which had been virtually abolished by Khrushchev (although many of them came back in the disguise of state committees) have been restored, and once again the industrial complex of the Soviet Union is run by a powerful network of ministries headed by a Council of Ministers. This is not to say that the exaggerated and unworkable overcentralization which characterized so much of Stalin's period has been fully restored. On the contrary an experiment in some kind of decentralization of planning responsibility to individual enterprises has been attempted, and many observers regard this as being the most important development in recent years in the Soviet economy.

By far the most important event after the fall of Khrushchev was the introduction for the first time in Soviet political history of genuine collective leadership. For the first time in very many years there is a genuine division between the leadership of the Party in the person of its General Secretary, as he is once again known, and in the person of the Chairman of the Council of Ministers. Not only are these offices held by different persons—a rare enough event in Soviet practice—but they are held by persons who apparently enjoy equal political status and equal responsibilities. Some would even argue that almost equal political status is enjoyed by the Chairman of the Presidium of the Supreme Soviet, the equivalent of the Soviet President, or Head of State, who has hitherto always been a very humble figure indeed. But the collective leadership is visible not only in this division of important offices. There would also appear to be a fairly clear division of functions between the Party apparatus on the one hand and the government apparatus on the other. The whole machinery of planning, the control of industry, and the control of foreign policy are clearly under the government machine headed by the Chairman of the Council of Ministers. On the other hand, such matters as ideology, control of the police, and relations with foreign Communist parties are under the jurisdiction of the Party. The division is not clear-cut —for example it would be difficult to say into which political field the important area of agricultural administration falls. Nevertheless there does seem to be such a division and a desire by the two incumbents of the dominating offices to maintain something of the nature of an equilibrium.

The natural political situation in the Soviet Union is the predominance of one man, however, and it is natural for this predominant figure to be the leader of the Party. If this situation was avoided for three years after Khrushchev, it must have been by a deliberate act of forbearance. It may well be a precarious balance—the ambitions of one or other of the top leaders, and particularly the General Secretary of the Party, could easily upset it. All that can be said is that at the time of writing (September 1967) there was no sign that this truce or balance had been upset. Now this is an innovation: It is the first time in Soviet history that a new solution has been attempted for this perennial conflict between Party and state, the conflict caused by the existence of dual authority at all levels. Khrushchev tried to solve it by making the Party predominant. There may be many who would like to solve it by abolishing the Party altogether—something of the kind may be on its way in Yugoslavia. But at any rate so far as Soviet experience in the past three years is a guide, it would appear that the solution adopted has been to try to maintain some kind of equilibrium between the two bodies, and therefore to reduce or avoid the conflicts which have bedevilled Soviet political life for so long. How long the balance will last no one who values his reputation would predict.

Another aspect of this attempt, probably a deliberate and carefully agreed upon attempt, to work out a truce between the Party on the one hand and the planners and administrators on the other, is seen in the network of soviets. The hierarchy of soviets, headed by the Chairman of the Presidium of the Supreme Soviet, may indeed be a third party to the "truce." It would be idle to pretend that these soviets play a significant part in the life of the country. In spite of rhetoric on the subject by the Chairman of the Presidium since he assumed office, it is difficult to believe that life in the Soviet Union would not go on exactly the same if the Supreme Soviet never met. Its decisions have always been unanimous, and its deliberations have never been of the slightest importance in the life of the country. Nevertheless, while the Supreme Soviet and its two chambers as such may be of little importance, there are signs of the growing importance of the permanent commissions of the two chambers. Their number has been increased and, especially at the local and union-republic levels, they seem to have some influence. Unlike the Supreme Soviet chambers, the commissions sit for very much longer and, most important of all, deliberate in private. They are therefore not bedevilled by the iron tradition of Soviet political life that all decisions arrived at in public must be unanimous.

A controversy has now raged for years among the lawyers on the question where control over these commissions should lie—in the Presidium or in the chambers themselves. This question would hardly have aroused the interest of the lawyers sufficiently for them to return repeatedly to it in the learned journals unless it carried some practical implications. At the union-republic level, the commissions are beginning to play a part in organizing public opinion, in coordinating local views, and indeed in bringing the local population into some kind of cooperation in the business of local administration. One cannot exaggerate all this activity. It is of a rudimentary kind and is very largely Party controlled. Moreover, since elections to soviets remain a completely Party dominated procedure in which the one candidate endorsed by the Party is necessarily elected, the democratic nature of this development obviously cannot be exaggerated. Nevertheless it is a small sign that efforts are being made to find some kind of avenue outside the Party for the expression of political activity.

SOME GENERAL REFLECTIONS

What stands out in this review of Soviet government and Party rule over fifty years is the enormous influence of the individual personality. At any rate, this seems true up to 1964, until the fall of Khrushchev. Since then, so far as can be seen, it is less the individual personality which matters than the partnership of two or even three persons. Some observers would say that the recent lack of decision, the meandering, the lack of purpose, the inability to adopt a clear-cut policy, have all been due to this feature of Soviet government. But it is perhaps too early to judge recent events. What is plain is that for the first forty-seven years, aside from two brief interregna, the system was dominated by one man who asserted himself by real authority (Lenin), or through terror (Stalin), or through a combination of force of habit and cunning (Khrushchev). This is not surprising. Emphasis on the need for a doctrine or theory according to which all policy must be pursued, requires one man to make decisions. How else can one decide which doctrine is "correct"? Besides, where disagreement is dangerous and majority decision is despised, the need for one-man decision becomes all the more imperative.

Neither the institutions of the Party nor those of the government have been able to take root in political life in the sense that they play an independent role which cannot be overcome by manipulation. Legality, even if much greater in extent than it was under Stalin, is still only tolerated legality, and is only allowed until someone changes his mind. Everything is in a state of suspension and uncertainty. On such soil institutions cannot develop, and the state retains all the traces of being simply an apparatus which primarily reflects the methods of rule imposed upon it, and through it, by one man.

At this point we may ask how appropriate the description "totalitarian" is to present-day Soviet Russia. Now it was obviously much more appropriate to the Soviet Russia of Stalin than to the Soviet Union of Lenin or the Soviet Union since Stalin's death. Yet in essence the system has remained the same throughout. In particular, it has remained an apparatus responsive to the rule of one man or perhaps to the rule of a carefully balanced duumvirate or triumvirate. "Totalitarianism" may really mislead more than it illuminates. There are and always have been forms of personal tyranny, and they tend to take on a strongly individual character which varies with the individual or individuals who impose his or their pattern upon it. If by "totalitarianism," however, we mean no more than the complete domination of all institutions in the state by the ruling elite, then undoubtedly Stalin's Russia was totalitarian; Lenin's probably was not, even if he intended to make it so; since Stalin's death it has remained such in essence, though the control is exercised with less open violence. It is perfectly true that the roots of this totalitarianism of Stalin lie buried in Lenin's utopian dreams of the state absorbed by society and in his doctrine of over-all Party control of all aspects of life which was developed in practice to its highest extent by Khrushchev, very much on the lines envisaged by Lenin. But Khrushchev's experiment broke down, and broke down comparatively quickly. This of itself suggests that a modern state, or a state that aspires to be modern in its technology and in the production of consumer goods, cannot tolerate the high degree of arbitrariness which over-all Party control necessarily implies. In the Soviet system the Party stands for the arbitrary element; the state and the law and the constitutional machinery when they are allowed to operate stand for the certain and predictable element.

Some signs of pluralism have been appearing, and greater observance of legality is evident—in spite of deplorable exceptions and a system of criminal law more severe than that of any civilized state. Soviet pluralism seems to be taking two forms. First, there has been some independent action by groups of people getting together on their own initiative, and not on the initiative of the Party. Such action has not been frequent, but has been all the more striking for its rarity. Groups of intellectuals, groups of churchmen, groups of students, have been able, in spite of the breach with tradition and of the serious risk to their own safety, to make a concerted approach, even exercise repeated pressure on the authorities.

Secondly, there is ample evidence that in many cases the ruling elite in formulating its policy takes some account of the opinion of certain groups of experts. But it cannot be emphasized too strongly that there is no evidence whatever to show that groups such as managers or generals or economists or lawyers, *acting in groups,* have been able to exercise influence upon decision making of their own accord and on their own initiative. Apparently they have been allowed to voice their opinions as individuals with much greater freedom than has ever been allowed before; as a result, decisions have sometimes but not always been taken in accordance with some of the opinions expressed. This is a very long way from the action of pressure groups or interest groups in our democratic societies.

In fact it is difficult to see Soviet managers or lawyers or economists as a "group" except in the broadest sense of a number of people to whom the same description applies. There is no evidence, so far as I am aware, which suggests that persons of this kind within Soviet society have in fact been allowed or given the opportunity to meet together or to act as a coordinated bloc. Therefore the description "pressure group" or "interest group" as applied to the Soviet Union is quite misleading. Nevertheless an important change has taken place in the sense that account is now taken of the opinion of those who are in a position to express an expert view, and that dissent from official lines is tolerated to a much greater degree than ever before. It may be that this represents incipient full-scale pluralism, but it has not arrived yet. The identity of state and society is still a fact in the sense that no area can escape control and in the sense that tolerance of dissent and the regard paid to opinion are not institutionalized: They can be switched off as easily as they can be switched on, and everyone who opens his mouth to express an unorthodox opinion takes the risk that the climate of toleration may have changed overnight.

This casts doubt on the validity of various theories of "convergence," of suggestions of growing identity between, say, the Soviet Union and the United States, on the grounds that economic and industrial pressures in both societies are leading to very similar results. The results do not seem to be similar at all, and there is a very considerable difference between the actual premises from which in each case state and society start. In the Soviet Union the state has absorbed society and, as it were, doles out or tolerates at its own discretion certain liberties. And what the state gives the state can equally take away. In the liberal democratic state the exigencies of a modern society lead to ever increasing state interference, and undoubtedly the state tends progressively to take more and more of one's liberties away. But it is not the all-embracing state *doling out* liberties, it is the state increasingly *taking away* liberties. Above all, in healthy democracies the state is faced with increasing and steady resistance from those whose rights are being taken away. The nature of this resistance is entirely different, and different in kind, from resistance in the Soviet Union. In the Soviet Union it is a process of wringing out of the state a few precarious concessions and without any institutionalized method of doing the wringing. The state has to be assailed by intrigue, by occasional acts of courage, by working behind the scenes, by wire-pulling, by playing off one section of the ruling elite against the other, and similar methods. In the pluralist state the long habit of resistance is there, the courts are much less easily made subservient to the policy-making elite, and there is a vast area of private enterprise which has not been subjugated as in the Soviet Union. Incidentally, it is also possible to escape abroad.

The significance of private enterprise in this context cannot be overestimated. It is true that private enterprise in the modern industrial society is increasingly being subjected to state control. But so long as private enterprise survives on the scale in which it does survive in most liberal democratic countries, the process of resistance to the state, the ability to stand up to its overall control, seems to make all talk of convergence or similarity between the industrial liberal-democratic societies and the industrial Soviet society of very little value. Incidentally, most so-called speculation in the Soviet

Union is little else than private enterprise. It is the attempt of the individual to escape the control which the state exercises by its control over all employment. The speculator, so called, who tries to live by his wits in the interstices of Soviet law, in the twilight between the illegal and the legal, and is tolerated for quite long times until for some reason or other the state decides to move in against him, is really the individual trying to assert some freedom against the stranglehold of the total state.

Finally, what evolution can be predicted with any degree of confidence for the Soviet Union in its present transitional stages? One overall word of warning is essential: All predictions are liable to be falsified in view of the extent to which the personality of one individual, or even the combined personalities of the type of committee now in power, affects the nature of the Soviet polity. There is, however, one respect in which the pressures generated in a modern industrial society, with a consumer economy, may operate in favor of pluralism and legality in the Soviet Union in the course of time. It is probably true to say that in every society which aims at economic efficiency, some rudiments of democracy are dictated by the practical needs of economic progress and efficiency. And there are some slight signs in the Soviet Union of recognition of the fact that both legality and participatory democracy, of a real and not of a fictitious nature, are essential elements of efficiency. Legality, for example, is essential in order to ensure some degree of certainty, some form of regularity, some hard core of predictability, upon which economic efficiency depends. On the other hand, participatory democracy is needed in order to ensure some enthusiasm in carrying a policy into effect. Similarly, there has been some recognition of the fact that variety of opinion and the freedom to dissent and discuss are an essential part of efficient decision making and political and economic planning.

I do not wish to overstate this cautious optimism, but the chances of the emergence within the Soviet system of some democratic features will probably be greater if the motive behind them is not ideological, not love of liberty nor desire for a more civilized form of polity, but the hard, materialist desire for increased production or efficiency. For it is the hard-headed materialists and not the intellectuals who will determine change for a long time to come. I do not wish to exaggerate this. The Party has a considerable vested interest in the arbitrary. There is a very natural fear of the whole system disintegrating if too much liberty is allowed. But with all these reservations, the rediscovery of the old virtues and wisdoms of political experience, so powerfully thrust aside by Lenin, still remains a possibility even in the Soviet Union.

THE SOVIET ECONOMY: RETROSPECT AND PROSPECT

G. Warren Nutter

To write an interpretive essay covering fifty years of Soviet economic history within the compass of less than a page a year, one must sacrifice something. If one were to engulf the reader with a flood of statistics and documentation, there would be no space left for interpretation, and the jumble of figures would mean little to anybody except the specialist. The other extreme—much comment and little information—also has little to recommend it. The middle course is obviously in order, and it will be followed here with due apologies to those who desire full substantiation of the facts in every scholarly essay.[1]

In the case of Soviet history, the line between fact and interpretation is a fine one in any event. As Michael Florinsky has said,

> The historian who values the integrity of his craft may well approach the Soviet period of Russian history with trepidation . . . [for] as far as history is concerned, the Iron Curtain is no mere figure of speech or figment of one's imagination but a stark reality: conformity in ideas and even modes of expression, censorship that amounts to the obliteration of all but official views, and nonintercourse with foreigners that borders on exclusion have erected around the Soviet Union a nearly impregnable barrier, a kind of Chinese or Berlin wall.[2]

This comment is nowhere more relevant than in application to economic data. What are seen as facts by one analyst may be seen as fiction by another, since there is always room for legitimate disagreement when basic statistics are ambiguous and otherwise unreliable. I will perhaps be excused for relating facts as I see them and for interpreting them in accord with my own judgments, while issuing the warning that other scholars may not share them.

THE ACHIEVEMENTS: AN OVERVIEW

Over the first half-century of the Soviet economy, production has multiplied about 5.7 times for the economy as a whole, 12 times for industry, 21 times for transportation, and 2.1 times for agriculture (see Table 1). As measured by man-years of employment, productive activity in other sectors multiplied about 4.7 times.[3] If the productive gains attributable to territorial expansion during and after World War II are eliminated, those multiples become, respectively, 5.0, 11, 20, 1.8, and 3.6. On this basis, production has grown at the average annual rate of 3.1 per cent for the economy as a whole, 4.7 per cent for industry, 5.9 per cent for transportation, 1.2 per cent for agriculture, and 2.5 per cent for other sectors.

Although the data are not reliable enough to permit an accurate estimate, it seems reasonably clear that, for the economy as a whole, more than half the multiplication of output is attributable to increased employment of resources and less than half to improved productivity in their use. If we consider labor alone, man-years of employment have multiplied about 2.7 times (see Table 2), or 46 per cent as much as output; improvement in labor productivity has accounted for the remaining 54 per cent. A significant portion of that improvement is traceable, however, to growth in the stock of capital, and the available evidence suggests that reproducible fixed capital has grown faster than output.[4] That is to say, the capital-output ratio has displayed a persistent upward trend, with a sharply accelerating pace in the postwar period.

The relation between input and output varies considerably from sector to sector: man-years of employment have multiplied about 40 per cent as much as output in industry, about 63 per cent in agriculture, and about 36 per cent in transportation. The capital stock, including land under cultivation, has grown more than output in both industry and agriculture, by a considerable margin in the former case and by a much smaller one in the latter.[5] In freight transportation, on the other hand, growth in output has far outpaced expansion in fixed capital.[6]

The restrictions placed by Soviet authorities on publication of statistics on living conditions make it impossible for anybody to assess with confidence what effect this growth record has had on levels of living, a fact that perhaps speaks more eloquently than all the figures one would like to be able to muster. By indirect and crude procedures, one may estimate that the volume of products available for consumption has multiplied about 3.3 times, or grown at an average annual rate of 2.3 per cent.[7] If this estimate is correct, consumption

TABLE 1

Production Indexes of Composite National Product by Sector (1913 = 100)

	Composite National Product				
	Total (1)	Material (2)	Industry (3)	Agriculture (4)	Transportation (5)
1913	100	100	100	100	100
1920	44	48	20	64	22
1928	103	112	102	118	106
1932	110	113	144	92	193
1937	178	179	285	113	373
1940A	181	183	286	116	414
1940B	213	206	318	134	434
1945	153	147	264	77	315
1950	244	232	393	125	615
1955	332	342	620	158	987
1960	450	472	886	188	1544
1965	574	613	1203	214	2074

SOURCES:

Col. 1–2: Index with 1937 income-originating weights (from A. Bergson *et al.*, "Soviet National Income and Product, 1928–48: Revised Data," RAND, RM-2544, 1960, p. 33): industry (including construction), 35.8 per cent; agriculture, 29.7; transportation (including communication), 7.9; and other sectors, 26.6. Col. 1 covers all these groups (output of other sectors is measured by man-years of employment, see Table 2); col. 2 covers only the first three groups.

Col. 3: For 1913–55, moving-weight index of all products; thereafter, extrapolated by industrial materials; from Nutter, *Growth of Industrial Production*, p. 196, and work in progress.

Col. 4: Index of production for sale or home consumption with 1958 weights; from unpublished study by Arcadius Kahan, and (for 1950 on) D. B. Diamond, "Trends in Outputs, Inputs, and Factor Productivity in Soviet Agriculture," in *New Directions in the Soviet Economy* (Washington, D. C., 1966) p. 346.

Col. 5: Unweighted index of ton-kilometers of intercity freight traffic; from E. W. Williams, Jr., *Freight Transportation in the Soviet Union* (Princeton, N. J., 1962), p. 14 (traffic for 1913 corrected to 28.5 billion metric ton-kilometers on the basis of later official statistics), and (for 1960 on) official statistics.

NOTE:

Current territory except 1913 and 1940A, which cover interwar territory. For comparisons with other indexes, see Nutter, in *National Security*, pp. 166 f.

TABLE 2

Population and Man-Years of Employment by Sector
(millions)

	Population			Man-Years of Employment				
	Total	Urban	Rural	Total	Industry	Agriculture	Transportation	Other Sectors
1913	139.3	24.7	114.6	38.6	5.9	24.2	1.0	7.5
1928	151.4			40.1	5.5	27.4	1.3	5.9
1937	165.2			62.8	12.9	34.0	2.7	13.2
1940A	175.6	57.7	117.9					
1940B	198.6	64.5	134.1	74.4	14.6	39.0	3.4	17.4
1950	181.5	70.5	111.0	75.8	17.6	33.9	4.1	20.6
1955	197.6	87.7	109.9	82.7	21.5	33.5	5.0	22.7
1960	214.4	104.7	109.7	93.0	23.6	33.7	6.3	29.4
1965	230.5	123.0	107.5	103.2	28.1	32.7	7.3	35.1

SOURCES:
Population from Nutter, *Growth of Industrial Production*, p. 519, and official statistics. Employment from G. W. Nutter, "Employment in the Soviet Union: An Interim Solution to a Puzzle," *Soviet Statistics*, April 1961, pp. 381 ff, and (for 1960 on) official statistics.

NOTE:
Current territory except 1913 and 1940A, which cover interwar territory. Population as of July 1. Sum and detail may not agree because of rounding.

approximately doubled per head of population, or grew at an average annual rate of about 1.4 per cent.[8] Part of this improvement in per capita consumption can be accounted for by the shift of population from the countryside to the cities. For example, if we suppose that per capita consumption before the revolution was about 70 per cent higher in the urban sector than in the rural,[9] total consumption would have had to double merely to keep per capita consumption constant in each of the two sectors. Given the estimate that total consumption actually somewhat more than tripled, we find that per capita consumption could have increased by about 60 per cent, or by 0.9 per cent a year, in each of the two sectors if in fact the percentage increase were the same in both. Put another way, such an increase for the rural and urban sectors taken separately implies the doubling of per capita consumption estimated for the country as a whole. How the over-all improvement in living conditions has actually been distributed between city and country and within each remains to be discovered if the necessary data are revealed in the future.

While average hours of work have declined in most sectors of the economy (not so surely in agriculture), a much larger fraction of the population has been put to work. The employed labor force, measured in full-time equivalents, amounted to 28 per cent of the population in 1913 compared with 45 per cent today. Hence it is not easy to state any meaningful generalizations about what has happened to leisure.

Changes in living conditions have, of course, varied widely in different respects. There has been vast improvement in health and education, as shown by the more than twenty-fold multiplication in the number of persons employed in these fields per head of population. On the other hand, housing conditions have deteriorated badly, the living space per inhabitant of the cities being only four-fifths of what it was before the revolution, to consider this aspect alone. The per capita supply of food, as indicated by domestic production, has increased by only 30 per cent, or at an average annual rate of 0.5 per cent. Consumption has increased slightly more since the Soviet Union has shifted from being a net exporter of agricultural products to being a net importer.

In industry, production of consumer goods has multiplied only 40 per cent as much as total production, so that per capita consumption of industrial products has roughly tripled. The increasing emphasis on investment and military goods is shown by the fact that consumer goods accounted for about three-quarters of total industrial production in 1913 compared with only two-fifths today. As a counterpart, output of products for the military and space programs seem to amount to about a quarter of total industrial production today, while similar products accounted for a very small fraction before the revolution.

It hardly needs to be noted that these fifty years of industrialization and urbanization have brought results in some ways similar to those experienced by other countries and in some ways unique. Soviet industrial production has risen from about a seventh of the U. S. level before the revolution to more than a third today. Urban population has multiplied almost five-fold while rural population has declined slightly, so that the former has risen from less than a fifth of total population to more than a half. The degree of urbanization is still rather far from that of the most advanced industrial nations (the United States was half-urbanized as early as 1920), but the relative shift from rural to urban areas has proceeded at a very rapid pace. For example, it took sixty years for the urban share in the population to move from 20 to 50 per cent in the United States, compared with fifty years in the Soviet Union.

Accompanying the rapid industrialization, urbanization, and expansion of health and educational services has been the radical decline in both birth and death rates normally associated with countries undergoing such developments, to the point of a drop in the rate of natural increase in recent years. Even more dramatic has been the sharp decline in the infant mortality rate from more than 270 deaths per thousand live births on the eve of the revolution down to fewer than 27 at the present time. Needless to say, there have been significant deviations from these favorable trends during the many crises that have recurred periodically during Soviet history. When all is said, the fundamental achievement of the half-century has been creation of an economic structure that makes the Soviet Union one of the great powers in the world. This has been the objective of economic policy over the decades, and it has been fulfilled. But the path has been tortuous and painful, as we shall see next.

THE TORTUOUS PATH

The modern Russian economy dates from the reforms of serfdom initiated under Alexander II over a century ago, reforms that made possible the creation of a broad market for hired labor. At that time the population of Russia was about 74 million, with 5 per cent in urban areas and 80 per cent illiterate. Economic developments over the next five and a half decades are reflected in the rapid growth of population, which reached 164 million on the eve of World War I within the imperial territory, more than double the size in 1860. Urban population grew to 18 per cent of the total, and the illiteracy rate dropped to less than 60 per cent. Industry expanded rapidly in both factories and workshops, production multiplying about 12 times between 1860 and 1913. The average annual growth rate was above 5 per cent, or faster than in the United States over the same period. Agricultural production multiplied perhaps 2.8 times, or grew annually at an average rate of about 1.9 per cent, with growth accelerating significantly in the last two decades of the nineteenth century and even more sharply after the Stolypin reforms in the first decade of the twentieth, when private farming was established as the general system for the first time in Russian history. Grain was the major product exported from tsarist Russia, and about a quarter of the crop was normally shipped abroad each year.

The latter part of the nineteenth century was a period of intensive railroad construction, and some 40,000 miles of roadway were laid by 1913 (there were only 1,000 miles of track in 1860), forming the basic rail network as it exists today. The average annual growth rate in railway freight traffic was more than 6 per cent from 1880 to 1913.

National product grew at an average annual rate of about 2.5 per cent over the last five decades of the tsarist period and about 3 per cent over the last three. Since population grew at about 1.5 per cent a year, per capita output experienced an average increase of about 1 per cent a year for the entire period and about 1.5 per cent for the last three decades. This peformance measured up to the European average but fell considerably short of that of the United States, Germany, and Japan.

When the Bolsheviks seized power in Russia in November 1917, the country was well advanced along the path of industrialization and economic development despite the generally miserable living conditions and the ravages of war. The substantial progress already made, in the face of formidable political and social obstacles, was immediately brought to a halt and thrown in reverse as the prevailing economic order was overthrown and supplanted by a disorganized and quasi-military system that the new rulers conceived as the logical outgrowth of Communist ideology. In rapid order they destroyed money, markets, and mobility, replacing them with rations, requisitions, and regimentation. The failures of the new order were compounded by the civil war that continued for almost three years and to which the Soviet leaders ultimately assigned blame for their own misguided policies by referring to these years as the period of "War Communism." One expects official historical accounts of the various phases of Soviet rule to distort reality, but one may wonder why so many Western historians continue to echo this myth. The fact is that "War Communism" was far more the product of ideology than of necessity; the myth is that such a system was forced on the infant Soviet state by the exigencies of war.

Whatever may have been the forces creating and driving this system, the results were chaos and disaster. Industrial production and freight traffic fell by four-fifths at their lowest points, and agricultural production by perhaps a half (see Chart 1). The civil war over, production in the economy stood at less than half of its pre-revolutionary level, and famine and pestilence now claimed millions more of

CHART 1

Production by Economic Sector: Soviet Union, 1913–1965

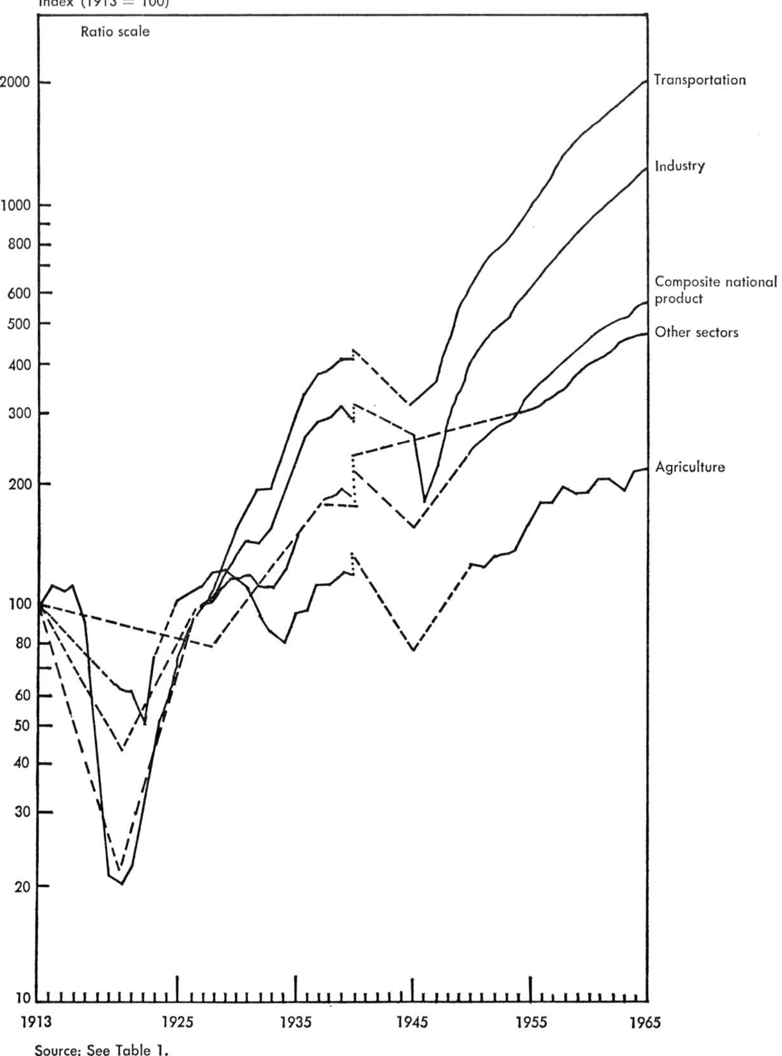

Source: See Table 1.

lives than had violence. The consequences would have been even more catastrophic if it had not been for the Hoover relief.

As a result of the separate peace concluded with Germany and the internal difficulties of the early postwar period, the Soviet Union had shrunk about 15 per cent in territory and population from the size of imperial Russia. Population within the new boundaries fell by an additional seven million between 1917 and 1922 (from 142 to 135 million), whereas normally it would have grown by perhaps twelve million. The tragedies of this period thus brought about a population deficit of almost twenty million persons, with the heaviest incidence on the male population. While under normal circumstances there would probably have been ninety-eight males for every hundred females in the age class of thirty years or over, only eighty-eight were recorded in the census of 1926, inaugurating a distortion in the sex ratio that has plagued the Soviet Union ever since, at times in even more exaggerated form.

In the face of economic chaos and open rebellion by the naval forces at Kronstadt, Lenin found it necessary to abandon "pure communism" and to re-establish a market economy in a broad region of activities, notably farming, small-scale industry, and trade. The so-called New Economic Policy was launched in March 1921 and quickly met with success. Factory production rose by 46 per cent in 1922, 23 per cent in 1923 and 1924, 38 per cent in 1925, 25 per cent in 1926, and 11 per cent in 1927. All told, industrial production multiplied about five-fold between 1920 and 1928, recovering approximately to its pre-revolutionary level. Agricultural production recovered in a similar fashion, although its low point was reached in 1922. By 1928 the economy stood roughly where it had been fifteen years earlier in the level of activity, but many profound structural changes had been introduced.

In the minds of Soviet leaders, N.E.P. was essentially an ideological retreat designed to provide a breathing spell during which the nature of the ultimate Soviet system could be worked out. In the background there lurked the idea of comprehensive centralized direction of the entire economy under the guidance of long-range planning, an idea that gained form and force during the period of highly centralized management under "War Communism" and continued to develop within the atmosphere of more decentralized control of the still large nationalized segment under N.E.P. Even as N.E.P. was being launched, commissions were being established for the purpose of developing comprehensive economic plans, Goelro (Commission for the Electrification of Russia) being instituted in early 1920 and Gosplan (State Planning Commission) in early 1921. The Goelro plan for electrification of the R.S.F.S.R. appeared at the end of 1921 and included in its long introduction a general economic plan for the next ten or fifteen years. Around the middle of 1922 Gosplan was entrusted with the task of preparing a long-range plan and an annual operational plan, and many drafts of partial plans for various sectors were prepared by that organization over the next few years. There gradually evolved a system of comprehensive annual plans, the earlier ones (for 1925/26 and 1926/27) being considered as control figures and the later ones (beginning with 1927/28) as directives. Already in 1925 Gosplan began preparing a five-year plan, starting with a project for the period 1925/26–1929/30. As each year passed, the beginning and ending years were moved forward until the plan for 1928/29–1932/33, published in its definitive text in the spring of 1929, was declared by Stalin to be the First Five Year Plan.[10]

These formative years were marked by much disagreement and debate among Soviet leaders on desirable ways to plan and direct development of the economy, but no substantial body of opinion visualized N.E.P. as more than an interlude. Recovery had been accomplished, and the economy was now to stride forward on the path to socialism. It was at this juncture that the economy took on its now characteristic nature with the introduction of the First Five Year Plan, aimed primarily at accelerating industrial growth. While a vast program of building new industrial plants and facilities was under way (largely under supervision of foreign engineers and technicians), workers were poured into existing factories to squeeze as much output out of them as possible. Employment in construction tripled, rising from about one million in 1928 to over three million in 1932. Between 1928 and 1933, industrial employment rose by 60 per cent in man-years and 40 per cent in man-hours, while output increased by 50 per cent. Hence labor productivity declined on a man-year basis and rose only slightly on a man-hour basis, a pattern that became common in the early years of forced industrialization of the Soviet type. Commercial freight traffic rose by more than 80 per cent, straining the existing system and facilities to the limit and creating a crisis in transportation that was alleviated by introduction of quasi-military controls, retained until very recently. Despite the magnitude of these gains and the unyielding pressure for more, they fell far short of the exorbitant goals of the plan, average fulfillment of the minimum goals for industrial output being no more than 75 per cent. The maximum goals were sheer pipe dreams.

The investment program bore fruit in the Second Five Year Plan, which began in 1933. Industrial production and commercial freight traffic both approximately doubled, showing a sharp increase relative to employment. Over the last four years of this plan, industrial output grew by 85 per cent while man-years of employment rose by only 40 per cent and man-hours by 45 per cent.

The burden of industrialization had to be borne mainly by the peasantry, the bulk of the population, and it was ruthlessly imposed by Stalin through forced collectivization of agriculture during the early years of the First Five Year Plan. The result was profound disruption of the rural economy accompanied by famine and massive destruction of capital. Herds of livestock and horses fell by more than half as the peasants, faced with confiscation of their meager property, slaughtered what they could and neglected care of the remainder. The loss of motive power alone was so heavy that not until the mid-1950's had the tractor park grown large enough to offset it in equivalent horsepower. When drought combined with the shock of collectivization, agricultural production fell to famine levels, reaching a low point in 1934 when net agricultural output was some 35 per cent below its 1928 level for a population that had grown by perhaps 6 per cent. Supplies available for consumption were even lower because grain was being exported to help finance imports. Over the next two years agricultural production moved upward and, thanks to extraordinary weather in 1937, reached about 95 per cent of its pre-collectivization level at the end of the Second Five Year Plan.

Success in stimulating industrial expansion was purchased through a sharp decline in the standard of living, so severe in some segments of the population and regions of the country that millions starved to death. The full history of this period remains to be revealed, but from the available data we can be reasonably sure that excess deaths amounted to at least five million persons by 1934 [11] and perhaps twice as many. Living quarters, already grossly inadequate, were further crowded as people flooded the cities in the face of almost no construction of housing facilities. At the end of the Second Five Year Plan, the real wage per person engaged in the nonagricultural sector was far below the pre-revolutionary level.[12] Of course, a larger fraction of the population was working than before the revolution, but it seems doubtful that there was any significant improvement in living conditions on the average. Although the national product had increased about 60 percentage points more than population since the revolution, the differential had probably been diverted into investment and military uses. The common man was surely worse off in regard to food and housing, and those fortunate enough to be alive would have been considerably worse off in all respects had not the suffering of the first two five-year plans levied its toll in dead.

It was against this background that the Third Five Year Plan was launched, scheduled to run from 1938 through 1942 but interrupted by the German invasion in mid-1941. During the three years preceding invasion, economic growth ground to a virtual halt, no doubt primarily as a result of Stalin's Great Purge. The costs of mobilizing for an expected conflict with Germany have usually been cited by both Soviet and Western commentators as the reason for economic stagnation at this time, but this explanation is essentially unfounded. The armament program had been under way within industry since 1934 at least, and there was no pronounced acceleration after 1937. It is now clear from Soviet sources that economic mobilization was half-hearted until shortly before the invasion, Stalin believing that he had averted participation in the war by his pact with Hitler in 1939. Full-scale industrial mobilization did not take place until after the invasion, and Stalin even undertook shipment of substantial quantities of grain and raw materials to Germany from September 1939 up to the attack in June 1941.[13] Moreover, the state of euphoria that followed the signing of the pact may well have led to a general slackening of effort throughout the economy. In any event, industrial production in the interwar Soviet territory apparently declined by about 8 per cent in 1940.

As provided by the Hitler-Stalin Pact, the Soviet Union gained possession of the Baltic countries, half of Poland, and other smaller territories after Germany marched into Poland in the fall of 1939. The acquired territories were about equal to France in size and held a population of around 24 million. This expansion gave the Soviet Union an additional 9 per cent of territory, 14 per cent of population, 17 per cent of agricultural production, 11 per cent of industrial production, and 5 per cent of transportation facilities. As events were soon to show, these economic gains were slight compensation for setting in motion the German military adventure that was to impose such heavy costs on the world, not least on the Soviet Union itself.

As for all the years of suffering in the Soviet era, a detailed account of conditions during and after World War II is yet to come, and we can therefore only surmise the broad outlines of what took place. By 1945 industrial production was almost a fifth below its prewar level, while agricultural production was more than two-fifths below. The food situation must have been desperate indeed since per capita output of agricultural products was 10 to 20 per cent less than at the nadir of the collectivization period. Starvation and pestilence were no doubt rampant, but we know few of the details. One German doctor, the late Wilhelm Starlinger, wrote in 1955 about an outbreak of bubonic plague that swept Königsberg at the end of the war, claiming the lives of nine-tenths of the population within a few weeks.[14] Perhaps a fifth to a quarter of reproducible tangible property was destroyed in the war, amounting to roughly $13 billion to $16 billion.

The most graphic measure of the cost of World War II is probably represented by wartime losses in population, which stagger the imagination. According to projections by Frank Lorimer that allow for declines in birth and death rates in accord with normal Western experience, Soviet population within the postwar territory would have been expected, under essentially normal circumstances, to show a growth from 1940 of about 18 million by 1945 and 33 million by 1950.[15] In fact, according to the more recent estimates of Western scholars based on official Soviet data, there was actually a decline of about 24 million by 1945 and 17 million by 1950, indicating a deficit of some 42 million over 1940–45 and some 50 million over 1940–50. Perhaps 5 million or so represent emigration that would otherwise not have taken place, but that still leaves losses attributable to war and its aftermath without parallel in history. These losses had their main impact on the rural population which seems to have declined by more than 20 million between 1940 and 1950. It has been estimated that excess deaths account for 25 million of the net losses up to 1950 and reduced births for the remaining 20 million.[16] How much of each was due to what cause—even how much was the inevitable cost of war and how much the avoidable result of internal policies—will probably never be calculable. We may merely point to the dreadful fact that the losses as of 1950, estimated in the described way, amounted to more than one person out of every five who presumably would have been living at that time if there had been no major calamity.

Western demographers, it should be noted, were not prepared for losses of this magnitude. Writing shortly after the end of World War II, Lorimer estimated the deficit to be about half that suggested by later official data. In calculating the deficit as of 1945, he supposed direct military deaths of 5 million, excess civilian deaths of 9 million, and deficient births and excessive deaths of infants of 6 million, assumptions that seem reasonably generous. It is fair to say that Western experts generally agreed on the figure of 220 million as the population for 1956, a figure that turned out to be 20 million larger than the official Soviet estimate for that year.

Where did the Western demographers go wrong? The obvious answer would seem to be that they grossly underestimated war losses, an answer they have apparently been willing to accept. They can hardly be blamed for failing to anticipate a wartime deficit of more than 40 million, since there was nothing in the experience of other participants in World War II or in information from Soviet sources to suggest such stupendous losses. One would feel easier if there were confirming evidence, and in its absence it would seem wise to explore other possible explanations of the miscalculations before reaching a final decision. There is, of course, one other logical possibility: the official count of population might be either too high for 1939 or too low for 1959, or both. There is little apparent reason to doubt the accuracy of the 1959 census, within limits of error normally associated with such undertakings. Aside from the fact that it is difficult to imagine any motive for understating population, the census findings have been published in sufficient detail to provide a variety of internal checks, none of which reveals obvious inconsistencies or inexplicable relationships.

The accuracy of the 1939 census is subject to much more doubt. Strong inducements to overcount were present, on the part of authorities anxious to justify earlier predictions and on the part of statisticians and enumerators anxious to avoid the fate of their predecessors in 1937. The census of 1937 was condemned as having been conducted by "socialist wreckers," the findings suppressed, and the principal statisticians liquidated. The apparent reason for this drastic action was that the census did not confirm the optimistic estimates of population growth that had been announced year after year during the first two five-year plans. There is therefore good reason to suppose that the 1939 census contains an overstatement of population, but this conjecture cannot be supported by independent evidence, not even by internal checks of consistency of data since the findings of the census have never been published in much detail. If the 1939 population is overstated, then to that extent the deficit now assigned to World War II should instead be attributed to upheavals of the interwar period.

It would be inhuman to suggest that the enormous losses of life, even when allowance is made for possible overestimation, could have been offset by any economic policies pursued by the Soviet Union in the postwar period, and there is something degrading about speaking of them in quantitative terms. At the same time, we must be willing to make a hard-headed appraisal of factors that mitigated economic losses entirely aside from the question of human costs. Within this category come the Lend-Lease deliveries that averaged about $3 billion annually, or more than a third of the prewar level of Soviet industrial production, and hence seem to have offset the wartime decline in industrial output completely and to have provided some slight relief in the food situation. Relief shipments under U.N.R.R.A. no doubt lessened hunger in the postwar years, though they were not large enough to cover more than a small fraction of the food deficit. Property losses were probably more than made up by the heavy reparations and other collections imposed on various countries after the war, the reparations alone amounting to at least $20 billion or almost twice as much as the Marshall Plan aid given by the United States to Western Europe. Finally, the reduced labor force was offset in part by use of prisoners of war, who were retained and employed on a large scale up to at least 1953.

Recovery was swift after the war, following demobilization of the armed forces and a sharp cutback in military production, as all efforts were bent toward reconstruction of the economy.[17] Military output continued to fall while damaged housing and productive facilities were rebuilt and civilian production raised, and the national product apparently regained its prewar level by about 1948. Living conditions improved slowly, but the average citizen was probably no better off in 1950 than before the revolution.

Production moved ahead rapidly during the Fifth Five Year Plan (1950–55), particularly in the period following Stalin's death in 1953. Industrial growth in the first few years was dominated by military preparations, resources being shifted from production of civilian machinery and other items to production of armaments for use in the Korean War. Over the period as a whole, military output seems to have multiplied almost twice as much as other industrial production, the leaders wasting little time in rebuilding military power once the economy was back on the path of expansion. With the death of Stalin, however, increasing attention was given to the civilian sector, and military output even declined somewhat after the end of the Korean War.

Let us pause at this point and consider the state of the economy at the end of the Stalinist period. The achievement in industry was impressive: with territorial gains eliminated, output stood at about 4.6 times its pre-revolutionary level. The story was quite different in agriculture, where net output was only some 30 per cent higher than the pre-revolutionary level including territorial gains or 14 per cent higher excluding them, and per capita output was actually lower than before the revolution. Livestock herds were smaller than they were before the collectivization drive, and the motive power lost through the slaughter of horses had not yet been replaced by tractors. The average inhabitant of a Soviet city enjoyed about five square meters of living space for housing, scarcely more than twice the size of a gravesite and about 40 per cent smaller than the figure before the revolution. It is difficult to believe that living conditions were significantly better for the average citizen at this point of history than they had been before the entire Soviet experiment.

Perhaps the most significant change in the years immediately following Stalin's death was the shift in attention toward the needs and wants of the common man, a shift motivated as much by political factors as anything else. It had also become clear that the perennially weak state of agriculture could not be tolerated if ambitions for continued economic growth were to be realized. The agricultural problem was attacked through the crash program of plowing up virgin lands in south central Asia, and within the span of two or three years crop acreage had been expanded by 25 to 30 per cent. At the same time, basic reforms in agricultural prices and in methods of organizing production were also instituted, and these reforms together with the expansion in cultivated land caused production to outstrip growth in population for the first time since the collectivization drive began. Housing construction was accelerated, and output of industrial consumer goods was expanded at a relatively brisk pace, even though heavy industry continued to receive top priority. For a while it seemed as if the economy might take a sharp turn away from its traditional path of growth, but events were soon to belie this initial impression.

The new regime faced a crisis quite early in the uprisings in Poland and Hungary, but the storm was weathered in the satellite countries, albeit at the cost of some significant changes in relations within the Soviet sphere. No sooner was this danger past than Soviet leaders launched, symbolically with the first satellite in space, a massive military and space program, requiring diversion of a large volume of resources from other uses. One of the first steps, typical of Soviet industrial mobilization, was to reduce the output of agricultural machinery by about 20 per cent in 1958 and 15 per cent in 1959, a shock that was to be felt quickly in the struggling agricultural sector. Growth in civilian production of industry was cut in half, from almost 10 per cent in 1957 to between 4 and 5 per cent in each of the three succeeding years.

Looking back we can see reasons why Khrushchev might have convinced himself that the military-space buildup could be supported by transferring resources from agriculture. This was the high point of confidence and optimism, fostered by the extraordinary harvest of 1958, and Khruschev almost daily boasted that the Soviet Union would soon outdistance the United States in per capita output of meat and milk. Confidence was so strong that the Soviet worker could be granted a reduction in his hours of work at the same time that strains were building up within the economy.

But it was soon apparent that agriculture stood on feet of clay. The weather turned bad, droughts became more frequent, and the virgin lands after some years of misuse began to dry up and blow away. The

Soviet leadership was now called upon to shore up a sagging agricultural sector that it had counted on to carry the military-space program, which was becoming increasingly burdensome. The cutback in production of agricultural machinery was reversed in 1960, and output climbed upward to its earlier level within the next two years. Those segments of industry dependent on agricultural materials began to falter. In the face of this doubled burden, something had to give, and the result showed up in a general slowing down in the rate of growth of industrial production, with a heavy impact on investment despite strenuous efforts to contain the decline within the consumer sector. For example, growth in output of construction materials fell from 10 per cent in 1958 to about 1 per cent in 1961 and 2 to 4 per cent in succeeding years. Even heavier demands were placed on investment with inauguration of the crash program for fertilization and irrigation of agriculture in 1963, and the dwindling supply of investment goods had to be spread more thinly. One result was a fall in the average annual rate of industrial growth from around 7.4 per cent for 1955–60 to around 6.3 per cent for 1960–65.

The growing strains on the economy seem to have focused attention on many long-standing problems and to have stirred up thinking about needed fundamental reforms. Perhaps most worrisome was the steady downward drift in the industrial growth rate, long evident to anyone who inspected the record carefully but nonetheless overlooked by Soviet and Western analysts alike. As can be seen from Table 3, growth of industrial production was retarded in the postwar decade of the 1950's compared with the interwar decade of the first two five-year plans, in the second half of the 1950's compared with the first, and in the 1960's compared with the 1950's. Intercity freight traffic shows a similar pattern.

It may be, of course, that the growth trend in industry was ignored because expansion of the economy as a whole seemed to be proceeding at a stable and satisfactory pace, but this illusion was created by the postwar spurt in agricultural growth that temporarily offset deceleration elsewhere. The lesson was driven home by the crop failure of 1963, when the growth in national product was only around 3 per cent compared with the accustomed average of 6 per cent.

It hardly seems a coincidence that public discussion of economic reforms burst forth on the Soviet scene in the fall of 1962, clearly under official encouragement and with official sanction.[18] The response to this invitation to air dissent was vigorous and threatened to get out of hand as deep-seated criticisms of the prevailing order, no doubt long felt but unspoken, were voiced more and more boldly.

TABLE 3

Average Annual Growth Rates * of Composite National Product by Sector (per cent)

	Composite National Product					
	Total	Material	Industry	Agri- culture	Trans- porta- tion	Other Sectors †
1860–1913	2.5 ‡	2.8 ‡	5.3 §	2.0 ‡	6.2 ‡	2.5 ‡
1913–1965	3.1	3.3	4.7	1.2	5.9	2.5
1913–1928	0.2	0.8	0.1	1.1	0.4	−1.6
1928–1965	4.3	4.4	6.6	1.2	8.2	4.1
1928–1940	4.8	4.2	9.0	−0.1	12.0	6.9
1940–1950	1.4	1.2	2.2	−0.8	3.5	1.7
1950–1965	5.5	6.7	7.7	3.7	8.4	3.6
1928–1937	6.2	5.3	12.1	−0.5	15.0	9.3
1950–1955	6.6	8.1	9.5	4.8	9.9	1.9
1955–1960	6.4	6.7	7.4	3.6	9.4	5.2
1960–1965	5.1	5.4	6.3	2.7	6.1	3.6

SOURCE:
Table 1, except as noted. Adjusted to eliminate gains from territorial expansion.

* Calculated from data for terminal years by compound interest formula.

† Measured by employment in man-years (Table 2).

‡ R. W. Goldsmith, "The Economic Growth of Tsarist Russia, 1860–1913," *Economic Development and Cultural Change*, April 1961, pp. 442 f and 471. For transportation, railway freight traffic only and 1876–1913.

§ 1870–1913. Nutter, *Growth of Industrial Production*, p. 229.

Before the authorities managed to bring the debate under control, centralized administrative planning had been harshly indicted by a number of Soviet economists. Internal criticism even had the apparent effect of modifying views of the Soviet economy held by some Western scholars.

The reform movement has come to be known as Libermanism, but it would be more correct to apply this label to the line of thought tolerated by the authorities. Liberman's proposals may properly be interpreted as an effort to save the essential features of centralized administrative planning by shifting various routine managerial functions to the enterprises. In this sense, Liberman represents the more conservative wing of thought from the official Soviet point of view. Far more radical reforms have been suggested by others and so far rejected by the authorities. The basic issue is how much administrative direction of the economy is to be displaced by markets and quasi-markets. This issue has been approached only obliquely in public discussion, but we may be reasonably sure that the situation is rather different behind the scenes, particularly in view of the example of candid debate being set in some of the East European countries.

Whatever may be the spirit of reformist thought, Soviet leaders have moved cautiously and experimentally, and the Soviet economy is entering its second half-century in essentially its traditional form, even though beset by agitation for basic reform. Progress toward reform has no doubt been restrained by the political consequences foreseen by Soviet leaders. Once again, the rulers of Russia are confronted with the "dilemma of the tsars." Like their predecessors, today's rulers recognize the sickness of their society, but they know equally well that to cure the patient is to kill the doctor. The economy can be made more efficient only through creating many decision-making centers, dispersing them throughout the economy, and letting them compete impersonally in the market place. How can the dispersal of power be kept from contaminating the political order as it did in imperial Russia? This is the specter that haunts the Soviet ruling class and paralyzes constructive action. Meanwhile, we witness much more talk than action.

AN APPRAISAL OF THE RECORD

To appraise, one must pass judgment. We face the question: What is golden about the fiftieth anniversary of communism in the Soviet Union? No doubt some will answer that the Communist regime has raised a backward, rural, uneducated country to a position of eminence as an industrialized, urbanized, and scientific power to be reckoned with in world affairs. This assessment is correct, and the record in this respect is impressive.

Yet, despite unbending efforts to outpace the record of the past, the growth of industry, agriculture, and transportation seems to have been no faster in the half-century of Soviet rule than in the last half-century of tsardom (see Table 3). Growth in the economy as a whole apparently accelerated from the one half-century to the other by virtue of the changing economic structure, but even here there does not seem to have been a rise in the tempo of growth in comparison with the last three decades of tsarist rule. The average rate of growth—around 3 per cent a year—matches the long-run performance of such countries as the United States if no account is taken of the accompanying trend in leisure and living conditions, but it is not exceptional in the annals of advancing economies. And what other country has paid such a high price for its economic growth?

If we focus on industry, the sector so heavily emphasized in the Soviet age, we see a remarkable similarity in the growth records of Russia and the Soviet Union relative to the United States (see Chart 2). The Soviet Union has outperformed imperial Russia in this race with the United States, but not dramatically. Moreover, long-run Soviet industrial growth, adjusted to exclude gains from territorial expansion, has not matched the experience of the United States over the years 1870–1920, a period of industrialization comparable to the Soviet era in a number of important respects. Of course, in its best years the rate of economic growth in the Soviet Union has exceeded the long-run average, at times by a wide margin, and it exceeds that average today. Hence the long-run average is being pulled upward. At the same time, the short-run rate is drifting downward, so that the differential may disappear or even turn in the opposite direction.

One might reasonably object that it is improper to judge the Soviet economy on the basis of its full record, the bad years counted with the good. Normal performance, one might argue, is represented by those years without crises and calamities, events not necessarily endemic in the system but more in the nature of historical accidents. Should we not, then, strike from the record the years of turmoil—the periods of "War Communism" and N.E.P., of forced collectivization of agriculture, and of World War II—and attribute such economic growth as has been achieved to the remaining "normal" years?

For some purposes, perhaps so, but not when we are supposed to appraise the record of fifty years of history. Here we are concerned with what was, not with what might have been. If Lenin or Stalin had it to do over again or if more moderate counsel had prevailed, perhaps the excesses of "War Communism," forced collectivization, political purges, and so on would have been avoided, and the course of economic growth might have been more smoothly upward. By the same token, wiser policies would have ameliorated the Great Depression in the West, or lessened the dips in Russian economic growth during the late tsarist period—or prevented World War II. Yet we seldom bother to correct history on these accounts. "Mistakes" are a normal and integral part of history, and there is no reason to expunge them from the record unless we are convinced that they will not recur

CHART 2

Industrial Production: Tsarist Russia, Soviet Union, and United States 1870–1965

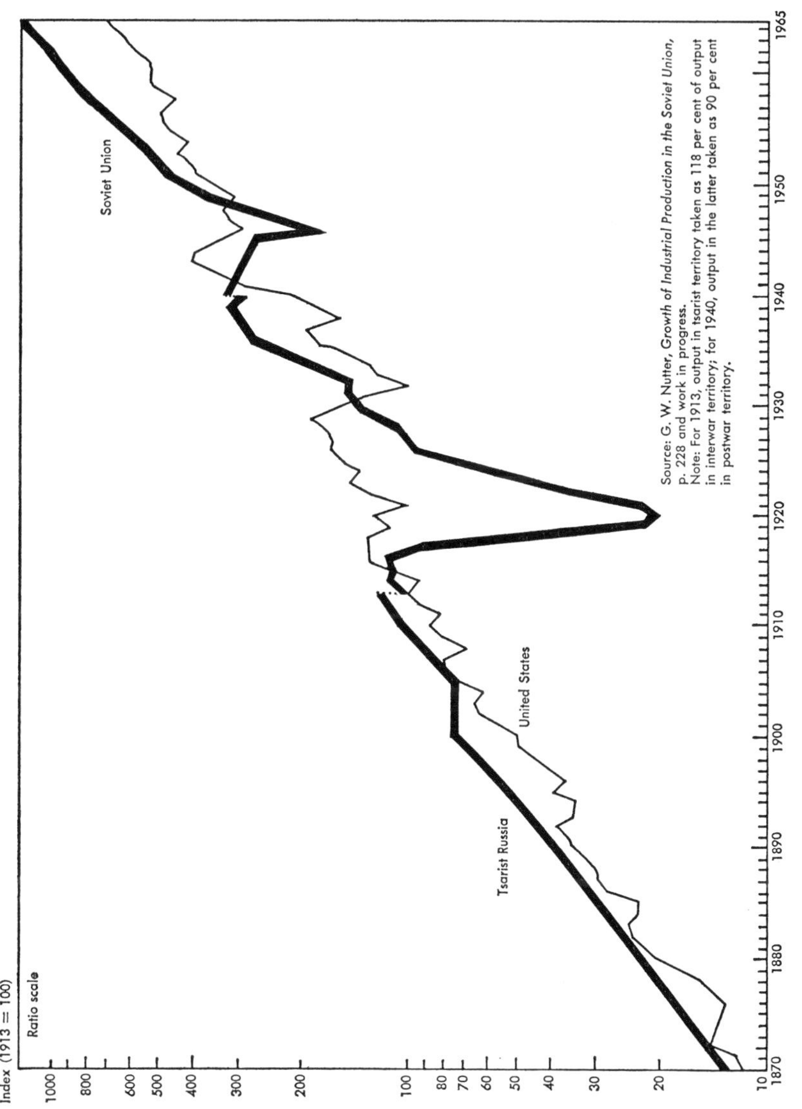

Source: G. W. Nutter, *Growth of Industrial Production in the Soviet Union,* p. 228 and work in progress.
Note: For 1913, output in tsarist territory taken as 118 per cent of output in interwar territory; for 1940, output in the latter taken as 90 per cent in postwar territory.

in similar form. Most fruitless of all is the effort to reconstruct the history of what might have been or should have been.

A stronger case can be made for special treatment of World War II, the product of many historical forces. While Soviet policy played a role in building up tensions over the years and in facilitating the outbreak of hostilities, it can hardly be blamed for the war. This event intruded in Soviet history with catastrophic economic consequences, and due allowance must be made in the economic record. But we must remember that other countries suffered from the war as well and, like the Soviet Union, managed to recover quickly and to experience subsequent spurts of growth. Calamities often have a way of generating the extraordinary effort needed to overcome them, at least in the short run. Although the Soviet Union no doubt suffered more than any other nation, it also resorted to more draconian measures to effect recovery.

Similarly, the tribulations of the period of "War Communism" made the populace more receptive to the stimulus of N.E.P., and so on. In the irony of history, even the terrible demographic calamities of earlier years had their positive side as they relieved the burden to the economy of supporting unproductive labor. With a surplus labor force, one way to increase production per head is to reduce the number of heads.

The matter may be put this way: suppose we subtract all the years of adversity and attribute Soviet economic growth over the last half-century to the remainder. Then we would assume that what has been achieved in fifty years could have, under more normal circumstances, been achieved in thirty to thirty-five years. The Soviet economy presumably could have stood in 1947 or 1952 where it stands now. On this basis, the effective average annual growth rate of the national product would be taken as around 5 per cent compared with the rate of 3 per cent actually recorded for the entire fifty-year period. I cannot accept this possibility, even leaving aside what has been said up to this point about the self-corrective forces of adversity.

Let me illustrate with the specific case of the first decade of communist rule. Suppose that, by some miracle of history, the revolution had imposed no costs of upheaval and that the First Five Year Plan had been smoothly introduced in the fall of 1917. Could the economy have achieved its actual 1937 level by 1927 instead? The answer must be no, for many things happened over the "lost decade" immediately following the revolution that raised the productive capacity of the economy even though aggregate production showed no significant advance. For example, illiteracy was significantly reduced, the structure of industry was drastically altered, and great technological advances were made in the outside world. The succeeding growth could not have taken place without these prior developments, all of which took time.

In one important sense, it is not worth debating how fast the Soviet economy has grown, whether at 3 per cent a year or 5 per cent, since growth in and of itself is of little significance. There is much more to economic development than sheer growth, regardless of direction: for example an economy proficient in producing empty pyramids or broken crockery contributes little to the welfare of its subjects. By the test of consumer welfare, the poor performance of the Soviet economy is visible to all without any need for sophisticated measurement.

It is important to keep in mind that Soviet economic growth has been the product of a system dedicated to enhancement of power—in effect, the power of the ruling elite. Relying on centralized administrative planning, that ruling elite has driven the economy forward along the path of least resistance, focusing on the easier tasks and bypassing the more difficult ones, utilizing a system that, through a process of natural selection, causes the most readily fulfilled targets to be realized. The basic objective has been to grow in military and political strength as quickly as possible while generating a rapid measured rate of economic growth, for its propaganda value as much as anything else. One can see merit in Leontief's description of the Soviet economy as the "input-input system."

While the helter-skelter rush for power has manifestly paid off for the ruling elite up to now, the longer-run prospect is more in doubt. What is to be done about all the tasks so long neglected: construction of adequate housing, building of modern roads and highways, provision of decent service trades, renovation of consumer industries, and so on and on? Where is the engine for generating innovation and progress across broad segments of the economy? How is the obsolete economic system, burdened almost to the breaking point, to be overhauled without threatening the survival of the autocratic political order?

A favorite sport of historians, professional as well as amateur, is to search for some necessity in otherwise ugly sweeps of history. Thus, as they survey the Russian past, some will argue that the cruel times of Ivan the Terrible and Peter the Great were after all necessary, first to build a nation and second to westernize it. In the same vein, they may increasingly argue that Stalin was needed to create a world power. The case for each is not convincing, but let it be granted. There remains the more important question of whether the things for which these inhuman and uncivilized reigns were presumably necessary were themselves necessary, and the answer must be no.

In any case, one can flatly state that Stalin and the Soviet system were absolutely unnecessary for overcoming economic backwardness and promoting rapid economic development. The route of despotic rule, centralized management, forced collectivization, and lopsided industrialization, far from producing economic miracles, has yielded less economic development in any meaningful sense than the many successful alternatives followed elsewhere, particularly those relying heavily on market places organized within a regime of private property. Viewed against the aspirations of the masses when they overthrew the tsarist order, the verdict must be even stronger: Communist rule, in its half-century, has betrayed the revolution. Recall the promises: land to the peasants, bread to the workers, and freedom, peace, and brotherhood to all. They have been swept into the ashcan of history.

There is a Polish saying that, under communism, only the future is certain: the past is always changing. We would do well to keep this in mind as we listen to official praise of achievements over the half-century since the October Revolution. In fact, the event whose fiftieth anniversary we commemorate was not a revolution but a reaction, one of the great reactionary events of all time. For centuries, Russia had drifted slowly and painfully away from a cruel and despotic order toward a humane and liberal one. The drift swiftened after the middle of the nineteenth century, bursting forth into the revolution beginning in 1905. The symbolic death of the old order came in February 1917 when tsardom was put to an end. But the Bolshevik coup of October and its aftermath threw the country back to conditions of despotism, terror, and serfdom unsurpassed under the worst of the tsars.

By all civilized standards, there is nothing golden about the fiftieth anniversary of the Bolshevik reaction, for a society must be judged ultimately by the kind of people it produces and the welfare it makes available to them. Yet, the slow tortuous drift toward liberalism still stirs beneath the surface, and once again we witness the cry for reform and freedom, perhaps someday to become as strong as it was half a century ago. What does the future hold for the suffering and enduring peoples of the Soviet Union? No one can say. But we can say that improvement will go hand in hand with reform.

THE SOCIO-PSYCHOLOGICAL TRANSFORMATIONS OF SOVIET SOCIETY

Lewis S. Feuer

When the United States emerged in world history, there was an outpouring of literature to describe the new man, the American. Crèvecoeur in 1782, asking what is an American, answered that this "new man" was one who, having translated himself to America, had left behind him "all his ancient prejudices and manners"; he was regenerated in the new environment; "new laws, a new mode of living, a new social system; here they are become men: in Europe they were as so many useless plants." A procession of travellers concurred (with various reservations) that the American was a new psychological type —free, industrious, his own master, self-reliant, indifferent to religious dogmas but yet religious, and with a sense of his own individuality and importance. Fifty years after Crèvecoeur, in the aftermath of the Jacksonian Revolution, de Tocqueville talked much with the defeated and disillusioned survivors of the old Federalist Party. From them he learned of another side of democracy, of their fear of a potential despotism when constitutional safeguards were obliterated.

The Soviet Union has had neither its Crèvecoeur nor its de Tocqueville. That has not been altogether the fault of the host of travellers who have gone to study the Soviet citizenry. The visitors to America found a people ready to talk, argue, and describe; they found an easy access to men of different parties; they did not have to bear in mind, as they arranged for interviews, the surveillance of a secret police. Conditions have been quite otherwise in the Soviet Union. Let us then, having stated the unusual methodological difficulty, still raise the question—how has the psyche of Soviet man fared during fifty years of Soviet rule?

THE OCTOBER DREAM OF A NEW MAN

The Bolsheviks of 1917 certainly believed that the new society, conceived in the October Revolution, would bring forth a wonderful new human being. Leon Trotsky believed the future would see men with noble gait and bearing, with beautiful speech and high intelligence. "Man will become immeasurably stronger, wiser and subtler; his body will become more harmonized . . . his voice more musical . . . The average human type will rise to the heights of an Aristotle, a Goethe, a Marx." [1] Lenin foresaw a blending of mental and physical labor which would make the workingman-ruler the realization of a philosopher-king. Alexandra Kollontai foretold a love of the sexes ennobled, free from cruelty and selfishness. Such were the dreams. What then were the realities of Soviet psychological evolution? Lenin insisted that every creative idea must have an element of the dream in it.[2] If so, what was achieved, and in what ways did the dream's superimposition do violence to human nature?

If there is one great achievement of the Soviet society, it is that during its first twelve years or so, it carried through a psychological revolution against the traditional masochist psyche of the Russian people. This first era might well be called the anti-masochist period of the Soviet evolution. Paul Miliukov once said that he regarded E. J. Dillon's *Russian Characteristics* as the best portrayal of pre-revolutionary Russia; it gave a picture of a flagellant people, fatalistic, immoral, dishonest, lying, superstitious, and given to alternate brutality and self-castigation; its passive perspective, its acceptance of its own sinful character, was summed up in the proverb: "What is to be, cannot be avoided." [3] When this same observer visited the Soviet Union in 1928, he was astonished by the transformation. The obsequious muzhik had changed, he wrote, into "a full-blown citizen, conscious that he has a country with whose interests he identifies his own, and a government which is largely of his own making." [4] Dillon went to the bookstores of Moscow. "I never anticipated anything like this," he wrote. "The notion that a large percentage of mooshiks were smitten with a mania for enlightenment . . . seemed hardly admissible . . . But the fact was undeniable. The stores were crowded, . . . and millions of volumes were circulating in the various Republics." The sight of these book-seeking peasants, he said, "opened my eyes to the completeness of the change that had come over the population." Scientific, technical, and medical films were being shown everywhere, *The Mechanism of the Human Brain, The Choice of a Profession.* The most popular medical film was entitled *Abortion;* produced five or six years earlier, it was still drawing well. This was not the Russian man whom Saltykov had satirized—the suffering-deadened, consciousness-blunted Russian man, who looked at his hunger, misery, and humiliation as predestined.

The Bolshevik personality-structure refused to take physical suffering as the law of existence. Insofar as man was beset by technical problems, there were technical answers, and the Marxist was at one with the Comtist in asserting confidently the power of science. "We shall win over all the Russian and European Archimedes, and then the world will have to change whether it wants to or not!", said Lenin.[5]

This hatred for masochism, for "self-castigation" as he called it, was a primary component in Lenin, and a dominant element in the ego-ideal which he transmitted to the first decade of Soviet history. This was the Lenin who ridiculed the Tolstoyan, "the exhausted hysterical, misery-mongering Russian intellectual, who, publicly beating his breast, cries: 'I am bad, I am vile, but I am striving for moral self-perfection; I no longer eat meat but live on rice cutlets.' " He mocked at even the Jamesian religious philosophy to which Gorky was attracted; its adherent, he wrote, "castigates himself in the worst possible way, because instead of occupying himself with 'deeds' he indulges in self-contemplation." Lenin as an ego-ideal stood for a categorical rejection of the Russian wallowing in suffering. As Gorky defined Lenin's role: "I have never met in Russia, the country where the inevitability of suffering is preached as the general road to salvation, nor do I know of any man who hated, loathed and despised so deeply and strongly as Lenin, all . . . suffering."

The anti-masochist vector in the Soviet psychology brought a liberation of energies and creativity; something like a Soviet Renaissance seemed to be in the making, an experimentation in art forms, an enthusiasm for progressive education, a popular cultural revolution. This liberation of energies was the phenomenon which enthralled the Western intellectuals who visited the Soviet Union during this era and touched them with its infectious hopes. Isadora Duncan, the votary of the new dance with its free bodily expression, spent three years in Russia from 1921 to 1924, "to dance for the people," and she regarded that time as the happiest in her life. John Dewey, America's foremost philosopher, came to the Soviet Union in 1928, and was stirred by its teachers, "some of the wisest and most devoted men and women it has been my fortune to meet." Never had he seen in the world, he wrote, "such a large proportion of intelligent, happy, and intelligently occupied children." He found the Soviet effort "nobly heroic, evincing a faith in human nature which is democratic beyond the ambitions of the democracies of the past," while the Russian intellectuals seemed to him "organic members of an organic going movement." His colleagues from the Teachers' College at Columbia University, William Heard Kilpatrick and George S. Counts, joined with him in these judgments. The noted social worker, Lillian D. Wald, found the Soviet achievement in public health "extraordinary" and admired the campaigns to teach the people the rules of hygiene. The economist Professor Paul Douglas sensed "the big, the spiritual fact" behind the Soviet material construction, and his faith in socialism was strengthened. The distinguished liberal thinker, Horace M. Kallen, saw the realization of a cultural pluralism in the Soviet setting; he found a thriving culture among his fellow-Jews; for them, he wrote, "more truly than for any people under the Soviets, a new life is beginning." [6] The American travellers, to be sure, were all affected by a social will to believe as far as Soviet society was concerned. Nevertheless, there was a large counterpart in Soviet realities to their observations. The revolt against traditional masochism was releasing hitherto suppressed or dissipated human energies.

THE BOLSHEVIZATION OF THE PERSONALITY

The anti-masochist period in the Soviet psychological evolution gave way in the early thirties to a new stage which might be called that of the Bolshevization of the personality, from an anti-masochist to a sadistic elitist personality-structure. Stalin's famous speech in February 1931 to the First All-Union Conference of Managers, the most eloquent he ever gave, placed the motive for industrialization primarily in overcoming the Russian masochist tradition:

> The history of old Russia is the history of defeats due to backwardness. She was beaten by the Mongol Khans. She was beaten by the Swedish feudal barons. She was beaten by the Polish-Lithuanian squires. She was beaten by the Anglo-French capitalists. She was beaten by the Japanese barons. All beat her for her backwardness . . . She was beaten because to beat her was profitable and could be done with impunity. Do you remember the words of the pre-revolutionary poet: "You are both poor and abundant, your are both powerful and helpless, mother Russia" . . . They beat her saying: "You are poor and helpless," . . . Such is the law of capitalism—to beat the backward and the weak. The jungle law of capitalism.[7]

Here was a version of Russian history not as class struggle but as repeated submission to beating by foreigners. The memorable iteration of "beaten" indicated above all the psychological motive power for industrialization. But then the sadistic component, emerging to dominance, chose of all the possible ways to industrialization that one which would enforce the government's will most harshly on the people.

The Russian ego-ideal in its fluctuation from masochism in effect now swung to sadism—from an exaltation of suffering to one of cruelty. There took place a remarkable psychological change in the Soviet ego-ideal structure. Already in the twenties, observers had often spoken of "Communist Puritans," of those who like Marxist Calvinists renounced the goods and joys of life, and lived with frugality, industry, and thrift. Thus Louis Fischer, writing from Moscow in 1924, in an article entitled "Communist Puritans," expounded their psychological similarity: "The Bolsheviks presume to tell the individual how to act and how to live. This is the 'superiority complex' which is one of the most essential characteristics of puritanism. 'I am perfect. Watch me. Go thou and do likewise.' The Russian Communists are puritans without religion." Cotton Mather, wrote *The Nation*'s Moscow correspondent, would have approved of Trotsky; also Lenin lived as an ascetic, and there was "something reminiscent of Christian self-abnegation in Chicherin's, Bukharin's, Radek's disdain for good clothes." [8]

It was in keeping with their initial Puritanism that the Bolsheviks began a campaign against the horrible swearing of the Russian people. The Russian oaths, generally involving their mothers, were said to make the worst product of the British navy look pale. Trotsky wrote that "one would have to consult philologists, linguists, and folk-lore experts to find out whether any people has such unrestrained, filthy, and disgusting oaths as we have." [9] Psychologically, the oaths of Oedipal maternal fixation are characteristic of people suffering from masochism, self-hatred, lack of manliness; American Negro leaders, for instance, strive to end the vogue of such oaths among their people. The dominant bearing of the government's campaigns in the mid-twenties was toward raising people's self-respect, and evidently they bore considerable fruit.

The Puritan virtues were appropriate to a revolutionary period in which pleasures were associated with the upper classes; to live like a proletarian was to live frugally. Moreover, these Marxist Calvinist virtues were validated by the needs of an era of industrialization; the people were being called upon to consume less and to accumulate more. It was also true that side-by-side with the liberating, anti-masochist component of the Soviet Revolution there had been co-present a strong, harsh, sadistic vector. Bertrand Russell, a keen psychological observer, perceived the sadistic component which moved Lenin's asceticism. The Bolshevik Revolution, as William H. Chamberlin wrote in his history, opened the gates to a tremendous mass release of hatred. Under these circumstances, men whose personalities were dominated by sadistic motives moved ahead into the highest positions of leadership. The conditions of the civil war, the frustrations of material existence, the accumulated personal envies of class existence, the bitterness of life where survival had become the primary end, while emotions and thinking became survival-emotions and survival-thinking, all this filled the interstices of social life with a free-floating aggression.[10] Political leaders who came from the most extreme sadistic segment of the spectrum of personality-types found a psychological climate in which they could forge to the top. The Bolsheviks of this time, to use Max Eastman's classification, were divided into the "softs" and the "hards." The "hards," the sadists, began to displace the "softs." Leon Trotsky was aware that one psychological type was gradually displacing another. He tried to explain the phenomenon of the rise of Stalin and his henchmen by reference to a psychological law—that there is a reaction of exhaustion on the part of the people to the great social and psychological strain of revolution, and that in this situation, the mediocrities push ahead, displacing the men of talent and genius. Stalin, in Trotsky's eyes, was "the outstanding mediocrity of the party." [11] But something more was involved than the rise of mediocrities. Even a mediocracy can take either malevolent or benevolent forms. John Stuart Mill wrote in *On Liberty* that "the general tendency of things throughout the world is to render mediocrity the ascendant power among mankind." A distinguished president of the United States, Harry Truman, did not regard himself as an exceptional man; Trotsky would have called him a mediocrity. The psychological character of the Stalinist era, however, derived not from the intellectual mediocrity of its leaders but rather from their qualities of emotion—their sadistic vectors. Whatever the social causes for the elevation of such a psychological type to the Soviet leadership, it expressed itself in the Bolshevization of the ego-ideal for the character-structure of the Soviet people.

The experiment in Bolshevizing the Soviet social character was carried out in large part through the figure of Lenin. Its use was as significant as that of Jesus' image in medieval Christianity. To be like Lenin, with busts and pictures of Lenin replacing the ikons, this was the summons of the Soviet order. And to be like Lenin was to possess the qualities which Gorky perceived in him, "self-discipline often amounting to self-torture and self-mutilation, in its most extreme form, amounting to a renunciation of art." [12] Like Lenin, the Bolshevized personality had to be prepared to stifle his emotions, his "social idealism," for the sake of the cause. Lenin, said Gorky, "kept silent about the secret agitation of his soul"; he sacrificed himself "to hostility and hatred, so that love might be at last realized." Hostility and hatred possessed, however, an autonomous valence for the Bolshevized personality. Lenin said he did not envy the next generation which would not know such cruelty, because cruelty went hand-in-hand with the making of history. The Bolshevik character-structure, on the more unconscious level, found in the making of history an occasion for massive cruelty which otherwise would have lacked the shadow of a historico-philosophical excuse. A personality less Bolshevized than Lenin's would have said how much he regretted the historical mission that had been thrust upon him, how much rather he would have preferred to have lived in the next generation. Even Trotsky in 1918, beholding "the heavy barbarism of Moscow," was reminded of Hamlet's lines: "The time is out of joint;—O cursed spite, that ever I was born to set it right!" [13]

Children in the schools imbibed the stories of Lenin's life. If American schoolchildren are taught the sentences of Lincoln's *Gettysburg Address* or the Second Inaugural with its "With malice toward none, with charity for all," Soviet children were the receptors of a political ethic which told of the renegade Kautsky, the flabby Mensheviks, and the lackey liberals. Self-mutilation and self-torture were extolled in a variety of Lenin parables. They told of a man ready to renounce any friend who was not a political ally, who misshaped his personal feelings to conform to a political test, who feared music lest it mellow his commitment to ruthlessness, who excluded any activity whether museum-going, chess, or ice-skating which might intrude on his revolutionary dedication. This was the self-mutilated man who found himself so upset by the probing of irrationality in Chekhov's "Ward No. 6" that he rushed from the house to wander under the skies.[14]

To have a Bolshevized personality was then to absorb into one's ego-ideal all the traits of historical self-mutilation, self-sacrifice, and historical sadism. It was to be dedicated to the Party, to make its will yours, to have comrades, not friends, to be indifferent to personal relations, unsentimental, a lover of hard facts, to write in a style that was as de-personalized as possible, to avoid subjectivism. The Bolshevized personality feared above all his unconscious which housed all the excluded humanistic components in himself. For this reason, Soviet psychology became increasingly hostile during the latter twenties to Freud's ideas, and by 1930 the concept of the unconscious was being ostracized; man's consciousness was emphasized as the director of human behavior. Corresponding to the Bolshevization of the ego-ideal which was taking place, the Soviet psychologists emphasized conscious control, discipline, and "self-training." If freedom was the recognition of necessity, then consciousness was the organon of freedom because it moulded the personality to the requirements of the party and the state. Soviet psychological doctrine mirrored what actually was taking place in Soviet personalities; its concepts, however, were an ideological reflection rather than a scientific analysis of the phenomenon. If the behavioristic environmentalism of the early twenties transposed the anti-masochist phase of the Soviet evolution, with its simple hope that the socialist environment would nurture a new socialist superman, then the voluntaristic doctrine of the primacy of consciousness, which became dominant from 1930 to 1936, corresponded to the requirements of the Bolshevization of personality. Whatever might upset the controls in the planning of Soviet personality structure was debarred from consciousness. By 1936, for instance, research which made use of questionnaires was altogether banned. "Such questionnaires as concern the subject's political views or probe into the deeper and intimate side of life," it was declared, "must be *categorically banned* from use." [15] "Spontaneous" processes were taken to be the road to "leftist" deviations. The kind of personality a man should train himself to have was dictated by the needs of the Five-Year Plan. It was as if each citizen was being assigned a personality quota to fulfill. He must repress troublesome questions, suppress his inner discontent, identify with the Party, and regard its edicts as his own. The Bolshevization of the personality on a collective scale thus involved a massive self-repression.

It was this massive self-repression which made possible the acquiescence of the Soviet people to the large-scale purges and liquidations of the thirties. The questioning intellectual, the recalcitrant worker, the writer insisting on his freedom, the obstinate peasant, each externalized motivations which the majority of the Soviet citizenry felt and expressed within themselves. Soviet citizens struggled to talk and behave as the official policy demanded. There developed that separation into two selves which Soviet thinkers now describe as the separation between the "official self" and the "real self." Every society has some degree of such a separation but in Soviet society it reached extremes. People found themselves intoning public speeches which they didn't believe; parents curbed their comments to their children lest they be quoted or reported for counter-revolutionary utterances. The atmosphere resembled that which the historian Ammianus Marcellinus described as existing in the Rome of the fourth century A.D. when things reached the point that people denied they even had dreams for fear that they would be held accountable for what they had dreamed.[16] It was the depth and extent of the division between the "real" and the "official" self which became the primary characteristic in the latter thirties of the Soviet personality structure. It was a harsh, disharmonious self rather than the harmonious self which Trotsky had foreseen. The decrees against abortion and divorce, the official notation of illegitimacy, were all aspects of the attempt to Bolshevize personality. The "spontaneous" individualistic concern with private happiness was out of keeping with the repressive temper.

Such a laceration and duality of selves was always in an unstable equilibrium, the maintenance of which required all the resources of social controls and threats to assure the individual's collaboration. For almost every person felt guilty, almost everyone repressed some discontent, some frustration, some clear insight into the workings of the regime. Every person knew he was guilty of sins, original and unoriginal, against the regime. The price of survival was successful repression. Every deviationist who was tried and condemned externalized one's own inner repressed deviation, and joining in condemning them was a collective easement of the aggressions which had accumulated in one's self. Every totalitarian system from the Spanish Inquisition on has seen the complicity of its people in the extirpation of heretics, for the simple reason that the modal personality structure which such systems require is based on every individual's repressing his angers and doubts into his unconscious; hence, every totalitarian system must cope with the accumulated aggressions issuing from the histories of individual repression and frustrations. To engage in any causal psychological analysis which might uncover the contents of the unconscious was *prima facie* evidence of a leftist deviation; the unconscious indeed was presumed by the Soviet regime to be a Trotskyist. Thus the popular play *Fear* produced in 1931 depicted the counter-revolutionary activities of an "Institute for Physiological Stimuli"; they consisted in the administering of questionnaires among the people which supported the conclusion that eighty percent were cowed into social submission by an "unconditioned response of fear." The play showed how the institute's director was unmasked and removed, and then repented.

Curiously Leon Trotsky had been the only important Soviet leader to defend the significance and fruitfulness of Freud's psychoanalytical method. Having been in contact with psychoanalytical circles in Vienna, he saw in Freud's work "a heroic break with all kinds of conventions." He wrote a letter to Pavlov pleading for a reconciliation with Freud's ideas, describing Freud as standing over the human psyche with a "penetrating gaze." [17] As the Soviet dictatorship, however, grew more and more into a totalitarian system, it was inevitable that Freud's concept of the unconscious would be proscribed. Consciousness, the censor, was apotheosized to a point where the censored unconscious was virtually liquidated. Thus the regime created its image of man, and decided it was good. When the great trials of the latter thirties took place, Bukharin warned from the dock that people should not try to use the Dostoyevskyan psychology of the Slavic soul (or unconscious) to understand the motives of the deviationists; no, it was simply that they had failed to Bolshevize themselves, to shape themselves as socialist construction required.[18]

A kind of hatred and suspicion of one's fellow-man came to pervade the emotions of Soviet people during the latter thirties. The goals of upward mobility were more available if one's bureaucratic superiors or rivals were "physically liquidated"; denunciation became a technique for rising in the bureaucratic hierarchy or for venting one's grudges; at the same time, one could claim the warrant of one's Socialist conscience.[19] The unethical, the envious mediocrity, the ambitious gifted, the time server profited from the removal of the ethical, the talented, the sincere. The insincere could Bolshevize their personalities most easily. Participant-observers, as the phrase goes, described the time as Machiavellian. Lev Kamenev, shortly before the shadow of the purges fell upon him, wrote about Machiavelli in the language of Soviet indirect discourse. "This servant of the Florentine oligarchy," he said, had not been afraid "to look at the political reality of his time and to reveal behind the broad banner and paltry finery its true countenance: an oppressive class of masters struggling amongst themselves for power over the laboring masses." [20] And Ilya Ehrenburg, recalling the character of the Stalinist era in later years, said it evoked Machiavelli and the chieftains of the Renaissance, when any means were regarded as justified in creating a strong state—poison, informing, stabbing in the back.

The Bolshevization of the personality carried with it as an indirect consequence a heightening of one's quantum of social guilt. To repress the guilt-anxieties, one talked about such questions as little as possible and never mentioned the names of destroyed or imprisoned persons, or the attendant circumstances. For the mentioning ignited one's sense of guilt against which reinforcements for repression would then have to be mobilized; the personality became all the more stilted, unspontaneous, colorless, harsh. The Bolshevized personality evolved into a structure of defence-mechanisms against one's inner self and the perception of external reality.

The war years from 1941 to 1945, for all their untold physical hardship, brought an easement of the psychological strains under which the Soviet personality lived. Ehrenburg has described the pre-war years: "In March, 1938, I had listened to the elevator with alarm; at that time I wanted to live, and like many others I had a small suitcase in readiness with two changes of linen." The internal enemy receded during the war years; the enemy became real and external, and every person felt needed in the struggle. From a psychological standpoint, the war helped the Soviet equilibrium by providing a target for the accumulated aggressive resentments. The aftermath, however, brought the renewed anxieties of Bolshevization. Exhausted and indifferent, people submitted. The second Bolshevization had an aspect of the *déjà vu*. "In March, 1949," writes Ehrenburg, "I did not think about linen, and I awaited the outcome almost with indifference . . . I had had time to grow tired, old age was setting in. Or perhaps because this was a repetition, and after the war, what was taking place was particularly unbearable. We would go to bed late—just before morning; the thought of their coming was particularly unbearable." [21]

STALIN'S LEGACY OF GUILT

The Stalinist era ended in 1953, but it left the deepest imprint on the Soviet personality-structure. The Soviet intelligentsia had sustained the worst psychological trauma—the blow to the sense of their own sincerity. For sincerity was what the pre-revolutionary intellectuals proudly felt to be their most distinct trait. As Kropotkin wrote, it was nihilism which had "impressed its stamp upon the whole of the life of the educated classes of Russia" and which would be "retained for many years to come." It gave to them, he said, "a certain peculiar character which we Russians regret not to find in the life of Western Europe . . . that remarkable sincerity, that habit of thinking aloud, which astounds Western European readers." This sincerity made the Russian intellectual refuse "to bend before any authority except that of reason, and in the analysis of every social institution or habit he revolted against any sort of more or less marked sophism." [22] The traumatic surrender of this sincerity remained in their memory for the Soviet intelligentsia to abreact. As Pasternak put it in Dr. Zhivago: "To conceal the failure [of collectivization] people had to be cured, by every means of terrorism of the habit of thinking and judging for themselves, and forced to see what didn't exist, to assert the very opposite of what their eyes told them. This accounts for the unexampled cruelty of the Yezhov period."

Second, there came to pervade Soviet society what we might best call a "Cain-Abel complex." The new society, the new elect of activists and Marxists, the new working class, had shown itself like Cain unable to guard its brothers; they had allowed the Abels to be destroyed. Each person had to come to terms with his share in the collective guilt. Some intellectuals said later with Ehrenburg: "Yes, I did know about many crimes; but it was not within my power to stop them." [23] They were met with the query: Why hadn't they spoken out as Tolstoi had spoken out against the crimes of tsarist Russia? They answered: the Soviet society was different, and in any case, who would have believed the protesting voice? But the Cain-Abel complex imposed an especial burden of guilt on a people professing a higher historical mission. That is why Khrushchev's speech at the Twentieth Party-Congress was the single most politically and psychologically therapeutic act in the twentieth century: "Like millions of my countrymen," recalled Ehrenburg, "when I read the materials of the 20th Congress I felt that a weight had been lifted from my heart."

The phenomenon itself and its psychological effects were not easily exorcised; on a less grandiose scale, they persisted. The meaning of the Cain-Abel complex was a reiterated statement: "We killed our comrades, we still destroy them." Revolutionary France got rid of its guilt by using the Directory and Napoleon to eradicate all the Jacobin Clubs. Napoleon, we must remember, was the first great anti-ideologist. In the Soviet Union, however, the Communist Party, unlike the Jacobin Clubs, pervaded every domain of social and economic existence. The Jacobin Clubs, in contrast, led ephemeral lives for a few years. The Communist Party was the primary social institution, and of forty years' standing. Naturally an effort was made to keep unsullied its collective image, and to make of Stalin an almost sole bearer and scapegoat of the collective guilt.

The Soviet Cain-Abel complex was qualitatively of a different kind from that of the Nazis. The Nazi ideology was to begin with filled with evil, hatred, and anti-reason. The German people had entered, as it were, into a united self-conscious pact with evil, emulating their national Faust-Mephistophelean legend. The Nazi intent (expressed in psychoanalytical metaphor) was: Where there was the ego, let the id prevail. The Soviet evil, however, was done in the name of Marxism—a doctrine with internationalist, rationalist, scientific, humanistic, and egalitarian aims. The Soviet intent officially was: where there was the ego, let the super-ego prevail.

The Nazis were in revolt against the whole humanistic tradition and super-ego of Western civilization; the Bolsheviks, on the other hand, claimed to be the inheritors of that tradition, and to be fulfilling its aims. They would therefore sense themselves as betrayers rather than neo-barbarians. The Soviet guilt, in a more passive form, spread from the society's vanguard to the masses through the Party which drew its members from all classes, and through the mass organizations like the trade unions which had contributed their punitive resolutions whenever asked. The Cain-Abel complex is that of a society which has condoned or engaged in a collective lynching. The ideological super-ego becomes discredited; the sense of being history's elect collapsed once Khrushchev gave his speech on the crimes of the preceding era.

The exposure of the Cain-Abel complex had a tremendous political consequence; it made it almost impossible for the Soviet Union to maintain its rigid control over foreign Communist Parties. Stalin had been able to enforce his will on foreign Parties through the use of a few agents so long as the psychological enthrallment of his Marxist apostolate was maintained. De-Stalinization, the dethronement of the epochal super-ego meant that a whole period's development had been contaminated with historically unnecessary evil; the psychological hegemony of the keepers of the doctrine was undermined. The Soviet Communist Party ceased to be the political super-ego of the world Communist movement. Political parricide destroys the continuity and transmitted authority of the tribal political doctrine.

Within the Soviet society, the Cain-Abel complex was always now in consciousness; returned, rehabilitated victims were perpetual reminders of a shared guilt. The Soviet regime hoped it could "decollectivize" the guilt; that it wanted to make the exclusive property of Stalin. For every personality to the extent that he was Bolshevized had contributed to the making of Stalin.

Almost every sojourner in the Soviet Union has noted three psychological phenomena which are symptoms of the collective psychological repression. First, there is what might be called the "peeling off effect." Discussions with Soviet citizens usually go through several stages; the first stage consists of a recitation of the "official line." The second begins as one gets to know the person better; the "official self" recedes; initially there may be slips of the tongue which break through the dull, official self, or sudden, shrewd, glancing remarks; then the dialectical qualitative leap to the third stage, sometimes gradually, sometimes abruptly; the citizen states his inner beliefs and feelings truthfully. Discussion with a Soviet citizen over a time-period thus has a geological aspect as one brings to view the series of repressed layers of thought and feeling. Second, there is the "three-person effect." You will be having a discussion in an institute room with a Soviet scholar; his metaphors are becoming freer, his words more personal. Suddenly, a third person opens the door. "You can stay," says the first Soviet citizen to the interloper, in a precautionary hearty tone, indicating there's nothing private in the discussion. At once, however, the words reassume a cliché-ridden aspect; the hackneyed, meaning-mauled phrases from *Pravda* reappear; personal metaphors are supplanted by the collective vocabulary. Third, there are the continuing circumlocutions and avoidance of names. It is not quite proper to mention Stalin's name; if it has to be done, do so by reference to the "cult of personality"; Soviet etiquette enjoins this as a rule of discourse. And if you want to bring to view the resistance-mechanism of a Soviet scholarly group, begin to mention with approval the work of some man whom Stalin killed, as for instance, Bukharin. The chairman, secretary, and audience will suddenly be at a loss what to do with the obtruding, unwelcome ghost. Why doesn't he remain in limbo? Why disturb the living? Moreover, a certain discomfort is inevitably experienced in blaming the several million injustices of twenty-five years on Stalin. For one thing, such an explanation attaches an importance to the individual which contravenes historical materialism. And as we have mentioned, the Soviet personage knows there is something of Stalin in himself, as the current saying goes. Thus, the way of expediency is still repression; the collective unconscious of Soviet society is probably the most outstanding, though most unstable, of its collective enterprises.

Above all, the coming to consciousness of the Cain-Abel complex has terminated the sense of being a member of an elect. Since Herzen's time, the Russian intelligentsia have been imbued with the feeling of their uniqueness, their mission. The pre-war intellectuals experienced the guilt of serfdom, the peasantry, the proletariat, but they had movements which served the function of expiating the guilt. The Soviet citizen, however, finds himself without such a mechanism for guilt-alleviation. Socialism exists. Where does one go from there? If socialism itself is guilt-ridden, does any class remain with whom an identification may restore meaning to one's life? We, the intellectuals (Lenin told us), brought socialist consciousness to the masses. Now that the naked guilt of our socialism is uncovered, what have we to bring? In the Khrushchevan era, like missionaries deprived of their mission, the Russian intellectuals began a search to restore the sense of moral stature.

Thus, the Cain-Abel complex has dissolved old myths and slogans of populism and messianism. Thirty years ago in his report to the Central Committee Stalin made his famous reference to the myth of Antaeus. He compared the Bolsheviks to the hero of Greek mythology: "They, like Antaeus, are strong because they maintain connection with their mother, the masses, who gave birth to them, suckled them and reared them. And as long as they maintain connection with their mother, with the people, they have every chance of remaining invincible."[24] When the Cain-Abel phenomenon, however, was brought to consciousness, it was hard to pose as Antaeus and the redeemer of the masses. Cain, after all, went wandering from land to land bearing the mark of his guilt.

Populist mysticism, whether in peasant or proletarian form, the notion of a mystic fusion with the oppressed, had always been an influential tenet among the Russian intellectuals. To go back to the people was the chief way of shedding one's individual guilt. The realization of socialism, however, had made populist mysticism obsolete. The latter had always involved an element of protest against the existing social system; one merged one's self with the lowliest who would some day rise against the system which exploited them. The socialist state, however, was in principle a workers' state and its bureaucrats not infrequently spoke with the voice of mass prejudice as when Zhdanov inveighed against Shostakovitch or Khrushchev against abstract art. The obsolescence of "back to the people" movements in a socialist society, forcing the intellectuals to return to social realities, made more poignant the sense of the permanence of the social order. One had to come to terms with it even if the terms were not one's own. Groups of young dissenters who arose in the Khrushchev era wanted more intellectual freedom for themselves; they thought little of the masses as a democratizing or liberalizing force.

SOCIALIST PESSIMISM

The philosophy which has thus emerged in the Soviet Union, the outcome of its fifty years of socialist experience, is best characterized as "socialist pessimism." What is pessimism? It is that frame of mind which arises when every desire we have tends to be frustrated by external material or human obstacles. Every attempt to gain pleasure becomes an occasion for anticipated pain. Pain, suffering, defeat, are taken as the law of things, and there is no real confidence or faith in an alternative. Pre-revolutionary Russia at its times of suffering still believed that the meaning of its experience lay near at hand. Vershinin in *Three Sisters* foreseeing the town filled with such folk as themselves, Irina firm in her faith that "a time will come when everyone will know what all this is for, why there is all this suffering, and there will be no mysteries," and Olga beholding the happiness which would redeem their suffering—much of this hope is gone from the Soviet consciousness. The resolution has been made. Lenin's notion of a society reconstructed like one big post office has been realized.[25] And now what oppresses the Soviet citizen is the sense of no alternatives. "The Cruel Words: No Alternative" was the way *Komsomolskaya Pravda*'s Institute of Public Opinion characterized the responses of one thousand Smolensk pupils to the content of the television programs which absorbed the free time of half of them: "The programs are dull. Can't they present new variety shows, new theatre productions and guest appearances by various foreign artists? If for all this they still watch television for three hours, it is apparently because they have no alternative . . . In time the feeling of dissatisfaction will disappear and will be replaced by omnivorousness or by habitual grumbling." [26] This phrase "no alternative" expresses the essence of the socialist pessimism. A Schopenhauerian-like theme of the *ennui* of Soviet life became a recurrent theme among Soviet critics. The tedium of party conclaves had long replaced the October exhilaration; the dullness of ideology was its refutation.[27]

The pre-war Russian system with all its oppressiveness had safety-valves of various kinds; a dissatisfied worker could migrate and choose a different society; or he might dream of opening an enterprise of his own. In the pluralistic American economy, the workingman's belief that he can leave the factory and buy a store or small business of his own has a psychological reality which diminishes the personal impact of corporate power. To the extent that a society is perceived as possessing such degrees of freedom, to that extent it is not experienced as a system. But in the Soviet Union, the sense of the System is omnipresent; there are no alternative modes of social existence for the different psychological tempers; one model of personality-structure, provided by the image of Lenin, is dominant, and other types, individualist, or apolitical, must strive to conform, re-mold themselves, or be regarded as, to some degree, deviant or idiosyncratic. Any system with minimal alternatives inevitably generates a sense of pessimism. When to this is added the influence of the loss of mission and the status of the elect, the ebb of the doctrine of the chosen class, and the involvement of one's ideology in the Cain-Abel complex, one can perceive the multiple vectors of Soviet pessimism.

For various reasons, furthermore, Soviet nationalism has failed to provide a sufficient antidote to Soviet pessimism. A nationalistic ethos thrives when there is the sense of a potential external aggressor who aims to destroy one's culture. Freud long ago raised the problem: against whom would the aggressive energies of the Soviet society be directed once the kulak, the deviationists, and the alleged foreign plotters were gone? For nationalism can serve to unify a people by providing an external object for emotions of hatred which otherwise are turned internally against themselves.

As the threat of Hitlerism has receded into the historical past, Soviet nationalism has looked for the stimulus of a new external enemy. But the current unsolved problem for Soviet nationalism is the lack of such an external object. Soviet propagandists have worked hard to instil in the people a fear of the United States as embodying the menace of imperialism. The people, however, remain unconvinced. At the height of the Cuban missiles crisis of 1962, President John F. Kennedy was still an adored figure among the Russian people, especially the youth. Too much is known about America to depict it successfully as successor to the Nazis. Soviet nationalism has, therefore, been beset by an emotional hollowness.[28]

Finally, it has proved difficult to integrate nationalism with Marxism; indeed, the amalgam has tended to reinforce the drift to socialist pessimism. The uncomfortable feeling has always persisted that every nationalist step forward is two steps backward from the original founding Marxist doctrine. Furthermore nationalist reality definitely impugns Marxist internationalism. The Soviet people learn, for instance, that in 1957 Mao Tse-tung, presumably in the name of Marxism, was prepared to envisage a global war in which one-third of the world's people would be killed, and that his followers today foresee the transfer of civilization's center to China. When a nationalistic bond arises from anxiety concerning aggression by a "Marxist" nation, it inevitably calls into question Marxist internationalism itself, and heightens a climate of pessimism.[29]

The most measurable consequence of Soviet pessimism seems to me to be the steady decline of the Soviet birth-rate. Population problems are a favorite subject for young Soviet sociologists; the materials lie ready to hand, are measurable, and actually provide a most basic criticism of Soviet society. Here after fifty years of Soviet power is the most dramatic sign of a failure of confidence—the refusal to reproduce one's kind. And population data cannot be exorcised by ideological clichés. A Stalinist ideologist who tried to do so at a candidate's public defence of a thesis on population quickly found himself discomfitted. By 1966 the birth rate in the Soviet Union was lower than that of the United States, a surprising contrast in view of the fact that the Soviet population is so much more rural in its composition. Thus, in 1966 the Soviet birth-rate, according to the most recent statement from the Central Statistical Administration, was 17.2 per 1,000 of population; the comparable American figure was 18.5. The decline in the birth rate has been a continuous commentary on the Soviet regime's official pronouncements of socialist optimism. From 44 births per thousand inhabitants in 1926, the rate sank to 36.5 in 1939; the decline continued during the post-Stalin era from 24.9 in 1960 to 18.5 in 1965. The net reproductive rate and that of natural increase diminished in concomitant proportions. The economist V. Perevedentsev therefore wrote: "Our demographers are well aware of the stable declining trend in the indices of population replacement." A compensatory stimulus from the post-war children has not yet taken place, the rate of growth steadily declined since 1960 from 1.6 per cent to less than 1.1 in 1966. The birth rate, wrote the leading Soviet authority, A. G. Kharchev of Leningrad, decreased by 25 per cent from 1940 to 1961. One-fourth of all families, according to the census of 1959, had no children, while of the remaining number, half were raising only one.[30]

The birth rate in the Soviet Union, moreover, is far lower than that of the United States when its percentage of rural population was equal to the present Soviet figure. In 1963, for instance, the Soviet rural population of 107,700,000 constituted about 47.5 per cent of the total. The United States had a corresponding rural percentage approximately in 1922, when its birth rate, we estimate, reached more than 26 per 1,000. When we read the complaint of a Soviet collective farm chairman that the milkmaids cannot find husbands, we can appreciate how serious the basis is for the declining Soviet figure.[31] Soviet social scientists have called for an institute of demography to study such problems; the absence of such an institute in a planned economy is itself evidence of a tendency to repress a problem.

To what extent, however, can the decline of the Soviet birth-rate be attributed to the workings of the Soviet planned system and a consequent pessimism? The kind of personal interviews in depth which would confirm this hypothesis are not available to Soviet sociologists. From time to time, however, an isolated voice calls attention to the correlation of the low birth-rate with poor economic planning. One economist, for instance, traced the low birth-rate in the country's textile centers to the high ratio of unmarried young women and the relative paucity of young men.[32] He attributed this discrepancy in the ratio of sexes to the low wages of the textile industry which failed to attract men. Thus the population decline for a specific industry and specific localities was tied to the industry's low wages. But the argument had a clear applicability for many sectors of the economy and for centers other than textiles—a latent suggestion, from which the economist himself may well have drawn back, of a failure in the system, of its members' loss of confidence in its promise of singing tomorrows. Probably the most melancholy expression of this socialist pessimism was the extraordinarily high abortion rate in the Soviet cities. Leningrad, which had not only the lowest reported birth-rate but the highest legal abortion rate, was estimated by Professor Kharchev to have three abortions for every live birth.[33]

Probably the most moving spokesman for the socialist pessimism has been Andrei Sinyavsky. Like all classical pessimists, Sinyavsky finds an intractable psychological wound in man's loss of religious faith, for man's sense of purpose is shattered without God, and Marx's socialist purposefulness itself rested on Purpose in history. As an ungrounded purpose became purposeless, the dialectic came to be regressive rather than progressive, as deceptive as the Schopenhauerian Will: "So that prisons should vanish forever, we built new prisons . . . So that work should become a rest and a pleasure, we introduced forced labor." Although communism approached realization, wrote Sinyavsky, "we do not find around us what we hoped to find." "To our new God we sacrificed not only our lives, our blood and our bodies. We also sacrificed our snow-white soul, after staining it with all the filth in the world." A vestigial historicism leads Sinyavsky to hope that the corruptions of socialism will prepare the way for a socialist efflorescence, even as the Inquisition preceded a great Christian culture. This effort, however, at a sociodicy to replace a theodicy, is a desperate measure. One recalls that the Inquisition prepared the way for decline in Spain and Italy, that a free culture and science prospered elsewhere. And Sinyavsky acknowledges: "Today's children will scarcely be able to produce a new God, capable of inspiring humanity into the next historical cycle."

Thirty years before, Nikolai Bukharin had also expressed concern that Soviet culture was becoming impoverished, that the "cultural style" of the new period was that of "technicism," that the vast majority of the new intellectuals would be technicians without the least idea of ancient Greek tragedy or even the nineteenth-century Russian writers. He trusted, however, that all this was an essential strategy of the Hegelian cunning of history, the required antithesis to the "Solovievs, Dostoyevskys, and Tolstoys," the "famous mystical 'Slavic soul'," the "slavish, Asiatic labor customs." [34] Bukharin, however, died one of the Abels, and to the socialist pessimist, history seemed to have lost most of its cunning. For the predicament of no alternatives, and the guilt of the Cain-Abel experience, went far beyond concern over the narrowness of technicism. American civilization too had seemed to Emerson, James, and Dewey, as it had to de Tocqueville, dominated by technical preoccupations. But always it retained the sense of freedom, of open alternatives, something which withered away in the Soviet evolution.

There is a hint in Sinyavsky's *On Socialist Realism* that the most intimate relations of men and women have been affected by the emotions of defeat. "Russian literature," notes Sinyavsky, "is full of love stories in which an inadequate man and a beautiful woman meet and part without achieving anything. The fault, of course, lies with the man, who does not know how to love his lady as she deserves, actively and with a purpose. Instead, he yawns with boredom . . . like Rudin, or else kills his beloved." Rudin was indeed said to have been modelled on Bakunin, who was talked about maliciously for his sexual inadequacies. Revolutionary action was indeed a way the "superfluous man" achieved a new vitality. Was Sinyavsky's remark about the inadequacies of nineteenth-century Russians intended for his Soviet contemporaries as well? We have, however, no sufficient evidence on which to base judgments concerning the character of sexual feelings in an emotional climate of socialist pessimism. Soviet novels do portray bureaucratic executives as men who are romantic failures with their wives. The personal lives of the higher echelon have been described as corrupted. But we are better informed about the Trobriand Islanders in these respects than we are of Soviet citizens, and Kinsey reports are not on the agenda for Soviet sociology.

The general theme of pessimism is one, however, which deeply worries the Soviet ideologists; what measure, they ask, can be taken to combat it? A play such as Arbuzov's *My Poor Marat* evoked so much criticism precisely because it conveyed a socialist pessimism. It is noteworthy that as with Peter Weiss's *Marat Sade* the concept of a revolution unfulfilled called forth a Marat symbol. Whereas Weiss's play depicted Marat in dialogue with the Marquis de Sade on the failures of the revolution, and the search for its erotic counterpart, the Soviet play depicted how spiritual hopes were defeated even though people realized their vocational aspirations. Three teen-agers in besieged Leningrad in 1942 dream of becoming a doctor, a bridge builder, and a poet respectively. Seventeen years later they have achieved their positions, but as the *Pravda* critic noted, "they have grown old in spirit—they live in a melancholy state of waiting for happiness. The play ends on this note of waiting"; the future has become vague, indistinct, unchallenging. A "mixture of 'neorealism' and 'neodecadence'," a critic called the play, and he cavilled at Marat's tragedy, the "abyss" between the ideals of the thirties and the realities of the sixties, and his haunting dream that these are two riverbanks which he can never join with a bridge; the protagonist falls back on silence: "I could say what I think, but I won't, so there." [35]

This is the source of Soviet pessimism—the socialist system realized but the Soviet citizen so "alienated" from himself and his fellows that he remains silent, the passive aggression of speechlessness. The Chekhovian pessimism never lost its verbal protest and hope; it kept alive the dignity of its character. The Soviet pessimism derives from a deprivation of dignity, and an abnegation on the social stage into silence. Or as with the hero in Ehrenburg's *The Thaw* wondering how his words pervert realities: "Isn't it comical!" he thought. "I get up on the platform and calmly prove that those things simply don't exist." The sociology of hypocrisy is an unstudied subject—how to measure not merely the gap between ideals and actions but the contempt for ideals which arises with their conscious misuse as endorsements for evil acts; then the ideals and words themselves are stamped with dishonesty. Hypocrisy is not ideological in character, for ideological processes are unconscious, sincerely self-deceptive; but the hypocrite consciously uses ideology for his purposes. The guilt of socialized hypocrisy is an ingredient of socialist pessimism.

The mood of socialist pessimism expresses itself in a mode of thought which is new for the Soviet Union; it might be called "anti-dialectical thinking." Russian thought from pre-revolutionary times through the Soviet era has been largely imbued with apocalypticism. There was the belief that a new type of humanity would emerge, a new intelligentsia, qualitatively different from the old. Russian apocalypticism merged with Marxist dialectic. "There is no fortress that Bolsheviks cannot take by storm," said Stalin, and the conviction was strong that with a new social base the bastions of restrictive laws, whether those of social psychology, of diminishing returns, or political behavior, would be superseded.[36] The pessimist mood, however, has always been conducive to a perception of the permanences in social relations, the social invariants in different times and places. So the Soviet sociologist today will explain the difficult housing situation by reference to similar problems in capitalistic and even underdeveloped countries; he will discuss the growing rate of divorce, the juvenile delinquency, the appeal of jazz, in terms of worldwide social trends; he will talk of the persistence of "zoological individualism" even under socialist forms; he will document the persisting structures of social inequality in the Soviet society.[37] And this type of thinking, "antidialectical" in character, the opposite pole to the "qualitative leaps" which were always anticipated from the kingdom of necessity to the realm of freedom, largely pervades and is increasingly manifest in published writings. The illusion of the "qualitative leap" was part of an eternal recurrence, the circulation of illusions; such is the mood of socialist pessimism at its extreme.

THE RETURN OF THE REPRESSED

By the customary criteria, the Soviet society is a stable one. Its planned economy, despite inefficiencies, can satisfy the basic needs of its population. Its social system offers rewards to those who have ability and talent, especially if these are combined with a psychological adeptness for dealing with bureaucratic superiors and a receptivity to the limits of discourse which the system imposes. The Communist Party above all is the potent instrument for what we might call the "systematization" of the divergent personality-trends in the society. Its ever-present scrutiny, if sometimes slipshod, is often meticulous; it weeds out the stubborn and the recalcitrant; it rewards the compliant and the talented with careers. No economic dialectic decrees the decline of the Soviet system; the Soviet citizen imbibes a sense of the massive social power which pervades the interstices of his society, and which makes pessimistic dissatisfaction seem wholly unreal, a purely subjective feeling without any possible objective consequences. And above all, the social power is getting things done, though at a lesser level of achievement, and is absorbing in some measure people's individual contributions.

What then of the future? Is socialist pessimism the final philosophic expression of the Soviet order? In the Roman world a pessimism weighed heavily on the citizenry so that many of them welcomed and even joined the barbarian invaders. In the Soviet Union there are many signs, on the contrary, of the emergence of a revived psyche: we might call it "the return of the repressed." The values of individualism, of questioning, of the religious spirit, of the ethical personality, of human relationships transcending Party discipline—all this is returning to the conscious Soviet psyche. They survived a long night in the unconscious of the Bolshevized personality; they came to first consciousness in the spirit of Soviet pessimism. Now in the growing self-conscious return of the repressed, they constitute the psychological basis of the major social changes which we shall probably witness in the Soviet Union. Social scientists have often tended to believe that every social system can shape the human personality to its requirements; this is the notion of what has been called the "over-socialized conception of man." What the Soviet experience indicates is the survival of basic psychological longings, alien to the mandates of the social system, and which assert themselves both in the interstitial and major problematic situations in the system. Let us review several typical manifestations of the return of the repressed.

The questioning spirit has begun to return. Many young Soviet citizens have become "questionnaire-happy." In 1963 the Institute of Public Opinion which a few bold spirits on *Komsomolskaya Pravda* had founded was experiencing great difficulties with party bureaucrats who were anxious about the consequences of public information. Liberal Komsomol leaders in various centers were pressing for the right to use questionnaires. For a quarter of a century research questionnaires had been interdicted. Now the youth seized upon them with the delight of a new scientific toy. An article of concern over the questionnaire-mania indicated its extent in 1966. "Questionnaires have become the fashion; after all, it looks so modern to conduct Young Communist League work on a scientific basis! It is very tempting: without even leaving your office you find out what is on the minds of hundreds and even thousands of people under your jurisdiction!" And the sociologist V. Shubkin declared that in the next three years Siberia would be covered by almost a triple layer of questionnaires.[38]

The workers in Novosibirsk enterprises were said to be "fed up with the amateur surveys conducted by all kinds of organizations and even by individual persons." Individual persons! This seemed to be the last straw. The work of professional sociologists, it was alleged, was being impeded. Poorly formulated questionnaires were becoming an object for jokes; "damage" was being "caused by this chasing after the fashion." Unprocessed questionnaires gathered dust, and were finally consigned to the waste basket. The amateur researchers were significantly accused of "subjectivism," of selecting isolated facts to fit preconceived premises. But this "notorious questionnaire mania" was evidently here to stay; the joy of questioning had been rediscovered, and the article hoped the questioners would observe sound procedures, and emulate the researchers who had contributed to an understanding of the work stoppages at the Yefremov Plant.[39] Clearly the younger generation has found in research questionnaires a methodology of tremendous potential for awakening a long dormant public opinion. In the beginning was the question.

The "questionnaire mania" is a social indicator of a potential for social change; its protagonists are challenging the mores of the Soviet system and are laying hands on its defence-mechanism of secrecy, on the psychological security system for collective repression. Such a sociologist as V. Shubkin complains about the fetishism of "state secrets" which makes it hard to get the statistical facts, for instance, on divorce. Meanwhile, the questioning movement embraces hundreds of workers, physicists, engineers, writers, jurists—all becoming amateur sociologists. Marx's last research in his lifetime was a sociological questionnaire on French workers' conditions of everyday life. The liveliest movement of Soviet Marxism today is precisely Marxist Questionnairism. "Amateur groups, centers, laboratories and even institutes are springing up everywhere" for this purpose, it was recorded in *Literaturnaya Gazeta.* Though the questions have a homely aura, almost nonideologically sounding, nevertheless they are portentous with ideological consequence. "How are friendly, neighborly and other unofficial relations developing in today's society?" queried N. Lapin: "This is an important subject for research." [40] Its importance is undeniable. Is the Soviet system making for enhanced aggressive attitudes in everyday relations? Are the bad manners about which everyone perpetually complains somehow rooted in frustrations of the Soviet system? "Sociology is a powerful instrument of the people's struggle," say the Marxist Questionnairists. Now that the world has been changed, how is it to be interpreted?

The younger generation especially has what *Komsomolskaya Pravda* calls a "fascination with polls." For they are a means of re-discovery of the importance of the individual, thinking in his own solitude, without the pressure of party collectivities. Three secretaries of Young Communist League committees actually said publicly in 1967 "that a Y.C.L. member is much more sincere when he is alone with himself than he is at times of a meeting." [41] The return of the repressed thus involves a return to the classical sincerity of the Russian intellectual. The party apparatus is naturally concerned by the correlation of sincerity with private thought and its use to justify questionnaires. What kind of a sincere person is it, they ask, "if he is only able to ponder the life of the organization in silence, if he is unwilling to state his position publicly." One secretary replied plainly: "The youngsters are afraid of criticizing their foremen at meetings. They are dependent on them. The foreman has the authority to deprive a fellow of a bonus, keep him in his pay grade or give him worse work. But in the questionnaires they write down, everything." The fate of the questionnaire is in some ways an index to the future of the Soviet recovery of the repressed.

The return of the repressed also has manifested itself in an attempt to reconstruct the Lenin ego-ideal. It would have been outside the permissible limits of the system for critics to have subjected the Lenin ego-ideal itself to higher criticism. What has been permissible, however, has been the humanization of the Lenin ego-ideal. Lenin, the self-described "gloomy ascetic," was allowed to become recessive. Instead, rifle clubs and shops for sporting goods display pictures of Lenin sitting with his companions beside a camp-fire, a rifle conspicuous across his legs. The chess club at the Institute of Philosophy featured a picture of Lenin engrossed in a game with Gorky, while a benign Krupskaya regarded them. A widely read story published in *Izvestia* in 1962 portrayed Lenin taking a perverse delight in outwitting his own secret police by helping his personal friend, the Menshevik Martov, to escape across the border. "Among the commissars" says Lenin "are some who are stronger Leninists than Lenin himself." [42] Though the story aroused criticism, it indicated the deep wish to reconstruct the Lenin ego-ideal which had forbidden any autonomous friendship with claims which might be independent of or even superior to political demands. A pamphlet on Inessa Armand suggested a more personal side of Lenin. Friendship and the family, as personal relationships distinct from Party ties, have become basic categories for what we might call a new "Soviet personalism." A booklet thus was printed on Marx and Engels, the story of a true friendship. Another booklet described Jenny Marx as an example of a devoted wife; still another presented Marx's daughters as examples of children's love. It all has had its pathetic side as hagiography, but these are the means whereby the rigidities of the Bolshevized personality are being eased, the means whereby the repressed has been fashioning for itself a new ego-ideal.

The return of the repressed, moreover, manifested itself in a new respect for ethical personality, quite outside the bounds of Marxist materialism. Classical Marxist texts ridiculed ethical ideas as nonsense or mythology, and as without significance in social change. On the death of Albert Schweitzer, however, in 1965, the Soviet press rendered him a tribute which was out of keeping with the old Bolshevist orthodoxy. Passing altogether over his political views on Africa which were at odds with the Soviet position, *Izvestia* declared that the doctor-missionary had been "a sincere friend and enlightener to the people of Gabon." It praised him for his "selfless efforts," for the hospital he had built, for the thousands of Negroes he had cured, and for his efforts to advance their education: "The Negroes lovingly called Schweitzer 'Oganga', meaning magician, and told legends of his miraculous cures." It concluded: "Albert Schweitzer, a great humanist and friend of the people of Gabon, devoted all his beautiful, heroic life to lightening the Africans' path to the sun." [43] It was remarkably different from what would have been said during the era of the Bolshevization of the personality. At that time, Schweitzer would have been ridiculed as a missionary-agent of Western imperialism, and his humanitarian efforts depicted as imperialist hypocrisy. In 1964, however, there was a longing for a revived morality and humanism, for a breaking of the political constraints which deformed one's human feelings. Only such an ethical-humanist renaissance can dispel the depression of socialist pessimism.

The recovery of sincerity has been a notable theme in the return of the repressed. The appeal of the critic V. Pomerantsev in 1953 for sincerity in literature was a landmark in this ethical evolution. Pomerantsev classified the forms of Soviet insincerity—the stereotype, the "slicking up of life," the "cunning" devices of omission, the avoidance of the controversial, and explained how useful they were for getting into print. He described the prescribed formula for the Soviet hero: "They even dream only logical dreams. Normal dreams are not for them. And how they talk to one another! In harangues taken from a radio recorder." People stopped reading novels because they were all alike in fraud. He described the "collective" pressures from the Writers' Union and the publishing houses to collaborate in insincerity, and he ventured the commentary: "I have heard that Shakespeare wasn't a member of a union at all, yet he did not write badly." Moreover, the ethical personality was an autonomous creation not determined by society's material foundation: "there is no direct line from these conditions into man's soul." He enumerated the ten sins of "playing it safe," and said it would require the ethical efforts of more than a generation to conquer them. The return to sincerity was a return to universal virtues, beyond a class-centered code: "Do not try to be anybody but yourself . . . Then do not fool yourself, follow your own path; otherwise disillusion awaits you." Naturally, the advocacy of sincerity called forth a scolding from the Bolshevized personalities who insisted that not sincerity but the ideological criterion was still controlling.[44]

Thus universal ethical categories are resurging as against political, ideological ones. It is becoming a mark of identification for the young Soviet liberal to say as one student did recently to Ehrenburg that whether capitalism exists is not important, but what is important is whether people are good or bad, and politics had become "simply hateful" to her.[45] The most dramatic statement of this supraideological, ethical universalism has been made by Svetlana Alliluyeva: "There are no capitalists and Communists, for me, there are good people, or bad people, honest or dishonest, and in whatever country they live people are the same everywhere, and their best expectations and moral ideals are the same." [46]

The recovered values of individualism in this last decade have found expression in people's preferences among films. In 1963 the two films which they were talking about most at the universities were two American ones—*Twelve Angry Men* and *Inherit the Wind.* Here were two motion pictures in which the individual was shown in conflict with the collectivity, and in which the collectivity turned out to have been wrong and the solitary individual right. To the Soviet viewer came the dramatic presentation that one isolated individual could be right against a near unanimity of eleven; he was acutely aware that he on the contrary had always had to suppress his doubts under the pressure of the group. Naturally the films were social criticism of American society; the first showed the living conditions of a Latin American immigrant family, the second the backwardness of a Southern town enforcing a law against the teaching of evolution. What the Soviet viewers perceived, however, was the message of the creative individual in conflict with an oppressive group. And this enhanced regard for individuality has been part of the return of the repressed. The pre-revolutionary liberalism, side-by-side with its populist ingredient, had esteemed Lavrov's notion of the "critically thinking individual"; the latter is reviving after the years of submergence.

Perturbed by the attraction of liberal individualistic values even in carefully selected American films, Soviet authorities from time to time assail their pernicious influence. But these very criticisms testify to the vigorous return of repressed values. The Russian Minister for Safeguarding Public Order recently bewailed, for instance, both the popularity and bad effect of the film *The Magnificent Seven.* The past generation, he noted, which went on to build a Communist society, was nurtured on such films as *Chapayev* and *We are from Kronstadt.* The present generation, on the contrary, is not so fortunate; although, averred the Minister guardedly, many good films were being made, "unfortunately, however, weak, tedious, and uninteresting films that are incapable of stirring the viewer are also being made." [47] He was especially concerned, he said, by the example which the American film *The Magnificent Seven* had set for several juvenile delinquents. He felt that if films with unusual types of heroes were in demand, Soviet producers should make their own "heroic film about Richard Sorge, their own spy, as a proper theme." If one asks why the young find Soviet films "weak, tedious, and uninteresting," and why, as the Minister acknowledged, they seek out foreign films, it is because the films with Bolshevized heroes fail to satisfy a generation in which liberal individualistic values are returning from their repressed status. The competitive market between Soviet and American films, limited though it is, is one of the few areas in which consumers' preferences, value choices, can make themselves felt.

The deep undercurrent of individualistic values is again evident in Soviet preferences among Western authors. "Surprisingly, the most popular and respected writer among the general public is Somerset Maugham," notes Mihajlo Mihajlov.[48] What the Soviet reader finds in Maugham is a universal psychological truth, not a dialectical, historically specific one. Such a story as "Rain" is not regarded as a criticism of British imperialism or the Protestant Ethic. Rather it is taken as a study of the psychological roots of fanaticism in all societies, in all places and times. Thus a Soviet critic of Maugham appends a universal moral which applies to his own society as well: "A fanatic is capable of anything, of both contemptible and heroic deeds. He himself may go to the stake, but he will not hesitate to send others to the stake as well." And Maugham's idea "that religious fanaticism is merely an expression of perverted sexual urges" carries with it for Soviet readers a corollary with respect to ideological fanaticism.[49] One can see why the Bolshevized personalities stand so firmly against Freud, and why Soviet liberals are eager to see a return of the repressed Freud. Above all, the Soviet reader finds himself fascinated by such of Maugham's heroes as Strickland in *The Moon and Sixpence* who forsakes bourgeois society for the "heavenly beauty of Tahiti," "still yet untrampled by the iron heel of civilization." The Soviet critic states the case with a generality which suggests a similar yearning in socialist society: "To this individualist who has always regarded with aversion civilized society's suppression of the individual, forcing people to conform to its standards, the freedom of the individual is a criterion of supreme importance."

The revolt against the model of the Bolshevized personality results in strange quests for the expression of personal temperament. For instance, a tremendous dedication has developed to individual hobbies. The ablest young philosopher of science told me, quite out of the blue, that his hobby was studying the history of the automobile industry in the pre-October days; he had exhumed pictures of Russian cars made in 1896. An able young historian of logic similarly told me he was making a hobby of the interrelations of Bacon and Shakespeare. The Bolshevik Puritans are naturally uneasy about these individualistic preoccupations. For what is a hobby? Psychologically every hobby is a retreat, a regression to childhood, sometimes to narcissism; the person becomes a collector again as he was in childhood, collecting stones, post cards, stamps, building a private ego-domain dissociated from the world. Thus the Bolshevik Puritans write polemics against the rise of the hobbyist movement:

> There has been wide publicity lately, fortunately without much effect, about another mighty filler of free time—the hobby. A hobby is an interest not directly related to a person's job. It doesn't matter what it is. It could be an interest in spearfishing, or it could be collecting cigarette boxes. Or thimbles. Or pink fish with transparent tails that seem to be of nylon. Or postcards. Advocates of the wider practice of hobbies usually cite Gorky's statement that eccentrics adorn the world. As if it were possible to mass-produce eccentrics by means of hobbies. After all, in unthinking collecting there is something of the miserliness of Plyushkin [in Gogol's *Dead Souls*], who was also an eccentric of sorts but who hardly adorned the world . . . I am railing at hobbies.[50]

The hobbyist, in his curious way, is a person in partial secession from the Soviet social system with its "over-socialized conception of man." The whole question of "free time" indeed raises the most acute difficulties for the Soviet social system. That is why the journals and newspapers abound with discussions of the "problem of free time." The social system previously had a rationale for the rigidities of the Bolshevized personality-structure; they were said to be required by the exigencies of construction, of primitive socialist accumulation. That period is now declared past, yet the regime fears the consequences of the relaxation of the rigidities of prescribed character-structure. Moscow has an outing club, but no poetry-lovers' club, or theatre-goers' society. Allow such clubs to come into existence, and their discussions, if uncontrolled, if spontaneous, might transgress Soviet canons; control them, and they cease to be enjoyable. This is precisely what happened with the outing club where, according to *Literaturnaya Gazeta,* the hikes were fitted "into a rigid scale of norms: so many days, so many kilometers and so many nights camping out." Thus free time sharpens the contradictions of the Bolshevized personality-system; as free time increases, there is increasing misery for the Bolshevized personality-structure; the personality-system becomes a fetter on the underlying, returning repressed values. This is the dialectical law, if one there be, of the evolution of Bolshevized personality-systems.

The reviving Soviet individualist is tired of the official pronouncements and technical bulletins. What Arthur Koestler in *Darkness at Noon* portrayed as the return of the "I," that personal pronoun whose use constituted a violation of the impersonal language-rules of Bolshevik political grammar, that "I" is re-appearing in Soviet society. When *Izvestia* queried its readers a few months ago as to which articles interested them most, the overwhelming majority, 87 per cent of more than 25,000 respondents, said they valued most those in which the problems of internal life were truthfully presented and "conflict" situations discussed. In the midst of the important Soviet economic reforms only three per cent indicated a preference for articles on economic subjects. Evidently as far as the economy was concerned, a certain fatalism had developed; the years of queues and shortages and the surly manners and indifference of sales and bureaucratic personnel had left their mark. One falls back on the individual and his problems, perhaps in a wounded narcissistic spirit, but then one remembers that the individual's conflicts also presumably mirror the contradictions of socialist existence. *Izvestia's* readership, it should be noted, is representative of the Soviet educated class, and fifty-five per cent of its readers are from thirty to fifty-five years old.[51]

As the sense of the "I" returned, an idiomatic contrast has sharpened between the "we" and the "they." Who were "they," asked one Soviet writer in 1967; "they include the factory big 'shots'—the director, the Party committee and the trade union committee. It is they who conducted socialist competition bureaucratically . . . Unfortunately, one still comes across them, and we are fighting them . . . Bureaucratism, callousness, indifference toward people—this constitutes a terrible and evil force." [52] In short, the "they" are the Bolshevized personalities, those identified as having an emotional stake in preserving the rigidities of the system.

The return of the repressed, manifesting itself in a variety of homely ways, also reveals itself on the most spiritual and philosophical level. For the first time in many years, young Soviet thinkers express a sympathy for idealistic philosophy. The young existentialists at the Institute of Philosophy will tell you that they find Berdyaev (apart naturally from Lenin) the most interesting Russian philosopher of the twentieth century. The trial of Andrei Sinyavsky was especially remarkable for the defendant's open profession of philosophical idealism: "I find it difficult to define my approach; in general terms it is idealistic." "If I were able to write from an idealist point of view here [in the Soviet Union]," he told the court, "I would do so." [53] The materialist idiom, so long identified with the Bolshevization of the personality, with the rationale for the repression of ethical feeling and spontaneous emotion, is experienced as a fetter; and thus among young intellectuals, there is a revival of philosophical idealism. It is a yearning for such an idealistic basis, for an anti-materialism, which lies behind the current vogue of the concept of "alienation" in the Soviet Union. We might say it is a philosophical idealism exhumed in the texts of the young Marx, and thus in protectively authentic Marxist garments. But as one professor of philosophy at Moscow State University said: "They are interested in Marx when he was not yet a Marxist." Alienation speaks of the universal essence of man, trans-historical, unobliterated by the repressions of social systems; as a universal essence, it is an anti-dialectical concept; with its emphasis on the human spirit's eternal quest, it assigns the latter an autonomous significance, independent of the mode of production, and suggesting a notion of free choice.

Especially in the sphere of religious feelings there are signs in the Soviet psyche of a return of the repressed. If religion were solely what Durkheim said it was, a collective representation in which society is engaged in worshipping itself, the Soviet Union would have had little difficulty in extirpating religious beliefs and practices. In the early years of Soviet society there was indeed a sustained effort to contrive a Bolshevik equivalent of religious ritual. On November 26, 1923, for instance, the first public "civil christening" was staged at the Free Opera House. It struck an American observer as the strangest spectacle of its kind since Robespierre fêted the Goddess of Reason before the Tuileries: "On a stage bedecked with red banners and slogans, a young father and mother brought a baby girl out to the footlights, before the table of the Executive Committee, and dedicated her to communism." The mother said she wished her own girl child "the same life of sacrifice as Rosa Luxemburg." Nikolai Bukharin received the baby, held it "tenderly, yet awkwardly," then said: "I dedicate thee, Rosa, little flower of human life, to the cause of Russian women, Rosa, sweetest of flowers; Luxemburg, honored name of a martyr-beauty and sacrifice." Then the dancer Isadora Duncan advanced to the center of the stage, and knelt "in an attitude of wonder over an image like that of the Christ child." [54] This was the time when Trotsky was re-discovering the universals in human nature and calling for their Marxist celebration: "the three great moments of the life of man

—birth, marriage and death," and the need for "marking and decorating the principal sign-posts along the road of life." [55]

A half-century later, it is clear that Soviet revolutionary atheism has gone through an evolution much like that of the Western anti-religion. Atheism is a satisfying creed so long as one is fighting *l'infâme,* an oppressive clerical organization. There is a joy in this fighting. But when *l'infâme* is gone, and one simply has one's irreligion to live by, with nobody around against whom to use it aggressively, a certain disaffection arises with atheism, a distaste for its dogmatism—an evolution begins toward a kind of religious agnosticism.

The Soviet atheist propagandists have labored hard to make of science an adequate emotional substitute for religion. Lecturers on popular science blend their facts with atheist doctrine. During the 1963 Easter Week, at the planetarium for instance, they interspersed the stellar spectacle with pictures of martyrs to science; Bruno was shown as animated flames consumed him at the stake, while churchmen watched approvingly. A kind of scientific martyrology was provided, with the stake as the functional substitute for a cross. The lecturer emphasized the infinitude of the universe, ridiculing the Abbé Lemaître for his theory of an expanding universe. Then he described the cosmonauts looking for a God and not finding any. The lecturer ended with a splendid confidence: man, with infinite time, would conquer infinite space; this creed of scientific progress bade the listening children suppress their sorrow at the fact of death and merge their longings for personal individual immortality into a potential collective immortality. One had the feeling, however, that the children endured the atheist sermon for the sake of the stars.

There are certain universals in human nature which can be suppressed by a social system only at the cost of emotional strains. The Soviet atheist socialization creates its own stresses. An American adolescent, fifteen years of age, experienced something of this while she was attending a Soviet school in 1963. She had gotten into her classmates' habit of passing notes to each other. One day she asked the boy next to her: did he believe in God? He wrote back: "We have to write an essay showing how evolution disproves the existence of God. They would make fun of me if I said I believed in God." An enforced anti-religious indoctrination engenders the feeling among the indoctrinees that they are being asked to collaborate in their own spiritual impoverishment. So the Soviet press continually publishes the complaints of the atheist propagandists at the negative attitude they encounter. "Atheist Day" was proclaimed at one of the factories, with "a solid arsenal at our disposal," wrote one atheist indoctrinator, "radio, cinema, factory newspapers, music." The atheist lecturer orated but there was "no act of shared experience": "I saw the people's faces. The majority of them were indifferent." Why, wondered the atheist lecturer, do church images appeal to people when they "suggest to a man that he is a nonentity, a slave, a worm"? [56] Curiously, the question suggested the source of atheism's psychological insufficiency, for if there is a religious masochism, there is also an atheist masochism: it goes against people's grain to tell them to take pleasure in the fact that their consciousness is a transient episode against the silent background of the infinite material universe. Soviet atheism trys to make people rejoice in their ephemerality. The Bolshevized personality, which internalized a certain self-sadism, a harshness and cruelty towards himself, a "self-surgery" toward his emotions, blended well with revolutionary atheism. With the return of the repressed, however, the hostility to religious feelings has noticeably declined. The atheist propagandist complained of the many people who were social agnostics, who said that religious belief was harmless: "It would probably be right to consider the man who professes indifference when it comes to religion Enemy No. 1." Especially a matter for concern was the indifference of the youth to the atheist indoctrination: "I gave a lecture at a production technology school. The young people weren't listening; they grew restive." The atheist indoctrinator tried to arouse their interest by encouraging aggressive forays against a religious classmate, to detach him from his parent. Generational revolt, he hoped, might be enlisted for atheism's sake.

Typical of the sympathetic religious agnosticism of the Khrushchev era was Alexander Solzhenitsyn's *One Day in the Life of Ivan Denisovich* which showed religious faith giving the highest fortitude to the much ridiculed Baptists. "On Sundays," the Baptist Alyoshka "spent all the time whispering with the other Baptists. The camp didn't worry them—it was like water off a duck's back." It was Alyoshka who was so clever at hiding the Gospels in a hole in the wall that it eluded the guards' search. At the day's end, the protagonist Shukhov acknowledges to Alyoshka: "I'm not against God, understand. I believe in God, all right. But what I don't believe in is Heaven and Hell." In the labor camp, in the setting where all ideology became obsolete, Marxism included, religious feelings revived as an expression of an elemental human dignity which no social system could destroy. The gang boss hearing that the Stalinist persecutors had themselves been executed thinks: "There's a God in heaven after all. He's long-suffering, but when he hits you, it hurts." [57] A longing for a religious, just order supersedes the social concept. Perhaps there is a cyclical movement from ideology to religion. In any case, revolutionary atheism withered away in the Arctic corrective camp, to be replaced by religious agnosticism or a religious standpoint.

Among the intellectuals a return of repressed religious feelings has been evident. Sinyavsky wrote in his *Thought Unaware* in rebuke of pure humanism: "We've had enough affirmations about Man. It's time to think of God." [58] One writer wrote openly in a recent public interchange that he refused to accept the materialist view that death ends our personal existence.[59] His critic, while asserting that it was impossible to prove personal immortality scientifically, still acknowledged that he too felt a certain desire to believe in it. Theology aside, the whole controversy was an indication of the rise of religious agnosticism as against revolutionary atheism. Above all, Biblical allusions have returned with a surprising frequency to the conversation and writings of intellectuals. When a writer, for instance, recently protested in *Literaturnaya Gazeta* against the tyranny of editors who excised every fresh phrase in favor of a hackneyed one, he spoke of them as "petty Herods who back away from human words as if from perdition." It was a crucifixion of the writer's language: "And the impassivity of some salaried Herod can crucify it on the spot with the sharp point of a fountain pen." [60] A long expelled religious imagery returns to describe the writer's status in the Soviet system. Once, at the end of an interview, I asked a brilliant young Soviet philosopher his age. "Old enough to go to my Calvary." No American would have answered that way. No Soviet thinker would have spoken that way twenty years ago. The official optimistic philosophy, of course, maintains that the System is the best of all possible social worlds, the Leibnizian doctrine in Leninist idiom. Sinyavsky, who called for a literature of grotesque allegory, for Soviet Candides in effect against their Dr. Panglosses, began one of his own stories with an allusion to Jacob wrestling with the angel, as God tests him.

Joban allusions are especially popular with the Soviet intellectuals, the vehicle of their protest on behalf of the Soviet man: where is the tribunal before which he can summon the omnipotent Soviet system? At the celebration of International Women's Day at the Institute of Philosophy, a festive occasion with students' skits on the place of women in the universe, one able institute member began to talk to me of his reading of the Bible. He liked the Book of Job especially, because, said he, "it deals with the problem of why good men suffer." He felt that God had not answered Job; in real life, he added, the problem has no answer either. With one Joban allusion, the young philosopher showed himself a dissenter from the official socialist optimism.

The Stalinist era also evoked Joban allusion from Ilya Ehrenburg. Stalin, he said, was like Jehovah: the God "was not only omnipotent but ruthless and unjust; he inflicted every type of grief on the righteous Job . . . God made a bet with Satan, and God won. The loser was Job." Thus a Biblical symbolism joins repressed religious feelings with socialist pessimism. The problem of evil has returned to the fore in a secular guise. The Bolshevik revolution, with its ideology and scientism, has effected some partial changes but otherwise only made more poignant the "alienation" of man in a socialist system. The dialect, thesis and antithesis, play with man as God and Satan did. But who will write the final chapter? The search for answers to ultimate questions takes on an unforeseeable aspect.

As religious feelings return, they are taking different forms from those of pre-revolutionary Russia. The anti-masochist years have borne fruit; the old Russian sects, notes a Soviet sociologist, have virtually disappeared—the Flagellants, Molokans, Dukhobors, Skoptsy, Subbotniki. The Baptists have been gaining ground. Their growth puzzles the Soviet sociologists. One of them who has read Max Weber tries to connect it with the growth of capitalism during the New Economic Policy.[61] The Baptists, however, have gained since the end of the Second World War; the best analogue is the strength of Baptists among the Negro storefront churches in the United States. The defeated, the alienated, in a socialist society as well as a capitalist one, turn to directly emotional and physical expression in the most democratically expressive sects. The Soviet Baptists flourish particularly among the unskilled laborers. The latter derive little solace from the official dogma that they own the factories. The revival of religion is especially related to the increase in socialist pessimism.

Soviet sociologists acknowledge that "religiosity is most actively manifested in everyday life" especially in the observance of ceremonies. As many as one-fourth of the children were reported in 1965 as having been baptized in previous years. Among the Leningrad workers, whose percentage of baptized was high, the highest in 1963 were the children of construction workers.[62] It was among the "unnoticed ones," it was said, that the religious feelings were high, and Soviet sociologists took some comfort from their interview data which allegedly showed that only eight per cent acted from religious conviction, whereas most of the others blamed their ceremonial observance on elderly relatives and grandmothers, or fell back on the *consensus gentium,* "We're all baptized; everybody does it." Of course a great margin of error, of under-estimation, must infect the Soviet interview data. For many people would be more than reluctant to admit religious views to atheist interviewers from the university. The Soviet sociologist, however, spoke wisely when he spoke of the "unnoticed ones."

The truth emerges that a totalitarian system may be unable to provide psychological reassurance to its defeated, its rejected, its alienated. The "unnoticed" are precisely those who have experienced a disproportionate share of the rebuffs, who know the anomie of Soviet bureaucratic existence, who would like to migrate, who feel held down. "Scientific atheists" urge that "civic organizations" concern themselves with the personal lives of the "unnoticed ones." But what conceivable comfort could the alienated derive from governmental social workers committed to maintaining the Soviet System and its dictatorship? In a pluralistic society, religious institutions often act as bases for the ethical criticism of the government, and in a sense they provide alternative communities to the economic and political ones. The Soviet system precludes such a functioning of religion. Nevertheless, as religious feelings revive in Soviet society, they are latent with criticism of the Soviet order. Religious persistence remains a surd, a center for an alternative world-view in the Soviet system.

THE PSYCHOLOGICAL IMPULSION FOR CHANGE

Our reflections on the psychological evolution of Soviet society bring us up finally to the central problem—the direction of change in the Soviet system. Any reflections of this kind, if they are to be more than pure conjecture, must be founded on some theory of the nature of societies, social systems, and social causation. We should like briefly and diffidently to indicate such a working model:

Every social system fulfills certain types of character more than others, and likewise frustrates certain character-types more than others. The feudal system, once it had solidified, frustrated many who had qualities of initiative, adventure, creativity, enterprise. And even given full employment, the capitalist system tends to frustrate those who dislike competition, or who feel it denigrates their status as intellectuals. The Soviet system likewise tends to frustrate certain personality-types—ranging from the creative individual who rebels against bureaucratic controls, to the person who would like to be a free economic agent making his own decisions without any supervening impersonal controls. It fulfills those personality-types who like to enhance their egos with bureaucratic legitimacy, those who are sadistic, those who are envious of individual ability. Those psychological types who feel themselves frustrated by the social system might be called the "alienated." They are the potential agents for social change, awaiting any weakness in the system, any strategic opening, for proposing alternatives which they would find more emotionally congenial. Every system runs into difficulties; they are not necessarily "contradictions"—but the "anti-system" group, the system's alienated, are ready to convert problems or difficulties into "contradictions." Some societies can repress their alienated as the Roman Empire did; but they are to that extent vulnerable before external enemies even as the Roman alienated threw their lot with the barbarian invaders.

Now the history of revolutions testifies that personalities with a harsh, other-destructive, and self-mutilating character-structure find the revolutionary experience a tremendous occasion; they can assume leadership under such circumstances. Such an elite usually has tended to hold the leadership only during a transitional period of stress: Cromwell was succeeded by the easy-going Charles II, Robespierre was followed by the hedonistic Directory and the anti-ideological Napoleon, the radicals of 1776 were superseded by the Federalists. In the Soviet Union, however, the Bolshevik personality-structures have had a longer dominance because their revolution has not been as successful as were the so-called "bourgeois revolutions." Theirs was a revolution against the psychological grain of a large segment of the spectrum of personality-types. For this reason the anxiety is present after a half-century that any relaxation of controls would be followed by a resurgence of bourgeois psychology. But in 1898, fifty years after the revolutions of 1848, no one feared a return to the repressive system of Metternich.

And the truth is that the Soviet fear is founded on psychological truth. The returned, repressed feelings are looking for their corresponding expressions and realizations in economic and intellectual life. The considerable controversy which Vladimir Dudintsev's novel *Not by Bread Alone* evoked was due to its representation of the individual inventor or entrepreneur as fettered by the bureaucratic economy. The manager expresses his dislike for the individual creator: "I have a hereditary aversion to all these—these irreplaceables." "There is no capitalist here to buy your ideas," he says, "and the people have no use for primitive passions that jolt the economic routine." The young high-school physics teacher takes heart from listening to Chopin and imbibing "the emotions of great fighters." A *deus ex machina* rescues him from "the 'invisible empire' of bureaucracy." Khrushchev acknowledged that Dudintsev's book "has true pages rightly and strongly," but he nonetheless complained vehemently of its presentation. If today Dudintsev lives in punitive poverty, it is because his novel expressed a widespread discontent.

What new economic forms will emerge from the return of repressed individualism is hard to forecast, but there will be a continuous psychological pressure for more enclaves of private enterprise and the extension of the economic reforms now taking place. A few months ago two physicians writing in *Literaturnaya Gazeta* called for private nursing homes standing outside the system of state medicine. "We need not fear the word 'fees'," they said. "There are polyclinics that charge fees; out of embarrassment we call them economic accountability clinics. These polyclinics are extremely popular, partly because here a person can choose his doctor according to his own taste and judgment . . . Incidentally, the term 'economic accountability' is employed only in official documents. The patients never call it anything but a 'paid polyclinic'." [63] Curiously, the previous year a questionnaire survey was made of such an enterprise in petty-bourgeois medicine at No. 15, Kirov St., Moscow; the results were published in *Literaturnaya Gazeta.* Fifteen hundred patients or so were visiting the clinic daily. When the 1,616 persons questioned were asked why they came to a private polyclinic, the greatest number, 443, said they liked to be treated as human beings; 416 said they wished treatment by older, more experienced doctors. The clinic was prospering despite petty harassment by the Moscow City Health Department; the clinic had to heat its hot water on a stove. The author of the article demanded the right of individual choice on a free market: "If thousands of people ask for the right to paid medical care, over and above free state medical care, it should be done." [64]

Such is the new individualistic spirit, the return of the repressed individual. More than any economic dialectic or even consideration of efficiency, it is the ethos which underlies the economic reforms and doctrine which go by the name of "Libermanism." The traditional centrally planned and controlled economy could continue indefinitely; the Communist Party need only cajole the citizenry, propagandize them with slogans, and punish the recalcitrant. If anything, the advent of computers and calculations would bolster the technical basis for a totally planned economy. It is precisely the ingredient of psychological individualism, however, the feared so-called "subjectivism," which impels in the direction of decentralization and free choice. There is restiveness with a totally planned economy because its workings require the driving activities of Bolshevized, sadistic personalities; people seek consciously and unconsciously for an economy which has no need of an elite of Bolshevized personalities. All the relative comparisons with American efficiency, the articles on the failures of planning to meet consumers' needs, are a projection in economic terms of an underlying psychological pressure.

The return of the repressed involves a return to the tradition of the grandfathers, a by-passing of the Stalinist generation of Bolshevized personalities. Thus the distinguished physicist, Pyotr Kapitsa, in his recent call for relearning the art of genuine debate, said: "Young people should learn the art of polemics from their grandparents, who made the Revolution." Speech was then meaningful; "the oratorical art was at a high level then because sometimes everything depended on a word." And Kapitsa linked this new spirit with the tentatives for the reorganization of the Soviet economy.[65]

If sociological determinism were the final truth, if a social system could shape the human character to its requirements, if a planned economy could regard psychological types as an output-element in the social flow-chart, then one would expect the indefinite continuance of what Mihajlov calls "homo Sovieticus," that blend of sado-masochist traits. Precisely here one meets the limits of sociological determinism. We might say that the "dialectic" of personality-structure determines that of social structure; the varieties of men's characters and aspirations find the "soviet man" a fetter; this may well be the theme of the next era of Soviet history.

RIGIDITY AND ADAPTABILITY OF SOVIET LAW

John N. Hazard

"Marxist literature on the general theory of law is very scant." [1] With this plaint a noted Soviet law professor in 1924 bemoaned the fact that he and his colleagues had little to build upon in creating a legal system for the world's first experiment in the application of Marxism. No outsider will challenge his judgment, for Marx and his colleague Engels bequeathed Lenin very little on the subject of law. What they left as a guide was a general foundation of political theory, a sentence on the specific subject of law in the *Communist Manifesto,* a treatise on the origin of the state which related law to the protection of class and the determination of class to property ownership, and a few phrases in the *Critique of the Gotha Program, Anti-Dühring* and the *Civil War in France.* In light of this paucity of doctrinal materials, what is the Marxist doctrine on law to which a jurist bent upon preserving "orthodoxy" might be expected to adhere? In short, is there a set of ideas to be found in what Marxists call their "classics" against which subsequent actions of Soviet lawyers can be measured as rigid application or adaptation?

The *Communist Manifesto*'s much-quoted sentence reads, "Your jurisprudence is but the will of your class made into a law for all." Lenin built on this to declare in a polemic over a Norwegian law that "law is a political instrument, law is politics." [2] These brief phrases put together and developed in a short study just prior to the "October" of 1917 in Lenin's *State and Revolution* have left a heritage which might be epitomized as the "class instrument" concept of law. For the Marxist, past or present, law represents no eternal good. It is not the essence of the wisdom of the ages, not the word of God transmitted to man through his prophets Moses or Mohammed or any other spokesman. It is a creation of man, but not of all men. It is an instrument fashioned and utilized by those who rule the rest of mankind by virtue of their ownership of wealth. It is a means of holding power.

Marxist inspired jurists are positivists, as the eminent legal philosopher John C. H. Wu recognized in defining "law" in the Catholic Encyclopedia. To him the law of the Marxists is "positivism pushed to its logical extreme." [3] But it is positivism of a special kind. It is positivism supplemented by the class idea.

The Marxist heritage instructs politicians in the steps necessary to maintain power. Engels devoted his *Origin of the State, Private Property, and the Family* to linking power to property ownership. Those who fashioned the legal system for revolutionary Russia in 1917 had clearly in mind that law must preserve the new regime's power, and this required for any lasting stability, reorganization of the property structure to deprive private owners of productive wealth. If there be any "orthodoxy" among Marxist doctrines concerning law, it is to be found here. Law is a class instrument, and Soviet law has to be an instrument of the proletarian class. From this premise developed the concepts of "proletarian justice" and "socialist legality," which dominated the thinking of Soviet jurists with varying degrees of intensity and with varying interpretations for more than forty years.

From this major premise flowed a conclusion which was to become a subordinate premise. Although less clearly stated, it was firmly believed by many of those who devised the legal pattern of the first few years. This was the idea developed by Engels in *Anti-Dühring* that law must eventually "wither away." To him and to all Marxists the logic of the conclusion, granted the major premise, was irrefutable. If law is a class instrument, useful in maintaining a ruling class in power, it will have no reason to exist in a society which eliminates all but one class by expropriating the bourgeoisie and prohibiting the employment of labor for personal profit. Just what this meant in application no one suggested, although Lenin in his *State and Revolution* repeated it as a major guideline of policy.

Three other guiding concepts, also dependent upon the first premise that law is a class instrument, became immediately apparent after the October Revolution when the jurists put pen to paper to draft the new laws and expound the new principles. They were the concepts of "simplicity," "popularity," and "flexibility." The first two sprang as much from distaste for the past as from doctrine, although they represented a combination of both. The legal procedures of the Russian Empire had, like the legal procedures in any long-established social order, become complex. A lawyer was necessary to the citizen seeking to invoke them in his own protection. Lenin is said to have felt this fact keenly as a result of his experience at the turn of the century in a St. Petersburg law office as an assistant working with a popular laboring man's lawyer. Woe unto the man who was caught in the net of tsarist justice without a good guide, for the law and its procedures were too complicated for the common man to understand. The new legal procedure had to be designed for proletarians; it had to be simple so that the citizen would require no lawyer to manipulate it.

"Popularity" was the second demand because the tsarist courts had been staffed by professionals whose attitudes and practices reinforced the complexity of the law. While this was most noted in the general courts of the Empire, it reached down into the Justice of the Peace Courts and the "volost" courts, where elements of popularity existed, but subject to the necessity in the Justice of the Peace Courts of keeping men on the bench who knew from practical experience what to do, and the policy in the "volost" courts of controlling peasants strictly through the Ministry of the Interior.

Finally, there was the desire for "flexibility" in the application of law. Revolution was characterized by dynamic change. In the absence of a blueprint for social reorganization, the men who guided the new Russia had to navigate their vessel along an uncharted passage. To have established a pattern for action in any detail could have prevented quick maneuvering to take advantage of unexpected opportunities and to counter unexpected opposition. Further, even if the leadership had thought it possible to establish precise guide lines for social control, the general public who had taken power into their own hands in each village and small town could not have been forced to conform to commands from the center. A revolutionary sense of the desirable and the practical necessity of leaving local Communists to their own resources in the absence of communications and discipline argued for a policy of "flexibility."

In sum, Marxist influence coupled with personal experiences created in Lenin, and in those of his colleagues concerned with evolving a new legal structure, a desire to develop the law as an instrument of policy, utilized in the interest of the new rulers, strengthening their position not only by striking a blow at the owners of productive wealth but also by popularizing Communists among the masses. This meant establishing a system that was simple, was administered by non-professionals, and indicated as clearly as possible that the new regime had at heart the well-being of the common man. Also in the back of their minds, and not so far back for some of the specialists, was the feeling that the new legal system must prepare the way for the ultimate withering away of the state and its handmaiden the law.

THE APPLICATION OF FUNDAMENTALS DURING WAR COMMUNISM

The denial of the past was complete in the first steps taken to install a new legal system in Lenin's Russia. The first decree on the courts, of November 24, 1917,[4] abolished all imperial courts, both the general courts and those at the local level, the Justices of the Peace and the "volost" courts. A "people's court" was established immediately for the civil and criminal process that would be of concern to the common man, while the problems held over from the old general courts were left for resolution by a decree to be prepared later when there was more time. The new "people's court" has remained the basic court of the Soviet state to the present time, although changes have been made in its structure and jurisdiction. In its original form it reflected the desires of the revolutionary leaders to establish a tribunal which would be nonprofessional, popular, and simple in its procedure.

Alongside the "people's courts" were "revolutionary tribunals." They were not conceived as courts of law, but recognition of the inevitable. When the wave of the revolution rolled over Russia, the aroused masses took the occasions to settle old scores. Drum-head tribunals sprang up everywhere to harass and sometimes to execute the local landlord before gloating peasants or to hound the "enemy" wherever he might be suspected. To regularize and in some measure control this pent-up fury, the new regime inserted in the first decree on the courts a formal sanction authorizing revolutionary tribunals to deal with cases of alleged counterrevolution,[5] although they had, in practice during the first weeks after the revolution, arrogated unto themselves wider jurisdiction: the administration of all measures of social order, both civil and criminal. It was the judges in these tribunals who declared that they were administering "proletarian justice," which became in their hands the law of revenge and survival. For five years they held sway, being brought increasingly under control through review procedures. Even in their demise, by decree of November 11, 1922 [6] to make way for the reorganization of the New Economic Policy, they left a lasting impress upon the general courts, which incorporated some of their features when they were absorbed.

These regular "people's courts" were conceived as the major instrument of the new legal system and have become the symbol of the Soviet legal system throughout the world, being copied in varying degrees by all states declaring themselves members of the socialist family. In the form established by the first decree they were composed of a judge chosen by local authorities, guided to the extent possible by the fledgling Communist Party which was not yet well represented in the villages. This judge was without legal education, but hopefully imbued with good common sense and when possible with political orientation as well. His service was to be full time, and in that sense he was professional, even though he had no legal education. To supplement his wisdom, and to help educate the community in the preservation of social order, he was to be flanked in each case by lay assessors, chosen by the community to sit in rotation for each session. This system symbolized the "popularity" of the new bench.

The popular ideal was so deeply fixed in the minds of those who made policy that they expected citizens to come forward to aid the court in considering all aspects of a charge. There would be the victim, supported by a member of his family or some local figure who took upon himself the burden of what might be called "prosecution," and in defense of the accused, be he criminal or civil defendant, there would be a member of his family, a friend, or some local figure willing to come forward to help his neighbor in his hour of need. "People's courts" were not for the trial of class enemies, but for resolution of disputes between workmen and peasants, and it was expected that fellow citizens would be easy to find to help in the performance of the functions of prosecution and defense.

Not even an investigatory arm was created at the outset to prepare the evidence for use of the court. The judge was supposed to search out his own facts both in support of the charge and in refutation of it. He was an "active" judge protecting society and the people brought before him, both at the same time. He was not a referee in a battle of wits between a professional prosecutor and a member of a professional bar. These institutions, as they had existed before the revolution, were abolished and replaced by the people's participation.

Aided by his two lay assessors, the wise man chosen to be judge was to make the law of each case as the circumstances seemed to require. No codes of law, either substantive or procedural were enacted to guide him. To the extent that he wished he was authorized by the first decree to look for ideas in the imperial codes, whose binding force was denied by the decree, but his major source of inspiration was to be his "revolutionary consciousness." This made for flexibility in that no preconceived notions of what was appropriate would bind a judge. He was free to meet the need of a case with whatever measures he thought fit to a society in process of development toward socialism.

A commentator [7] later explained that the authority to innovate was given by design, because it helped develop in each locality around the nucleus of the court a concept of social discipline. It helped create a sense of what was necessary to preservation of order, among people not expected to acquire it if rules were dictated from the center. Such a system was expected to nourish the social consciousness necessary to the ultimate withering away of the state. Thus rejection of formal legislation met two aims of the revolutionaries: a court system that could act with complete flexibility and one designed to prepare the way for its ultimate withering away. Outsiders may speculate that it met still another need: social order at a time when Lenin and his colleagues were too busy to give thought to detail, and too uncertain of what they wished to create beyond a society structured without the personal ownership of wealth but with the guidance of the Communist Party.

While wisdom was expected to flow from the local judge, supported by his lay colleagues, practice soon established the need for more guidance than that given by the first decree. It took two forms: (1) establishment by a second decree on the courts of a second system of courts to be called "district courts" for cases held over from pre-revolutionary court calendars, and (2) establishment by the Commissar of Justice of procedural principles designed to facilitate trial. By the second decree of February 1918,[8] the district court was to take the form of the abolished general courts of the Empire, with multiple judges and a jury. For civil cases the judges were to be three professionals and four lay assessors, and for criminal cases a professional judge to serve as chairman of a group composed of twelve lay assessors and two alternates.

In practice this district court recruited judges trained in law to facilitate decision of the pre-revolutionary matters which had arisen under the old law, and professional lawyers from the old regime were authorized to appear. In addition a college was established in the form of a list of individuals from which the court might choose prosecutors and defenders to assist with its work. A panel of judges elected by the various district courts would review records but not conduct new trials, and a supreme court would have final jurisdiction. The review procedure was never instituted, however, nor did the district courts function throughout the whole country. In many places hostility to them was so great that even when they were created they soon ceased to sit.

The district courts were really doomed before they began to function, for they had been established under the direction of a Left

Social-Revolutionary, I. N. Shteinberg, then serving as a representative of his party in Lenin's short-lived coalition government.[9] Even while he was working, his Communist associate, P. I. Stuchka, began working on a draft law under which the people's courts would absorb the district courts. In some provinces this was happening without formal law, as the district courts were disliked because they smacked of legalism and of pre-revolutionary times. Soon after Shteinberg's departure on March 4, 1918, a third decree [10] on the courts incorporated the Communist draft to increase the jurisdiction of the people's courts and to reduce correspondingly that of the district courts. This was but a first step, for on November 30, 1918 the first People's Court Act [11] abolished the district courts entirely, and gave the people's court the whole gamut of civil and criminal cases, except for those in which counter-revolution was charged, these latter being assigned to the revolutionary tribunals as political.

The district courts were gone, but their influence lingered on in a reform of the people's courts to assume their functions. The bench of the people's court was augmented for serious crime from the single professional judge and the two lay assessors to a bench of one professional judge and six lay assessors, but for all other cases, the standard people's court bench was to prevail.[12] There would be no more multiple professional judges in civil suits, but only the people's court bench of one professional judge and two lay assessors sitting in rotation. Not until 1922 were the supplementary lay judges for serious criminal charges eliminated to reduce the bench for all cases, civil and criminal to the standard three, two of whom were lay assessors.

With the absorption of the district courts, the people's courts also underwent a revision in attitudes toward procedure. A set of simple procedural rules had been issued by the Commissar of Justice in July 1918.[13] For the first time the judge was authorized in complex criminal cases to call upon an investigating commission created by the second decree on the courts. For the first time a "police" type agency entered the Soviet legal system, but it was still subject to judicial control, for no investigation could lead to trial without the judge's consent. The rules were to be only aids, for the hostility to formality was reaffirmed: "In hearing both criminal and civil cases, the local people's court is not cramped by any formal considerations." The July rules also established for the first time a system of court costs.

Substantive law was beginning to creep into the statute books along with procedure. While judges were left free to decide most issues in accordance with their revolutionary consciousness, a family [14] and a labor code [15] were adopted, and individual decrees on crimes of major concern to the state were issued. These were gathered together in a single volume during the summer of 1918 as an indication of what a judge must know.[16]

No formal system of judicial review was introduced at the outset for the people's courts, yet some coordination of the various attitudes of local judges was soon felt. The first decree had authorized the gathering of a congress of people's judges from time to time in each county or city to discuss common problems and to review judgments in excess of 100 rubles in civil cases or seven days detention in criminal cases. This was not a retrial but a discussion of the record. It provided the opportunity to reconsider the wisdom of the judges, but not their adherence to procedure. Even with the introduction of the July rules in 1918, demonstrating the first interest in procedure, there was to be no reversal for failure to follow procedural rules. The People's Court Act of 1918, however, reformed the congress of people's judges into a "council" to sit permanently in each province as a reviewing court, it also established procedures from which judges were not to depart. Even with this step, procedure was not to dominate the trial. Retrial was possible, but only if the "council" thought procedural irregularity had "created an injustice."

The Commissar of Justice was proud of the 1918 Act, for he thought the new courts, as heirs of the local people's courts established by the first decree, were near to the people, were in a position to act quickly, need no longer look at the imperial codes even for inspiration, and were free from any rules of evidence.[17] They were much less simple than those established by the first decree, but in his mind nothing had been sacrificed in greater formalization. In early 1919 the Commissar said exultantly, "Neither Roman law nor subsequent bourgeois law gave such authority to a judge. Perhaps we can find some analogy in more ancient primitive law." [18] The Communist Party reiterated his thoughts in its first post-revolutionary program, adopted in 1919, when it stated, "The Soviet Government has replaced the former endless series of courts of justice with their various divisions, by a very simplified, uniform system of People's Courts, accessible to the population, and freed of all useless formalities of procedure." [19]

The Communists of 1919 thought that they had conformed essentially to the doctrine passed them sketchily by the Marxist classics, making adaptations only to create helpful institutions desired by the judges, such as the department of investigation and the college of accusers and defenders. Also they had presented simple, almost informal, rules of procedure to facilitate the gathering of evidence and the reaching of decisions so as to assure a measure of uniformity throughout the vast country in the application of revolutionary consciousness.

The "perfect" Marxist system had been installed by 1919 but from that moment erosion set in. A series of events occurred which either initiated a trend toward centralization of direction and complexity in the legal system, or brought an end to what was no more than a compromise with reality at a moment when the central government was weak and could take no initiative, when communications were primitive, and when Communist Party discipline was as yet unenforcible. Historians may well debate the causes of the change during 1919 from simplicity to the beginning of complexity, from popularity to the beginning of professionalism. Indubitably, the civil war was a factor. Admiral Kolchak, advancing from Siberia, captured Perm and Ufa on the threshold of European Russia in the spring of 1919. General Denikin moved toward Moscow in mid-May and captured Kharkov in June. General Yudenich attacked Petrograd from the Baltic and reached a suburb. Within the Communist Party, factions competed for power, and the hosts of new members could not be given the discipline Lenin had demanded when he established membership qualifications in 1905.

The powers of the agencies designed to curb counterrevolution were extended. The extraordinary police, the Cheka, was authorized to continue to act through three-man tribunals to suppress those thought guilty of armed insurrection; [20] military tribunals were created on the model of the revolutionary tribunals to keep order in the Red Army; [21] local police were centralized by putting their financial requirements on the national state budget, and all appointments had to be approved at the center.[22]

When the counterrevolutionary danger had passed, these exceptional measures were not revoked, and the policy makers moved toward strengthening the central government. The foundations of the first national criminal code were laid by adoption of a "basic aid" in criminal law on December 12, 1919,[23] which was in 1922 to become the general part of the first criminal code of the Russian Republic.[24] The Commissar of Justice in January 1920 also undertook a unifying role, complaining of the lack of uniformity in the application of law. He indicated that many sentences pronounced by individual judges were too light.[25]

In the face of this clearly defined trend toward centralization, there was a reaffirmation of the desire to preserve the concept of mass participation, which meant fostering local initiative. The conflict came to the fore in debate over retaining the institution of lay assessors.[26]

Some criticized them as unnecessary in a people's state where by definition the professionals acted in the people's interests. The proponents of preserving the institution were criticized for "liberalism," which to Marxists is a form of reactionary counterposing of the people to the state. Nevertheless, the second People's Court Act adopted in 1920 retained the institution,[27] partly to evidence popularity, but also because without mass participation "it will be impossible to instill in the political laggards of the population a proletarian concept of law." [28] Here again was preparation for withering.

As a measure of centralized guidance, a systematized publication of 268 pages was issued to provide the courts with a handy manual of the decrees issued by the central government,[29] and the People's Court Act gave the Commissariat of Justice supreme control over criminal sentences and civil judgments of the people's courts and the provincial councils of people's judges. Two years later this provision was called by a Soviet historian, "the prelude to the organization of a supreme cassational court." [30] A department within the Commissariat functioned as a Supreme Court at the pinnacle of what became a three level judicial system, and the way was open for eventual installation of a Supreme Court in traditional form.

The People's Court Act of 1920 also took a long step in the direction of creating a professional prosecuting staff. The experiment of 1918, a salaried pool of persons from whom individuals were indiscriminately assigned to assist a judge as prosecutor and as defender, had failed. The "civil service" bar was unworkable. In consequence the People's Court Act separated the defenders from the prosecutors and assigned the latter to a new institution to be organized in each province by the provincial executive committee's department of justice. The emphasis remained on summons by the judge before assignment was made. There was as yet no professional prosecutor's staff working closely with the court in ferreting out crime and bringing suspects to the attention of the court. The Cheka was concerned with counterrevolution, but the routine violations of law were still left for disclosure by the enraged community.

For the bar progress was a bit slower than it was for the prosecutors. Although the combined state-financed panel system had failed, there was still a spirit of experimentation. The 1920 act made legal aid a public duty, like service as a lay assessor. Registers were established of all who could be presumed to know the law. When needed, a lawyer would be called to serve a case. He received no fee, it being presumed that his regular employment continued, although the self-employed received a *per diem* from public funds. Relatives were still permitted to appear for parties, as well as representatives of labor unions to which the party might belong. This kept before the people a symbol of the primitive tribunal of 1917 to which all might turn, but it was little more than a symbol. The Soviet courts were fast moving away from the form which had appealed to the Communist Party and its Commissar of Justice in 1919. The way was being prepared for the major retreat from some of the doctrine thought compelling in 1917 and 1918, namely the compromise of the New Economic Policy.

GREAT LEAP TO REALITY—THE N.E.P.

Lenin's great leap over the mountain of doctrine to the valley of reality, known to the world as the New Economic Policy, had a profound effect on the stabilization of Soviet law, and its effect lingers even today. After promulgation in March of the primary decrees partially restoring capitalism, namely the decrees on the tax in kind and on the restoration of private trade. Commissar of Justice Kursky called his colleagues together in a congress to announce the momentous change in policy. Speaking at the very end of December 1921, he tried to keep a stiff lip, but the truth slipped through. He opened his speech by saying that the slogans of 1918 were still valid.[31] The aim was to create revolutionary legality and to administer it through a single people's court, but "deep internal economic reasons . . . make these already well rooted methods of deciding questions give place to that great question which stands before us today, the task of installing a regime of law." To cheer his glum companions, he hastened to add that the new regime would, of course, be completely original, but the ring of authenticity was weak, for he had to add that British Prime Minister David Lloyd George, in discussing an agenda for the Genoa conference to bring Russia back into the concert of Europe, had demanded that Russia establish a known system of legal norms which would permit other countries to conduct permanent relations with her.

The Commissariat's draftsmen set to work on a set of substantive and procedural law codes, and Kursky's colleague, Nikolai V. Krylenko, took charge of reforming the court system, the prosecutor's office, and the bar to meet the new needs. The keynote of the reform was professionalism. Obeisance would be made to simplicity, popularity, flexibility, but the accent was in the other direction. A new bourgeoisie was being given its head, and its demand that the legal system protect investment required that rules be firmly applied by judges who understood their task and who were willing to listen to the arguments of trained lawyers organized in a conventional bar.

The courts were reorganized in a three-stepped hierarchy, resting on the people's court at the bottom, but supplemented by a series of specialized courts. At the intermediate level a court replacing the council of people's judges would not only hear appeals from the people's courts, but take original jurisdiction over cases of great importance. In this court the distinguishing feature was the higher educational qualifications of the professional judge. The Judiciary Act of October 31, 1922[32] authorized the professional judge to sit alone in hearing moderately serious criminal cases, whereas state crimes, economic crimes, crimes of violence, civil suits for more than 500 gold rubles, and suits against state agencies as well as those to be expected in the business community, such as disputes over partnership agreements, copyright, patent, trade marks, firm names, or protected industrial patterns were to come before a bench augmented by two lay assessors. In the drafting committee some had argued for exclusion of lay assessors, but Krylenko had insisted that they appear to preserve uniformity throughout the court system, and to carry out the Communist Party program of 1919 which had sought to attract the people generally into the judicial process.[33]

There was to be a general upgrading of judges, for Krylenko insisted that they be appointed by the provincial soviets for one year terms and be removed from the influence of the local soviets; also that they must have proved their worth by experience in a state or Party office for two years or on the bench for three. Even the lay judges represented something of a "blue ribbon" panel, for they were to be selected by a committee.

At the top was to be what Krylenko called "a strong fist, a judicial center" to overcome any laxity such as that shown by the councils of people's judges. This took the form of a Supreme Court of the Republic, no longer a department of the Commissariat of Justice but an independent body of the judicial branch of government.[34] Like other European supreme courts it would be organized in specialized colleges of three professional judges to hear matters coming up from the provincial courts, but it would also have original jurisdiction for both criminal and civil cases of extreme national importance. All thirty judges would sit as a "plenum" to consider judicial policy and issue rulings on interpretation of the codes. It was to have no power over the constitution, but only over the codes of substantive law and procedure. Its affairs would be directed by a steering committee, called a "presidium."

One year later, with creation of the Union of Soviet Socialist Republics, the hierarchy was capped by still another court, the Supreme Court of the U.S.S.R., to hear protests brought to it by the Union Procurator against decisions of the Supreme Courts of the Republics, to try suits brought by one Republic against another, and to try criminal charges against members of the U.S.S.R.'s legislature and executive in their official capacities.[35]

The court system was no longer the simple one of which the men of 1917 had dreamed, nor was it popular in spite of the continuing presence of lay judges in trials. No one was applying his revolutionary conscience, for every judge held in his hands full fledged codes of law, drafted by men trained for the most part in European law schools and utilizing models chosen from among the most modern of European enactments. The bar was to be the representative of the bourgeoisie before the courts.[36] No Bolshevik seems to have been happy with the return to favor of professional lawyers, and efforts were made to keep them from regaining their pre-revolutionary independence. Each province was to organize a "college of defenders" under the supervision of the provincial agents of the Commissariat of Justice who constituted the departments of justice of the provincial soviets. The court, which the lawyers wanted as their control, was given no such power. No one could be admitted as a charter member of the bar unless approved by the provincial soviet's executive committee, on motion of the provincial department of justice. Thereafter, the hand-picked charter members could add to their numbers, but the provincial soviet could subsequently order dismissal of any new member. Leaders were to be chosen by the college, but the first reports indicate what might have been expected, they were picked by the communist members. Leaders of a college could exact disciplinary fines which could be appealed only to the provincial soviet's executive committee.

Fees were the primary source of income, for the state financed civil service concept and the public duty concept had failed as a means of recruiting defenders. Capitalist methods in payment of fees were restored, but not in full, for the penniless were to be served gratuitously, while workers and employees were to be charged in accordance with a fixed tariff. Only the bourgeoisie could be charged whatever the traffic would bear, and of course it was here that the major legal business was expected. One remnant of the past appeared in the decree: the bar was given no monopoly. Close relatives, trade union representatives, and those of other public organizations had a right to appear, and others might appear when permitted by the court.

The bourgeoisie seemed to be regaining its lost position, and indeed this was Lenin's aim, for he expected them to regain sufficient confidence in his system to produce, market, and generally restore the wrecked economy. But there was to be a watchman at their door, the procurator. It was no longer enough to rely on an aroused citizenry to bring forward the individual who seemed to have violated social order. It was also necessary to have an office to watch other state offices. The problem was how to organize. In this the old guard with an eye to popular participation demanded that the procurators be responsible to the provincial soviets, but Krylenko was for centralization of authority, so that local officials could not escape by bringing pressure to bear on local procurators. The debate waxed hot, eventually at the highest level of the Communist Party, its Political Bureau, where Lenin argued in favor of centralization.[37] He wanted none of the "dual subordination" which existed elsewhere in the administrative apparatus, under which there was a direct line of communication with the center, but also responsibility to the soviet at the same level. He had no fear of the re-emergence of "bureaucratic centralism." Local concerns would never be ignored, because the procurator could not punish. He could only go before a court, and the court remained subject to local controls. The Politburo accepted Lenin's proposal, and the statute of May 26, 1922 [38] freed the procurator from all local influences, and he remains free today. The only structural change has been the superimposition upon the procurators of the republics of a Procurator General of the U.S.S.R., established as an office after the formal organization of the Soviet Union.[39]

Procedural stability was another desideratum of the New Economic Policy, but it was so unpopular that the Communist Party assigned its defense to one of the most popular Party members, the former peasant Mikhail Kalinin, president of the legislature to which the draft codes of court procedure were sent for enactment. In his speech of January 28, 1922 [40] he ridiculed those who thought that a return to procedure meant capitulation to the bourgeoisie. He noted that although "legality" had been given little importance in the preceding four years, "at the present moment it has for us very great importance." He even buttressed his arguments by reference to bourgeois England where a powerful government found it desirable to adhere meticulously to procedural forms to maintain public respect for the courts. He felt that the new Soviet regime could foster respect for its courts in the same way. To tie his remarks to his political philosophy, Kalinin added that the Soviet state wanted to inculcate the principles of the new society in the subconsciousness of the working and peasant masses. In short, his message seemed to be that communism was not chaos, it was discipline, and respect for procedure was an important lesson to be learned by citizens in the courtroom school. Thus, procedural conformity was not being established for the good of the bourgeoisie, but in the long run for the good of the proletariat.

Stability of substantive law and procedure had become the slogan of the Communist leaders with the introduction of N.E.P., but they feared the wily bourgeoisie who were being given rein by Lenin's new policy. The procurator needed some escape from the rigidity being written into the new codes. In the criminal code the loophole was a revival of the old principle utilized by the tsars and abandoned in 1903, namely the rule of "analogy" by which a judge could punish as criminal whatever he thought socially dangerous.[41] For the civil code [42] it was Article 1, which authorized the judge to refuse to apply the law if its application would do an injustice to a worker or peasant. In the legal language of the article, no code provision would be enforced if its application would violate its socio-economic purpose. Although popularity and simplicity had faded away under the reform measures, flexibility remained. But the accent was on stability; the concept simply remained, unsung, in each code so that a court could always refuse to apply its provisions to the benefit of some member of the bourgeoisie.

Krylenko had a hot temper, and it was fired by criticism that Soviet law in its new phase was but a product of the neo-capitalism of the New Economic Policy. To those who thought that everything could be explained by the N.E.P., he retorted: "This can be said only by people who have lost so completely their balance wheel, and most of all, respect for our collective creativeness that there is no possibility of talking to them." [43] His explanation was quite different: namely that the flowering of codes in 1922 was but a final stage in a progression of events set in motion by the first decree on the courts. To Krylenko, "N.E.P. provided only the atmosphere, facilitating it is true and hastening the exposure of this inescapable phase of development of our court work, but it never did more than that. It never foreordained the content of the work." To Krylenko the 1922 system was a natural phase in the development of socialist society, and it would remain for a long time until the next phase could begin, that of withering.

REASSERTION OF DOCTRINE: THE PASHUKANIS EPOCH

Krylenko was a strong defender of what Lenin had done to create a stable legal system for the N.E.P., but like all Bolsheviks he was also a strong believer in social change through the dialectic of history.

Krylenko never expected the N.E.P. and its legal system to last forever. It was only a phase, and he was soon to put his hand to preparing what was to follow. Still, he was not a theorist at heart but rather a man of action. He never expounded a philosophy. For this he relied on a contemporary who had been one of the judges in the Moscow people's courts of 1918, namely Eugene B. Pashukanis.

It was this Latvian Bolshevik who devised a theory which would support the introduction of codes copied in large measure from bourgeois states into an incipient socialist society. This he did in a noted work published in 1924,[44] beginning with a complaint that Marxist literature on the general theory of law was scant. Pashukanis' exposition was complex. He examined the course of law, as sketched by Engels in his *Origin of the State, Private Property, and the Family,* and supplemented by Marx's *Civil War in France,* to conclude that law had reached its most developed form under the bourgeoisie in support of a market economy, from which the bourgeoisie derived not only their economic but their political power. Contemporary law in the early twentieth century was, therefore, essentially bourgeois in both form and content. As such, it had no lasting place in a socialist society, but must wither away in fulfillment of the prophesy of Marx and Engels.

The task of Marxists in the mid-1920's in the U.S.S.R. was to utilize the forms created by the bourgeoisie while imbuing them with a new content, a socialist content, and as this process progressed the forms would wither away. The process was to be gradual but inevitable. As bourgeois society with its class structure was replaced by socialist society, composed only of workers and peasants, law would cease to function as an instrument of compulsion; without their "operative clauses," that is, without their sanctions, its rules would become the foundation of what Engels had called "the administration of things." Some of the rules, such as those relating to the ownership of private property, would cease to have any application. Since these were centered in the civil code, it would be the first to become an empty shell, rules and sanctions without applicability to anything, and the code would "wither away."

Pashukanis' ideas had relation to the criminal law as well. His philosophy led him to conclude that the structure of the criminal code, with its definitions of socially dangerous acts or crimes, followed by the punishments for those who committed a prohibited act, was also a product of the market place. It was a study in equivalents, a bill of fare, a store tariff. Every act had its price. In his view this relationship between act and precise penalty would have to be severed. At this point Krylenko, with his major concern for criminal law, joined him. Together they drafted model codes of criminal law and procedure to be discussed and eventually utilized.[45] They stated what was to be prohibited, but they left it to the judge to determine the measures of social defense to be taken and to do so without serious procedural restraints. In short, flexibility and simplicity were to be restored to the judicial process.

In civil law, Pashukanis' influence was destructive. He concluded that the old form was being given socialist content so fast that the subject was losing practical value, above all for the young men and women being trained in the law schools. Courses in civil law were replaced by a course in a new discipline called "economic law" designed to approach as near as might be to what Engels had called the "administration of things." When the Supreme Council of National Economy was created in 1918 to administer state owned industry, Lenin had called it the prototype of the instrument to administer things. Economic law, as Pashukanis and his colleagues conceived it, was to be the set of rules of relationship to be administered by the Supreme Council and followed by state enterprises in producing for the plan. Disputes would go before a special tribunal applying not a well defined law with civil sanctions, but a rule of reason to be applied in negotiation with the parties so as to assure fulfillment of the plan.

For Pashukanis and Krylenko the "withering away" of law was not a remote possibility, much less an end justifying severe interim restraints, but a workable doctrine needing only imagination to put into practice. The doctrine of 1917, as they understood it, needed to be reasserted and implemented. One might say, in terms of the theme of this book, that in 1927, with the five year plans moving into the drafting stage, and with the phasing out of the New Economic Policy, it was time to return to doctrine and stop adapting Soviet law to the reality of shortages and lack of discipline which had inspired the New Economic Policy.

The Supreme Court of the U.S.S.R. was also preparing the way for withering by reinstituting stability into the application of both the criminal and civil codes. Without changing the text of either, the court directed judicial practice toward a reassessment of the importance of finding "guilt" in the commission of crime and "fault" in the commission of tort. The codes of 1922 had been drafted with terminology that looked in the opposite direction. In civil law the attitude had been one of "soaking the rich" in the event of accident: "In circumstances when the person causing injury is not required to repair the injury under the provisions of Articles 403–405, the court may, however, require him to repair the injury, taking into consideration his wealth and that of the injured party" (Article 406). With the passing of the New Economic Policy, the rich were no more, and the article fell into disuse. The court began to demand that a suit against a person charged with causing injury be decided in favor of the plaintiff only if there had been "fault" as well as "causation." [46]

Likewise Article 1 of the civil code, which had been applied frequently to deprive owners of property of legal protection if they failed to use it productively, passed out of use with the end of N.E.P. By 1930 there were no longer any decisions based upon it.[47] The civil code, however, was still being applied to the letter when matters it treated continued to be of social concern. Its function was educational as well as remedial. It helped preserve order among workers and peasants by resolving their civil disputes, but in so doing it educated them in proper socialist behavior and prepared them for the time when no sanctions would be needed because they had learned self-discipline.

The trend in criminal law was similar. The 1922 code had adopted a theory that its purpose was to rid society of social danger, to be determined in large measure by the judge with reference to the Special Part of the code, but if the circumstances seemed to him to require an individualized approach to a given charge, he could set aside a penalty required by the code or establish a penalty under the "analogy" provision when the code made no such prescription. The theorists argued that no draftsman could have anticipated the wiliness of the bourgeoisie, so the judges had to be left free to take measures of protection as dangerous acts were identified.

With the passing of the N.E.P. the courts began to emphasize the factor of "guilt," not in any moral sense, because an atheistic state could espouse no concept with moral overtones, but as a measure of danger.[48] Members of a socialist community were expected to be free agents, unencumbered by economically determined proclivity to crime. Being free agents, those who committed socially dangerous acts were especially dangerous if they did so deliberately. By fitting penalties to intention, the criminal code could serve an educational function and thus prepare the way for its ultimate withering away.

Ironically the end of the New Economic Policy was an exhilarating moment for those jurists who thought that the evils caused by capitalism in society were about to be overcome, to be replaced by a social order maintained by self-discipline amid abundance, rather than by compulsion established by codes and enforced by courts and police. All anticipated, as Lenin had warned, that there would be a transitional period while people learned their new roles, and production soared to the level necessary to meet their needs, but the work of the courts would soon taper off.

STALIN'S NEW LINE

As Stalin crept up on Pashukanis and his colleagues, they hardly realized what was happening. The Sixteenth Party Congress in 1930 provided the platform for announcing that a basic change was to be made. Already the collectivization campaigns were forcing reluctant peasants into collective farms by the millions. To get the food needed by the cities and to finance economic modernization, Stalin had to eliminate those peasants most likely to resist, the relatively well-to-do; he announced his plan with the slogan "liquidate the kulaks as a class." The impact of this new policy fell heavily upon the law, and the first blow was struck at Pashukanis' legal philosophy.

At the Party congress Stalin inserted the blow into a paragraph following his discussion of a quite extraneous subject, the national-minority policy. He argued for an eventual merger of all cultures within the multi-cultured U.S.S.R. into a single amalgam with a single language, but in the meantime the separate cultures should be encouraged to flower as never before through considerable investment in their individual languages and art forms. Having said this at some length, he added in a paragraph, by way of comparison, his new doctrine on the state: [49] It must become the strongest the world had ever known. Only by becoming strong could it eventually wither away. This was an example of the dialectic process, Stalin said, just as a unitary culture would grow from strengthening first a multi-culture society. This new theory prepared the ground for a policy of increasing severity, while appearing to preserve the doctrine of the withering away of the state. Nothing was thrown away; it was only adapted to what Stalin claimed were the realities of the time.

The law was applied with a rigor not observed since the period of war communism. Hundreds of thousands of the newly discovered enemies, the so-called "rich peasants," were herded by the police without trial to the salt mines and forests of Siberia to perform hard labor. Those who fought back and committed acts which could be identified as criminal under the code were penalized severely for counterrevolution. A law of August 7, 1932,[50] permitted capital punishment for theft from collective farms and from transport and was used eventually to punish all those who took state property or pilfered from state stocks; it became notorious as the symbol of "socialist legality," the harsh new policy designed to make of the state apparatus an instrument poured into the mold Stalin had established by his 1930 speech.

Stalin's policy of severity regardless of guilt, his revived theory of class warfare, directed against the kulaks, marked the end of preparing society for self-discipline. It marked the end of rationality in the administration of justice and the reintroduction of terror to force acceptance of whatever rules the leader might make to industrialize the economy and consolidate his power.[51] The policy had another facet which paralled the first: subordinate state and Party officials must accept rigid discipline. On the Party side this had always been Lenin's rule, but he had not been able to prevent and perhaps did not want to stop considerable debate within the Party. Now Stalin halted all debate by criticizing his opponents as violators of discipline and creators of factions. On the state side, subordinates who failed to accept discipline in performing what was demanded of them were subjected to severe penalties.

What had begun as a campaign against the kulaks was pushed to its logical extreme. With no link between guilt and punishment, the legal system moved off whatever base it had established during the 1920's. Stalin purged those whom he disliked and those whom he had never heard of and turned his police loose to obtain evidence in whatever manner they saw fit, even by the use of torture. After he had eliminated his party opponents of long years standing through a series of simulated trials, he turned on his military officers and finally his engineers. In spite of the menacing shadow of Hitler across the frontier, the purge reached from the ministers of various branches of industry down to plant directors.

Stalin began to prepare his purge in 1934. In November he created within the Commissariat of Internal Affairs a new administrative tribunal, called a Special Board, with authority to banish to work camps for periods of up to five years persons deemed socially dangerous.[52] The code of criminal procedure was waived for these hearings. Then in December 1934 came the assassination of Sergei Kirov. For the lawyers it was an event of immense importance. Stalin decreed immediate amendment of the code of criminal procedure to deprive persons accused of terrorist acts of the right to counsel, the right to be present at their trial, and the right to appeal.[53] Also he ordered shot in prison a group of dissidents who had, so it was presumed, been held there for some time on suspicion of dangerous hostility to the regime. There was no effort to relate these shootings to the commission of any crime; they were intended to make clear to the general public that opposition of any sort would bring swift destruction, even if no crime were charged or proved.

Into this trend toward terror, came the curious interlude of the enactment of a second constitution, which appeared to be its negation. As has happened on various occasions in Soviet history, apparently quite contradictory positions can be taken at the same time. Stalin had appointed a drafting commission in 1935 to work out revisions of the first constitution, but it announced that an entirely new document was required. This it presented to the Central Committee of the Party, and eventually to the All-Union Congress of Soviets, but not until an extensive campaign had been conducted during the summer and autumn of 1936 to popularize it with the masses.

From the lawyer's point of view, the second constitution was a milestone because it included for the first time a chapter on "Fundamental Rights and Duties of Citizens." Here appeared in somewhat revised form the rights defined by the Russian Republic's Constitution of 1918, supplemented by a novel set of "economic rights," headed by the "right to work." The political rights were phrased in much the same way as before, but were less obviously restricted. The 1918 document had preceded the political rights with an article qualifying their use solely "in the interest of the socialist revolution," and if exercised contrary to that interest the user might be deprived of them. The 1936 chapter omitted any specific article limiting the application of the rights, but each one was preceded by a brief phrase "in accordance with the interests of the toilers and for the purpose of strengthening the socialist structure." Although all knew that this meant control over freedom of expression, if necessary, the very fact of the right's restatement in the new constitution gave hope to some Soviet citizens that a lessening of severity was in sight.

Few yet understood the deep meaning of the severe measures adopted in December 1934, so that when the new constitution was promulgated on December 5, 1936, it was generally interpreted as a first step toward easier times after forced collectivization. All were warned however, that Hitler's increasing threat precluded any serious innovations, such as multi-candidate elections to the Soviets which some had expected Stalin to permit when he gave an interview to Roy Howard in the summer of 1936.

A new blow was struck at the law in a decree of September 14, 1937.[54] Like the one following Kirov's assassination it waived articles of the code of criminal procedure, this time for those accused of "diversion" and "wrecking," the offenses usually charged in the purge of engineers and managers. Under this decree, persons accused of such offenses were to receive their indictment only twenty-four hours before trial, could not appeal, and were to be executed immediately if their plea for mercy were denied.

Lawyers vanished with the law. Krylenko had been appointed Commissar of Justice of the U.S.S.R. and Pashukanis Director of the Institute of State Construction and Law in the Academy of Sciences. Both disappeared in 1937 and were soon attacked as "enemies of the people." No clue was published to indicate what they had done specifically, if anything, but a philosophical attack upon Pashukanis appeared in the Communist Party's principal theoretical journal, centered upon his interpretation of the nature of Soviet law.[55] His conclusion that Soviet law was a new content poured into old bourgeois forms was attacked as impossible philosophically, because content and form are in dialectical unity; if content is changed, so also must form change. Had Pashukanis understood this rule, his critics argued, he could not have supposed that law as a bourgeois form would wither away. It had become socialist in form because of the new socialist content that had been created, notably with the ending of the New Economic Policy. Pashukanis with his interpretation of "gradual withering," or replacement of civil law by economic law, was said to have made a serious mistake. Though the criticism did not say so, it gave the impression that he had taken his position to cause havoc in society as compulsion withered away, and this had been planned with criminal intent to unseat Stalin. No clue was ever given of any precise violation of law, and Pashukanis was never tried publicly; only much later was it disclosed that he had "perished," whether in a prison camp or at the hands of a firing squad has never been revealed. The same cloak of secrecy was thrown over Krylenko's removal and death.[56]

Andrei Y. Vyshinsky was given Pashukanis' old post as chief legal theoretician in 1937. He had been the chief prosecutor in the purge trials of Stalin's most prominent Party enemies. As a Menshevik, turned Bolshevik, he seemed always on shaky ground, and his activities suggested that he leaned over backward to support the man who had made him prominent. He was ruthless in his attack upon Pashukanis' memory and upon those remaining law professors who had shared his views in any way.[57] Those who had been arguing for elimination of punishment by analogy as unnecessary in a period of socialism dared speak no more. Those who had argued that the code of criminal procedure should be strengthened to introduce a presumption of innocence were silent. Vyshinsky espoused the theory that confessions were the supreme evidence, although he followed the doctrine of earlier times by adding that the prosecutor should seek to corroborate the confession with outside evidence lest it be made to protect others.

Vyshinsky's hand was heavy. He almost silenced all debate with a speech of 1938 to the legal profession. Although his new definition of law was published "as the basis for discussion," no such discussion was ever held. His "normative" theory, as it came to be called, emphasizing that the law was composed of rules established to be obeyed as norms, left no room for consideration of social good, social danger, or social welfare. The men of the law were to become automatons, enforcing the policy set by the Party, under Stalin's direction, and enacted into law by the Supreme Soviets of the U.S.S.R. and the republics.

During World War II no one criticized Vyshinsky, but after the war a few brave men, some of them of considerable age and dignity, again began to urge that the principle of analogy had no place in a modern code for a socialist society, and that the presumption of innocence should be stated in so many words as an earnest of fair trial, but Vyshinsky silenced the reformers again. After 1947 theoretical discussion and proposals for reform disappeared from the law reviews, and the reform movement remained dead until March 1953 when the heavy hand stifling thought was lifted by Stalin's death.

SOCIALIST LEGALITY AFTER STALIN

Fears of revolt when Stalin's death was announced proved shortlived. Once his heirs realized that the people accepted the new regime, the Party leaders began to undo what Stalin had done. The first institution to go was the Special Board, abolished almost surreptitiously in September 1953.[58] When the problem of succession was settled by Nikita Khrushchev's triumph over Malenkov and Beria, Khrushchev initiated a retreat from Stalinism in its naked form. His secret denunciation of Stalin at the Twentieth Party Congress in 1956 laid bare atrocities, use of terror to gain confessions, falsification of evidence during the purges, and damage to theory in making the noted interpretation of 1930 on manner of withering. Khrushchev called patently absurd any theory that required the state to become stronger before it withered away. He expressed his determination not to let terror reign again and set in motion a chain of events which was to have profound impact upon the law. The codes which had been promised by the 1936 constitution to replace the old ones of the New Economic Policy were entrusted to drafting commissions again. Reform was demanded on the legal front to establish "socialist legality" in its true form, not as a misnomer for terror.

Institutionally the Soviet system of government remained unchanged: the Party remained unique, the hierarchy of soviets remained the same, and elections were conducted with but a single candidate. But there was ferment on the legal side. The role of the procurator as protector of legality was reaffirmed in a new statute,[59] and his practice indicated that he was prepared to act within his reaffirmed authority. Perhaps the most promising development was the appointment of Roman Rudenko as Procurator General. He had been prosecutor for the U.S.S.R. at the 1946–47 Nuremberg trials of the Nazi war criminals, and many of those from the West who worked with him in Nuremberg were impressed by his determination to function within a system of "socialist legality" in its new sense.

When the draft statutes enunciating new fundamental principles of criminal law and procedure appeared in 1958, the measure of the reforms could be gauged.[60] Of major importance was adoption of the long-standing proposal of the reformers to eliminate the analogy provision. To this was added an article interpreted to mean confirmation of the 1953 abolition of the Special Boards of the Ministry of Internal Affairs. In the field of criminal procedure the reforms did not go as far as the reformers had hoped, but they were a step in the direction desired. While the new statutes did not say in so many words that the presumption of innocence existed, they placed the burden of proof of guilt on the prosecution. This was hailed by the proponents of an express statement as the equivalent, and they began to build immediately upon this foundation to establish the presumption in the eyes of the public.

The other major change was recognition that the accused should have counsel well before his trial began, although the proposal that counsel be authorized from the moment of arrest was rejected. The preliminary investigation, which is of major importance in any continental-type proceedings, during which evidence from both sides is examined, was to be conducted without benefit of counsel to the suspect until the indictment made him formally the accused. This was late in the proceedings, and some thought it too late to help, but it permitted the accused some time before the trial to organize his case and obtain witnesses who might not have been heard by the preliminary investigator. This was certainly better than during Stalin's epoch.

Among the numerous changes in detail, some indicate dramatically the desire to introduce a more moderate system of criminal law. The age of criminal responsibility of minors was raised from 12 to 14 for the most serious crimes and from 12 to 16 for lesser crimes, and special labor colonies for juveniles were established. The maximum period of confinement was reduced from 25 to 15 years; confiscation of property was limited as a penalty to crimes against the state and certain serious crimes committed with mercenary motives. The number of crimes for which capital punishment might be ordered was reduced sharply. Parole was authorized under more circumstances than previously for exemplary prisoners. Definitions of crime were made more precise, although the crime of "sabotage" continued to appear under a definition which was so broad as to permit the court considerable freedom in determining whether it had been committed, but the maximum penalty was reduced from death to imprisonment. The phrase, "counterrevolutionary crime," which had overtones of the revolutionary tribunals of early years, was replaced by the traditional "crimes against the state" with its implication of unimpassioned trial.

Not every move was toward moderation, for some new crimes were introduced, the most notable being leading minors into a group which, under the guise of preaching religious beliefs, caused sexual dissoluteness or harm to health. Also a penalty was established for persons who failed to render aid to a person in danger of death. Official acts exceeding the law, especially those in violation of procedural guarantees, were defined specifically as criminal, instead of falling under the previous general heading of official crimes.

One feature of the new fundamentals was within a few months to open the door to intensification of a policy of severity for criminal repeaters. The new code reflected a new attitude toward hardened offenders and spoke of maximum prison terms for "especially dangerous recidivists." The discussions of the 1920's had stressed the educational role of the criminal law; crime was expected to disappear as class enemies were undermined economically and suppressed, for the workman and peasant would understand their opportunities and duties and live according to a system of self-discipline. The repeater in crime upset this expectation; clearly explanations in Marxist terms blaming relics of capitalism were no longer valid.

Hot heads, among whom Khrushchev seems to have ranged himself, took the easy answer: increased severity to frighten the repeaters. The death penalty was extended to a whole series of serious but nonstate offenses. In a number of amendments to the 1958 fundamentals, most of which were crowded into the years 1961–62, capital punishment was introduced as a maximum for six offenses, and ten new crimes were defined. Those for which death was authorized were counterfeiting, violation of rules on currency transactions, stealing state or social property in especially large amounts, group rape, taking of bribes by officials, and disruption of correctional labor institutions. In one case a new rule of 1958 prohibiting retroactive application of new criminal penalties was set aside by special act of the Supreme Soviet to permit punishment of currency regulation violators.

But the law professors were not prepared to rely upon such blind action. One of the seniors, Sergei Golunskii, who was on his deathbed with advanced tuberculosis, wrote a final piece for the Academy of Science's law journal: He noted that the concept of "the state of the whole people," enunciated in the Communist Party's 1961 program in replacement of the theory of the dictatorship of the proletariat, required a new approach to legal research. His colleagues should "risk their reputations" to bring an end to study in a formalistic and dogmatic manner. He denounced what had been common practice during the years of Stalin's terror, namely "the repetition of formulae taken from the Marxist classics." [61]

Some of those who survived Golunskii took up the challenge. In 1963 a well known criminologist, Dr. B. S. Nikiforov,[62] was willing to risk saying that "to pretend to explain anti-social acts and all other human conduct uniquely by social factors would be a simplistic generalization." He argued that human beings were not automatons; that they had a certain freedom of choice, and that this was related to traits of character, of temperament, and ability to adapt to changed situations. His conclusion was revolutionary among Soviet authors: crime is not created by a capitalist society but is due to individual character. It could be eliminated, he thought, by improvement in material and cultural conditions, by education, and by the development of a new social conscience.

What began as the speculation of individuals moved closer to the sources of power with an editorial in the journal of the Procurator General in 1965.[63] It established three general causes of crime: the consequences of World War II, inadequate educational work in the family and school, and shortcomings in ideological work among certain categories of citizens. Only the latter smacked of the old explanation that capitalism lingered on in the minds of men. The first was a recognition of shortages, and even of Stalin's harmful influence, for the editorial spelled out the fact that during Stalin's cult of the individual there had been a nihilist attitude toward legality; he had tolerated if not authorized violations of both Party rules and state law. The editorial singled out for special attention what it called violation of socialist principles in the conduct of the economy, especially in agriculture. While these were not identified, it is tempting to suppose that the authors were thinking of the headlong campaign against the "kulaks," the law of August 7, 1932, the extortionate collective-farm policies, and the general brutality shown to peasants.

An All-Union Institute for the Study and Prevention of Crime was established to conduct serious research and not to footnote Marx and Engels. This is made clear by a 1966 study of the Vice President of the Supreme Court of the U.S.S.R. who denounced the measures taken to extend the death penalty in hopes of frightening repeaters. He said, "An individual who is not sufficiently versed in criminology will sometimes assume that intensification of judicial repression is sufficient to eliminate crime completely. This is the result of feeble legal propaganda." [64] This sharp comment suggests that research conducted in many parts of the world is gaining a hearing in Soviet legal circles.

Further proof that modern sociological findings are to be used is offered by a report from the same institute on the causes of juvenile delinquency.[65] With considerable statistical materials in support of its conclusions, it blames shortages of material resources, parental neglect, setting of bad examples by parents, heavy drinking, school deficiencies, lack of moral tempering of the personality, shortcomings in job placement, frequent job turnover, and delayed arrests by the police permitting first offenders to repeat and increase the severity of their crimes before apprehension.

An investigator of sex crimes has added his bit to argue that youths, including the victims, have no concept of love other than the sex act; they have read no great love stories, have received no sex education from parents but only from the gutter, and live in a society where little thought is given to the social causes of rape because trials, to protect the individuals involved, are kept secret and, therefore, teach no lessons. He concludes that "everything was mixed up" among the delinquents who are in the great majority youths and adolescents: "everything was encrusted with licentiousness and cynicism, bravado and indifference, thoughtless imitation and ordinary boorishness." [66]

But in spite of these examples adaption to reality has not been complete. Doctrine still excludes genetics. A geneticist who discussed using data on twins to determine the influence of environment on criminal tendencies was roundly criticized by one of the most senior Soviet penologists for failing to familiarize himself with the party program, Lenin's basic statements, and the fundamental tenets of

Soviet jurisprudence. No genetic reasons can be given, in the senior's view, for lingering crime, for only social causes can explain the phenomenon. The critic clinches his argument with a doctrinal statement: "As is known, in a communist society a process of the withering away of both the state and the law, and hence of juridicial legislation occurs." [67] The specialist is saying that if the crime were explained biologically, there could never be an end to legislative repression, for Marx's explanation of its necessity only in class warfare would be invalid.

ECONOMIC REFORM AND LAW

Denunciation of egalitarianism as a petty-bourgeois utopian idea [68] in 1930 signalled Stalin's change of attitude toward civil law. Kursky had found it necessary to explain the introduction of a civil code in 1922 as a means of stimulating private investment; in 1930 there was no more private investment, but law remained. Pashukanis still held sway in 1930, and he seems to have failed to appreciate the results for law of what Stalin was doing. Civil law was taught in the law schools only as part of a course on economic law, and books on the subject treated it likewise. Not until Pashukanis was purged was there full realization in the legal fraternity of the implications of the new policy. In 1937 a full course in civil law was restored to the curriculum, and the textbooks were rewritten. Pashukanis' treatise on economic law disappeared from the library shelves, and his colleague Dotsenko, who taught the subject, was banished to Siberia, not to return until after Stalin's death.

A text from the Marxist classics was used to justify the civil-law reform. Marx had established two slogans to describe the steps through which society must move in its progress towards communism. The second of these, "from each according to his ability and to each according to his needs," was so firmly impressed on the minds of those who made policy that during the period of war communism distribution according to needs began. Apartment rents were abolished, as were fees for postage and telegrams. Distribution of free food took place in many factory shops, and communism seemed close at hand with the promised end of "commodity exchange."

The New Economic Policy ended such measures and reintroduced payment of wages in accordance with work done. But the egalitarian goal re-emerged in some minds as the N.E.P. was phased out and the five-year plans introduced. It was to stop such dreaming that egalitarianism was denounced and Marx's other slogan stressed: "From each according to his ability to each according to his work." This defined the first stage of development and was variably called the slogan of socialism or the first stage of communism. Whatever its designation, it meant close relationship between wages and work done. In the early 1930's, Morris Viteles of Philadelphia spent months in the U.S.S.R. explaining how to set up piece-rate systems of wages and how to select workers for assembly lines in accordance with their abilities. Books and pamphlets on accounting for piece-rate work appeared in the bookstalls. An Austrian specialist on the subject, Rudolf Uviro, became one of the innovators of the new era.

With the return of material incentives as a major factor in stimulating individual production, civil law's emphasis upon protection of what was earned became important again. Tort law abandoned the "soak the rich" policy of the 1920's and introduced careful determination of fault before ordering the payment of damages. Those who were becoming relatively rich because of high earnings were not to be unreasonably penalized in favor of those who did little for society.

Material incentives required more than protection of the right of the individual to enjoy them. New attention was paid to inheritance, yet inheritance had been looked upon by socialists around the world as the embodiment of privilege related to property ownership. One of the first steps of Lenin's government in 1918 had been to abolish the tsarist law of inheritance and introduce a form of temporary social insurance.[69] Under the new law, the heirs received property used by the deceased, e.g., dwelling, furnishings, and workmen's or peasants' tools, so long as their value did not exceed 10,000 rubles. Any excess was to be taken by the local soviet as its own, to be administered, however, for the benefit of heirs not having a subsistence income. Such heirs were defined as disabled relatives in a descending or ascending line, full and half brothers and sisters, and the surviving spouse. A social insurance law to replace inheritance law entirely was promised but never materialized, for the treasury was low. On the contrary the inheritance law was strengthened with removal in 1919 of the formal restriction of 10,000 rubles if the heirs were a working family having a communal economy.[70] This removed the last limitation on the peasant family, and it reverted to the customary rules that had applied for generations to govern the passage of property.

The New Economic Policy was the occasion for the enactment of a civil code, and a chapter on succession appeared as was traditional for all civil codes. The concept of inheritance as a means of insurance of the disabled passed partly from view, for heirs of all types, whether needy or not, were authorized to take property, but only up to the top limit of 10,000 rubles. Any excess was to escheat to the state, but only if it could be separated from the whole without causing economic dislocation or inconvenience. If this were a problem, joint administration by the state and the heirs was to be arranged, or the heirs were to be permitted to buy the excess from the state. The circle of heirs was narrowed to exclude able-bodied parents and brothers and sisters, but expanded to include any disabled and needy persons who had been dependent in fact upon the deceased for a year prior to his death.

By 1926 the limitations upon estates had proved unworkable. People were giving away the excess before death, and the gifts could not be traced. The top limit was removed,[71] and such limitation as remained was only on the designation of heirs: No property could be bequeathed to persons outside the circle of statutory heirs unless it be to a state agency or a public corporation, and a parent was not permitted to disinherit a minor child.

No further changes were needed to meet the needs of the new policy of emphasis upon incentives to stimulate individual production. No change became change, however, for the civil code was designed to permit the accumulation of profits from the private enterprise authorized under the New Economic Policy. When N.E.P. was phased out of existence, the inheritance provisions should have disappeared along with the reason for their being. Instead they took on a new function and perhaps, in Marxist philosophical terms, they acquired a new form with their new substance. This was the argument used by the proponents. A new socialist inheritance had come into existence, differing in kind because of the nature of the things that could be inherited. These people saw a difference between an inheritance law passing to heirs productive property, and one passing only consumers' goods.

Wartime inconvenience caused the next change in inheritance. The state could have received by escheat a considerable amount of property in devastated areas where no members of an immediate household remained after the Nazis had completed their destruction. To avoid the inconvenience of administering these small properties at a time when the state had no spare administrators, the inheritance law was amended to enlarge the circle of heirs.[72] Parents, even though completely able bodied, were permitted to inherit in the absence of descending heirs; and if parents had not survived, brothers and sisters of the deceased. Further, the right to bequeath by will was enlarged to permit bequests in the absence of heirs to any individual.

With the post-Stalin reform of the civil law, inheritance law was made still more liberal, for a testator may leave his property to any individual, even if heirs at law are living, and also to the state, or to state, cooperative, or public organizations.[73] This excludes only the right to leave property to a religious organization, since it is not categorized as public. Arbitrary rules assure minor children of no less than two-thirds of their statutory share, however, and any heir unable to work, and any persons who were in fact dependent receive likewise. Household furnishing go to those actually sharing the home and form no part of the estate.

While inheritance law symbolizes the new freedom granted the property owner, doctrine still supports restraints thought necessary to avoid a bourgeoisification of society. The aim is to eliminate the possibility of gaining what Marxists call an "unearned" income from property classified as consumers' goods and held within the constitutional guarantee of protection of personal property. A prohibition upon the ownership of two houses or two apartments precludes rental income. If a family inherits or otherwise acquires a second dwelling or apartment, it must sell it within a year or separate into two families to occupy both. If this is not done, the house will be sold at auction by the local soviet and the proceeds transmitted to the owner. To this restriction there is an exception for summer cottages are not considered homes within the meaning of the law, but a tariff is established which owners may not exceed in any temporary rentals.[74] Houses privately owned for a family's use may not exceed in size a norm established in each republic by the civil code to prevent rentals of excess rooms. Exceptions to the norm may be made by a local soviet on explanation of need.

Sales are restricted to avoid the purchase of houses, their repair and resale to make profits. Since the determination of appropriate mark-ups to represent the value of repairs cannot be done without examination of each case, the contract of sale has to be submitted for verification to a state notary, and it is his task to determine whether speculative profits are being made. Further, except to dispose of a house received by inheritance, sales may occur only once in three years. Should illegality escape the notary's inspection, a criminal prosecution may be brought for "speculation" when there has been a systematic practice of selling houses.[75] Privately owned automobiles are similarly controlled. They may be sold only through a state commission store which controls the prices.[76]

Restraints such as these upon what an owner may do with his property indicate that Soviet policy-makers have a keen sense of the corrupting implications of their doctrine of property incentive. He who earns may spend and pass to his heirs or friends, but he may not use property for gain. To this rule there is an exception, justified as necessary to finance the state's national economic plan, and also to reduce the likelihood of run-away inflation at a time when consumer's goods are in short supply: State savings banks pay interest on deposits.[77] Alongside this are the mass state loans. Originally purchasers could choose between an interest bearing bond and a lottery bond, the latter dividing the sum of money set aside as interest on the total of the loan through a lottery rather than to each purchaser as a fixed percentage of interest on his investment. The relationship between capital and income is obscured by the lottery feature. With the passage of time the lottery bond has replaced the interest bearing bond, so that this source of return on capital has been altered in form to remove its capitalist features, but the savings banks continue to function under their original rules.

NOSTALGIC FLASHBACKS TO SIMPLISTIC IDEAS

Stalin's death encouraged not only those who opposed terror, but those who hoped for signs in their lifetimes of the beginning of a withering away of the state. Khrushchev's 1956 denunciation of Stalin's 1930 speech on the way in which withering would occur, saying that it was absurd to think that a state would wither away only after it had first become the strongest state the world had ever seen, opened the way for discussion. Khrushchev himself stressed Lenin's concept of institutionalizing mass social pressures and proposed reactivation of the "comrades' court."

The comrades' court was a conception of Lenin to provide a simplistic method of enforcing discipline in the factories and in the multiple dwellings which had become state-owned under the nationalization decrees of 1917–18. Workers or tenants met in assembly to choose a panel of men and women from their own ranks to hear complaints of a minor nature against fellow workmen or residents and to warn, censure, order to repay light damage, and even to levy fines. The system worked well in the early days, although it sometimes led to petty tyranny in the apartment houses directed against those remnants of the bourgeoisie who found themselves the butt of pent up ill will among the worker families who had taken over most of the former owner's apartment and shoved him or her to the end of the corridor to occupy the smallest room in the place.

During the war these comrades' courts had been allowed to expire, partly because they were unnecessary. Stalin's legislation on labor, requiring workmen to remain at their jobs and subjecting them to severe penalties for tardiness in arrival at work,[78] transferred disciplinary responsibility from the workers' collective to the courts. For whatever reason, these bodies were not revived for the remainder of Stalin's lifetime after the war. Khrushchev re-established them and extended their jurisdiction to more serious complaints. Still, they remained essentially instruments of social persuasion. Only minimum rules governed their proceedings, and the persons chosen to serve had no legal education. A statute of 1961 provided a new charter[79] confirming what they had been doing since Khrushchev's revival of their moribund existence: They were revealed to be primarily social courts dealing with drunkenness, disorderly behavior, insults to women, abusive language, violation of apartment regulations, petty destruction of communal quarters, but hearing civil cases if the amount demanded was small. A measure of their success from Khrushchev's point of view was a statute of 1963 expanding their authority.[80] They might punish first offenders if the prosecutor thought this procedure suitable, and also acts resulting in impairment of health, circulation of a libel, insult, and theft of inexpensive articles of consumption and everyday life if the victim was a member of the group served by the comrades' court. The comrades' courts even expanded their jurisdiction without statutory authority, for they acted on their own initiative to punish first offenders for all crimes except those of violence.

In a measure the comrades' courts were a return to the people's courts of 1917 in their simplicity and popularity, and as such they prospered, especially in crowded living places. They gave tenants of the great state-owned apartment houses a chance to express their grievances against neighbors, and these grievances were many, as only one who has shared a common kitchen, bathroom, and toilet with a host of fellow tenants can appreciate. They were especially fitted to shame the drunkard, both in the apartment and in the shop, and many reports of the activities of these bodies indicate that this was a primary function.

Khrushchev introduced a second institution which was not so well received. This was the "social assembly," not a tribunal but a gathering of people. It was given the task of enforcing what was called the "parasite law."[81] The law itself was an effort to implement the constitution's requirement that everyone work. Khrushchev was prepared to leave it to the members of each peasant village, small producing unit, or dwelling unit to decide which of their number were not working or only appearing to do so. His formula was supremely simple: The Communist Youth League, the trade union, or a tenants' committee would call a general meeting. The group would elect a chairman to keep order, present the witnesses against the accused, and ask for a vote. The group voted orally on whether or not to banish the "parasite" from the locality. The only restraint upon this form of mass "persuasion" was that the executive committee of the local soviet had to confirm the order of banishment before it could be applied. The "social assemblies" represented "people's justice" in the simplest and most objectionable form; even during the period of war communism, the revolutionary tribunals chose a bench of individuals to decide on guilt and did not leave it to the mob.

RESTORATION OF A DUAL SYSTEM

The men with legal training were upset by Khrushchev's return to simplistic forms. Some noted that this was no manifestation of the withering away of the state. Force was retained in the form of penalties, and orderly application of law by a court was passed to a disorderly group functioning with none of the procedural safeguards established as the result of long struggle. The men of the law had gained considerable prestige in the years following Stalin's death, and they used it to erode Khrushchev's "withering" policy. They could not face his argument head-on, for it was a popular one and had a revolutionary ring. They did the next easiest thing. They pointed out that with expanded duties the members of comrades' courts required knowledge of substantive law and procedure. Night school classes were opened under the title of "people's universities" to which the individuals honored by election to the comrades' courts were invited to come for elementary training.[82] Reports indicated that classes were generally well attended, and that the sessions of the courts, although extremely informal, had a simple dignity about them. Since the people of the U.S.S.R. are showing their determination to protect procedural rights lost under Stalin, the outlook for legalization of the comrades' courts is relatively bright. They are becoming a second popularized system alongside the increasingly formal people's courts, and they probably will themselves become more formal although not to the same degree as the general courts.

The fate of the social assemblies has been quite different. The men of the law attacked them from the start as meeting none of the criteria of the procedural reforms of 1958 which provided that there be no punishment unless meted out by a court. The lawyers were dissatisfied, and they successfully enlisted the support of other elements among the leadership to effect a change. This came in limiting the scheme to situations where the accused "parasite" was a member of the work group which tried him or her, and the case could be heard only if a prosecutor decided that this was desirable. The second step came when the system was abolished by a decree of 1965.[83] In the principal cities of Moscow and Leningrad, only courts may now hear cases, while in other areas the executive committee of the local soviet may now banish a "parasite." There is no prior action by a social assembly. The 1965 revision still allows for punishment by a body other than a court and is not acceptable to the legally trained Communists, but they cannot obtain more from their colleagues at this time.

CONCLUSION

Soviet law has moved far from the first decrees of 1917. Its procedure, its substance, and the tribunals that enforce it bear little resemblance to those of fifty years ago. Perhaps the clearest measure of changed attitudes is Soviet denunciation of current Chinese legal methods for manifestation of the very features formerly revered by the Bolsheviks. Even before emergence of the Red Guards, which the Soviet communists detest, Soviet polemicists were denouncing the Chinese communists for having no law at all because they applied sets of rules so elastic as to negate the first element of law.[84]

This is not to say that Soviet law has evolved to a position deserving the Chinese epithet of "bourgeois." There are clear indications of progression away from simplicity, popularity, and flexibility, and the 1961 Party Program ends discussion of law in terms of class content, but there are still limitations designed to prevent society from slipping back to capitalism and to the rule of law which Westerners espouse. The most notable are in substantive law, although the procedural limitation on right of counsel before delivery of the indictment stands out on the procedural side.

The substantive law has been changed most notably with regard to property ownership. From a private enterprise system, the U.S.S.R. has been transformed into a state enterprise system, and this has left its permanent imprint upon the law. The civil code in its 1964 form has lost its chapters on business organization, and even those having to do with contracts, torts, the enjoyment of property, and inheritance have been changed in emphasis. This has occurred not by extensive alteration of legal principles in these fields, but because the provisions of the civil code have come to apply only to the relatively but by no means wholly insignificant quantities of personally owned consumers' goods.

The state has not withered away, nor even begun to do so, although since Stalin's death there has been an effort to make a start. At least it is no longer ruling primarily by terror, as it did in Stalin's time. Since Khrushchev's ouster, Soviet lawyers have chosen not to place the "accent" upon withering which he thought necessary, but there is a readiness to continue with popularization of justice through expansion of the jurisdiction of the comrades' courts.

But this commentary on the evolution of fifty years cannot close without reference also to what the visitor's eye can see. When an outsider enters a Soviet courtroom, with knowledge of court rooms in other lands, the impression is strong that it is still a "people's court." Judges have not become officials on pedestals. They sit on raised platforms in chairs backed with carved state seals, but they wear no gowns, nor do they adopt a sophisticated attitude. Most are now women in the trial courts, and they look like the mothers and elder sisters of those brought before them. They are not yet separated in sympathy from the majority of those with whom they deal. They show discouragement with the foibles of the average man and woman which bring him or her before the court. Only when they have to face the hardened criminal, does a hardness ring in their voices and the look of the stern disciplinarian freeze on their faces. At that point their anger shows through their patience. Woe unto him who arouses the anger of men and women steeled by Communist doctrine to fight those who undermine the regime.

Factors such as these serve always as a check on conclusions based upon analysis of documents, no matter how detailed. While they introduce an element of sentimentality into a framework reserved traditionally for hard headed analysis, they cannot be overlooked. Fifty years have brought great changes, but a Soviet courtroom provides a glimpse of a social drama which retains many constants from the early revolutionary days.[85]

SOVIET FOREIGN POLICY

Ivo J. Lederer

Half a century after the Bolshevik Revolution, the Soviet Union finds itself in a paradoxical situation. Militarily and industrially it is the most powerful Communist state, leader of a large "socialist" bloc. With its archfoe—the United States—it is co-arbiter of the destiny of the world. At the same time, however, the Soviet Union is in an impasse, with no readily visible way out. It is embattled on two diverse fronts, each of which tests the Soviet imagination while it consumes enormous Soviet energies and resources.

Within the socialist world, the Soviet leaders are in a state of quasi-war with China. They are groping for ways to harness Communist energies throughout the world, to forge unity in their movement, and to achieve or recapture the position of moral, ideological, and political leadership they once held. In relation to the West the Soviet position today is no less discomforting. No significant advances in the struggle against American "imperialism" have been achieved in some years. In fact, Soviet horizons in 1967 were not nearly so bright as they were a decade earlier when Sputnik, flashy diplomatic gambits in the Afro-Asian world, and Western disunity combined to augur a tide of success.

Soviet inability to achieve strategic gains at the expense of the United States and the West, and the uncertainty over how to deal with Communist disunity and with the threat of China have doubtless produced in Soviet ranks a sense of frustration and uncertainty. Such a frame of mind, however, should not obscure the reality of Soviet strength, power, and potential.

Viewed over the span of the past half-century this reality of power and standing in world affairs quite probably represents the greatest achievement of Russian communism. In spite of numerous misadventures and the current tribulations, it is in the spheres of world politics and diplomacy that the Bolshevik experiment turned into a success story that cannot be matched in Soviet domestic affairs. Foremost, of course, is the fact that within one generation the Soviet Union progressed from the position of an isolated and beleaguered outcast to that of a superpower capable of swaying the destiny of mankind. Considering the territorial expansion of the Soviet state, the communization of adjacent countries, and the extension of Russian influence into four continents, the Soviet regime has thus made spectacular gains, of a sort which in the mid-1920s even the most optimistic soothsayer in Moscow would not have dared predict. Many of these gains were occasioned by a world war and by Western disunity, miscalculation, and inhibition in the post-war years, but this does not detract from the overall picture of success.

That Soviet power and diplomacy since 1945 have not achieved superiority over the combined military and economic strength of the West should not be viewed as a mark of failure. Soviet military and economic capabilities, after all, are sufficient to give pause to any and all Western powers. In all, Moscow's power position in the world today—its dilemmas notwithstanding—is historically unparalleled since the first half of the nineteenth century.

ADJUSTING THEORY TO PRACTICE

Before and during World War I, Lenin gradually developed the body of theory that called for the destruction of the nation-state system. To this aim he attached as much importance as to the principle of revolutionary social transformation. Indeed, in Lenin's view the two notions were interlocked, for it was the nation-state system that maintained through its international network the capitalist social-economic order—in Russia and elsewhere. The foreign policy and diplomacy of the great powers together with finance thus formed the bulwark against revolution. For revolution to succeed that bulwark had to be destroyed. At the same time Lenin believed that if revolution were to succeed in Russia, it would have to occur in Central Europe and elsewhere. In any circumstance, the European state-system in pre-1917 Bolshevik eyes was foredoomed.

Consistent with this view, and following in the anti-tsarist tradition of Marx and Engels, Lenin condemned Russian foreign policy—objectives, methods, and results alike. During the World War he attacked tsarist war aims, including the historical goal of access to Constantinople and capture of the Bosphorus and Dardanelles. In all, before October 1917, the Bolshevik view of revolution was synonymous with the destruction of the nation-state system and destruction of an international community governed in its relations by agreed upon and accepted standards of behavior and diplomatic practice.

This revolutionary world-view received practical expression in the very birth process of the Bolshevik regime. The "Decree on Peace," issued on the morrow of the seizure of power, on November 8, 1917, in effect called for a revolutionary chain-reaction and promised the dismantlement of traditional diplomatic institutions. Trotsky's oft-quoted statement, made as head of the Commissariat of Foreign Affairs—"I will issue a few revolutionary proclamations to the peoples of the world and then shut up shop!" [1]—bespoke the then characteristic Bolshevik blend of exuberance and naiveté. This combination, of course, could not and did not endure very long.

Two Soviet attitudes toward the outside world took form in the three or four years following the October revolution. First and foremost was a genuine expectation—actually a gross miscalculation—that the events in Russia would set off a revolutionary chain elsewhere, especially in Germany and elsewhere in Central Europe. This conviction was prompted perhaps by years of Bolshevik self-indoctrination, and perhaps by the unexpected suddenness of success. To some extent it was justified by actual revolutionary stirrings in Central and Eastern Europe. That these stirrings were misread by the Bolsheviks, taken as portents of an impending tidal wave, led on the one hand to exuberance and, when the portents proved illusions, to bewilderment and disappointment.

Disappointment and the Bolshevik adjustment to reality led to the second attitude. Civil war, economic chaos, and Allied intervention forced a practical approach to the problem of survival. The European state system was not about to collapse, in Germany or elsewhere. If anything, it threatened to throttle the revolution in Russia. The Bolsheviks could no longer maintain that the need for conducting state-level foreign relations had disappeared. The need was pressing and real and quickly found expression in the development of a Bolshevik-Russian diplomatic apparatus. With the signing of the Treaty of Brest-Litovsk on March 3, 1918, Trotsky, whose approach to the negotiations had failed to gain Lenin's support, accepted a new assignment as Commissar of War. The People's Commissariat of Foreign Affairs (Narkomindel) passed into the hands of G. V. Chicherin, an astute and urbane man of superior talent who understood and appreciated the potential usefulness of conventional diplomacy. With his deputy and eventual successor, Maxim Litvinov, Chicherin developed an able Bolshevik diplomatic corps, and a pattern of diplomatic tactics, with which the Soviet regime succeeded in breaking the virtual quarantine imposed upon it by the anti-Bolshevik West.[2]

The establishment of the Comintern in 1919 formalized one aspect of the Bolsheviks relationship with the outside world. From this point on, the Russian Revolution became structurally committed to the cause of "world revolution." This created certain moral, doctrinal and political ambiguities for Soviet leaders which they have never quite resolved. In the long run, the compatability between the interests of an existing Communist national state and those of a visionary universal proletarian state proved impossible to maintain, except in the realm of slogans. In the early years of the revolution, however, the two sets of interests appeared not only compatible but mutually reinforcing. Thus the Comintern sought to promote world revolution through agitation and subversion while the Narkomindel served Bolshevik state interests by seeking recognition and trade agreements through diplomatic channels. The two approaches were in no sense antipodal; they rather reconciled the increasingly evident inconsistency between expectation and actuality, between theory and fact. Or, to put it differently, expedience and utopianism could not remain co-equal while the battle for survival was being waged. As Alexander Dallin aptly observed:

> The months following the Russian Revolution saw the confluence of two trends: the increasing reality of power and the increasing power of reality. Seizure of the reins of state gave the Soviet leaders an awesome awareness of the need to preserve and maximize power: this was the key to shaping the universe in alliance with history; power not as an end in itself but as a means toward the attainment of a better tomorrow. At the same time, the retreat (or advance) from naive faith in revolution to a more sober assessment of opportunities injected into the situation a sense of politics as the art of the possible.[3]

Several months after the revolution, Lenin, Trotsky, and others still thought that the Bolshevik cause in Russia could not succeed without a chain of revolutions elsewhere. By 1919, however, pleased but also surprised by their own survival, they adapted theory to reality, and "one could detect the essentials of a reorientation which would make the international victory of Communism contingent on the flourishing of Soviet might in Russia." [4] Gradually the Comintern and the cause of the world movement came logically to be viewed as extensions of the Russian Revolution, to which indeed they became increasingly subordinated. Ultimately the logic turned grotesque as, years later for example, Manuilsky with straight face argued that assistance "to the U.S.S.R., its defense, and cooperation in bringing about its victory over all its enemies must . . . determine the actions of every revolutionary organization of the proletariat . . . of every Socialist, Communist, toiling peasant . . . who desires that socialism should triumph throughout the world." [5]

Students of Soviet policy and diplomacy have for decades displayed a penchant for posing seemingly unresolvable questions. To what extent have theory and ideology and to what extent have state interest and exigency governed Soviet foreign policy? Has the Soviet Union served as a geographic headquarters for world revolution or has Moscow primarily used foreign Communist parties to further the security interests of the Soviet state? Is "peaceful coexistence" inconsistent with a policy of advancing the collapse of capitalist societies or with promoting revolution abroad? And so on. Such questions will of course continue to captivate the mind and to elude full and satisfactory answers. And even though fifty years of Soviet diplomatic history provide few (if any) examples of occasions on which state interests were sacrificed to theory or in the name of the world movement, it would be a gross error to conclude that pragmatism alone has dominated the field since 1917.

If we return to the formative years we shall find, I think, that from the very first Bolshevik international behavior and the Bolshevik world-view reflected a compound of varied emotions. These ranged from a fanaticism born of years of underground struggle to the confusion of inexperience and to a profound sense of grievance at foreign intervention. With fuel such as this, the stark necessity to improvise abroad as well as at home created a rather special mood, or a particular psychology in dealing with the outside world. Thus diplomacy and anti-diplomacy became two faces of the same phenomenon, and the slogans of coexistence and revolution its twin languages.

The issue of whether ideology determines policy or not is, on the whole, artificial. For the Soviet regime, ideology has rationalized the imponderables of historical processes and, as one student of Soviet diplomacy recently put it, has "functioned as a theory or strategy of action, i.e. as a framework for the analysis, mobilisation, and manipulation of social and political power in a variety of conditions and circumstances . . . Furthermore, ideology serves to justify and rationalise Soviet behaviour and . . . serves as the foundation of legitimacy upon which Soviet rule reposes and provides ethical sanction for the extension or intensification of Soviet power." [6]

Coexistence and revolution have thus not been antithetical; they have always been complementary techniques for the advancement of the same goal. The concept of coexistence never involved the element of permanence.[7] It rather developed as a corollary to Lenin's axiom that "to accept battle at a time when it is obviously advantageous to the enemy and not to us is a crime." [8] The history of Soviet foreign policy has thus been a skilful harmonization of the offensive and the defensive, of the challenge and the reassurance, of adjusting—temporarily—to the very international system which it meant to destroy ultimately.

SOVIET DIPLOMACY IN PRACTICE

In the Soviet view, as in the classical Western pattern, diplomacy is a means and not an end. Policy defines the end and diplomacy is but one of the instruments for bringing the end about. Over the decades Soviet diplomacy has evolved into a technique of conducting international affairs markedly different from Western practice. This difference derives from various sources, some of a historical character and some of Bolshevik making. The proverbial Russian suspicion of foreigners and the sense of having been victimized by the hostile West had, already in the nineteenth century, led many Russians (mainly outside government) to question why the game should be played by Western rules. Then too classical Russian diplomacy had already tempered Western conventions with certain oriental traditions in outlook and behavior which in the Soviet era assumed ever-larger scope.[9] This is not merely a case of atavism. The Bolshevik commitment to world revolution and the more immediate needs of the Soviet state produced special requirements for communicating and dealing with the outside world. Conventional diplomatic instrumentalities had to be adapted to the purposes of the revolutionary cause, both international and national.

By instinct as well as by calculation, Soviet diplomatic behavior thus evolved as a function of diverse needs and, perhaps, certain historical habits of thought. After 1917 the Western policy of quarantine and the image of the "Bolshevist-anarchist," regarded with a mixture of fear, contempt, and condescension, did little to stimulate a Soviet desire for "normal" diplomatic behavior. Most important perhaps, on the Bolshevik side, was the necessity of demonstrating through revolutionary conduct the irreconcilability of ideological and class differences with the capitalist world. So long as that world was the stronger, defiant behavior, disruptive tactics, loud and pious propaganda also represented a kind of corporate whistling in the dark.

In the classical pattern diplomacy is a process for the resolution of conflict. Negotiation and compromise are its essential ingredients. In the Bolshevik view diplomacy developed as one specific weapon in a variegated arsenal the sole purpose of which was the attainment of victory. Compromise, in this context, becomes anathema. When circumstances dictated compromise, it was regarded as a transient tactic. Negotiation was therefore approached as a game in which the result was either victory or defeat; it was not intended as a search for solutions. As defined in the 1948 edition of the *Diplomaticheskii Slovar',* Soviet diplomacy

> in its general purpose and its methods differs categorically from the diplomacy of the feudal epoch and the epoch of bourgeois domination. The principal goal of Soviet diplomacy has been and will be concentrated on the study of factors of social importance. For this purpose, Soviet diplomacy has at its disposal unsurpassed Marxist-Leninist methods of perception of world conditions and to a certain degree also of conditions . . . connected with the economic, political, historical, class and other problems of the countries with which it deals.[10]

This, in effect, has meant that Soviet analyses of national and international conditions proceeded from given assumptions and were not based, especially during the Stalin era, on a deeper understanding of the actualities and processes of non-Communist societies. Misconceptions, and not infrequently actual ignorance, have thus helped shape Soviet policy and conduct.

The doctrinaire world view, the power structure in the U.S.S.R., and for a quarter century the special role and personality of Stalin, have on the whole made of the typical Soviet diplomat an unessential functionary, deprived of meaningful latitude and individuality. An engineer rather than an architect, his virtues have been displayed in compliance with instructions and skill in confounding his adversary, not in breadth of knowledge, imagination, or personal style. Those Soviet diplomatic traits that have driven many a Western diplomat to exasperation and despair—imperviousness to logic, nonresponsiveness to personal or official gestures of courtesy or concession, enduring *sitzfleisch,* endless repetition, pettiness over procedural detail, distortion and the half-truth, recourse to public opinion, a messianic tone as well as invective, to mention but a few—have, however, produced many a Soviet diplomatic "success." At the same time, by incorporating revolutionary rhetoric into their diplomatic jargon, Soviet leaders have maintained the appearance of fulfilling their obligation to history, and have perhaps soothed their conscience when compacts with the enemy were struck. There may have been some unintended subtlety in Stalin's observation that "Words are one thing, deeds an entirely different one. Good words are like a mask to cover up nasty actions. A sincere diplomat would be like dry water or wooden iron." [11]

Soviet diplomatic techniques were tailor-made to a variety of needs of the state and the universal cause. Quiet and business like negotiations could be and were conducted when the need arose, as in numerous cases involving trade; or at critical political junctures as in August 1939. Propaganda, showmanship, bluff, threats, or extravagant promises were brought into play in other contingencies, for example when it seemed useful to strike a popular pose ("total disarmament," aid to undeveloped states), or to cloak domestic crises and/or likely failure abroad (the offer to aid the Czechs in 1938), or possibly to gain easy victory (the Berlin ultimatum of 1958). To capture and hold center stage and to create the illusion of greater significance and power than the U.S.S.R. actually possessed has, on occasion, also been a feature of Soviet diplomacy (Litvinov at Geneva). Summitry as practiced by Khrushchev has not been a standard Soviet tactic, though, despite its perils, it did produce certain transient and some durable successes, particularly in the Afro-Asian world.

Over the half century as a whole Soviet diplomacy has been more versatile and inventive, albeit not more successful, than that of the Western powers.[12] This may partly derive from the fact that actual Soviet might lagged, at nearly every stage, behind its principal rivals. Hence, diplomacy was called upon to reduce or bridge the gap. Moreover, Soviet diplomacy has sought to maintain a complexion of revolutionary universality while defending traditional great power interests. Basically, however, the instruments of diplomacy have been used to exploit existing and to contrive new differences and divisions within the capitalist "camp." Proceeding from Lenin's axiom that "the existence of the Soviet Republic side by side with imperialist states for a long time is unthinkable. One or the other must triumph in the end," it followed, again in Lenin's words, that

> The more powerful enemy can be conquered only by exerting the utmost effort and by necessarily, thoroughly, carefully, attentively and skilfully taking advantage of every, even the smallest, "rift" among the enemies, of every antagonism of interest among the bourgeoisie of various countries, and among various countries, and among various groups or types of bourgeoisie within the various countries, by taking advantage of every, even the smallest opportunity of gaining a mass ally, even though this ally be only temporary, vacillating, unstable, unreliable and conditional. Those who do not understand this do not understand a particle of Marxism, or of scientific modern socialism in general.[13]

THE INTERWAR YEARS

During the interwar years the two periods of greatest Soviet diplomatic skill and ingenuity were the years 1920–22 and the eleven months after Munich. Both were periods of high adversity; both culminated in spectacular agreements with Germany. Considering the special place that Germany held in Bolshevik revolutionary thought and activity, the outcome was rather ironic.

Immediately following November 1917, the Bolsheviks set out to encourage general anti–great-power risings. Their exhortations, as such, had little practical effect. After the Armistice of November 1918, however, Lenin and his associates made specific efforts to bring about a revolution in Germany. With the help of Karl Radek and others, German Communists worked to this end for nearly two years, only to have success elude them in the aftermath of the Kapp Putsch of March 1920.[14] During this period, the Comintern, which was controlled by Russian Communists, proved a useful instrument for implementing the policies of the Soviet leaders.

At the same time, Soviet policy was directed at the supreme objective of protecting the revolution in Russia, which was under attack both at home and abroad. The Narkomindel under Chicherin unfolded a diplomatic drive to neutralize the anti-Bolshevik camp. After the turn of the tide in the civil war in favor of the Bolsheviks, toward the close of 1919, Soviet diplomacy stood a reasonable chance of success, and in 1920 Moscow established relations with newly independent Estonia, Latvia, Lithuania, and Finland. Soon these precedents were followed elsewhere. Thus in 1920 the pattern of Soviet policy was to simultaneously pursue world revolution (especially in Germany) while normalizing diplomatic relations and securing commercial agreements needed for the hard-pressed Russian economy.

The Bolsheviks could vary the doses in the mixture of diplomacy and revolutionary anti-diplomacy. They did so in response to changing circumstances. Yet they also misjudged events. Probably their gravest blunder was seriously to expect revolution in Germany and elsewhere in the West.[15] By late 1920, however, they had recovered sufficiently from disappointment to concentrate, for a while, on diplomatic instrumentalities. The dilettante Lenin of 1918 showed by 1920 a sophisticated appreciation of diplomatic and commercial strategy and tactics. Aware of the differences in Western attitudes towards Bolshevik Russia, and particularly the British predisposition for trade, the Soviets turned to exploiting these "capitalist contradictions," in part by dangling before Western interests the prospect of a lucrative Russian market. Diplomatic recognition and the end of anti-Bolshevik action, however, were tied to it.[16] The formula on the whole worked and on January 16, 1920, the Allied Supreme Council ended the blockade of Russia. On March 16, 1921, a trade agreement was signed with Great Britain. This was the prelude to formal recognition which before long was granted by all major powers save the United States. As for trade, credits, and commercial concessions, L. B. Kamenev demonstrated how revolutionary purpose could combine with practical results, when he said, on the day before the British agreement was signed: "We are convinced that the foreign capitalists . . . will dig their own graves . . . With every additional shovel of coal, with every additional load of oil that we in Russia obtain through the help of foreign technique, capital will be digging its own grave." [17]

With the ice of Western hostility cracked, and the imminence of revolution in Germany gone, Soviet attention now focused on Berlin in a different way. The niceties of trade relations and de facto acceptance aside, Russia remained isolated and endangered by the anti-Bolshevik consortium. To break down the isolation and further disarm the Western powers, the Soviets determined to make common cause with Germany—the other black sheep of the European community. In a series of adroit diplomatic moves, Chicherin successfully played on Anglo-French differences toward the German problem as well as on various divisions within German governmental ranks. The signing of the Rapallo agreement on April 16, 1922, during the European conference at Genoa, was the high point of Soviet diplomacy in the 1920s.[18] Rapallo as such was harmless enough, but it did demonstrate the flexibility of the Soviet leaders and their ability to undermine British and French designs. From this point on, in fact, the Soviet Union became a material factor in European calculations.

By 1922 the interests of the Soviet state were further advanced than those of world communism. This remained essentially the pattern throughout the 1920s. Indeed, after 1922–23 it may be said that Soviet diplomacy was somewhat hindered by revolutionary activities abroad. The tensions that developed with England and France, for example, did little to help the Soviet state or the Communist movement in general. The Narkomindel and the Comintern came in fact to work at cross-purposes.[19] That this should have become the case was due to several factors: the gradual withdrawal of Lenin following his first stroke in May 1922; the rise of the diplomatically inexperienced but politically zealous Stalin; the jealousy between Chicherin and

Zinoviev and the fact that the latter, though not because he was head of the Comintern, stood higher in the hierarchy of power within the Party. After Lenin's death, Soviet purposes and behavior abroad were naturally affected by the bitter succession struggle, and some of the confusion that prevailed at home was reflected abroad, especially in relationships with non-Russian Communists. Stalin increasingly intervened in matters affecting foreign Communists and managed in the early 1930s to bring the Comintern under his direct control. Long before then, however, at the height of his struggle with Trotsky in 1926–27, Stalin bungled in China so dramatically that Soviet influence with the Chinese Communists was damaged for a generation, perhaps permanently. In the later 1930s foreign Communist parties, and hence the world revolutionary cause, were profoundly affected by Soviet domestic developments and few of the older non-Russian leaders survived Stalin's purges.

The impact of internal struggles and policies was not so visible on official foreign policy and diplomacy. Expanded commercial and stable diplomatic relations continued to be sought in the years following Lenin's death. The rupture of relations with Great Britain in 1927 was more the handiwork of British Conservatives than of Soviet official policy; in 1929 with the return of Labour to power relations were resumed. The Soviet diplomatic bureaucracy, too, remained relatively stable until 1937, mainly because the diplomats as such had no power base at home and were not centrally involved in the personal and doctrinal struggles at the top. In 1930 Litvinov succeeded Chicherin. He enjoyed somewhat higher status in the Party than his predecessor and eventually became the Soviet personality best known to the outside world.[20]

During the years 1929–1933, Moscow tried to avoid diplomatic complications abroad while occupied with collectivization and the first Five Year Plan at home.[21] And new perils arose on the international horizon in 1933. The assumption of power by Hitler, his suppression of German communism, his shrill anti-Bolshevism, and his rapprochement with Poland in 1934 all spelled danger for the Soviet Union.

In looking nervously abroad, the Soviet leaders were hardly reassured by the timidity with which the Western democracies responded to the political offensives of Hitler and Mussolini. The Soviet response seemed more energetic, though there is reason to wonder whether Stalin might not have welcomed some understanding with Hitler early in the game. But the ostensible Soviet policy between 1934 and 1938 was consistent and clear. It tried to bring into being a league of collective security against Hitler by persuading Great Britain and France that they were threatened as much if not more than the Soviet Union. In pursuing this end, Moscow brought everything into play: diplomatic channels, the podium of the League of Nations—which the U.S.S.R. joined in 1934 and in which Maxim Litvinov quickly emerged as a leading figure—and all the resources of *agitprop*. Between 1934 and 1936 Moscow negotiated and concluded mutual assistance treaties with France and Czechoslovakia, and in the summer of 1935 the Seventh Congress of the Comintern was directed to ratify the Popular Front policy which required Western Communists to make common cause with their former Socialist foes against Fascists and Nazis and to further pressure the democracies into opposing Hitler and Mussolini. The logical culmination of this approach was Soviet and Comintern participation in the Spanish Civil War.

Collective security, however, did not work. And *part* of the reason for this, ironically, was its Soviet sponsorship. The specter of Bolshevism—so effectively exploited by Hitler—continued to ward off the democracies. The Soviet presence in Spain and, more important, the show trials in Moscow made cooperation with Stalin distasteful in the extreme. Furthermore, the purge of the Red Army led many in the West to discount Soviet military potential in the event of a confrontation with Germany.

The rest is well known. By the settlement of Munich, the democracies, in concert with Hitler and Mussolini, in effect excluded Moscow from European affairs and placed it virtually in strategic-political quarantine. For the Soviet leaders Munich was a trauma. I think it would be difficult to exaggerate its intensity. Munich demonstrated the bankruptcy of four years of Soviet diplomatic efforts and revived the total isolation of the grim years after 1917. Munich was also taken in Moscow as re-confirmation of the inexorable conflict between the Soviet Union and capitalism and, so far as that struggle was concerned, of the essential lack of difference between the democratic and the fascist powers. With little to expect from either side after September 1938, Moscow was in no position to play off one against the other. That changed in March 1939, however, when Hitler occupied Prague and tore up the agreement he had signed less than six months previously. Hitler's action destroyed the last illusions in Paris and London, and the British guarantee to Poland followed on March 31. From this time on Stalin was courted by both sides. In August he turned to Hitler largely because Germany, once again, acted more decisively than Britain and France, offered substantially more than the West for Soviet cooperation, and in effect made it possible for Moscow to stay out of the impending war—at least temporarily. Anglo-French tepidity in negotiating with the Russians in the summer of 1939 and Chamberlain's performance a year earlier at Munich also provided an apparent justification for Stalin's course.

For the Soviet Union the arrangement with Germany was a triumph of skilful diplomacy that accomplished a number of ends at once. It broke the isolation imposed on Russia eleven months earlier; it allowed Moscow to stay out of the European war that by this time seemed inevitable; it offered much needed time to prepare Soviet defenses; it presented a possibility of the European powers wearing each other out; and, failing that, the understanding with Hitler based on a division of territorial spheres could be expected to last for a while. Taking the eleven months after Munich as a whole, Stalin showed masterful skill in combining passivity with cautious initiative and in gradually manipulating both Hitler and the Allies into believing that Soviet cooperation was important—and in Hitler's case indispensable—to their respective designs.

THE ERA OF EXPANSION

Diplomatic historians customarily divide the years after 1939 into three distinct periods: the two years of the Nazi-Soviet alliance, the wartime years of the so-called Grand Alliance, and then the era of the Cold War which began, by various accounts, in 1944, 1945, 1946, or 1947. As an alternative I suggest that the entire decade from 1939 to 1949, that is from the occupation of Prague until the end of the Berlin blockade, represents one integral period. To be sure, this decade involved the formation and the breakdown of two rather diverse alliance systems, but the same inner logic animated both: to advance Soviet security through territorial expansion.

There is little evidence that Stalin's eyes were fixed on specific territorial acquisitions in the west prior to the summer of 1939. But as soon as the European rivals began to court him, Stalin seized upon the territorial issue and began to equate it with Soviet security. The development of a Soviet "security zone" in Eastern Europe—to use the words Molotov put to Ribbentrop—formed the basis of the Nazi-Soviet alliance. Once it was agreed upon and in good part materialized, the very same issue, namely the Soviet "security zone" in Eastern Europe, disrupted the alliance.

Stalin—specifically and personally Stalin—neither desired nor expected the collapse of the arrangement with Hitler and was, by all accounts, stunned when Hitler struck in June 1941. Circumstances now led him into a different alliance whose raison d'être at the outset was purely military. But once the Soviet capability to survive the onslaught was established in Stalin's mind, the alliance increasingly began to turn political.[22] And the political basis for an understanding with his Western partners was to be, once again, the establishment of a Soviet "security zone" in Eastern Europe and ultimately in the Middle East and the Far East as well.

As happened with the Germans, the second alliance also broke down over territorial issues. But while Soviet motives and objectives may have been much the same, the two situations were vastly different. To begin with, the Soviet-German partnership quickly proved unequal since Hitler's Reich suddenly became the overwhelmingly dominant partner with the collapse of France. The incorporation of Polish, Rumanian, and Baltic territories was achieved with German agreement, but the foray against Finland produced only negative results; and all through the partnership with Hitler, Stalin and Molotov found Berlin unmoveable on the subject of a Soviet sphere in the Balkans and bases at the Turkish Straits.

In his German alliance, Stalin's basic conception of expansion was the classical pattern of annexation (Eastern Poland, the Baltic states, Bessarabia), sphere of influence (Bulgaria), and the establishment of military-naval bases (the Straits). In his Anglo-American alliance, Stalin began with the same conception but in practice ended up with a quite different scheme. First of all, Stalin's territorial sights were raised to include the entire Soviet periphery—Central Europe, the Balkans, Northern Iran, Manchuria, Korea, and, not long after, China. Second, the new scheme involved a novel form of expansion: a chain of pseudo-independent states whose societies were to be totally transformed by communization. This process would guarantee the greatest possible security for the Soviet Union. In addition, of course, Moscow continued to press for bases at the Turkish Straits and even for a trusteeship of former Italian colonial territory in North Africa. Western resistance to Stalin's demands and Western—especially American—refusal to legitimize the Soviet system in Eastern Europe created in the post-war years the principal problem of Soviet foreign policy and diplomacy.

But before turning to problems of the Cold War, let us dwell a moment longer on the war and immediate postwar years. If we regard the decade from 1939 to 1948 as a whole as marked chiefly by efforts toward territorial expansion, the German takeover of Czechoslovakia started this expansion, and the failure to take Berlin in 1948 established its geographic limits, at least temporarily, in Europe. Stalin frightened both his Nazi and Western allies by his territorial ambitions. With Hitler his negotiating strength decreased in direct ratio to German successes. With the Western allies, on the other hand, his negotiating strength increased in direct ratio to German failures and Soviet and Western military successes. The logic of the anti-fascist coalition, moreover, resting as it did on military exigency and in the American view on a political moratorium—or, better said, the separation of military from political strategy—opened up unexpected opportunities. These were quickly exploited.

It remains a question as to whether and how Soviet ambitions and behavior might have been constrained at the end of World War II. The magnitude of the Soviet war effort and sacrifices and the mentality of a victor provided a certain legitimacy for Stalin's ambitions. The U.S.S.R. was clearly entitled to security. But what were the reasonable limits? With the Red Army in physical control of Eastern Europe and large parts of Germany and Austria, and in the face of America's precipitous demobilization, Stalin could only feel emboldened. The turmoil in Western Europe and the emergence of strong local Communist cadres even unfolded a prospect of gaining the industrial West. In Western Europe, of course, the game was spoiled by the Marshall Plan and Allied resistance on Berlin. The summary Russian refusal to take part in the Marshall Plan and thus to influence or undermine its course represents one of the grossest miscalculations of postwar Soviet diplomacy. In Eastern Europe, however, Soviet hands remained essentially free; largely so because the Red Army was in effective control. Sovietization of the region was the result.[23]

As between diplomatic and military instruments of policy, Soviet successes at the close of World War II clearly resulted from the circumstance of war and the exercise of military power. The agreements of Yalta and Potsdam did *not* give the U.S.S.R. carte blanche,[24] but Western preoccupation with internal problems provided the necessary latitude. Furthermore, the West's reticence or inability or unwillingness to regard the sovietization of Eastern Europe as a *casus belli* made it reasonably safe for Moscow to carry out a coup in Czechoslovakia in 1948. But outside Eastern Europe neither military threat nor diplomacy was able to advance Soviet objectives. In Western Europe, in Iran, in Turkey, and in Greece Stalin failed to carry the day. And when in 1948 he attempted to physically oust the Western powers from Berlin—out of overconfidence and perhaps frustration—all lingering Western uncertainties came to an end.

Nevertheless, for the Soviet Union the situation in 1947–48 was fundamentally gratifying. Despite international storm signals, within one generation of the Bolshevik Revolution the Soviet regime had achieved an intoxicating position. The days of isolation were forever gone. The eastern half of Europe was firmly secure in Communist hands, while in the Far East the communization of China was in the offing. In historical terms, the future was anything but bleak.

STALEMATE AND EXPERIMENT

Turning to the past twenty years, here too the customary periods warrant some rethinking. Generally speaking, students of Soviet affairs are inclined to view the death of Stalin in 1953 as a turning point and the passing of Khrushchev in 1964 as yet another. No one can deny that Khrushchev's style was radically different from that of Stalin, nor that in vital respects the content of Soviet policy changed after 1953. These changes are particularly notable in the gradual, albeit limited, acceptance of polycentrism, and most recently the conversion of Eastern Europe into something more akin to an alliance —which is maintained by the ultimate dependence of most of the local Communist parties on Moscow. Changes are also notable in Soviet cooperation with the anti-colonialist, quasi-socialist leaders of Africa and Asia (Sukarno, Nehru, Ben Bella, and others), and by the stress on coexistence (which, however, clearly excludes ideological coexistence).[25] Khrushchev also blended theory and practice by stressing a policy of avoiding thermonuclear war and revising the Leninist doctrine of the inevitability of war with the capitalist world.[26] And on the surface the appearance in the late 1950s in world councils of a new-style Soviet diplomat (gregarious, on occasion "witty," veneered in urbanity) who no longer conformed outwardly to the solid Stalinist stereotype, represents yet another change.

These differences in style and content, however, seem to me to derive more from the deep and rapid transformation of the international environment than from the changing of the guard in the Kremlin in 1953. I would rather think that there is good reason to regard the fourteen years from 1948 to 1962, that is from the Berlin blockade to the Cuban missile crisis, essentially as a period of continuity.

Several elements characterize this continuity. The first involves the globalization of Soviet interests, power, and influence (with due regard to the interplay of advances and retreats). Ideologically this process began in 1917, if not before; with respect to foreign policy it began during World War II. But Stalin gave it decisive impetus in 1950 in Korea, while Khrushchev completed the process by a variety of ventures in all parts of the world. The second element involves the technological transformation of Soviet power—a significant factor in its globalization—and the decision to challenge Western, mainly American, technological-military supremacy. This undertaking was launched by Stalin (development of atomic and hydrogen bombs) and carried forward by Khrushchev. It permanently altered the character of the Cold War and, since the late 1940s, has been a cardinal feature of Soviet policy and strategy. Paradoxically, another element that characterizes the period after 1948 is a relative retrogression in the position of the U.S.S.R., due partly to the material strains imposed upon its resources by globalization and the new technology, and partly by the fragmentation of the Communist movement. The result, between 1948 and 1962, has been a series of probing skirmishes.

Even though the U.S.S.R. had been bled white in World War II, it is possible to argue that the Soviet position in the world has never been so solid as it was early in 1948. While Soviet technological capability has moved forward at a surprising rate, it appears to have remained at every stage behind the United States (except in the field of rocket thrust). And while Soviet influence has been extended into South Asia, Africa, and Latin America, the drain on Soviet resources and the vagaries of the Russians' Afro-Asian partners have involved sufficient political costs to raise a serious question about the practical returns. While Communist-ruled territory was increased by the revolution in China, Soviet influence within the Communist world—and in Communist parties out of power—has suffered significantly largely as a result of that increase. Indeed, the monopoly of 1948 that was first broken by the Yugoslavs is a thing of the irretrievable past. In short, the relative situation of the Soviet Union has in some ways retrograded in the past two decades.

After withdrawing from Iran in 1946 and after provoking American intervention in Turkey and in the Greek Civil War in 1947, Stalin made a final effort in the West in the face of general American opposition to Soviet designs. But when the Berlin blockade misfired and instead helped produce the North Atlantic security system and a viable West German republic, Stalin—at this point all the more incensed because he was unable to thwart the Yugoslav secession—called a temporary halt to Soviet efforts in Europe.

In this context the Korean venture in 1950 appears as a diversion from Europe, as well as an attempt to apply pressure on the United States in another theater.[27] But Korea misfired, too, not only because it ended in stalemate but because it created a powerful American base on the Asian mainland and brought the Chinese Communists into the picture as an autochthonous Communist factor. Stalin's death in 1953 did not interfere with the logic of the next step, namely to revert to Europe. While internal adjustments of power were underway in Moscow, Khrushchev and Bulganin made effective use of itinerant diplomacy—in Belgrade, New Delhi, London and Geneva—all the while courting and recruiting an auxiliary of vaguely socialist but distinctly anti-Western leaders in Africa and Asia. In 1955 the Soviets confounded the North Atlantic powers by withdrawing from Austria, thus lending credibility and, seemingly, substance to the slogan of coexistence.

But soon after the Twentieth Party Congress in early 1956, suddenly and explosively, the entire Soviet dominion in Eastern Europe was threatened. The situation was saved by vigorous military intervention in Hungary which maintained and even strengthened the Soviet position. American passivity with respect to Hungary in 1956 could be viewed as de facto recognition of the Soviet sphere of influence in Eastern Europe, and the natives had been taught a lesson they would not soon forget.

The desire for Western concurrence and official sanction remained, however. Had it been obtained, the problems of the local Communist parties and of the Soviet Union in Eastern Europe would have been somewhat alleviated. But so long as the idea of an eventual redemption of Eastern Europe continued to be mentioned in the West, neither Moscow nor the local parties were able to feel fully secure. The language of roll-back and liberation may have seemed a genuine threat—particularly since it was backed by strategic nuclear and delivery superiority. And the experience of 1956 demonstrated that the domino principle might very well become operative in the Soviet "commonwealth"!

Once Hungary was pacified and the issue of internal power in the U.S.S.R. resolved in favor of Khrushchev, the probing abandoned by Stalin at Berlin in 1949 was resumed. From this point on the scope so enlarged as to make it global in scale and extra-terrestrial as well. After the launching of Sputnik and especially in 1959–60, Western Europe felt exposed and imperiled and America confused on the issue of the missile gap. In outer space a series of spectacular feats seemed to lend substance to Khrushchev's claims, while his pronouncements on peaceful coexistence made Soviet policy appear responsible and restrained. The U-2 incident was adroitly used to portray the Soviet

Union in the role of an aggrieved victim, ringed as it was by N.A.T.O., C.E.N.T.O. and S.E.A.T.O. bases plus American submarines.

At the same time, Khrushchev launched a diplomatic-economic campaign to break the American "stranglehold." In the Middle East, in Africa, and in Asia his flamboyant diplomacy produced such an effect that a tide of success seemed close at hand. That Soviet diplomacy was riding the crest of an anti-imperialist (or anti-Western) frenzy in Africa and Asia, a frenzy stimulated by the Suez crisis and by Soviet encouragement, did not seem to matter at the time. The penetration of the Western hemisphere through Castro's entry into the Soviet fold, and the concommitant humiliation of the United States, produced an aura of inexorable victory. It may well be that the mirage of triumph tipped the scales of prudence and in 1962 could have led to Armageddon in Cuba.

The language of Marxist-Leninist theory is global and so has been the practical language of revolutionary movements and the so-called "national liberation" movements. Still, despite all of Khrushchev's fireworks elsewhere, all the evidence seems to suggest that over the past twenty years the highest Soviet priority has continued to be assigned to one issue, to the root problem of Soviet security in Europe, in short to the question of Germany whose division may be indispensable to continued Communist rule in Eastern Europe.

The problem of Germany had become aggravated since 1948. The Federal Republic had turned into a viable and prosperous state in which communism stood no chance of taking hold. By contrast, Eastern Germany remained in shambles and became more expensive to maintain—economically and politically. The West Berlin enclave was in fact and not only in word an intolerable magnet and a beacon of Western light. As East Germany became the weak link in the Soviet bloc in the late 1950s, Khrushchev and Ulbricht settled upon an orthodox but effective move—raising of the Berlin wall and hermetically sealing off of all East Germany. Whatever one might be inclined to say about that, one elementary fact stands out: there is no longer any danger of Eastern Germany becoming depopulated.

One other point should be made about Germany and its significance for the Soviet Union. The Soviet leaders have sought Western recognition of East Germany with compulsive perseverance. They have sought it for two related reasons. First, because it would help stabilize the Ulbricht regime and, by extension, Communist rule throughout Eastern Europe. Second, because it would settle the question of the Oder-Neisse line. The issue of this line is cardinal, for any tampering with the German-Polish frontier would surely call into question the Russian-Polish frontier, and potentially other East European boundaries as well. In the delicate postwar balance of Central and East European frontiers and in the face of existing national passions throughout the region, the German question thus involves Russia's own frontier with Europe.

These are some of the main elements that kindled Soviet diplomatic efforts from 1948 to 1962. Though the field of activity was global the central concern lay in the heart of Europe. Here the basic objective was not achieved, for the Western powers did not abandon Berlin, recognize the East German regime, or, in the case of the United States, forever renounce the possibility of a liberated Eastern Europe.

AT THE HALF-CENTURY

The past half decade, in contrast to the preceding years, has been essentially a period of consolidation. The Cuban affair exposed the degree to which Khrushchev had become overextended. It punctured the illusion of tidal Soviet success and jolted policymakers in Moscow into a more realistic assessment of Soviet capabilities. It also appears to have hastened the downfall of Khrushchev, though foreign policy was not the main catalyst of that event.

As might have been expected, during the post-Khrushchev interregnum, the regime has exercised caution on all diplomatic fronts. Actually, Kosygin and Brezhnev have been in a dilemma since 1964. Soviet policy has been dominated by the problems of China and inter-bloc relations, and during the last two years by the issue of Vietnam.

The problem of China, which in the end had mesmerized Khrushchev, attracted Soviet attention increasingly each year after 1957. By 1960–61 Soviet-Chinese relations began to have a tangible effect on the East European bloc, and of course on Communist parties around the world. Mao's criticisms of Soviet conduct cut deeply, especially when charges of Soviet self-centeredness and conservatism fell on receptive revolutionary ears. Polycentrism was one thing—with Moscow still *primus inter pares*—but indictments of betrayal something else. The escalating pressures of Peking have had a paralyzing effect on the Soviet political and diplomatic imagination.

To oust China from the fold, even if that were possible and even if it mattered, would rend Communist ranks, perhaps forever. To proceed without regard to China, and wait out the passing of Mao in the hope that it might bring basic change, would be to disregard and by implication to admit Chinese charges. But the ideological image of the Soviet Union—is it revolutionary or not?—is not all that is at stake. Strategic considerations are not to be ignored, and China as the adjacent great power, with demands on Soviet territory and an eye to primacy in Asia, has become a serious security problem. While it would be easy to overstress the point, the modest Chinese nuclear arsenal could inflict more damage on Vladivostok than on San Francisco. In all these respects, the question of China has loomed larger in recent years than that of Germany and Eastern Europe. But recent developments in Eastern Europe may cause the center of gravity to shift westward once more.

As for Vietnam, it is too early to assess its role in recent Soviet policies. While it is clear that Hanoi has received substantial Soviet aid, including most if not all of the sophisticated weapons, it is far from clear whether Soviet aid was rendered reluctantly or not. For Moscow, Vietnam has greatly complicated relations with the capitalist as well as the socialist blocs, and there is much evidence to suggest that Soviet policymakers have been divided on any given course. Much as it may have been desirable to involve the United States in a costly, demoralizing, and seemingly futile war in Asia, in view of its potential for spreading beyond control, the end of this conflict—with no loss for Hanoi—may well produce a sense of relief in Moscow.

One of the questions to which this symposium was addressed is whether the promise of the Bolshevik revolution has been consumated. The Revolution promised to do away with diplomacy and inter-state relations, a pledge that has yet to be fulfilled. More seriously, the balance sheet of the past half century is a record of remarkable success, tempered by notable failures. The promised universal Communist state has not materialized; moreover, the communist movement is today in such disarray that, despite its common goals, it would be foolhardy to forecast recovery and reunion (much as it would be foolhardy to forecast collapse). As a state and great power, though, the Soviet Union advanced from outcast to superpower within one generation.

During the era of greatest trial—the 1920s and 1930s—Soviet diplomacy displayed the greatest ingenuity. During those embattled years wits and skill substituted for superior military power. But Western disunity then, and ever since, contributed substantially to Soviet success. And the emergence of the Soviet Union at the head of a large socialist bloc was primarily a result of World War II and the destruction of the earlier balance of power. Negotiation alone could not have obtained what the Red Army already occupied. What might have been in 1945–47 if the Anglo-American partners had been disposed to use force or exploit fully their atomic monopoly, we can only conjecture.

When Stalin failed to exploit the Marshall Plan, he unwittingly released Western Europe from a potential Communist grip. From the Truman Doctrine on through the Berlin airlift and the foundation of N.A.T.O., attempted Soviet inroads in Europe were blocked. Khruschev enlarged the field of action and scored several diplomatic coups in the undeveloped world. But their full value was compromised by the gamble with missiles and in a number of cases (in Ghana, for example) by local turns of policy. In the Middle East, of course, Soviet influence appears to have enduring qualities.

Today the Soviet Union stands in an ambivalent though not an unpromising position. Its strength at home and abroad is materially greater than it has been at any point since 1917. At the same time, however, it is plagued by grave challenges from the capitalist and socialist worlds alike. As these are not likely to abate, the possibilities of the future remain, anti-climactically, unclear.

PROLETARIAN INTERNATIONALISM

Jean Laloy

Two ruptures marked the life and thought of Lenin. In his youth he broke with the liberal world and became a disciple of scientific socialism. He found in Marxism (as he understood it) both complete intellectual satisfaction and, he believed, a guide to action. Until 1914, despite his unceasing polemics and quarrels, Lenin remained a member of the Social-Democratic movement. He considered himself a better member than others, but did not repudiate the movement. After August 3, 1914, however, he broke with the Social Democrats too. Observing the patriotic attitudes of the parties of the Second International, he was confronted with a dilemma: either accept the fact that the international proletariat had failed to rise above national divisions, and that socialism was an ideal but not the sole key to a necessary future; or continue to maintain that class struggle was the one scientific truth. In that case the division of the international proletariat into opposing nations could only be explained by some accident, in this instance by the perfidy of the Social-Democratic leaders. He alone and those who followed him were the true socialists. The movement must be completely rebuilt. The extent of the catastrophe was a measure of the upheaval to come. From world war would spring world revolution.

As we know, Lenin took the second course. In the autumn of 1914 he unhesitatingly proclaimed the need for a new International, a world revolutionary movement organized and disciplined to promote an ultimate revolution. The war would end not in peace but in civil war. Step by step the revolution would gain ground, would break out in the belligerent countries, spread to the colonies victimized by imperialism, and finally engulf the earth. But during those three decisive years from 1914 to 1917, Lenin was the object of indulgent pity on the part of all socialist militants who were in touch with the masses. The latter, from the depths of their misery, were able at most to grasp the idea of peace. Explaining to the soldiers in the trenches that they must add to the sufferings already endured the horrors of a civil war was a hopeless undertaking.

Lenin's internationalism, however, did not stem from contact with the masses or a strictly objective analysis of reality. It was rather a raft that he used to preserve his convictions while the storm raged. His pamphlet *Imperialism, the Highest Stage of Capitalism* was an a posteriori study designed to prove that the Entente and Triple Alliance amounted to the same thing, and his discussions with Inessa Armand in 1916–17 on defensive war, as conceived by Engels in 1891, had the same character.[1] Lenin sought to prove that everything had changed between 1891 and 1914. Everything had changed because he, Lenin, did not wish to accept reality: the power of nationalism which belied proletarian internationalism. To accept this fact was to renounce his essential ideas, to join up with all those whom he had been fighting for twenty years. It was better to plunge on in pursuit of a Universal Idea which would never let him down.

Lenin's exacerbated internationalism of course had objective origins. After 1905 and 1912 it was hard for a Russian socialist to back Nicholas II, his court and ministers. It was more difficult than for Jules Guesde to accept Poincaré. Lenin's extremism was due in part to the nature of the tsarist regime. But its deeper origin lay elsewhere: in his desire to preserve intact the system of ideas on which he had founded his thought and actions. Lenin's internationalism was a thing of the mind (*ens rationis*) projected onto reality. It was not an objective idea drawn from an unceasing confronting of doctrine with reality.

Lenin is always presented as a great realist, and he was indeed a master tactician. But his revolutionary ideas were primarily the fruit of a frenzied ambition to transform society, for which Marxism was his guarantee. It was rightly said that "Lenin is Marxist because he is a revolutionary." Rather than revise ideas inherited from Marx when events contradicted them, he invented an explanation to protect the revolutionary theory: If the masses follow their national governments and go to war instead of uniting against their oppressors, argued Lenin, this doesn't mean that internationalism is wrong but rather that the masses are deceived by the Social Democrats. The Bolshevik should therefore break with other socialists and the masses will see their mistake. Internationalism will be reborn. Such internationalism divides in the hope of reunion, but reunion is postponed, rejected, until later—the important thing is first to divide. Through the split the world revolutionary movement will advance.

Of all the splits that Lenin authored, the one he provoked in the name of internationalism was the most radical and enduring. It was done in three stages: the seizure of power and dissolution of the Constituent Assembly, i.e., refusal to cooperate in any way with other socialist parties inside Russia; the peace of Brest-Litovsk, i.e., the break with all "imperialist brigands"; and finally the creation of the Third International which split the international socialist movement. These three acts, which Lenin later called the three irrevocable gains of the revolution, isolated the Bolsheviks in Russia and led first to a civil war, then foreign wars, and finally to deep hostility among socialists.

The first effect of the new International was to cut the Russian revolution off from any kind of relationship with the outside world. At the same time those responsible for this revolution were awaiting with feverish impatience the spread of their movement to Europe. They kept a sharp lookout for the least signs of this event, which they were counting on to save them. The Bolsheviks were trapped in a contradiction. Their movement, by its very nature, was supposed to be universal. It was not merely to reform Russia that Lenin had seized power. It was, as he incessantly repeated, for the purpose of lighting a fire that would spread everywhere. At the moment, however, this universal movement was confined to the Russian provinces of the old Empire. Lenin spoke Russian, was defended by an army of Russian peasants, had to solve Russian problems.

How would these two elements fit together? Would the universal at a given moment detach itself from the particular, take on a supranational character? Or would it be reabsorbed into the particular, gradually assuming a strictly Russian character? There might be a socialist movement which, while clearing a path for the new regime, remained independent of it—or a Russian regime which, gradually losing interest in the socialist movement, would again become a state like any other. The first possibility would have required similar successful revolutions elsewhere, and a merging of the new regimes in an association of equals—or for Lenin to recognize as socialist the German revolution of 1918. For realization of the second, the Bolshevik leaders would fairly quickly have had to renounce their international hopes and confine themselves to trying to run, as well as they could, the country in which they did hold power. In both cases some tolerance would have been needed: tolerance of other socialist parties in the first, tolerance of other nations in the second, but tolerance was not one of Lenin's virtues.

Once in power, the intolerant Bolshevik leaders rapidly arrived at a third formula: The particular state they had taken over, with its traditions, geographic and historical heritage, became in their eyes the "prototype state," a revolutionary state with a *unique* character not identifiable with any other. And this unique state did have a *universal* function: inspiring and supporting a movement that would spread over the entire earth. Unique and universal, established on a particular territory but chafing at its boundaries, the Soviet state was to be neither a traditional state, circumscribed and stable, nor a pure movement setting the world on fire. As Trotsky had predicted in 1916, it incarnated "the national-revolutionary Messianic mood" which viewed "its own nation-state as destined to lead mankind to socialism."[2]

As Lenin had put it in 1919 at the Eighth Party Congress, "for the moment the Soviet Republic exists only within the borders of the old Russian empire." It was not a Russian republic with a socialist character, but a unique socialist republic temporarily confined within the boundaries of Russia. The primacy of class over nation, so clearly affirmed in the Manifesto of 1848 and in Lenin's writings, was to lead not to the disappearance of the state but to the creation of a class state whose function would be to draw unto itself all the revolutions to come and thus gradually substitute itself for the old political forms. "A world state in the middle of a world of states."[3] But the internationalism of the revolution's early years aroused the hostility of other states and other socialist parties. Instead of igniting the universe, it remained locked within the limits that it itself had erected and within which it organized its followers into a "monolithic" movement. Neither purely national nor truly universal, the October Revolution profoundly roiled the waters of world relationships which have not quieted to this day.

The history of the movement unleashed in 1917 can be divided into two great periods, each subdivided into two phases. In the first period, from 1917 to 1945, the Soviet state was alone against the world. The tension between nation and class, diversity and unity, was confined to the borders of Soviet Russia. The citadel of socialism was encircled by capitalism. In that first period there was a phase of expansion which ended in failure, and a phase of relative stability and coexistence which terminated in the catastrophe of 1941.

The end of World War II saw the dawn of a new period. The expansion interrupted in 1921 resumed and led to the formation of a "socialist camp" of several ostensibly sovereign states. This was an entirely new phenomenon which changed all the problems. The contradiction between nation and class which had been relegated to the sidelines in 1918 was now introduced into the socialist system itself. The resulting crises induced Stalin to reestablish, by terror, a seeming unity. But the problems remained. And Stalin probably, like Lenin, died disabused and disappointed. After his death the new leaders sought to limit the crises, both internal and external. They endeavored to redefine the idea of coexistence, but without sacrificing the idea of the uniqueness of their state and of the movement directed by it. This second phase did not end with the fall of Khruschev, though his fall did signal an important break.

At present the world Communist movement is undergoing fragmentation but not collapse. A need to rethink all the problems is recognized but meets with an instinctive defensive reaction. The Communist Party of the Soviet Union vacillates between accepting the national tradition and upholding the universal idea. The compromise of Lenin and Stalin, that of the revolutionary state, no longer applies when other revolutionary states exist. This problem underlies all the present difficulties: the Sino-Soviet crisis, the crisis of the "People's Democracies," and the relations of the U.S.S.R. with the countries of the Third World. It plays a role too in international crises: Vietnam, Cuba, Latin America, the Near East, Germany, Europe, nonproliferation.

THE REVOLUTIONARY EXPANSION

Trotsky, who became Commissar of Foreign Affairs in November 1917, believed that within a few weeks he would have nothing left to do; the revolution would establish a new world order. And during the first months, their anticipation of this world revolution was the principal concern of the Bolshevik leaders. The men of 1917 considered themselves less Russian than socialist, citizens of a future world polity. In contrast the first leaders of the French Revolution had only wanted to improve the institutions of France. If their new institutions happened to catch on elsewhere, well and good, but their basic aim was not to change the universe. Ironically the victorious Bolsheviks remained prisoners of their world movement, while the defeated French Jacobins saw their movement spread to many countries.

Lenin and Trotsky did not confine themselves to waiting, however. From the beginning they worked through two channels: The one—that of the Party, later of the Comintern—transcended boundaries and states; the other, the state, had to take nations and boundaries into account but only up to a point. The two channels were different but not separate. The first was not purely revolutionary: Zinoviev shouted loudly, but Radek did not neglect the state's interests; the second was not purely national: Chicherin defended the new state but also participated in Party action. For purposes of analysis the two have to be distinguished, but in reality they are two arms in the service of a single authority, that of the Party, which governs the state and the revolution simultaneously.

In the first period, that of the "forced march toward socialism," which lasted in Russia from November 1917 through the end of 1920 (roughly from the armistice of Brest-Litovsk until the armistice at Riga), Lenin attempted to foment revolution by direct action. He used the Communist parties then being founded, and was especially hopeful of the one in Germany. As soon as the fall of Wilhelm II opened the prospects for revolution, Lenin had despatched Radek to Berlin. The founding of the Third International in March 1919 served the same end. It was necessary to create an instrument with which to control the revolutionary forces that were soon to topple the edifice of parliamentary democracy. In actual fact, there was very little for the International to control. Radek was to return from Germany convinced that the revolution was a myth. In Hungary Bela Kun lasted only three months, and 1919 saw not the triumph of revolution in Europe but only that of the Bolsheviks in Russia.

By 1920 Lenin was at it again. On the one hand, at the Second Congress of the Comintern, he established tight control over the foreign parties, intervened in their internal debates, and made the split in the workers' movement permanent. On the other hand, in the war with Poland—for which he was not responsible, but which he used to his own ends—Lenin tried a new method: revolution by means of the Red Army. This attempt also failed as Trotsky (and Stalin) had foreseen. The Communist government set up behind Red-Army lines vanished from the scene, and Lenin negotiated with Pilsudski.

From that point on, instead of being produced directly, either by Communist parties and their coups d'état or by armed forces and their victories, revolution was to be brought about indirectly. The direct attempts became rare, and Soviet leaders came to rely more and more on the diplomatic machinery of the Soviet state, acting sometimes as a traditional state bent on increasing its power (Straits Convention, commercial treaties, etc.), sometimes as a revolutionary state seeking to undermine or upset everything beyond the border of the U.S.S.R. (coalition of the pariah states against the victorious ones, support of anti-imperialist governments, etc.). In 1922 Lenin preached prudence, study and wisdom to the Comintern while pursuing at the same time a Genoa policy (promotion of national interests) and a Rapallo policy (dividing the "imperialists"). This was the beginning of a transition toward a policy that remained ideologically internationalist but accepted the idea of a pause, i.e., the simultaneous existence of "imperialist" states and of one that was different.

This development was precipitated in part by internal events, the crisis between the Bolshevik Party and the masses that resulted in the N.E.P., and also by experience in the Middle East. After some hesitation, Lenin became convinced that the nationalist regimes of that area would make better allies of revolutionary Russia than nonexistent Communist parties. Turkey, Persia, and Afghanistan being anti-British played an "objective" role in the anti-imperialist revolution regardless of their form of government. This concept, which started to take shape in 1920, tended to distinguish among the "encircling" states those that were less imperialist than others. Class struggle developed not only between classes inside national boundaries but among states, some exploiting the others. This was a return, under new conditions, to the Marx-Engels distinctions between progressive and reactionary states. Soviet policy sought to create around the prototype state a kind of league of have-nots which would divide the outside world and strengthen the citadel of socialism. In his last two years Lenin, who had defined the status quo as "permament change," was enchanted with the opportunities opened to his tactical genius by the international game placed in the service of world revolution. Not only did he see Germany as "forced" to ally itself with Russia, but he rejoiced at the idea of an alliance within Germany between the nationalists and the proletariat.[4] In this he was no doubt influenced by Radek.

At the time of Lenin's death in 1924, the revolution had failed everywhere outside the old Russian Empire. Nevertheless, although the revolutionary movement was marking time, the universal idea had been preserved as the guiding star of the new state. Lenin had dreams of one day bringing India and China into his movement, but this ambitious plan was less a hope than a consolation. In theory he had brought about an international socialist revolution; in fact he headed a state that was far from socialist, and did not even include all the territory of the old Empire. Internationalism was in a sense his alibi: One day the onward march would resume; until then one had to stand firm.

A "WORLD STATE" AGAINST A "WORLD OF STATES"

Stalin was only too inclined to push this line. As early as January 1918, during the debates on the peace of Brest-Litovsk, he voiced doubts about revolution in Europe. Like Lenin, he believed that the essential question in revolution was that of "power," but his conception of it was narrower than his master's. For Stalin, power meant the power to compel. Lenin had sought to blend persuasion and coercion, even if he did more often use the latter.

Stalin followed the line laid down by Lenin, but, being more concerned with order than ideas, he simplified and dulled it. Beginning in 1925, the year in which the doctrine of coexistence was proclaimed, internationalism emerged in the following garb: The world Communist movement was a kind of extension of the Soviet Communist Party. Rather than carrying to it any echoes from the outside world, however, it relayed to the outside world the orders and instructions of the Soviet Politburo (and reflected the latter's internal disputes). The Third International ceased gradually to play any role of its own, assuming rather the function of enforcing on foreign Communist parties the directives inspired by the twists and turns of the Soviet Government's policies.

The Soviet Union was not a state like others. Its "coexistence" strengthened "socialism" but was designed to weaken "capitalism." Abroad, its policies were essentially the ones that Lenin had followed at the end of his life: keeping the imperialist nations divided through the agreement with the Weimar Republic, promoting a national-revolutionary breakthrough in China, and attacking and weakening Social Democrats. The results are well-known: failure in Germany; failure in China, success against the Social Democrats who were weakened (to the advantage of fascism). When in 1934 Stalin was obliged to correct his orientation, he sought a rapprochement with the least dangerous enemies, France and Britain. He also attempted a reconciliation with the Social Democrats, through his policy of the popular fronts. But he failed in 1934–38 too.

At the time of these dramatic events, these about-faces and gambles, most foreign observers agreed that Stalin had cast aside any revolutionary spirit and had become, as it was called, the "preserver of the revolution." Only a small though influential minority continued to depict him as bent on convulsing the universe. Both schools were probably wrong. Stalin had domesticated and to some extent crushed the revolutionary movement and was probably delighted to rule an immense country. Still, he had not renounced the universal idea. True, he did not think in terms of "world revolution" but rather of a Communist movement controlled and therefore slowed down—but a movement nevertheless in the service of the Soviet Party and state, "whose very existence revolutionizes the world." He was less expansionist than the pessimists feared, because he was in no hurry and did not want to take risks. He was less nationalistic than the optimists hoped, for he did not renounce the idea that the state he ruled had a universal mission. This, then, is what Stalin's idea of internationalism boiled down to. Why did he remain so faithful to it? Would not his job have been easier if he had conceived his policies in purely national terms?

One reason for sustaining the notion that the Soviet State was a state with a unique mission was given in his letter to Ivanov. In 1938 one Ivanov, an obscure Communist, was kicked out of his party cell for declaring that capitalist encirclement was still a danger. He appealed to Stalin, who had him reinstated: "You are right, Comrade Ivanov, capitalist encirclement does still threaten us." How could he renounce the idea of this threat while the purges were being advertised as a defense against capitalism? How could one explain the threat except in terms of the uniqueness of a new society encountering universal hostility? For Lenin internationalism, at least in the beginning, was a hope; for Stalin it became the justification for power. Without a universal mission founded on the idea of class struggle there would be no justification for the one party and its absolute power in Russia. So Stalin clung to the idea. But he was no prophet out to set the world on fire. He would content himself with a few successes showing that his method was the right one. Whoever gave him those, would be accepted as a temporary partner.

We thus descry the outline of what coexistence meant in Stalin's day. It allowed of international alignments of all kinds, no matter how bold or brazen. But it never reached the point where the Soviet State was threatened with the loss of its unique character. Similarly, on the party level, with the policy of the fronts, the Communist Party was never to submerge its own individuality.

We can understand how in the final years of this first period, when the U.S.S.R. faced the outside world alone, Stalin could see himself as remaining true to Lenin. He made a pact with Hitler, but Lenin had dealt with Ludendorff and Hindenburg. Stalin annexed the Baltic countries, but Lenin had attempted to do so in 1919. During the war Stalin created a Polish National Committee at Lublin, but Lenin had created a similar committee in 1920, on which (among others) sat Dzerzhinsky. Stalin mistrusted Churchill and Roosevelt just as Lenin, while negotiating with young Bullitt in the spring of 1919, had regarded Wilson with the deepest distrust. In 1939–41 Stalin extended the territory of the U.S.S.R. Had not the Second Congress of the Comintern spoken of the Russian Republic as a state "whose frontiers expand as the counterpressure relaxes"? Stalin did not innovate; he hardened and shrank Lenin's ideas. By the end of the war proletarian internationalism, to which he remained faithful in his way, had become an ever thinner reed, ever more tightly locked within the U.S.S.R., and sealed there within the Communist Party. The universal idea had become the property of a particular state; the revolutionary conflagration had dwindled to a sacred flame with Stalin as its jealous keeper. As Dimitrov said to Djilas in 1944, "the main force behind the spread of Communism in the world today is the Soviet Union, no longer the Communist movement as such; all forces must therefore rally around the government of the Soviet Union." The dissolving of the Comintern in 1943 was a formality, doubtless decided upon long before. It did not signal the end of internationalism but its incorporation into the Soviet State.

True, this created difficulties and problems, but they were kept within bounds, the more easily as diversity—the very essence of internationalism—was absent from this type of internationalism. The Soviet state, being the only socialist state, ran no serious risk in claiming to be the guardian of international socialism. But what would happen if events should conspire to inject the problem of diversity into the socialist camp itself?

INTERNATIONALISM AND SOCIALIST NATIONS

A new phase for the Soviet Government and Party began in 1945. Within four years the territory of the "socialist camp" had come to include half of Europe and a large part of Asia. As Molotov was to say in February 1955, the lands of the socialist camp extend from "the shores of the Pacific *almost* to the Atlantic." True, the outside world was becoming a difficult problem. It was armed with the atomic bomb and, far from splitting apart, was actually uniting. But this did not induce Stalin to change his general outlook. Inside the U.S.S.R. vigorous re-establishment of firm controls restored some order to a society shaken and fragmented by war. Outside the "camp" the complete obedience of the Communist parties made it possible to maintain intact the internationalist doctrine elaborated before and during the war.

But the new states gravitating around the U.S.S.R. gave rise to difficult questions. We do not really know why Stalin elected to ring the borders of the U.S.S.R. with technically independent states. We do know that after 1920 he had envisaged a special status for Communist Poland and Germany within the Soviet federation. Lenin had vetoed this suggestion.[5] We know also that the policy of a patriotism to be steered by Communists acting through fronts survived the 1939–41 years. In 1943 young Wolfgang Leonhardt, deep in the Soviet Union, began to receive training in how to form national-front groupings in the future "liberated" Germany. Finally too, we know that Stalin liked to advance "without provoking the enemy fire." He did not wish to provoke his allies unnecessarily. Hence his remonstrances with Tito and Djilas, who in their hot-headedness foreshadowed Castro.

For all these reasons together, the Soviet advance—translated into reality by the accession to power of totally disciplined domestic Communists—took place under the name of "national road to socialism," under the banner of "people's democracy." In two cases, as we know, this national road was not entirely a fiction. Tito had no thought of being anything but loyal to the U.S.S.R., but he did want some allowance made for the interests of his own country. Mao, ignoring all advice, established his power over China, owing little or nothing to Moscow.

The crises soon blossomed. With Tito in 1945, Dimitrov in 1947. In 1948, on the heels of the success in Czechoslovakia, came the Yugoslav crisis, followed by the first measures against the proponents of the "national road"; 1949 saw the triumph of Mao, the first trials in Eastern Europe. Stalin reacted vigorously everywhere. He isolated Tito, having failed to destroy him, and purged the Communist parties of all the satellite states. For months he negotiated with Mao to work out an accord between the two Communist giants. But even at the peak of his power, Stalin was unable to establish complete unity with the Communist government of China.

Before his death the problem of internationalism was presenting itself anew in a virtually insoluble form. What was the true measure of internationalism? Was it fidelity to the U.S.S.R.? In that case, socialism meant the hegemony of Soviet Russia. Was it fidelity to the socialist movement? But how could there be a movement comprising several states without acceptance of some diversity? In that case the U.S.S.R. must acknowledge that socialism could have different national aspects. But if there existed "different roads to socialism" (as Tito claimed, and as Mao's experience showed), where exactly was the borderline between capitalism and socialism? On which side was Nehru? Erlander? Even Attlee? Where would it all end? Suddenly the entire edifice built up since 1917 threatened to collapse. Was the U.S.S.R. to be just one more state among others? Revolutionary yes, but less than some, more than others? Was its form of socialism, then, no longer to be the only answer to the crisis of the twentieth century?

If so, what would become of the Party, the very structure of the regime?

We see the implications of the questions raised by the events of 1945–53. We understand why, after 1946, Zhdanov had to crack down so brutally in the U.S.S.R. If internationalism ceased to be the prerogative of a single country, a single party, a general relativism would dissolve all the power built up over thirty years. With prestige and terror Stalin succeeded in preserving the façade, but he never found an answer to the question. He died (his daughter tells us) disappointed, disgusted, prey to a persecution mania, and bequeathed to his heirs a somber heritage.

THE DOCTRINE OF THE DIFFERENT ROADS TO SOCIALISM

The debates that agitated the Soviet leaders from 1953 to 1956 bore upon many subjects, one of the most important being the "different roads" to socialism. At stake, as under Stalin, was the relationship with Tito and Mao. Some (one thinks of Malenkov) favored a graduated pragmatic rapprochement with Yugoslavia, a cautious adjustment of the aid-to-China program, hence as painless a revision as possible. Others (Molotov comes to mind) agreed to a rapprochement with the Yugoslav state but warned against reconciliation between the parties. They desired the least possible change. Still others (especially Khrushchev) wanted to strike a great blow, to accept the principle of the "different roads" in hopes that this concession would re-establish the authority of the U.S.S.R., i.e., that Yugoslavia would rejoin the "socialist camp" and that China, bound by increased economic aid, would play within it the role of leading substar. The July 1955 debates of the Central Committee showed the importance of the Yugoslav case. Should one acknowledge the "legitimacy" of the Yugoslav road? If so, how was the unity of the "camp" to be maintained? Should the Soviet leaders limit themselves to tolerating this road as a temporary phenomenon? If so, how could Tito be brought back into the family? Yet if he were not brought back, how could one launch a grand policy toward the socialist parties and underdeveloped countries?

The doctrine settled upon at the Twentieth Congress in February 1956 was a compromise. Yes, "different roads" did exist, but they must not diverge from the Soviet model except within certain limits, those of "scientific socialism." The revolution could be peaceful, if the adversary did not fight. "National conditions" might color this or that development, but not deflect it from the direction that the Soviet revolution had taken. One might cooperate with Social Democrats, not to reach agreement but to guide them. To use a graphic image, the "general line" was no longer a thin line walked by a few initiates whom the troops followed blindly, but a rather broad ribbon along which the armies of socialism were advancing, some more to the left, others more to the right, but all keeping discipline and all going the same way.

The doctrine of the Twentieth Congress was an attempt to make some allowance for the diversity of the real without sacrificing the primacy of the U.S.S.R. Like all compromises, it solved some problems only by creating others. These surfaced that same year, 1956, in connection with the Stalin issue, and led to the crises of the autumn. The Polish episode showed that some diversity was admissible. The events in Hungary revealed where the limit was. But the basic problem was raised by China starting in 1957. To what extent could a sharp turnabout like that of February 1956, made independently by the Party of the U.S.S.R., be imposed on all the other parties? Why should the internal problems of one party have to upset all the parties? This question, asked by Mao from the very beginning, allowed only one answer, the answer that the Soviet leaders were unwilling to give. If they conceded as common sense required that each party was master in its own house, that only by agreement among them (the rule of unanimity) was a change of orientation permissible, the Soviet leaders would no longer be the leaders but prisoners of the movement—in this case prisoners of China. Since 1956 the question of internationalism, which is to say of the primacy of the U.S.S.R., has been at an impasse. Taking advantage of the impasse, the parties (even the ones not in power, like the Italian party) began to declare their independence. Crisis followed crisis: Albania in 1959, China from 1959 on, Rumania from 1962 on, Cuba in 1962, the Italian party in 1964. The remedy, an international conference, could not be applied, since convening one presumed a unanimity that did not exist. Proletarian internationalism, as conceived by Lenin and Stalin, seems to have had its day. The Leninist notion of a pre-established harmony among the Communist parties of all countries has been belied by events.

Has the moment arrived for a grand mutation? Are we to see the Communist parties acknowledge themselves disciples of a certain type of socialism without denying that other, entirely different types may exist? Are we, in other words, to witness the gradual birth of a certain unity from acceptance of fundamental diversity in place of the opposite that we have watched for more than twenty years: the assertion of absolute unity in collision with growing diversity? Can the relation between these two terms (which, generally speaking, is the secret of peace) be inverted? Instead of postulating a unity ending in rebellions, may one not posit a diversity ending gradually in a greater unity or unities? These questions, as we see, transcend the communist movement and present themselves to all of mankind. On the answer will largely depend the type of peace which, little by little, can be established.

PRESENT AND FUTURE

The answer depends on two other questions. Firstly, are we certain that the disintegration is an irreversible process? In opposition to the centrifugal forces, is there not another set of forces working consciously for cohesion? On the other hand, what is the likely outcome of the relaxation process that we see at present? Is there no choice between the socialist monolith and a proliferation of sovereignties? Is nothing else conceivable?

Khrushchev's successors have probably made it their mission to stem the decay of the system. They have decided to put up with Rumania's gibes, swallow Cuba's rebuffs, tolerate from French or Finnish Communists criticisms formerly inadmissible. Above all, they have tried to mollify the Chinese monster. The excesses of the "cultural revolution" have accentuated the break, but they have helped the Communist Party of the Soviet Union re-establish some of its authority. Independently of this more objective attitude (or more "scientific," as they say), the new leaders are taking advantage of a certain *de facto* solidarity among most of the groups in power. Each well knows that if it goes too far in its fits of independence it may be obliged to yield power to more turbulent or less compromised rivals. Within each party there is a regulating mechanism which those in charge know exactly how to manipulate. The fact that they now enjoy more freedom enables them to adjust this sensitive mechanism to fluctuations of opinion and/or the impact of events. To this extent the Communist system by growing suppler has in a way grown stronger.

On the other hand, among the ingredients comprising the elixir that is communism, internationalism continues to play a major role. If it really began to look as though these fifty years were going to end in a total breakdown of unity, the Communist regimes would have the greatest difficulty in maintaining themselves. This is why they all so assiduously keep warming-over the myth of imperialism (German in

Europe, Israeli in the Near East, American everywhere), which is still one of their best cements. Not one of the affected governments tolerates the least political manifestation that could embarrass it. They still control all expression of opinion, and the most independent among them, the Rumanian party, is one of the most rigorous at home.

Finally, the Communist Party of the U.S.S.R., even if it does show a velvet paw, does not hide the fact that it also has claws. Not only is it powerful and indispensable to its allies but, in the realm of principles, it strives to uphold the rules that have been fixed for fifty years. "Under present circumstances," declare the theses published for the fiftieth anniversary of the October Revolution,

> the question of a proper blending of the national and international tasks of the great army of Communists is of essential importance. One cannot fulfill one's international obligations, independently from the struggle to solve the national problems, without close contact with the basic interests of the toiling masses in each country. Yet solution of the national problems is impossible without every unit of the Communist movement taking active part in solution of the problems common to all. Fidelity to proletarian internationalism is one of the essential lessons learned by the Communist movement in the half-century since October.[6]

Moscow is probably hoping that China's present disturbances will give rise to some event making it possible, if not to turn back the clock, at least to have tolerable relations with Peking. That would be a great change, even if today it does seen quite unlikely. We may look forward, therefore, neither to an irreversible disintegration of the "socialist camp" nor to an evolution free of crises. There will probably be new jolts whose nature cannot yet be foreseen and which may involve numerous complications of every kind.

The answer to the second question is found in part in the present trend of the "socialist camp." What we are witnessing is less a pure and simple return to national selfishness (though many examples of that can be cited) than a series of attempts to regroup. Mao rants not in the name of Eternal China but proclaims a Chinese conception of world communism. Castro declares his independence of Peking and Moscow, but thunders against the Latin-American Communists who do not follow him. Tito seeks to preserve privileged ties with Cairo and New Delhi. Each, in other words, tends to form a group around himself. Mao and Castro are tending more and more to set up messianisms in competition with that of the U.S.S.R. Nationalism is a powerful force which Mao and Castro exploit, but they exploit it in the interest of a larger cause. Thus for the moment the Communist movement tends more toward fragmentation into rival messianisms or autonomous groupings than toward a pure and simple return to the nationalist tradition of the nineteenth century. Is this a "sign of the times," or is it one more step on an inexorably downward staircase? One cannot say.

On the other hand, we may pause to ask ourselves what national Communist states would be like. To take the two most imposing examples, China and Russia, the idea of these enormous entities—animated by a powerful national will, out to "say something new to the world" (like Dostoevski) or to "teach respect to those barbarians of the West"—inspires a certain dread. National communist or National-Communist (not to say National-Socialist) states would perhaps produce a turbulence still greater than that which they have caused as bearers of an idea, questionable though it may be, but which does at least conform to certain rational standards.

And so here we are back at the beginning. Between pure revolutionary expansion, the supreme form of proletarian internationalism, and pure and simple acceptance of other states—between the primacy of class and that of nation—the experience of the last fifty years shows that many intermediate forms are possible. The one assumed by the Leninist movement after 1917, the revolutionary state with a messianic calling, is today in collision with rival messianisms. But several messianisms, by their very existence, ruin the messianic idea itself. Many unexpected episodes are possible in the process, however. Our understanding is still very poor of the relationships that arise between a political idea of universal character and the political forces claiming to embody it. Do political ideas spread by means of movements which monopolize them and are thus led to try to impose on others their versions of them? Do not political ideas find more favorable ground in free competition with one another? A necessary quality of ideas being their free circulation, do they not gain by breaking out of the matrix of party and state? Does not a politics founded on reason presume inter- or supra-national institutions that preclude both the state as an absolute sovereign entity and the freezing of movements into fanatical pseudo- or anti-churches?

Instead of answering these questions, which merit no doubt research and development, let us simply observe that any reflection on the subject of proletarian internationalism almost inevitably leads to thoughts about internationalism in general. All those hoping that the great phenomena unfolding in the East will proceed with a minimum of disturbance and calamity would do well to ponder the concomitant evolution of the non-Communist world. If little by little the latter could orient itself toward international institutions, first regional but with a broader potential, thus assuring a balance more stable than hitherto between desirable unity and necessary diversity, this movement in the long run would probably have profound effects not only in the West but in the East too.

The problem is not one of going back to the days of Theodore Roosevelt or Raymond Poincaré nor of confining ourselves to a choice between Lenin and Wilson. Are not human societies capable of going farther, of rising above the selfishness of Poincaré, the juridic pedantry of Wilson, the fanaticism of Lenin? They might orient themselves toward *organizing international relationships.* The organization would be based upon the real, upon nations. It would not ignore the goal: an end to traditional or ideological rivalries; mutual understanding, founded at worst on awareness of the common peril in any total war, at best on the notion of a human family existing above nations and ideologies. We are still very far from that goal. The experience of the past, particularly with proletarian internationalism, may enable us to grasp a simple truth (but not an easy one to practice): If internationalism is to benefit all, it cannot be the privilege of any one.

MILITARY THEORY AND PRACTICE

Raymond L. Garthoff

The Bolshevik conception of politics assumed unremitting conflict until complete victory. The successful seizure of power in Russia in 1917 was seen by the Bolshevik leaders as a great and incomparable achievement—but also as only a step in a continuing global struggle of the proletariat against the ruling capitalist class. The entire world-system of states—the "state" itself (an administrative tool of ruling classes)—was expected to be swept away by the triumph of the Revolution throughout the world. And this triumph was considered imminent, once the process had begun with the success of the Revolution in Russia. Hence the Bolsheviks assumed all traditional state attributes, and inter-state relations, to be obsolete and soon irrelevant. The fundamental fallacy of this image of history has never been faced by the Bolsheviks or their contemporary Communist heirs. But the need for adjustment of early expectations to reality was gradually recognized. Although the objectives of the new Bolshevik leaders of Russia were universal, they soon found themselves compelled to accept the constraints of a national state, both internally and in terms of the international order.[1]

The leaders of Soviet Russia had, moreover, to realize that while the "imperialist" war had made possible the overthrow of the old order in Russia, it was a live legacy threatening their own continued existence. From the very outset, the Bolshevik leaders had to accept the interdependence of internal and international political relationships, to face political realities defying ideological expectations (though *not* beyond ideological rationalization), and to deal with traditional international military confrontation.

The principal, immediate Bolshevik aim was ensuring the survival of the revolutionary base in Russia. This required military power to put down increasing armed opposition, and both military power and political action (since their military power alone was quickly demonstrated to be insufficient) to counter German pressure. The Germans were quite prepared—indeed, anxious—to sign a peace treaty with Russia, but only on the terms of a victor. The Bolshevik leaders were disoriented and divided on grounds of principle, since signing a treaty would mean "recognizing" and dealing with an "imperialist" power, and on more practical grounds as well, since the treaty would mean giving up vast, rich portions of the Russian patrimony. Lenin favored realistic expediency; he realized that peace was imperative to preserve the revolutionary base. But Lenin at first was unable to bring a majority of his colleagues to agree, one of the very few occasions that his leadership was not effective; most of the Bolshevik leaders favored a call for "revolutionary war" which they believed would galvanize German workers and soldiers into overthrowing their government. A compromise proposed by Trotsky, "no war—no peace," was at first decided upon. The German negotiators at Brest-Litovsk were indeed dumbfounded, but German troops merely resumed their advance, and the Soviet Government finally had to accept even more onerous peace terms. As Lenin said openly at the time, the Bolsheviks had no intention of abiding by the treaty any longer than they had to, but two lessons were clear: first, until the World Revolution succeeded, the Bolsheviks had to operate as leaders of a state in an international system of states; and second, defensive military power was a key and necessary element to prevent the destruction of the sole "Socialist" state by the surrounding capitalist states.

The Bolshevik seizure of power was a coup d'état rather than a "revolution." It succeeded not because the Bolsheviks were strong, militarily or politically, but because the Provisional Government and all other aspirants to power were even weaker. While the Bolsheviks had been very active in both propaganda and subversion, their preparations for waging armed conflict had not been extensive. Moreover, Marx, Engels, Lenin, and other Marxist theoreticians had devoted their attention almost exclusively to critical analyses of capitalism and its institutions rather than to the problems of organizing the state—and the armed forces—under socialism. Hence neither in theory nor practice were the Bolsheviks prepared to organize and use military power.

In the absence of any realistic alternative, the Soviet Government accepted the Peace of Brest-Litovsk with Imperial Germany. But while the Bolsheviks had seized nominal power with little difficulty, within a few months opposing "white" and regionally separatist armies began to take the field, and for the next three years the main efforts of the Soviet regime were focused on defeating opponents in the Civil War. The principal White Armies received assistance in men and materiel from the Entente Powers, particularly Great Britain, France, and the United States, and in the Far East Japan. Some other opposing forces were for a time assisted by the Germans. Because of general war weariness, foreign intervention was not pressed vigorously, but it reinforced the lesson taught by the Germans early in 1918—that the Soviet state needed military power to defend itself against foreign threats. This experience reinforced ideological presuppositions on the hostility of capitalist states. Conversely, the failure of foreign intervention gave some Bolshevik leaders an exaggerated idea of the effectiveness of their propaganda abroad.

While survival was perforce uppermost in the minds of the Bolshevik leaders in the first few years after seizing power, they nevertheless made every effort to extend the Revolution throughout the world. Indeed, initially the two were believed to be inseparable: From 1917 to 1919, at least, probably no Bolshevik leader (except possibly Lenin) thought that Communist rule could survive in Russia if the Revolution were defeated in Germany and elsewhere. The Marxist classics had all presumed the indivisibility of the Revolution on class, not national, lines. The Brest-Litovsk Treaty and the whole idea of temporary "coexistence" with capitalist states had to be rationalized as transitory phenomena, tactical concessions compelled by the given relation of forces, but not the basis for the prolonged existence of a single socialist state. It would have been considered serious deviation if not indeed ideological treason, to have been so perspicacious as to have foreseen half a century of coexistence, or acceptance of peaceful coexistence as the Party's general line.

As Marxists, the Bolsheviks expected the Revolution to arise naturally from the conditions of capitalism. Germany, with its developed proletariat, had produced the leading socialist theoreticians and the largest socialist party. Apart from having their hands full at home, the Russian socialists thought they would have to do no more than lend a secondary helping hand to their German comrades. This, of course, they tried to do. At Brest-Litovsk the Russian delegation actively engaged in agitation and propaganda among the German soldiers to the consternation of the German command. And subsequently, the first Soviet diplomatic mission abroad, in Berlin in 1918, was so actively and openly involved in spreading subversive propaganda that it was sent packing by the Germans in less than a year.

Groping their way through unanticipated situations, the Bolsheviks had no clear guidelines on how their developing military power might aid the Revolution abroad. Although they were disposed to use all of their resources to that end, expediency was the real guide. The conflicts in Finland, Estonia, Latvia, the Ukraine, and the Transcaucasus in 1918 and 1919 were practically indistinguishable from the Civil War in Russia proper. But the year 1919 marked a turning point from near-defeat to near-victory for the Bolsheviks in Russia, and from near-victory to complete defeat for the Communists in Central Europe. Barely prevailing in the heart of Russia itself, the Bolsheviks were in no position to give military or any other aid to the Spartacist revolt in northern Germany, or the Soviet Republic briefly established in Bavaria, in 1919. In the case of the short-lived regime of Bela Kun in Hungary, the Commander-in-Chief of the Red Army in Moscow did order "direct, intimate contact with the Soviet armies of Hungary," [2] but a serious turn in the civil war at home prevented the move, and the defeat of the Hungarian Communist regime rendered the whole question of Russian aid academic by the time the Bolsheviks had emerged victorious in the central Ukraine. In October of that same year, Lenin prevailed in divided Bolshevik counsels in deciding not to follow the defeated White army of General Yudenich into newly independent Estonia.[3]

The key decision on the role of the new Red Army in spreading Soviet rule was taken in 1920. The Poles, now independent, had intervened in the Ukraine, but had been defeated there. Although the White army of General Baron Wrangel was still a threat in the Crimea, the Bolshevik leaders recognized that the question of expanding their successful counteroffensive into an invasion of Poland involved broader questions. Again the leaders were divided on the issue, and even Trotsky (who, for example, had earlier advocated moving into Estonia) opposed an advance into Poland. But Lenin and the majority decided to advance and transplant a Polish Communist government from Russia. While the causes for the subsequent failure were mixed, and included Stalin's and Budenny's insubordination and French support of the Poles, Lenin recognized that the fundamental one was the unreadiness of the Polish people, and that revolution could not be exported.[4] He later told Trotsky that Soviet troops should "never again" be used directly to aid a revolution abroad.[5]

In 1920 and 1921, the Civil War was won, and in its wake the Red Army did assist in taking the Transcaucasus.[6] A "Soviet Republic of Gilan" was even established in northern Persia, beyond the borders of the old Russian empire, and supplied with arms and military advisers. But in a 1921 treaty with Persia Moscow agreed to withdraw its support, and the "republic" quickly collapsed.[7] Satellites were also created in 1921 in Outer Mongolia and Tannu Tuva. These areas had never been part of the tsarist empire, but they had been Russian protectorates from 1912 to 1917, and Soviet forces intervened against a White Russian warlord, Baron von Ungern-Sternberg, who had delusions of reconstituting a mighty Mongol empire including portions of Siberia. Once drawn into a political vacuum in defense of their own territories, the Bolsheviks used the opportunity to extend Red rule.[8]

Meanwhile, although the Civil War had been won (apart from lingering guerrilla warfare by the Central Asian Basmachi), two new internal threats required vigorous military measures: a peasant uprising centered on Tambov province in 1920–21, and a naval mutiny at Kronstadt in 1921. Here the enemies were not led by hostile class elements nor supported by foreign powers; the sailors of Kronstadt had been a key pillar of the Revolution, and now were rebelling in its name. The flower of the Communist Party in the armed forces was mobilized into special shock units to take Kronstadt,[9] while seasoned troops from distant areas were brought to Tambov to bolster security police in ruthlessly suppressing the peasant rebellion.[10]

Thus the Bolshevik revolutionaries in power found that they required some of the institutions of traditional states, including armed forces, in order to maintain external and even internal security. At the same time, they concluded that attempts to extend socialist rule by "exporting revolution" on Red Army bayonets could endanger their new-found state interests and the interests of Socialism (they still do not distinguish between the two). The Communists thus had to accept the armed forces as a subordinate, though essential, element in preserving the socialist base of the Revolution in Russia during the temporary period of coexistence until the World Revolution should prevail.

FORGING THE RED ARMY

At the time of the Bolshevik seizure of power, the Party commanded only a motley force of a few thousand armed men scarcely organized in any fashion. It had slogans, élan, sympathizers, arms, above all it had a disciplined Party machine with Lenin at its head—but it did not have an army. Virtually the whole Bolshevik effort prior to October 1917 had been devoted to speeding the disintegration of the old Russian army. Some two months after the Petrograd coup d'état, the "Workers' and Peasants' Red Army" (hereafter, as usual in Soviet writings, termed simply "the Red Army") was formally created by a decree of January 28, 1918. A veteran Bolshevik military leader of that period has recently stated that the total armed forces at that time only amounted to about 50,000 men.[11] The official "birthday" of the Soviet Armed Forces, however, is February 23, 1918 when the fledgling Red Army is said to have been victorious in an engagement with German forces near Pskov. (The actual facts of this alleged engagement are obscure, as even some debunking Soviet scholars have been bold enough to note, but this is of interest only because it underlines the role of historical myths in Soviet historiography and propaganda and a slightly freer opportunity lately to relate history to facts.)[12]

The new Red Army was initially recruited entirely on a voluntary basis, and although many Bolsheviks entered military service, many others were required for other duties too (on January 1, 1918, there were only 115,000 members of the Party). As the Civil War began to unfold, general conscription was introduced on May 29, 1918;[13] the Red Army grew, until by late 1920 it reached a peak of 5,300,000 men. Many of these had served in the old army, indeed, according to official Soviet statistics, some 314,180 officers, non-commissioned officers, and rated medical personnel including 48,409 commissioned officers up through the rank of general. Moreover, 10,339 civil servants of the old Ministry of War were absorbed, as were the major part of the General Staff and military academies.[14] The Party leaders were divided over the wisdom of relying so extensively on officers of the prerevolutionary army, but Lenin and Trotsky (then People's Commissar of War) fully appreciated the need to make use of the expertise of these "military specialists," as they were termed. At the same time, in addition to constantly screening them, political officers or "military commissars," usually Party members, were introduced in 1918 to control the regular officers, particularly those drawn from the old army.

A controversy also developed over whether the new army should be a "regular army" more or less on the pattern of discipline, command, and career of other armies, or whether an entirely new form of army, proletarian, closer to the people, could develop. In practice, the degree of discipline and "regularity" within the Red Army varied greatly, ranging from guerrilla cavalry bands living off the land (and sometimes antagonizing the local population) to highly disciplined regular units. Naturally, differing personal experience and career had a great deal to do with diverging opinions on the general question.

It is unnecessary for the purposes of this analysis to review the course of the Civil War. The Red Army emerged victorious because it had a central position, a coordinated command, a crucial modicum of popular support, a number of talented military leaders, and a cohesive and determined political leadership. The White Armies were divided geographically and otherwise, poorly coordinated, politically nondescript and therefore subject to being tarnished with the sins of the old order and of their foreign support, and, despite probably richer overall military experience and some very able generals, without cohesive political direction.[15] In their unanticipated dual role as representatives of an international revolutionary movement and rulers of a state, the Bolshevik leaders combined appeals to Russian patriotism with calls for proletarian internationalism. A number of "international detachments" of Germans, Poles, Chinese, and many other nationalities fought as "ideological mercenaries,"[16] while among the former imperial officers who served the new regime, many, like General Brusilov, saw it simply as the new Russian government, no matter how different its ideology.

After the Civil War the swollen Red Army was no longer needed, and the difficult problems of internal reconstruction cried out for the resources, manpower, and leadership previously required for the conduct of the war. There does not appear to have been any objection to a drastic reduction of the regular army to about 500,000 men (ten per cent of peak strength, but there were sharp disputes over doctrine and organization. Proponents of a unique "proletarian military doctrine" and a militia lost to the concept of a "unified military doctrine" based essentially on traditional military science, although with emphasis on experience in the Civil War, and to the idea of a regular army and supplementary militia. (Incongruously, a former Imperial Guards officer and nobleman, Mikhail Tukhachevsky, called for a general staff and standing military forces for the Communist International, apart from the Red Army of Russia.[17] But this proposal attracted no serious support, and even the existing "international detachments" were dissolved.)

SOCIALISM IN ONE COUNTRY

By the close of the Civil War or shortly thereafter, the Soviet leaders had come to realize that the "world revolution" was not coming soon and that temporary coexistence would continue indefinitely (not permanently but for a prolonged period). The chief task of Soviet diplomacy was seen as avoiding a clash with the capitalist states and, above all, preventing a coalition against Soviet Russia. Although leaders in Moscow considered the interests of the Revolution, of Communism, in the rest of the world dependent on the fortunes of the one socialist state, this very consideration forbad Soviet military involvement—with attendant risks to the Soviet state—in attempts to extend the Revolution elsewhere.

The attention of the leadership from the early twenties on was turned inward, to economic and political consolidation at home. In December 1922, the Union of Soviet Socialist Republics was established. The New Economic Policy from 1921 until 1928 allowed the economic rehabilitation of the country. In this same spirit, the Red Army also underwent reforms, particularly in 1924–25, placing it on an appropriate basis for the long pull. By 1924 the regular armed forces numbered 560,000 men (about half of the pre-World War I Russian Army strength), a level maintained for the next decade. Modernization of the ground forces, more slowly of the air arm, and most slowly of all of the navy, proceeded in step with the gradual industrialization of the country, particularly during the 1930's. After 1933, with the rise of Nazi Germany and the general increase of tension in Europe, the Red Army was gradually built up, to 1,513,000 men in 1938 and 4,207,000 by June 1941.[18]

One interesting development during the 1920's and early 1930's was extensive cooperation between Reichswehr and Red Army in circumventing Allied controls on Germany and building Soviet military technology and weapons production facilities. German assistance was given in production of tanks, aircraft, and munitions (and abortively poison gas); several German military training centers were established in Russia, and a number of Soviet officers studied in Germany.[19] Ironically, this clandestine military cooperation paralleled the last-gasp efforts of the Bolshevik leaders—acting as leaders of the Comintern—to spark a revolution in Germany itself. Several hundred Red Army officers were secretly sent as advisors to the German Communists, and in 1923 a poorly coordinated Communist uprising in Hamburg was quickly suppressed by the Reichswehr, at that very time receiving munitions from the Soviet Union under the secret military cooperation agreements.[20] The utter failure of this, the third Communist revolt in Germany, also marked the last attempt to stir up the Revolution in the West.

During the 1920's and 1930's it became an axiom of Soviet policy that war should be avoided as long as possible. Stalin outlined this policy in a speech to the Central Committee of the Communist Party in 1925 (not made public until 1947), declaring that the U.S.S.R. should avoid war or "enter last. And we must enter in order to throw the decisive weight onto the scales, the weight which can tip the scales." [21] During the 1920's and 1930's Soviet strategy was defensive, insofar as avoiding war was concerned. Eventually diplomatic maneuvers culminated in the Nazi-Soviet pact of August 1939 which allowed the Soviet Union to stand aside while the Axis and Allied Western powers went to war.

In the shadow of German victories, the Soviet leaders found their first opportunities in nearly two decades for direct territorial expansion. Military power was used for diplomatic pressure and then occupation in the Baltic States in 1939–40, for threatening Rumania and gaining Bessarabia and northern Bukovina in 1940, and for occupying eastern Poland after the defeat of that country by the Germans. Only in the case of Finland did unexpected refusal of Soviet demands lead to an undesired, unanticipated, and embarrassingly difficult war in the winter of 1939/40.[22] If Stalin believed that these moves bolstered the strategic defenses of the Soviet Union, he was wrong. The deeper defensive glacis led to committing the Red Army too far forward, virtually abandoning the former frontier defense line, involved the acquisition of substantial and largely hostile populations, and ensured that Finland and Rumania would join the Germans in their attack.

Meanwhile, the Red Army had been involved directly in several limited engagements in the Far East. In 1929 after the new local Manchurian warlord, Marshal Chang Hsueh-liang, adopted a pro-Nationalist (Kuomintang) and anti-Soviet posture, Red Army forces occupied part of Manchuria to prevent nationalization of the Soviet-owned Chinese Eastern Railway. Once the railway was secured, however, they withdrew. Japan entered the scene two years later, and in 1935 the Russians sold that vulnerable foreign asset to the Japanese puppet state of Manchukuo. From 1929 on, a semi-autonomous Special Far Eastern Army was maintained, and in the late 1930's several border incidents occurred between Soviet and Japanese troops. Large-scale engagements took place in 1938 at Changkufeng and in 1939 at Khalkin-gol' on the Mongolian border. It is not clear whether Soviet forces provoked the fighting in a successful effort to discourage any designs by the Japanese Army on eastern Siberia or whether the Japanese were probing to test Soviet reactions. In any case the Soviet forces were victorious.[23]

Although these were the only instances of direct employment of Soviet military forces during this period, Moscow supplied arms and advisors to several states. A beginning was made in northern Persia in 1921, but this was in support of a Communist dominated regime. The "prototype" case was the supply of arms, money, and military advisers to Kemal Ataturk in Turkey in 1921. Lenin himself decided on this ideologically controversial scheme of aiding non-Communists (over Trotsky's objection, but with Stalin in support of the idea).[24] No attempt was made to subvert the new Turkish movement which soon succeeded and remained grateful to Moscow although it suppressed local Communists ruthlessly. The new tactic proved more effective in serving Soviet interests than the attempt to export Communist revolution.

The most ambitious assistance was furnished to non-Communists in China. An intimate relationship was established with the revolutionary but non-Communist Kuomintang. Sun Yat-sen sent his Chief of Staff, General Chiang Kai-shek, to Moscow in 1923 to arrange for military assistance and advisers. These advisers, including "General Galen" (later Marshal of the Soviet Union Blücher), played a considerable role in instruction and operational planning and also created a system of political officers. In 1927, however Chiang suppressed the Communist and left-wing elements in the Kuomintang, and the Soviets withdrew their advisers.[25] Parallel but separate Soviet aid was given to two Chinese warlords in the north, Generals Feng Yu-hsiang and Kuo Sun-lin, but these ventures also ended in failure for the Russians. (General Kuo requested Soviet troops in 1925, but Moscow wisely decided against that course as unduly risky.) On the periphery of China, however, the Russians achieved better results—for a time. Secret agreements with two successive Chinese warlord governors of Sinkiang, Chin Shu-jin and General Sheng Shih-ts'ai, made that province virtually a Russian protectorate from 1931 until 1943. Advisers and arms were provided, and in 1934 and 1937 Soviet military forces were called in for direct support against rival warlords; one Soviet regiment of police troops, in Chinese uniforms, remained at Hami in eastern Sinkiang from 1937 to 1943. But in 1942 General Sheng (who had become a clandestine member of the Soviet Communist Party) thought the Russians would be defeated by the Germans; he expelled the advisers and executed a number of local Chinese Communists including Mao Tse-tung's brother, Mao Tse-min.[26]

During two important conflicts in the late 1930's, Moscow provided arms, advisers, and even "volunteers." About 2,000 Red Army advisers and specialists aided the Loyalists (and tested new weapons and tactics) in the Spanish Civil War of 1936–39. The Comintern also acted as a recruiting network for the International Brigades which many Western Communists (but no Russians) entered. Soviet and Comintern agents mobilized "anti-Fascists" everywhere, purged rival leftists, and sought to control the whole Loyalist government.

They succeeded in their infiltration, subversion, and propaganda—but the Loyalists lost the war.[27]

Although Chiang had turned on the Communists in 1927, the U.S.S.R. resumed diplomatic relations with China after the Japanese occupation of Manchuria in 1931. In the following years, Soviet diplomats in China seized every opportunity to urge resistance to Japanese aggression. Shortly after hostilities finally broke out between Japan and the Chinese central government in 1937, Soviet Foreign Commissar Litvinov had a long conversation with Leon Blum, the French Socialist leader: His government, said Litvinov, was

> perfectly delighted that Japan had attacked China. He believed that Japan would be so weakened financially and economically and would have such enormous difficulty in digesting a conquered China that the Soviet Union was now completely assured of peace in the Far East for many years to come. Litvinov had added that the Soviet Union hoped that war between China and Japan would continue just as long as possible and would result in an attempt by the Japanese to swallow just as much of China as possible. . . . Litvinov had said that whereas before the Japanese attack on China, Japan had been most hostile and aggravating, today the Japanese were all politeness and butter in their relations with the Soviet Government.

To help keep the Japanese tied down in China as long as possible, Moscow gave the Chinese Nationalists a credit of $250 million and about 1,000 aircraft and also sent some 2,000 "volunteer" airmen. Thus, despite the earlier Nationalist anti-Communist campaigns, after 1937 Moscow was more concerned to prevent Japanese domination of China and the Far East than it was to see the Chinese Communists win. Soviet assistance continued until June, 1941, when the Russians could no longer afford it.[28]

Although of interest these few direct and indirect uses of military power underline the peripheral and relatively unimportant role of military policy in the Soviet Union over the formative decades from 1921 to 1941. Similarly, military leaders played little part in Soviet policy-making during this period. The Red Army was neither favored nor neglected relative to other institutions of the Soviet state. It was, necessarily, starved in the 1920's and gradually developed and built up in the 1930's as resources, and the need, grew.[29]

The officer corps developed into a highly professional but politically indoctrinated cadre. Nevertheless the prerevolutionary professional officers long retained an important role. They reportedly constituted 76 per cent of the total officer corps in 1918, and still accounted for 10 per cent by 1930.[30] As early as 1921, in the initial reductions in force, of 37,954 officers who were released from service, a surprising 14,390 had at one time served in the *White* armies.[31] While the numbers of officers from the Imperial Army declined fairly rapidly, those who remained were for the most part highly placed and very influential. A survey in 1929 showed that 80 per cent of all military writers were former Imperial Army officers, one-third of them former colonels or generals. And of the one hundred contributors to the 1929 *Field Service Regulations,* seventy-nine had been officers in the old army.[32]

A roughly parallel process was the increasing proportion of the officer corps with membership in the Communist Party. As late as 1924, only 32 per cent were affiliated with the Party; by 1928, some 65 per cent were members.[33] This rapid rise in Party affiliation, however, was due more to application for membership by career officers than to any change in the composition of the officer corps. As late as 1926, "higher officers" (i.e., generals) were 7.3 per cent of worker origin, 31.2 per cent peasants, and 61.5 per cent "others." [34] Similarly, while the number of Party members at the elite Zhukovsky Air Academy more than doubled, from 35 percent in 1922 to 77 per cent in 1927, the proportion of those of "worker and peasant" origin only rose from 40 to 50 per cent.[35] The Soviet regime did not, of course, rely upon Party membership to provide Party control. The "military commissars" introduced as an expedient in 1918 (in fact, derived from the Provisional Government) were retained as "deputy commanders for political affairs."

The new professional officer corps was stabilized during the period of Tukhachevsky's rise from 1931 to 1937. Gradually traditional privileges were conferred. In 1935 the old ranks were restored, except for general officer grades which also reappeared in 1940, and even the rather imperial-sounding grade of "Marshal of the Soviet Union" was established. Good pay and other special prerequisites were also granted the new officer corps. But then in 1937 the political purge struck. The military was not singled out, it was simply not spared the terror which Stalin visited upon all major institutions and above all on Party members. The percentage of Party and Komsomol affiliates in the armed forces as a whole was no higher in 1939 than it had been in 1931, about 50 per cent, whereas in 1933 it had stood at 60 per cent.[36] Old Bolsheviks in the army were harder hit than former Imperial Army officers. But the senior levels, regardless of origin, were virtually wiped out: 3 of the 5 marshals, 13 of the 15 with the rank of army commander, 57 of 85 corps commanders, and 110 of the 195 men of division-commander rank. In all, up to half of the entire officer corps were adversely affected.[37] On the other hand, the other half advanced rapidly, sometimes replacing "dead wood" among senior ranks, but in general at some cost to the professional competence of the corps.

The buildup of the armed forces moved ahead notwithstanding the Great Purge. The last of the territorial militia were fully integrated into the regular army by 1939.[38] Modern aircraft and tanks were being produced in large numbers in the late 1930's, and the army was acquiring both new technology and new professional expertise. Military doctrine emphasized a unified, combined-arms approach centered on the infantry.[39] In line with the lessons of the Spanish Civil War and the repulse of the Japanese in Mongolia, tank and mechanized forces were assigned to direct support of the infantry, as were artillery and the air force. A passing interest in long-range heavy bombers in 1935–37 had been dropped by the late thirties, partly as an incidental consequence of the purge of its few major enthusiasts in the air force and partly because of failure to develop a satisfactory successor to the slow four-engine bombers of the mid-1930's. A major naval building program began in 1938, stressing submarines and intended to provide battleships as well as heavy cruisers by the mid-1940's, but Stalin vetoed the proposal of Admiral Kuznetsov, the People's Commissar of the Navy, for aircraft carriers.[40] In general, air and naval power was designed to support the ground forces.

By the beginning of the 1940's, Russia had returned to the European scene as one of the four major powers, with commensurate military power (despite the poor showing in the Finnish "Winter War") to support its diplomatic role. Stalin had successfully maneuvered "to enter last." He had reached an agreement not only with Hitler in the west, but also Tojo in the east. The capitalists were at one another's throats. Stalin expected at least one more year of peace for completing his tank, aircraft, and certain naval programs. Then something went wrong: The German Army struck on June 22, 1941.

THE TRIAL BY FIRE

The German attack was highly successful, but the campaign failed because Hitler and his generals had underestimated the sheer size of the Soviet military machine and the logistic and other requirements for the attacking forces as well. One of the cardinal issues not yet resolved in Soviet historiography is the responsibility for the initial

German success. Since the issue is so intimately tied up with judgments regarding the high command, Stalin's personal role, and ultimately the political system itself, it will probably continue to be a bone of political controversy. But it is clear that the Soviet Union was caught badly by surprise, both politically and militarily, if not with respect to Hitler's ultimate intentions, at least with respect to an attack in the summer of 1941.

The German-Soviet campaign revealed to the Russians (Stalin, the military, and the man in the street) that their vaunted and massive armed forces could be largely destroyed and that a numerically inferior invader could advance to the gates of Leningrad, the suburbs of Moscow, and the banks of the Volga. And to the bitter surprise of the Germans (and also to the surprise of most disinterested Western soldiers), notwithstanding the scope of their victories—beyond any known in modern times—the enemy did not collapse either politically or militarily; after absorbing the crushing blows of 1941 and 1942, the Red Army was capable in 1944 and 1945 of driving back to Berlin. Despite the pride of the Russians in their victory, and one-sided historical credit to themselves alone, Soviet political and military leaders remember how near they came to defeat, despite having built up what then was the largest military force in the world. They are, therefore, fearful of possible enemy attack, disinclined to overestimate their own military strength, and determined to avoid another total war.

There is no need to recount here in detail the causes of the initial Soviet reverses, or of their subsequent stubborn defense and shift to the counteroffensive.[41] It is, perhaps, worth noting that the Red Army certainly did not fight more effectively because of socialism or "proletarian internationalism"; on the other hand, the large-scale surrenders of 1941 and 1942 were not due primarily to political disaffection but to military collapse. What did inspire the Soviet soldier to fight, and to fight well, was patriotism in defense of his homeland, and Stalin and the other Soviet leaders understood this well. Accordingly, for example, the army was given medals for valor named for eminent pre-revolutionary military commanders, officers again wore golden epaulettes, elite guards units were formed, and political officers were resubordinated to commanders after 1942. A number of young and very capable officers rapidly rose to top staff and command positions; most of the senior army and army-group commanders were in their early forties. Also, the war brought these professional soldiers into closer contact, under circumstances not disadvantageous to the military, with leading political figures who were involved either in managing the war effort from Moscow (such as Malenkov, Mikoyan, and Kosygin) or as senior political officers with the armed forces (such as "Generals" Khrushchev and Brezhnev).

The first three and a half years of the "Great Fatherland War of the Soviet Union" were required to check the invader's advance and expel him from the country, but even then the new alliance with the Western Allies and the prospect of the complete defeat of the Axis powers opened possibilities for postwar political gains by the U.S.S.R., and Stalin never lost sight of this. The Soviet leaders later subordinated purely military considerations, such as calculation of casualties, to such political objectives as liberating Berlin, Vienna, and Prague before the Western Allies (who were less aware of the political significance of these actions in the postwar world). Soviet-created Polish and Czech units accompanied the Red Army into their homelands and provided much of the cadre for later Communist seizures of power. (Conversely, Stalin deliberately permitted the rival Polish Home Army to be slaughtered in Warsaw by the Germans without any attempt at assistance by General Chuikov's army just across the Vistula, and even denied the Western Powers the chance to air-drop supplies to the Poles.) Finally, aware of the imminent Japanese surrender, the Soviet leaders hastily entered the war in the Far East after the first American atomic bomb had been dropped, and thus gained their minimum political and territorial objectives in the Far East.[42]

THE AFTERMATH OF WORLD WAR II

As the war ended, the Red Army was at peak strength—some 11,365,000 men in about 550 "divisions"—but it also was scraping the manpower barrel and had exceeded its logistic and general military capacity for combat against any but an equally exhausted and decimated opponent.[43] Indeed the whole Soviet Union badly needed peace and recuperation. Despite this temporary weakness, the Soviet Union emerged from the war with its defensive position greatly enhanced by the complete defeat of the two great rival powers to the west and east, and with opportunities to determine the destiny of a number of lesser neighboring states then under Soviet military occupation. The U.S.S.R. could, however, only exploit such opportunities short of risking a clash with the Western powers—or, to be more precise, with the United States.

As one consequence of the war, the Soviet Union consolidated and even extended the prewar territorial gains in Eastern Europe, acquiring a little more of Finland and Poland, the Carpatho-Ukraine from Czechoslovakia, and the northern half of East Prussia. The Red Army only reluctantly withdrew from northern Norway and from the Danish island of Bornholm. Withdrawal from northern Iran, where again (as in 1921) an effort was made to create a new independent satellite in the northwestern province of Azerbaijan, was forced in March, 1946 only by strong pressure from the United States, acting both in the new United Nations organization and directly.

In the Far East, even before the war had ended and without a ripple of world attention, Tannu Tuva, a protectorate since 1921, was formally annexed by the U.S.S.R. in 1944. By wartime agreement with the Western Allies, the Russians regained the former Russian territories of southern Sakhalin and the northern Kuril islands, and the southern Kurils too, which had never been Russian. Outer Mongolia, a Soviet dependency since 1921, was (in August, 1945) reluctantly admitted by the Chinese Nationalist Government in Nanking to be independent of China. Finally, the U.S.S.R. received a lease on the Chinese Eastern Railway and on the former Russian naval base at Port Arthur in Manchuria.[44] But the Russians did not attempt to establish satellites in Manchuria or Inner Mongolia during their year's occupation as they subsequently did in northern Korea.

Occupation of the major part of Central and Eastern Europe offered still wider opportunities. Soviet military occupation was the key factor allowing the gradual Communist take-over and consolidation of power in Poland, Hungary, Rumania, and Bulgaria during 1946 and 1947, and the later formation of a puppet regime in East Germany. Although the Red Army left Czechoslovakia in late 1945, its shadow (and the contrasting absence of a strong Western military presence plus memories of Munich) played a role in the success of the Communist coup d'état in Prague in February 1948. In Finland, which the Red Army did not occupy, a similar coup on the Czech model was prepared for about the same time, but failed when a key Communist who had been installed as Minister of the Interior proved to be more a Finn than a Communist and disclosed the plot.[45] In Yugoslavia and Albania, the wartime indigenous Communist-led partisan movements established themselves in power. In Greece, indigenous Communist guerrillas attempted unsuccessfully to seize power in a four-year civil war. In Austria during their ten year occupation, the Russians could not establish a Communist regime in their occupation zone without risking a new *Anschluss* of the Western zones with West Germany.

In areas never occupied by the Red Army, efforts to extend Soviet power were few, cautious, and invariably unsuccessful. Strong diplomatic pressure was levied on Turkey to surrender the formerly Russian provinces of Kars and Ardahan, and less directly for shared control over the Straits, but to no avail. Active seizure of power by subversion was not attempted in Western Europe, and in the late 1940's attempts by local Communists in many other areas—e.g., Burma, Indonesia, the Philippines, South Korea, and Malaya—failed without the U.S.S.R. raising a finger to help. Only in China, against Stalin's advice, and to some extent in Indo-China (where the Communists had assumed leadership over much of the nationalist movement), did success follow—without Soviet assistance.

Moscow exerted direct pressure in the Berlin blockade in 1948–49, but stopped short of military action. Only in Korea in 1950 did Stalin resort to military action, and then by proxy rather than the use of Soviet armed forces, and only after he had concluded that the United States would not intercede militarily to defend South Korea. The unexpected American response was met by Chinese Communist forces without commitment of the Soviet Union to the conflict. As in Berlin, the Communists failed to achieve their objectives and settled for the *status quo ante*.

The fundamental strategic fact of the postwar period for Moscow was the unfavorable geostrategic situation of the Soviet Union vis-à-vis the United States. The modest gains noted above were crumbs left over from the Soviet wartime counteroffensive. Even though the Western powers had speedily demobilized their greater military power, and did not attempt to roll-back the Communist gains, the Soviet Union could neither threaten the United States nor avoid being under a potential American atomic threat. Other political, economic, geographical, and technological considerations favored the United States in all of the world beyond the "socialist camp." All this reinforced Stalin's caution with respect to foreign policy. What did it mean for the development of the Soviet armed forces?

The absence of immediate military threats permitted priority to be given to economic rehabilitation of the country. As after the Civil War, the swollen military machine was sharply cut back in size, from 11,365,000 men in 1945 to 2,874,000 in 1948,[46] and gradually modernized. In addition to general modernization of traditional armaments, a long-range air force with World War II-style bombers (copied from four American B-29A's, which had made a forced landing in Siberia in 1944) was rapidly built up in the late 1940's. A large-scale conventional submarine construction program was also launched. Research and development for advanced weapons systems led to the first atomic bomb test in September, 1949.

The "Workers and Peasants Red Army" was even given a new

name in 1946, the Soviet Army and Navy, titles more in keeping with the development from the revolutionary army of a civil war to the national armed forces of a mature state. This change paralleled a de-revolutionization of other institutions: "Peoples' Commissariats" became traditional European (including Russian) "Ministries." Hence the Ministry of Defense administered the Soviet Army and Navy (the latter briefly having an independent ministerial status from 1950 to 1953, as it had during the war).

The army ground forces remained dominant in the military establishment and the high command despite the increased importance of the offensive bomber force, strategic air defense, and the submarine fleet. During the Korean War, the army was built up to 175 divisions, and reequipped with modern arms, and the air force was built up too; by the time of Stalin's death in 1953 the armed forces totalled some 5,763,000 men.[47]

Soviet military doctrine, however, continued for a number of years virtually unchanged; military thought was stagnant. During the war, doctrine had been modified in particulars, but it remained on the whole cast in the traditional prewar mold. By 1953 military doctrine was little more than the doctrine of 1945; Stalin preferred it to remain a mere elaboration of the formulas which had emerged under his nominal leadership in the "Great Fatherland War." A misguided and intensive censorship led to a virtual silence on military writings and thinking about the nature and implications of the new military technology born in the war: nuclear weapons, jet aviation, rockets, and the like. New weapons were being developed, but the arsenal of Soviet —or, as it increasingly came to be called, "Stalinist"—military doctrine was considered adequately stocked.[48] This situation was not as serious as it might otherwise have been only because of the virtually unchanged and single-minded role of the military in Soviet policy: defense in the unlikely case that an enemy should attack the Soviet Union, and garrisoning the new Soviet empire. The only *use* of Soviet military power had been the rather conservative one of remaining in many of the places occupied during the war and serving as a background to the political means used to acquire control over much of that territory.

THE NUCLEAR AGE

With the death of the autocrat Stalin, all other major Soviet institutions automatically increased in relative importance. Initially, the members of Stalin's old Politburo (that venerable body had been diluted and expanded into a Presidium in October, 1952) rallied together and divided among themselves the major executive and administrative functions. Nikolai A. Bulganin, a Marshal though essentially a political figure, was given the now consolidated Ministry of Defense, but his three "first deputies" were the key senior professionals: Marshals Georgy Zhukov and Aleksandr Vasilevsky and Admiral Nikolai Kuznetsov. With the drastic purge of Beria and the security police less than three months later, the military again by default gained in standing. But more generally, rivalry for power between factional political alliances over the next two years saw the governmental and economic bureaucracies, under Prime Minister Georgy M. Malenkov, opposing the Party machine led by First Secretary Nikita S. Khrushchev. In this contest, Khrushchev was supported by Bulganin, and moreover courted the military by criticizing both the modest military retrenchment undertaken by the economic rationalizer Malenkov, and the related turn by the latter toward mutual deterrence and peaceful coexistence. In an unusual argument between newspapers representing the competing factions, the military press of course supported the Khrushchev line on the dangers of war and the need for giving precedence to heavy industry (and defense industry) over consumer goods. In short, without seeking an independent political role, the military nonetheless became involved in a supporting role on the political stage.[49]

With the victory of the Khrushchev faction in February 1955 and Bulganin's designation as Prime Minister, Marshal Zhukov succeeded to the post of Minister of Defense. That same month, the military budget (which had been trimmed) was increased, and the next month saw the first series of belated high-level promotions of generals and marshals. Within a few months, however, despite Khrushchev's and Bulganin's rhetoric in the debates with Malenkov, the new government began to reduce the size of the ground forces, which still were at or near the Korean War peak. By 1959, the forces had been cut by about two million men, about the maximum without altering their basic framework as a combined ready force and mobilization base. At the same time, "peaceful coexistence" became the general line.

In May 1955, following the admission of the Federal Republic of Germany into N.A.T.O., Moscow created a multilateral military organization of the Communist states of Eastern Europe under the Warsaw Pact. The formal organization is modest, and it has been centered in Moscow, with the successive commanders-in-chief and chiefs of staff of the organization always Soviet marshals. The one occasion in the postwar period in which Soviet troops were called to battle came in the fall of 1956. Stirred up by precipitate de-Stalinization and the uncertain relaxation of controls within the Communist empire in Eastern Europe, popular dissatisfaction with an inept and repressive regime in Hungary erupted in October, 1956 in a successful popular revolution. Imre Nagy, the new Hungarian Prime Minister, was prepared to surrender control by the Communist Party and attempted to withdraw from the Warsaw Pact. Apparently the Soviet leaders decided that acceptance of such developments would lead to anti-Soviet uprisings and the overthrow of Communist regimes throughout Eastern Europe. Seven Soviet divisions crushed the revolution and Nagy government in November 1956.[50]

Coincident with Marshal Zhukov's rise to the Ministry, a renaissance of Soviet military thinking began. As we have noted, stagnation of such thought had marked the postwar Stalin years. The most important element in this revitalization of thought was the belated recognition of the significance of the continuing revolution in military technology. Beginning in 1954, the Soviet military leaders began a systematic effort to inform themselves and lower-ranking officers (and, on occasion, high political leaders too) of the nature and effects of new weapons and technical developments and their strategic and tactical potentialities. A debate on "the laws of military science" from late 1953 to 1955 in the secret General Staff journal *Military Thought* disclosed a lively interest in questions of military theory. In answer to the question whether "the laws of military science" apply equally to the armies of socialist and capitalist countries, the conclusion was that the same laws do apply, but Soviet leaders were superior in understanding and utilizing the objective laws. The main issue in the debate, however, was whether military science should limit itself to studying the "laws of war as armed conflict," or should also consider a whole complex of political-military questions. The conclusion was that military science should concern itself with the narrower range of problems, although of course accepting broader Marxist-Leninist views on war as a political-military process.

Soviet military doctrine has never been expressed in a list of "principles of war" similar to those usual in Western armies. There is, however, a partial equivalent. From 1942 until 1956 it was formulation by Stalin of "the permanently operating factors" which, he said, "decide the course and outcome of wars." These factors were contrasted with so-called transitory factors such as surprise or advance mobilization. After 1956 the stereotyped formulation of "permanently operating factors" was discarded, but not the "decisive" factors themselves.

Along with the unfreezing of doctrinal discussion, increased attention was paid to the importance of surprise in the nuclear and jet age. Early in 1955, it was recognized that under some conditions surprise could be decisive in a nuclear war. Even more important, at the same time the concept of preemptive action was developed in an attempt to deal with the fact, of which the Soviet military leaders now suddenly became acutely more conscious, that the Soviet Union was highly vulnerable to American nuclear striking power. This concept was not discussed in the open military press, but the discussions in *Military Thought* make clear that this idea was specifically distinguished from the idea of a preventive war. A preemptive strike was conceived as the last-hour seizure of the initiative to weaken an enemy's surprise attack. It meant forestalling an enemy's surprise attack, at a time basically of *his* choosing. At the same time, it was concluded that surprise by itself did not ensure victory even in the thermonuclear era. Unless countered by combat readiness and vigilance of the other side, surprise could be decisive; but against a prepared major power it could not succeed without superiority in the decisive political, military, and economic factors. "Blitzkrieg" was, therefore, specifically rejected as a feasible strategy for either side.

The doctrinal adjustments to the nuclear age in the early post-Stalin period did not question belief in a long war, requiring combined operations of all military components, waged in large-scale campaigns, over extended periods of time. Soviet military doctrine continued to stress campaigns in which victory would finally be won by destruction of the enemy's armed forces and the seizure and the occupation of his territory.[51] What occurred was essentially a readjustment of traditional doctrine to the nuclear age, rather than a reexamination of its bases. Marshal Zhukov supported an enrichment of military thought and substantial investment in further modernizing the military forces, but there was no basic recognition of the implications of a near future with almost unlimited quantities of nuclear and thermonuclear weapons and intercontinental missiles nor any questioning of the fundamental role of military power in such a world.

Meanwhile, advanced weaponry was becoming available as the fruit of the research and development program started by Stalin. Although the first Soviet nuclear device was tested in September 1949, the Soviet armed forces did not begin to get an operational inventory of atomic bombs until about the time of Stalin's death. In August 1953, however, the first Soviet thermonuclear test followed only by nine months the first U. S. test and actually preceded American testing of an air-delivered hydrogen bomb.

Similarly, in 1954 and 1955 medium and heavy jet-bombers began to enter service in the Soviet Long Range Air Force, not long after their counterparts had in the U. S. Air Force. In 1955 an integrated Air Defense Command was established, with anti-aircraft missiles as well as jet interceptors. Although the Soviet Navy launched a new program of modernization of smaller surface vessels and construction of advanced conventional and nuclear-powered submarines, the cruiser and medium-range submarine programs ended suddenly in 1955, and Admiral of the Fleet Kuznetsov was retired early in 1956. In August and October 1957, the first Soviet ICBM was test-fired and the first artificial satellite launched into orbit. These developments had tremendous impact although in military terms not for some time. October 1957 also witnessed another major development directly affecting the Soviet military. Marshal Zhukov was preemptorily removed, and a propaganda campaign reasserted the dominance of the Party over the military. What had happened?

"Politics," or the adjustment of differences with respect to power and policy, pervades Soviet affairs. Although internal political conflicts seldom erupt into the open, they are constantly active beneath the deceptively calm surface. The military as an interested institution, and its leaders as its representatives and as individuals, play a part in this political process. Ordinarily the military are concerned chiefly with getting their share of the available resources, but when political differences among others become sharp they (and the police, when they are powerful) have unique potential. The military had acquired increased importance in this period simply because of the change in the relationship and relative weight of other Soviet institutions.

Marshal Zhukov had strongly supported Khrushchev in June 1957 when various opponents of the First Secretary had joined in an effort to depose him. Zhukov is reliably reported to have told the Central Committee that the Soviet armed forces would not "permit" anyone to "bid for power." Subsequently, as a full member of the Party Presidium, Zhukov spoke "on behalf of the Armed Forces" in pledging continued support of the Party leadership under Khrushchev.[52] But Khrushchev did not want to be beholden to a marshal who could make political statements "on behalf of the armed forces." Too, Zhukov evidently began to speak more authoritatively in the Presidium on the strategic implications of various issues before that body. Finally, under Zhukov the military had acquired a substantial degree of autonomy. The whole trend of his administration of the Ministry of Defense was non-Party although not anti-Party. "Military science" itself was defined in terms stressing purely professional military competence.

This development clashed with Party policy, not because the military sought to usurp political prerogatives, but because it threatened to become a self-contained professional body within the state. Khrushchev and the Party refused to accept this, since their whole aim was to revitalize the Party as the driving force in all activities of the state. The Party has shown great concern over the growing tendency toward an autonomous, professional governmental and economic bureaucracy, a would-be independent intelligentsia, and a professionally autonomous military establishment. At present, some 93 per cent of officers, and 85 per cent of the entire personnel of the armed forces, are affiliates of the Communist Party or its youth adjunct, the Komsomol.[53] But Party membership is no longer very significant—not very different from an American businessman's membership in the Chamber of Commerce. The Party can still claim the primary loyalty of its full-time officials, but not necessarily of its nominal members.

Marshal Malinovsky, who succeeded Marshal Zhukov (and held the post until his death in 1967), was not accorded Presidium/Politburo status or a corresponding voice in national policy-making, nor has his successor Marshal Grechko. But the perennial problem of Party-military relations has not again become critical.[54]

MISSILE AGE AND MUTUAL DETERRENCE

In 1960 Khrushchev opened a new period in Soviet military policy and strategic doctrine. In a speech to the Supreme Soviet on January 14, 1960, he announced plans for a reduction of one-third in the personnel strength of the Soviet armed forces (then numbering 3,623,000 men). It was necessary to retrench on the cost of a large standing army while adding expensive new strategic offensive and defensive weapons systems. At the same time, and related to the change in force levels, Khrushchev endorsed the doctrine of mutual deterrence. *Either* military super-power, he said, could always devastate the other even if the attacker launched a surprise nuclear-missile strike. This implied security for the Soviet state, but also severe limits on any forceful Soviet use of military power.

Soviet military theory, however, bore little relation to this new military policy. During the several years following this pronouncement by Khrushchev, debate among Soviet military men—stimulated this time by the political leadership—led to a deeper reconsideration of the nature of modern war than had the revisions of the 1950's. But the debate in the early 1960's continued to reflect a slowly shifting compromise between more radical "modernist" and traditional military viewpoints on the nature of war and on military doctrine. The possibility of a brief but intensive intercontinental thermonuclear missile exchange has been added to the possibility of a protracted general war requiring major land campaigns. Differences arose between the high command and Khrushchev over the precise military share of national resources, and in a more subdued way they continue under the Brezhnev-Kosygin regime. These differences tend to transcend and replace the traditional frictions over Party controls in the military establishment.

The Soviet leadership has come to recognize, in the case of the military leaders rather reluctantly, that general nuclear war would be mutually devastating. Nonetheless, the military leaders have held that wars, even general nuclear war, might require large armies, and that it is necessary to hedge against the possibility of war however improbable. Too, in recent years and especially since the ouster of Khrushchev, the military have given increased attention to nonnuclear or limited nuclear warfare. Throughout the concern of the professional military leaders has been to meet the shifting requirements for *waging* a war if war should occur. Khrushchev and his colleagues and successors, on the other hand, while not unmindful of the need to hedge against war, regard that contingency as very remote and are more concerned with holding military outlays within acceptable limits in their inevitable competition with other political and economic programs to which the leadership also gives high priority. The military leaders realize that they can not get their optimum "requirements," and for their part the political leaders also recognize that in peacetime military power also serves political purposes beyond deterrence. Hence actual military programs rest on a compromise, constantly subject to review, affected by internal and international developments, by changes in personalities in the leadership, by developments in military technology, and by fluctuations in the level of international tension.[55]

The structure and strength of the armed forces has followed the main course of this shifting compromise on military policy. The substantial reductions announced by Khrushchev in 1960 were carried out about half way before being suspended in the course of military demonstrations and counterdemonstrations in the Berlin crisis of 1961. Since then the size of the Soviet armed forces has fluctuated and in net increased slightly; it stands today at about 3,300,000 men (since 1966 second to the United States in the number of men under arms). The ground forces were trimmed back for the nuclear battlefield, but have since had their dual capability for nuclear or nonnuclear warfare again enhanced, all within a framework of about 140 light divisions, of which about half are at relatively high strength and considered "combat-ready"; the remainder, at low or cadre levels, would require mobilization of reserves before commitment to combat.

The tactical air force was cut sharply in combat aircraft in 1960, by about half, and the naval air force by two-thirds (being entirely shorn of its fighter component). Since then, the strength of these forces, and the air defense interceptor force, has remained approximately the same with gradual modernization improving their combat capabilities. The Long Range Air Force has been slowly declining in size but with a slower phase-out of medium bombers than occurred in the U. S. Air Force. The Air Defense Command acquired large numbers of antiaircraft missiles in the late 1950's and early 1960's, and in the late 1960's is now getting advanced defensive missiles including ballistic missile defenses (ABM's) in the Moscow region.

A separate Strategic Rocket Forces Command was established in 1960, giving form to Khrushchev's stress on strategic missiles and incorporating a large number of medium and intermediate range missiles mainly concentrated against European targets. But it had few intercontinental ballistic missiles (ICBM's) until the latter half of the 1960's.

After a cut-back in older conventional units in the early 1960's, the navy has been building up a nuclear submarine fleet, cruise and ballistic missile launching submarines, and rocket launching cruisers, destroyers and smaller craft. A modest marine corps was resuscitated in the mid-1960's.

By the end of 1967, the Soviet Union was closing the gap but was still inferior to the United States in the quality and numbers of its strategic military forces. It was, however, building up a deterrent, "second-strike" capability to match that of the United States.

During the early 1960's four world crises arose. Although at least two resulted from Soviet initiatives, they were not necessarily intended as crises by the Soviet leaders; certainly none of them ended to Soviet advantage. The first arose in November 1958 when Khrushchev attempted to capitalize politically on the Soviet priority in developing strategic missiles. He demanded a change in the status of West Berlin within six months. The Western powers ignored the implied ultimatum and rejected the proposal. After keeping the issue simmering for almost three years, Khrushchev suddenly heated it up in the summer of 1961, perhaps not so much because the prospects were promising as that it might be his last chance, for—as he well knew—the United States had already outstripped the Soviet Union in operational strategic missiles. The effort failed, after a strenuous series of demonstrative military moves such as budget increases, reinforcements, and partial mobilizations on both sides, climaxed by a 60-Megaton nuclear test by the Russians (who had broken the tacit three-year moratorium on nuclear weapons testing), and finally by the disclosure in Washington that the alleged "missile gap" in favor of the U.S.S.R. was in fact a sham.[56]

Khrushchev then sought to restore the image, and something of the substance, of strategic parity or even superiority to the Soviet Union; the emplacement of Soviet medium and intermediate range missiles (abundantly available) in Cuba, would provide a substitute "intercontinental" missile capability to supplement the still very limited Soviet ICBM force. In the event, however, Moscow faced Washington's resolute determination (fully supported by the O.A.S. and N.A.T.O.) to force the removal of the missiles from Cuba by whatever means were found necessary. Moscow capitulated and withdrew them under humiliating U. S. naval escort. Thus American strategic superiority was doubly confirmed: The attempt to install the missiles in Cuba showed the Soviet need for such substitute intercontinental missiles, and its failure bore impressive witness to the American superiority which compelled the Russians to capitulate.[57]

The third crisis was essentially political but has military implications. Sino-Soviet differences had been growing since 1956, and in mid-1960 the Soviet Union abruptly recalled all its economic, technical, and military advisers from China. Sino-Soviet military relations, never as close as generally assumed, were virtually severed. With recurring border clashes it also became necessary for Soviet military and political leaders to think in terms of possible military operations against Communist China, and they have stationed additional forces along the border.[58]

The fourth case, though in the first instance involving others, has been the Vietnam war. As a matter of principle, the Soviet Union has always favored "national liberation wars," all the more when one protagonist is Communist, as in Vietnam since 1946, and more specifically in South Vietnam since 1960. But there is no evidence to indicate, and much reason to doubt, that Moscow instigated or even favored the turn to guerrilla warfare in South Vietnam in the early

1960's or the later infiltration of regular armed forces from North Vietnam. Khrushchev had, in fact, virtually washed his hands of Vietnam by 1964, but his successors believed the Communist insurgents would win and wanted to attract them and the North Vietnamese to the Soviet side in the split within the Communist movement, so they began to provide direct military and economic aid to North Vietnam. Precisely at that juncture, in retaliation for attacks on American bases in South Vietnam, the United States began bombing North Vietnam. Yet the Russians have limited themselves to continued economic aid and arms supply, and to strident protestations of support for the Vietnamese Communists and verbal attacks on the American role in Vietnam. Presumably Soviet leaders feel they can do no less without losing all influence on the international Communist movement.

Among the significant indirect uses of military instruments has been the extensive supplying of arms to countries outside the socialist bloc. In the decade after the first instance in 1955, the U.S.S.R. provided three billion dollars' worth of military equipment, chiefly to the U.A.R., Iraq, Algeria, India, and Indonesia, but on a lesser scale to a number of other countries. After the Middle Eastern crisis of 1967, in order to regain standing with the Arabs without becoming directly involved, Moscow promptly sent arms to the Arab countries to replace those captured or destroyed by Israel. By furnishing arms, the Soviet regime gains friends (what this friendship is worth is another matter), stirs up trouble abroad without any risk to the U.S.S.R., and in some cases even secures badly needed foreign exchange. Within the "socialist camp" arms aid has been used not only to strengthen the recipient countries, but sometimes, notably in the case of China, to limit in certain important ways the military forces and thus the policies and freedom of Soviet allies. The Russians have not supplied nuclear warheads or strategic weapons systems to their Warsaw Pact allies or to anyone else. The U.S.S.R. has also avoided distant and risky commitments or even extensions of its own military presence. The attempt to establish intermediate range ballistic missiles in Cuba in 1962 was the only exception, and the disastrous failure of the attempt helped to dissuade the Soviet leaders from the temptation to try such a move again.

WAR AND REVOLUTION, POWER AND POLICY

As we survey half a century of Soviet military theory and practice, the most significant questions which stand out are those relating to the basic underlying aims and policies of the Soviet leadership. What in the view of the Soviet leaders is the role of the Soviet state in realizing the proclaimed goal of a Communist world? What is the Soviet view of the role of their military power in that process? Have these views significantly changed over the years, and what if any major changes appear likely in the future?

Marxism-Leninism was always a blend of confident historical determinism and stress on the need for voluntary, disciplined action to further the "inevitable" historical process. Ever since the early years of the Bolshevik regime in Russia, for half a century, the successive leaders of the Soviet state have tied their aspirations to history but based their actions on politics—the "art of the possible." "What's good for the Soviet Union, is good for the World Revolution" is not an inaccurate epigram summarizing the whole span of Soviet policy, more obviously as time went on. And over the years, particularly the decade and a half since Stalin, the investment—on behalf of Socialism and the World Revolution—in the Soviet State has made it more necessary than ever in the eyes of those responsible for its destiny not to hazard the revolutionary base by any gamble.

Soviet leaders presumably still believe that eventually the entire world will become Communist. That belief makes it difficult for other countries to deal cooperatively with the Soviet Union, but so long as we do not share that belief, it does not really need to alarm us. What *does* make a difference is how the Soviet leaders act on the basis of that expectation—what do they *do* to try to advance the cause of the World Revolution? If one approaches this question from the viewpoint of the Soviet leaders, it can be largely restated in terms of what they do to advance the interests of the Soviet Union. For the purpose of this discussion we need only consider the question of the use of Soviet *military* power to advance the interests of the Soviet Union and, to whatever extent it may differ, to extend communism to the rest of the world.

The Marxist-Leninist theoreticians, including Lenin, had not visualized this question because they had failed utterly to imagine any Socialist state existing for half a century in a capitalist world. There is neither doctrinal guidance, nor burdensome extra baggage in the way (as there is in so many fields where the Marxist theoreticians *did* pronounce!), when one turns to the military field. In short, the only ideological prescription is expediency.

At no point in this half century has the Soviet Union had even remotely sufficient military power to attempt military conquest of the world for "Socialism," and in fact a rather strong tradition has grown up regarding Soviet military power as a defensive element of the state, or at most discouraging the "imperialists" from resorting to military means to meet the nonmilitary revolutionary wave. This does not, of course, mean that Soviet military power, when its use for acquisitive purposes seems expedient, will not be used offensively as in 1939–40 and, more indirectly, 1945–48.

The question does not pose itself in moral terms to the Soviet leaders, for expediency in serving their interests (and therefore those of "Socialism") is the only relevant moral term for them. But since it is often expressed in other terms in the West, we should so address it. The Soviet leaders, as it is often said, will do anything to advance Communism (or, "for world domination"). That is true; there are no a priori moral restraints on what they would do. They are ready to do anything if it is expedient—but not everything is expedient. And in particular, successive Soviet leaders from Lenin through Brezhnev and Kosygin have emphatically not considered it expedient to risk the existence of the Soviet state by the offensive use of Soviet military power.

This analysis should not, of course, be misread to say that the Soviet Union would do nothing aggressive with its military power. In the future, *if* the Soviet leaders came to believe that they could use Soviet military power directly for some decisive gain without great risk to the Soviet Union, they *might* so use it. It is, therefore, highly incumbent on others to take the necessary measures to insure that the Soviet leaders will continue to regard any aggressive military action as inexpedient. But even in cases where the risks have been low and the stakes not unattractive, the Soviet Union has not resorted to overt military means; to note a few: Finland after World War II, Yugoslavia in 1948, Poland in 1956, Albania in 1961, and Rumania in 1964. Indeed, Hungary in 1956 is the only case (other than the 1939–40 division of Eastern Europe with Germany), and in strategic terms (though not, of course, legal or moral ones) the move in Hungary was to retain an established part of the Socialist camp and prevent the rest from unraveling. Had the Soviet leaders tolerated a non-Communist government in Budapest, certainly Poland and probably most of Eastern Europe would have gone up in anti-Communist flames.

The real question at the close of this half century, then, needs to be approached in terms of concrete political and military rather than ideological factors. The Soviet leaders recognize that the risks in global thermonuclear war would be ominous in the highest degree; they do not want nuclear war. They also appreciate the risks of escalation in limited direct military confrontations with the United States, and wish to avoid them too. The Soviet Union now has incomparably greater capabilities than ever before in its history to visit destruction on opponents anywhere in the world—but not without suffering comparable destruction itself. And preservation of the U.S.S.R. would be accorded a higher priority in Soviet policy than expansion of Communist dominion, if ever they were weighed against one another.

The Soviet leaders see no deadline for the final triumph of Communism in the world, though they probably expect it eventually. They do not see any predetermined or necessary role for military power in reaching that goal. Indeed, the thrust of their thinking has been entirely in the direction of holding off war, and assisting the spread of communism by demonstrating its successes. In the words of the Central Committee's Theses On the Fiftieth Anniversary of the Great October Socialist Revolution, "The great goal of the Soviet people, the building of Communism, is at the same time its main international cause. . . . The main task of Soviet foreign policy is to insure favorable conditions for the building of Communism." [59] As other authoritative Soviet sources have put it: "The socialist countries exert their main influence on the development of world revolution by their economic successes," and indeed "building communism in the U.S.S.R. is the main Soviet contribution to the world revolutionary process." [60]

What, then, of the role of military power? Again it may be useful to cite the C.P.S.U. Central Committee's own Fiftieth Anniversary Theses: "The might of the Soviet Union, of the socialist countries, creates a real counterbalance to the aggressive forces of imperialism. It emerges as a most important factor in the struggle to avert a new world war and for the preservation of peace." Finally, as authoritative Soviet sources have made explicit in recent years, the Soviet leaders reject "the use of *military* means to force revolutions in other countries, or the 'export of revolution' by means of military intervention." [61] The reason is not a priori morality or doctrinaire ideology, but simply recognition that military means on an interstate level involve risks to the state; the Soviet leaders do not consider it necessary or expedient to use Soviet military forces, and thus to hazard Soviet security, in order to advance the Revolution.

At the same time, military power has political uses short of major war: deterrence, counterdeterrence, political pressure, various psychological-political effects, and possible use in limited military actions. Today, political uses of military power, at least among the great powers, have indeed become their primary actual uses.

The limited, indirect, sometimes subtle political exploitation of military power has thus moved to the fore. There is always a risk of miscalculation, as in the North Korean invasion of the South in 1950 and the attempt to establish a Soviet strategic missile base in Cuba in 1962. On the other hand, as those and other cases show, the Soviet leaders are able to adapt—if necessary by accepting a defeat—if such local aggressive moves prompt more vigorous and effective countermeasures than had been anticipated. Soviet support for "national liberation" struggles will probably remain largely verbal with little concrete assistance and without irrevocable commitment of the Soviet state through overt involvement of its own armed forces.

On the other end of the spectrum, arms control agreements and even limited disarmament measures may play a larger role in Soviet military as well as foreign policy. While one-sided propaganda and political considerations still dominate, there have already been a few concrete indications of interest in arms control restrictions of mutual benefit.

Military power has never played the central role in Soviet expectations in international politics. Nonetheless, military power has always been regarded as an essential element of state power as a deterrent and a defensive last resort, and also as a useful many-faceted instrument in support of an active and frequently assertive foreign policy. Soviet military (particularly naval) leaders have recently mentioned a major mission of the Soviet armed forces: "to protect the *state interests of the Soviet Union*" (and occasionally also contribution to "the international prestige of our country").[62] The "state interests" of the U.S.S.R. may, of course, sometimes be construed as justifying an aggressive forward initiative. But this is hardly the term to describe support for revolutions elsewhere in the world.

The future will, no doubt, include occasions of tension and perhaps crises in Soviet and American political confrontations, backed by counterpoised military power and possibly even involving the limited use of military force. Changes in the political and even the military elements of the balance of power in the world may prompt assertive Soviet moves leading to confrontations. Clearly, the United States and other nations (democratic or non-democratic, non-Communist and even Communist) must be prepared to deter or if necessary to defeat aggressive military challenges. During the past half century, however, the Soviet ideology, system, and several successive generations of leaders have not been committed, or even inclined, to seek a military solution to the problem of the future of world society.

FIFTY YEARS OF SOVIET SCIENCE

John Turkevich

The importance of science in the twentieth century is obvious to everyone. Nuclear energy, rockets and missiles, increased productivity of agriculture (due to better fertilizers, pesticides, and farm machinery), plastics, faster transportation and better communication through radio and television, healthier and longer lives—all these advances have taken place since the Bolshevik Revolution of fifty years ago. It is the writer's thesis that those spectacular successes that the Communist Party has achieved in Russia are particularly due to the favorable time the Bolsheviks happened to carry out their political, social, and economic experiment. Furthermore the tragic mistakes, the heavy price that was paid in this experiment are all the more culpable and onerous since they occurred when the capacity of modern science and technology to reduce suffering was increasing every year.

The story of fifty years of Soviet science is an exciting story—beyond the ability of the writer to present either in its completeness or in proper perspective. It must be approached with humility. We may, however, know more about what the Russians have accomplished in science than in any other field of endeavor. Scientific publications coming from Russia are voluminous, and the merit of the work is easily verified by critical reading or by repetition of the published experiments. More Soviet scientists have had contact with their Western colleagues than members of any other group in Soviet society. We have met their science leaders, we have visited their institutes, laboratories, and universities. We have not visited all of them, but certainly those where work is carried out that has contributed to the world pool of scientific knowledge. We would not worry about the U.S.S.R. if Soviet science and technology had not been so effective in making Russia one of the two major powers of the world. The advances of science and technology, however, may be destroying the basic tenets of Marxism-Leninism: the proletariat is disappearing, a world war would be suicidal even for the chief Communist state, and colonialism has been eliminated without any collapse of the colonial powers. The philosophical basis of Marxism has become more and more antiquated, based as it was on nineteenth-century science which has been so thoroughly revised in the last fifty years. The Soviet leadership has been forced to base its plans more on science and technology than on communism.

Soviet science and technology received a firm and broad heritage from imperial Russia. The Communists hate to concede this, but the old regime of the tsars, the old Russian intelligentsia, gave the new regime of Lenin scientific experts and scholars in every field of human knowledge, an educational system that was both advanced and thorough, and a small group of laboratories up to the standards of most West European countries. The Soviet Union also inherited a great tradition in science: Leonhard Euler, one of the world's greatest mathematicians; Mikhail Lomonosov, the fiery encyclopedist, both chemist and poet; Nikolai Lobachevski, who broke one of Euclid's postulates; Dimitri Mendeleev, who ordered the chemical elements and showed which were yet to be discovered; Ivan Pavlov, the physiologist who made the concept of conditioned reflex a common word. During the last decades of the Empire, in spite of the steady deterioration of the internal political situation, intellectual life flourished in St. Petersburg, Moscow, Odessa, and, to a lesser degree, in other cities. Widespread knowledge of Western languages, familiarity with the most recent political and philosophical ideas of the West, a high tradition and unexcelled performance in the arts, music, ballet, painting—all created a stimulating environment for Russian scientists. The capital investment in laboratories and equipment was not great, but at that time the same was true of the United States.

THE REVOLUTION

The Revolution of 1917 affected scientific and scholarly life as it did all activity in Russia. Many scientists emigrated permanently to the West and made significant contributions to world science in their adopted countries: Igor Sikorsky and Alexander de Seversky in aviation, Vladimir Zworykin in television, Vladimir Ipatieff and George Kistiakowsky in chemistry, George Gamow in physics. Thousands of other members of the White emigration, while not receiving world recognition contributed markedly to various branches of knowledge all over the world. Their contributions testified to the high quality of science and education in imperial Russia.

During the period of militant communism and civil war some scientists were in territories controlled by White armies. Others were in Petrograd, Moscow, and Kiev. All suffered privation and annoyance. Their basic aim was to survive themselves and preserve whatever basic facilities were left from the revolution. During this period the Soviet government gave special rations to scholars. The Academy of Sciences, a small but highly prestigious organization of forty-five academicians, continued to function undisturbed for almost a decade even though its secretary and executive officer (until 1934) was Prince S. F. Ol'denburg, a former Minister of Education in the Provisional Government of 1917. Universities and higher education suffered greater damage. In an attempt to develop a whole new class of scientists, scholars, and managers from the proletariat, the Party made "proletarian origin" the only requirement for entrance to universities. All grades and discipline in secondary schools were abolished by educational "reforms" of 1918.

During the years of the New Economic Policy, the lot of the scientists improved. They were allowed to visit West European centers, and research resumed in universities and in the newly established institutes: of Physics and Biophysics in Moscow, the Physico-Technical Institute in Leningrad, the State Optical Institute in Leningrad, and the Karpov Physico-Chemical Institute in Moscow. The basis of future success of Soviet science was laid in this confused period, but the interaction of scientists and government was still weak. In 1918 Lenin proposed a "sketch of a plan of scientific technical work" outlining the relation of science to the development of the Russian economy. A number of scientific expeditions found important deposits of iron, oil, phosphate, and potash. The great Russian famine of 1921 also provoked Lenin to organize research in plant selection and animal breeding under the direction of N. I. Vavilov. Different fields of science, genetics, mathematics, physics, physical chemistry, rapidly developed to positions of world leadership. The control of science by government was minimal, while discussion of the implications of Marxism for science was limited to philosophical gatherings.

THE STALINIST PERIODS

During the period 1927–41, of five-year Plans, industrialization, and collectivization of agriculture, science and technology were of paramount importance in attaining state and Party goals; research and development were reorganized in the service of the Soviet state and the foundation was layed for the spectacular advances after World War II—aviation, atomic weapons, missiles, space exploration. The years 1927–41 also saw the first phase of the interaction of Marxist philosophy with science which culminated in the great genetics controversy of 1948.

The first dramatic change was in education. The disorganized school system was now strictly regimented, and secondary school was made compulsory. Attempts to create a new proletarian intelligentsia were abandoned. The Communist Party gradually took over the Academy of Sciences. In 1926 the Soviet press criticized the Academy for not serving the needs of the new Communist state, and in 1927 a new charter was adopted under the pressure of the Council of People's Commissars. The authority of the president and permanent secretary was replaced by that of the General Assembly of Academicians. The number of academicians was increased from 45 to 270. Furthermore they could be nominated by organizations outside the Academy. The Party took advantage of these new election rules and elected a number of Communists to membership: the Marxist philosophers and historians V. V. Adoratski, N. I. Bukharin, A. M. Deborin, and V. P. Volgin; the chemist V. A. Kistiakowski, electrical engineer Krzhizhanovski, and a number of engineers. In the next step (1929–31), the Party purged the Academy of undesirable academicians and staff members, mostly in the social sciences and humanities. A new constitution was drafted in 1931, and the post of Permanent Secretary was given to the Party member V. P. Volgin. He proceeded to consolidate institutes, eliminate activities which were considered remnants of the old regime, and defined by statutes the objectives and organizational structure of each institute. In 1930 the Academy of Sciences was given an educational function, graduate instruction of young scientists and scholars supplementing the instruction given by the new Soviet universities. In 1934 the Academy with most of its institutes was transferred from Leningrad to Moscow, and the following year it received a new charter which determined its character for many decades. The number of institutes increased, and the Communist Academy was incorporated into the Academy of Sciences. During the 1936–38 purge, however, half the Party members in the Academy were reportedly sentenced to death or sent to forced labor camps.

The fourteen pre-war years witnessed important contributions in every field. Soviet mathematicians, the most outstanding in the world, influenced the development of their subject abroad and also trained the future leaders of Soviet science: O. Ya. Shmitt, the Arctic explorer, I. G. Petrovski, rector of Moscow University, A. D. Aleksandrov, rector of Leningrad University, N. N. Bogolyubov, director of Dubno Nuclear Institute, M. A. Lavrentiev, the organizer of the Novosibirsk science city, and M. V. Keldysh, President of the Academy of Sciences.

Astronomical observatories were built and the skies explored, while geodesic and geological teams mapped the Soviet Union. Seismic methods of exploration for oil were also developed. Arctic exploration was led by the mathematician, explorer, and astronomer Otto Ya. Shmitt. Attempts to make a northeast passage by the ship *Chelyuskin* (1934) captured the attention of the world press as did the ice drift station "Severnyi Polyus."

Developments in physics covered the whole field; theoretical work was carried out by V. A. Fok, N. N. Bogolyubov and Nobel laureates I. E. Tam and L. D. Landau. The first cyclotron in Europe was built in the Radium Institute in Leningrad, and I. V. Kurchatov, the leader in Soviet atomic research after the war, discovered nuclear isomerism (1935); P. A. Cherenkov, I. M. Frank and Tam found the Cherenkov radiation for which they received a Nobel Prize. The discovery of uranium fission by Hahn and Strassmann in Berlin provoked great activity in the Soviet Union. Theoretical calculations were carried out on the mechanism of the process and on modes of utilizing it for power and weapon production, but the war seems to have forced suspension of work in this area until after the Stalingrad battle.

The optical industry was built up and spectroscopy flourished. Two Soviet scientists, L. I. Mandel'shtam and G. S. Landsberg, barely missed being the first to discover light scattering by liquids for which C. V. Raman received the Nobel Prize. Low temperature physics has been an area of Soviet excellence for the last three decades, undoubtedly due to the leadership of Peter L. Kapitza, a Russian-born professor of Cambridge University who was "persuaded" to stay in the Soviet Union when he went there on his vacation in the summer of 1935. His forced stay in the Soviet Union created a world-wide furor. Solid state physics developed under the leadership of A. F. Yoffe and served as a basis for the development of the large variety of solid state devices that dominate the present-day electronics industry—transistors, television, radar, lasers, computers.

The bulk of chemical work was devoted to building up a chemical industry: large plants for sulfuric acid, ammonia, soda, potash, and fertilizer; small plants for dyes, medicines, explosives, solvents, and fine chemicals. Outstanding work was carried out on explosions and combustion by N. N. Semenov (Nobel laureate) who trained, in addition, a large number of outstanding physical chemists. Another important "school" of chemistry was that of A. N. Frumkin who studied processes involving interaction of electric current and chemical reactions, then important in batteries and now in fuel cells. Organic chemistry had a brilliant history in imperial Russia, but during the last fifty years the great developments have occurred in the West: petrochemicals, medicinals, vitamins, unraveling of complex compounds of plant and animal origin, chemico-physical interpretation of chemical bonding—all these were missed in the U.S.S.R.

Engineering training in which advanced mathematics was coupled with sound science later produced spectacular results in the strategic areas of missiles, aviation, atomic energy, electrification, radio communication, machine construction, and metallurgy. Rocket research was seriously pursued at this time by K. E. Tsiolkovski (1857–1935), I. V. Meshcherski (1859–1935), F. Tsander (1887–1959), and V. P. Glushko. In 1933 Sergei P. Korolev (1907–66), later the chief Soviet designer of space vehicles, joined the rocket group and published a book on *Rocket Flight in the Stratosphere*. The Zhukovski Central Aerohydrodynamics Institute in Moscow became world famous for training and research; its graduates included such well-known designers as A. N. Tupolev, S. V. Il'yushin, Artem I. Mikoyan, A. S. Yakovlev, and S. A. Lavochkin.

The story of Soviet genetics, of the interaction of science and Marxism, of the rivalry of Vavilov and Lysenko begins in this period. Soviet agriculture was and still is a major concern of the Communist Party. Lenin realized the importance of basic research in plant selection and animal breeding. He selected N. I. Vavilov to organize a program along these lines. Vavilov, an unusual organizer and inspiring leader, had been well trained in imperial Russia and in England. He proceeded to build a large organization and made Soviet work in genetics in the thirties the most outstanding in the world, attracting to Soviet laboratories prominent scholars from all over the world.

Undoubtedly Vavilov's success irked some of the old-fashioned biologists who taught at the Timiryazev Agricultural Academy and who espoused the "practical approach" to the problem as exemplified in the work of the Russian Burbank, Ivan Michurin. They found a leader in T. Lysenko, a Ukrainian agronomist, who in 1929 proposed rapid unorthodox methods for improving Soviet agriculture: "vernalization" (converting winter wheat into spring wheat) and later "vegetative hybridization" (changing genetic characteristics of a plant by grafting). His ideas that genetic characteristics can be changed by external conditions and that these changed characteristics can be transmitted to the progeny had long been discredited in the West and were tolerated but not accepted by Vavilov and the other reputable geneticists in the Soviet Union.

In 1932 Lysenko obtained the support of a Marxist theoretician, I. I. Prezent, and started publication of the *Bulletin of Vernalization* in which he propagandized his theories and started attacking Western genetics. Lysenko was elected to the Academy of Sciences in 1934 and intensified his attacks on orthodox geneticists, a number of whom were arrested. On December 28, 1936 a special session of the Lenin Academy of Agricultural Sciences was called by the Party to discuss the problem of genetics and selection. At the meeting Lysenko criticized Vavilov and his colleagues for ignoring Lysenko's practical work, for engaging in "nonproductive" academic research, and for ignoring the teachings of Michurin. Vavilov defended himself, but a resolution passed at the end of the session supported Lysenko. More Vavilov supporters lost their positions, were arrested, or disappeared. Vavilov himself lost his directorship of the Institute of Plant Breeding and of the Institute of Genetics and the Presidency of the Lenin Academy of Agricultural Sciences. Lysenko replaced him in these key positions. An International Genetics Congress, originally scheduled to be held in Moscow in 1937 but cancelled by Soviet authorities, was held during August 1939 in Edinburgh, Scotland. Although Vavilov had been elected President of the Congress and had already accepted this honor, neither he nor any other Soviet geneticist appeared in Edinburgh.

Six weeks after the Edinburgh congress, a meeting was held in the U.S.S.R. to discuss the two conflicting points of view of Vavilov and Lysenko. The official evaluation in *Pravda* of December 7, 1939, again supported Lysenko. Vavilov disappeared from public sight at the end of August 1940. He was reportedly kept in prison in Moscow and Saratov and then transferred to a labor camp at Magadan in Eastern Siberia where he died in 1942. Just before World War II Lysenko was firmly entrenched in important scientific posts and had strong backing by the Party leadership. A number of classical geneticists, however, such as A. Serebrovski, P. Dubinin, and I. Zherbas continued to work along classical Western lines.

During the four years of war with Germany, over six hundred scientific research institutes were destroyed. The pride of Russian and Soviet astronomy, the Pulkovo Observatory near Leningrad, was pillaged and gutted, while the Crimean astrophysical observatory was looted and burnt. The main scientific establishments were evacuated beyond the Volga and the Urals, to Kazan, Sverdlovsk, Frunze, Tashkent, and Alma Ata. Under new conditions and often without the necessary equipment and supplies, Soviet scientists and technicians carried out war research in artillery, tanks, and radar. A surface-to-surface artillery rocket was used effectively, and a number of antiaircraft rockets were also produced.

Apparently there was no special wartime organization in the Soviet Union such as the National Defense Research Council or the Manhattan Project. Neither was there any scientific liaison between the Soviet Union and Anglo-American groups. One American mission was sent by the Rubber Reserve Board to study the synthetic rubber process developed by Lebedev and highly publicized by the Soviet regime. This mission was unsuccessful; the Lebedev process has been discontinued if it was ever actually used in the Soviet Union. Conversely, Western research and development in atomic energy, radar, and explosives was the target of intense Soviet espionage activity.

After the war Stalin seems to have had two main objectives in mind: the development and production of atomic weapons and intercontinental missiles. V-2 rockets, blueprints, tools, and manufacturing facilities captured by the Red Army, together with a group of German experts kidnapped by Soviet intelligence, provided a solid basis for development of liquid fueled rockets. Research was carried out secretly at a number of centers, at Khimki near Moscow, at an island in a lake two hundred miles northwest of Moscow, at a rocket-motor station near Kuibyshev, and at a rocket proving ground 150 miles east of Stalingrad. The chief administrator of the space work was D. F. Ustinov, the Minister of Armament, and the chief designer of the space vehicles was the late Sergei P. Korolev. Other prominent Soviet scientists also participated: Leonid Sedov, an expert on aerodynamics, shock waves, and astrophysics; Mstislav V. Keldysh, a theoretical aerodynamist and mathematical physicist, now President of the Academy of Sciences; Peter Kapitza, an expert on the production and handling of liquid oxygen; Nicholas Semenov, a Nobel laureate in chemistry, honored for his work on combustion and explosions. The German specialists were Wilhelm Fischer, a navigation and guidance expert, and Helmut Grottrup, the former executive assistant to the director of the Peenemunde rocket establishment.

This work bore fruit in the Khrushchev era, but atomic weapons research produced results much earlier. Soon after the capture of Berlin, a team of Soviet nuclear scientists persuaded a number of leading German nuclear specialists, Nicholas Riehl, Baron von Ardenne, F. Hertz, and their assistants to go to Russia to work on the atomic weapon project. The general supervision of this project was placed in "The First Main Directorate of the Council of Ministers" under Lavrenti Beria, the head of the security police. The immediate supervisor was General Boris Vannikov, while the scientific direction was under Academician Igar Kurchatov (1903–63). The work was carried out near Moscow, in the Crimea, and in Siberia. Other leading members of the team were A. P. Aleksandrov, A. I. Alikhanov, I. K. Kikoin, S. I. Sobolev. Helped by the Germans and by information brought in by intelligence, the Soviet team rapidly developed an atomic weapon which was tested on September 25, 1949.

During this period the Academy of Sciences had a major reorganization and came completely under the control of the Party. Soon after the war, the elderly President, V. L. Komarov (1869–1945), resigned and was replaced by S. I. Vavilov (1891–1951), a physicist and the brother of the geneticist N. I. Vavilov. The Academy took an ambiguous position in the Vavilov-Lysenko controversy, supporting both camps, but during the genetics discussions of 1948 it had to publicly acknowledge its mistake and dismiss some prominent Academicians. In addition, in July 1948 steam-roller tactics elected a Party nominee, A. V. Topchiev, not only as Academician but also as secretary of the organization. The Academy structure was changed by the government to place complete control in his hands.

The immediate postwar years saw a tightening of the controls relaxed during the war. An ideological campaign was instituted which culminated in a veritable witch hunt. The Party line stressed idealism, nonsubservience to Western ideas, and proper respect for the Russian cultural heritage. Underlying this was an attempt to reconcile the discoveries and concepts of modern science with the philosophical ideas of Marx, Engels, and Lenin which were based on antiquated scientific information. Undoubtedly another objective was to isolate Soviet scientists from the West, conceal the work on atomic weapons and missiles, and prevent the outside world from realizing how weak the Soviet Union was after the ravages of World War II.

The opening salvo of the ideological war was fired by A. A. Zhdanov with a scathing attack on A. A. Aleksandrov's *History of West European Philosophy*. The most dramatic confrontation between ideology and science took place in genetics. During the war and in the early postwar period an accommodation existed between Western and Lysenko genetics—both were supported by the Presidium of the Academy. After several articles in Western scientific journals and polemical articles in Soviet periodicals, a session of the Lenin Academy of Agriculture was called by its President Lysenko on July 31,

1948 to discuss the validity of the two genetics. In a long address Lysenko attacked the Western concept of the gene and the chromosome as idealistic; he accused the classical Soviet geneticists Zavadovski, Dubinin, Schmalgausen, and others of being subservient to Western ideas and of neglecting the Soviet heritage of the plant physiologist Timiryazev and the plant breeder Michurin. Lysenko further claimed that characteristics of species, even species themselves, could be changed by environment and this change was inherited by their progeny. He further claimed that his techniques of "vernalization," "shattering of heredity," and "vegetative hybridization," produced results useful to Soviet agriculture while the classical Western approach based on production of pure strains by inbreeding was false in principle and impractical in the field.

Although Lysenko's propositions were supported by many Soviet agronomists, they were also rebutted by both cautious and outspoken criticism. Prezent, Lysenko's ideological guide, concluded the debate by saying "there can be no compromise between Michurinism and Mendelism; minor concessions to Michurinism are worthless." At this point Lysenko read a statement: "A question is asked in one of the notes handed to me, 'What is the attitude of the Central Committee of the Communist Party to my report.' I answer: 'The Central Committee of the Party has examined my report and approved it.' " He then declared that the principle of inheritance of acquired characteristics has been "once more fully confirmed by the actual factual material presented at this session." The meeting ended with several of the critics, Zhukovsky, Alikhanyan, Zherban, and Yuri Zhdanov, recanting and enthusiastic general approval of the Lysenko position.

And on August 24–26, 1948, when the Soviet Academy of Sciences held a session to discuss the status of biological sciences, President Vavilov admitted that the presidium and the biology section of the Academy had erred in supporting Western genetics. Academician L. A. Orbeli, secretary of the biology section and renowned pupil of Pavlov, defended the policies of his section, however: "I regard it as essential to respect the views of others and not bar the way to those who disagree with my personal scientific views," he declared. He considered the struggle between Lysenko and supporters of Western genetics as "a struggle of views on a purely biological question." But Academician A. I. Oparin, Director of the Biochemical Institute, S. V. Kaftanov, the Minister of Higher Education, I. A. Benediktov, the Minister of Agriculture, N. A. Skvertsov, Minister of State Farms, and Academician G. F. Aleksandrov supported Lysenko and criticized Orbeli. The presidium of the Academy formally admitted its mistake on August 26, recognized Lysenkoism as the only true genetics, dismissed Orbeli and Academicians Shmalgausen and Dubinin, and abolished or reorganized those institutes still working according to the findings of Western genetics. The same day S. Kaftanov, the Minister of Higher Education, forbade the teaching of Western genetics in the Soviet Union and ordered the rewriting of all the textbooks.

A Soviet biologist, G. B. Lepeshinskaya (1871—), an ardent revolutionary and friend of Lenin, had formulated in 1933 a theory that cells could arise from non-cellular substances. Lysenko and Oparin took up her cause and organized two conferences on "Noncellular Forms of Life and the Origin of Cells" in May 1950 and in April 1952. After the second conference the presidium of the Academy of Sciences passed a resolution confirming the validity of the views of Lepeshinskaya.

Meanwhile the witch hunt had proceeded to other disciplines. A combined session of the Academy of Sciences and the Academy of Medical Sciences to consider the "Physiological Problems of the Teaching of Academician Pavlov" was held from June 28 to July 4, 1950, with 1500 attending. Orbeli was strongly criticized, and others mildly, for distorting Pavlov's teaching. Orbeli was dismissed from his remaining post and orders were given to revise all textbooks to make them more consistent with Pavlovian teachings and less reflective of Western ideas. In chemistry the theories of Linus Pauling on resonance were criticized as being "idealistic." M. E. Dyatkina, G. K. Syrkin, M. V. Volkenshtein, and A. I. Kiprianov were severely criticized for espousing resonance theory and for neglecting to give due credit to Butlerov (1828–86) who had formulated a "materialistic concept" of the structure of organic compounds. Mild criticism was leveled at as high a personage as A. N. Nesmeyanov, the President of the Academy of Sciences; his collaborators, Syrkin and Dyatkina, disappeared for a number of years from the scientific scene, while Academician A. Balandin, a prominent catalytic chemist whose work was highly esteemed in the West, was arrested and sent to a labor camp.

In physics polemical articles attacked the Heisenberg Principle of Indeterminacy, the causality principle, relativity theory, and the significance of the Einstein formula for equivalence of matter and energy. V. A. Fok and D. I. Blochintsev attempted to keep the discussion of these problems on a high scholarly level; however they did not escape criticism which was directed primarily on scholars whose books were popular in the West such as Y. A. Frenkel (1894–1952) A. A. Andronov (1901–52), and S. E. Khaikin.

KHRUSHCHEV AND HIS SUCCESSORS

The death of Stalin initiated a new relaxed era. The iron curtain that separated Soviet and Western scientists gradually rusted enough to allow a freer flow of periodicals, increased participation by Soviet scientists in international conferences, and the introduction of cultural exchange programs. Even before Stalin's death, the organic chemist A. N. Nesmeyanov, rector of the University of Moscow, had planned and supervised the construction of a vast complex of university buildings on the outskirts of Moscow. He later became president of the Academy of Sciences which grew rapidly in size; by 1955, 2,800 research institutions with 97,000 staff members were under its jurisdiction.

After Beria's arrest in 1953, the First Directorate of the Council of Ministers which managed the atomic energy program became the Ministry of Medium Machine Building. This organization is still in charge of the atomic weapons program in the Soviet Union though it had a rapid succession of leaders in its early years: V. A. Malyshev who died in February 1955, General Zavenyegin who died in December 1955, Mikhail Pervukhin who lost his post during the Molotov-Khrushchev power struggle, and finally Y. P. Slavski who was appointed in April 1956. The first Soviet hydrogen bomb was tested on August 12, 1953, and was followed by a succession of explosions until the Atomic Test-Ban Treaty was signed on August 5, 1963. But underground tests are still carried out by the U.S.A. and the U.S.S.R. and both countries have built a fleet of atomic submarines.

The "peaceful uses" program was split off from the Ministry of Medium Machine Building in 1956 and organized as the State Committee of the Council of Ministers on Peaceful Uses of Atomic Energy. V. S. Emelyanov, chairman of this committee during the Khrushchev era, was an articulate spokesman and canny negotiator in the Soviet campaign of "peaceful coexistence" with Western Europe and the United States. The Soviet Union took an active part in the first (1955), second (1958), and third (1964) Geneva Conferences on peaceful uses of atomic energy, disclosing research and engineering work in all phases of utilization of nuclear energy. The first Soviet nuclear power plant was built in 1954. At present the Soviet Union has nine hundred megawatts of capacity while the United States has more than a thousand. The Russians have a nuclear icebreaker, *Lenin,* while the Americans have built a nuclear cargo ship, *Savannah* and an aircraft carrier. Both countries started off on a race to be first in power production from nuclear fission, but the difficulty of the problem has turned rivalry in this field into cooperation. The rivalry still continues in particle accelerators, however with America's present lead being challenged by the large accelerator in the last stages of construction at Serpukhov.

The most spectacular achievements of Soviet science and technology have been in space. The first earth satellite, the first dog in space, the first hard landing on the moon and on Venus, the first human in orbit, the first view of the back of the moon, the first soft landing on the moon—all these achievements attest to the strength of science and technology in the U.S.S.R. Behind them is a powerful rocket motor which gives the Soviet designer a luxury that his American counterpart does not enjoy. The Soviet space spectaculars have been the by-product of a military objective which was also attained: to make the continental United States vulnerable to nuclear attack.

Soviet science has not scored such obvious successes in other fields, though its excellence is attested by the interest in Soviet scientific literature by scientists of the West. Pure mathematics has continued the great tradition of the past. Areas of applied mathematics which were disdainfully ignored during the Stalin era, such as cybernetics, theory of games, linear programming, and operation theory, were "discovered" during the Khrushchev period. These disciplines are the basis behind computers and automation; modern science cannot exist without electronic computers, and modern technology cannot do without automation. Computers are particularly necessary for calculation of missile trajectories and rocket behavior. Automation is the answer to shortage of highly trained personnel for a modern industrial state. The Khrushchev period saw the development of the first series of Soviet electronic computers and the start in automation of industrial processes such as rolling railroad rails.

During this period Soviet chemistry turned to synthetics to replace the natural textiles that were in short supply. But the chemical industry still has insufficient capacity for fertilizers, insecticides, fungicides, and herbicides. Nor has synthesis of drugs, medicinals, and antibiotics been developed in the Soviet Union. In isolated areas such as electrochemistry, however, the work of individual scientists such as that of Academician Frumkin, has been outstanding.

Physics has been a strong science in postwar Russia. Every branch of physics—cosmic rays, nuclear physics, low temperature physics, spectroscopy, electronics—has had able practitioners who have made significant contributions. Astronomers were active in both optical observation and radio astronomy. The Soviet Union embarked in this period on the construction of the largest optical telescope in the world and has built extensive radio-telescope installations which are used not only for astronomical work but also for tracking satellites. Oceanographic research, Arctic and Antarctic exploration supplement the thorough study of the mineral resources of the vast expanse of the Soviet Union. A spectacular result of these explorations has been the discovery of diamonds in Siberia.

In the autumn of 1951, opposition to Lysenko became articulate in several critical articles in the *Botanicheski Zhurnal;* but the editor and the authors were reprimanded by the Presidium of the Academy of Sciences. In the fall of 1952, however, just before Stalin's death, *Botanicheski Zhurnal* under the editorship of Academician V. N. Sukachev published articles by N. V. Turbin and N. D. Ivanov criticizing Lysenko's ideas on transforming one species into another and particularly the results reported by Lysenko's associates in changing a hornbeam tree into a hazelnut tree and a fir into a pine. Lysenko's supporters came to his defense and the controversy continued through 1954 when the Presidium of the Academy called a halt.

In 1954, however, V. S. Dmitriev of the Genetics Institute and Chief of the Agricultural Planning Administration of the Ministry of Agriculture presented to the State Higher Certifying Commission a doctor's dissertation entitled "Primary Sources for the Origin of Certain Types of Weeds." In this dissertation Dmitriev claimed that plants themselves give rise to weeds that plague the plant that originated them. The official reader of the dissertation, S. Stankov, recommended rejection of the dissertation. This recommendation was accepted by the Presidium of the Certifying Commission, and the thesis was rejected on February 13. But Lysenko called for a reconsideration by the full membership of the Certifying Commission which met on February 20. Lysenko defended his protégé, called the readers of the thesis "Weismannists," and forced the Certifying Committee to give Dmitriev the Doctor of Science degree. Stankov in turn wrote a letter to *Pravda* complaining about this action. It appeared on March 25 and seems to have caught Khrushchev's eye; soon a note in *Pravda* stated that the Certifying Commission had rescinded its action of February 20 and deprived Dmitriev of his doctor's degree.

In November 1955 Lysenko received the Michurin Gold Medal, but a half a year later in April 1956 he was relieved as president of the Lenin All-Union Agricultural Academy. During this period Khrushchev became interested in hybrid corn and sent a team of experts to the United States to study American agricultural practice. The geneticist N. P. Dubinin, one of Lysenko's earlier victims, reappeared in print as an editor of a Russian translation of an American book, *Hybrid Corn.* Dubinin was also named director of a newly organized Institute of Genetics in Novosibirsk Science City. Criticism of this appointment by Khrushchev led to a speedy dismissal, but Lysenko's influence was definitely on the decline. In October 1964 he lost his post as director of the Institute of Genetics of the Academy of Sciences, and in 1965 the Presidium of the Academy had a formal investigation of Lysenko's management of the experimental farm. He was found guilty of gross mismanagement and retired.

Numerous organizational changes in the Soviet science establishment occurred during the Khrushchev era. A 1957 reform decentralizing the large ministries and transferring authority to regional councils (sovnarkhozy) did not affect the gigantic Academy establishments. From 1959 on, however, there was increasing pressure on the Academy to define its role in Soviet society: Was it an institution for basic research with no responsibility in creating the new socialist state, or should its activities be devoted solely to applied research? The Central Committee of the Party and Khrushchev called for reorganization, but the Stalin-era stalwarts of the Academy, President Nesmeyanov and Secretary Topchiev did not offer a satisfactory plan. Finally on April 9, 1961 the Central Committee and the Council of Ministers announced "A Measure for Improving the Coordination of Scientific Research in the Country and the Activities of the U.S.S.R. Academy of Sciences." This decree created a State Committee for Coordination of Research at the Council of Ministers level. The Academy was relegated to a subsidiary role with its president being merely a member of the committee. Many of the institutes of the Division of Technical Science, the largest division of the Academy, were transferred to various state committees and industrial ministries.

The State Committee on Coordination of Research did not fare well during the following years, however. Its first chairman, M. V. Khrunichev (former Deputy Minister of Military Uses of Atomic Energy) died several months after assuming office, and he was succeeded by K. N. Rudnev (former Minister of Defense Technology). The Committee had a difficult time building up an organization parallel to the well-entrenched Academy organization. Furthermore, its prestige suffered drastically when Oleg Pankovski, one of its high officials, was convicted and shot for espionage. It did organize a series of scientific councils (nauchnye sovety) responsible for specific scientific or technological problems, with personnel drawn from different sectors of Soviet research and development activity.

In the Academy there was a change in leadership. Nesmeyanov was replaced on May 19, 1961 by the applied mathematician M. V.

Keldysh. Topchiev was promoted to Vice-President and given responsibility for foreign relations of the Academy; he died in December 1962. His post of Main Scientific Secretary was filled successively by the physicist E. K. Fedorov, the biochemist N. M. Sisakyan (died March 1966), and the agronomist Ya. V. Peyve. Peyve had been (1958–66) the President of the Council of Nationalities (the Soviet Senate) and President of the Latvian Academy of Sciences.

On April 11, 1963 another decree of the Party and government thoroughly reorganized the Academy structure. The Academy remained subordinate to the State Committee on Coordination of Research and its role in planning, guiding, and coordinating basic research was recognized; but the decree also emphasized that the Academy should concentrate on "scientific problems directly connected with the development of production." The Academy's nine divisions were reorganized into fifteen and these were grouped in three sections, each in charge of a vice-president: (1) a section of physiotechnical and mathematical sciences, (2) a section of chemico-technological and biological sciences, and (3) a section of social sciences. The important science administrator of the Party apparatus, V. A. Kirillin, was elected Vice-President of the Academy. After Khrushchev's dismissal, the Committee on Coordination of Research was replaced in 1965 by a State Committee on Science and Technology. The chairman of the dissolved committee, K. N. Rudnev, was made responsible for instrument production, automation, and control systems, while V. A. Kirillin resigned his Academy position to become a Deputy Prime Minister and chairman of the new State Committee on Science and Technology.

What is the present status of Soviet science fifty years after the Bolshevik Revolution? In evaluating the science of any country, one must keep in mind that the influence of one outstanding scholar such as Fermi or Bohr far transcends that of a thousand pedestrian workers. Nevertheless, the Soviet Union definitely has the second strongest science and technology in the world. Although it leads the United States in a few very important areas, it is behind in most but is ahead of the United Kingdom, France, Germany, and other countries. Soviet work in mathematics, astronomy, physics, electronics, and mechanics is outstanding, but work in biology and chemistry is not as impressive as it is in other countries or in other branches of science in the Soviet Union.

In space, the Soviet Union has led in the power of its rockets. This gives greater payload with higher destructive power, and multiple warhead potential increases the difficulty of interception. In the field of intercontinental missiles, the race has awesome implications. According to the Institute for Strategic Studies as reported by the *New York Times* on September 14, 1967, the United States had 1,054 Minutemen and Titan ICBM's while the Soviet Union had 460, rising to 550 by the middle of 1968. The Americans have 650 Polaris-type missiles while the Russians possess 130. And the death of a Russian cosmonaut and three American astronauts has had a sobering effect on the heady enthusiasm of both countries in their race to the moon.

In the atomic energy field, the race between the two nations is also carried out on two levels: military and the peaceful. Since the Test-Ban Treaty, nuclear weapon testing has been carried out underground, and is periodically reported by seismic stations close to the U.S.S.R. Both countries have built atomic submarines which are deployed in the oceans of the world. Nuclear power plants are satisfying the growing Soviet needs for energy, and extensive research is carried out on all phases of nuclear physics, chemistry, and biology, particularly at the Joint Institute of Nuclear Research at Dubno, at the Kurchatov Institute for Atomic Research, and at many other laboratories and universities throughout the vast reaches of the Soviet Union.

Organizational changes seem to have subsided with the current absence of strong personalities such as Stalin and Khrushchev. The State Committee on Science and Technology formulates policy, supervises planning, and allocates funds for science and technology. Basic research is carried out by the traditional Academy institutes and at special "science cities." Successful work at the science city at Novosibirsk has encouraged Soviet planners to create one at Serpukhov some fifty miles south of Moscow. At Serpukhov the largest particle accelerator in the world is nearing completion and extensive laboratories for biology and biochemistry have been activated. University research is still limited to Moscow, Novosibirsk, Leningrad and Kiev. Industrial laboratories are also lacking in the Soviet Union; at present emphasis is placed on building pilot plants to facilitate the introduction of new technology.

The ideological problems of Marxism and science have been relegated to their proper place: the implications of science for philosophy rather than the implication of philosophy for science. Although attempts are still made to fit new concepts relating to automation, computers, and cybernetics into the Procrustean bed of Marxism, the discussion has lost its harsh polemical character, and vituperative personal attacks are no longer made. The audience has been extended from the limited group of readers of the monthly *Voprosi filosofii* to the much more numerous readers of the weekly *Literaturnaya Gazeta*. The latter has a full-page discussion of current philosophical, educational, and public questions by scientists.

Khrushchev attempted to "proletarize" the new generation of university graduates by requiring two years of practical work before a boy or girl could enter an institution of higher learning. The attempt thoroughly disrupted the Soviet educational system just at the time when some American leaders were praising it as the basis of Soviet preeminence in space. Recent reforms have repaired some of the damage, however, and more and more attention is placed on early identification of unusual ability and special schools for the gifted.

Communication with Western science and scientists has been restored to what it was before the Revolution. Extensive information scanning service, thorough abstracting and indexing of scientific publications, and reprinting of Western journals and textbooks give Soviet scientists wide access to the results of work done abroad. Many Soviet scientists also visit the United States and other Western countries under the auspices of cultural exchange agreements. The language barrier still hinders Western scientists, however, though this barrier has been lowered by a widespread program of translating Russian periodicals into English.

During the fifty years since the Bolshevik Revolution, science and technology have become the dominant forces in Russia. They have replaced Marxist doctrine as the weapon of the Soviet leadership for world domination and as the hope of the Russian people for a happy life of the future.

THEMES AND VARIATIONS IN SOVIET LITERATURE

Max Hayward

One can say without much fear of contradiction that the only significant work produced in the fifty years of the Soviet period is in the Russian language and is a continuation of the pre-revolutionary Russian tradition, however distorted or mutilated it may at times have been. The Soviet claim to have created a "multinational" literature must be disputed. Only Russian literature had the metropolitan concentration, the inherited richness and variety, to survive in the rigorous post-revolutionary climate. Other cultural traditions within the Soviet Union faced impossible odds, and any promise that they might have resisted strong pressure to assimilate to Great-Russian models was extinguished in the late twenties and early thirties by brutal campaigns against "bourgeois nationalism" and the application of the principle "nationalist in form and socialist in content."

Neither is there much sign, in the Soviet period, of any fructifying influences on Russian literature from the non-Russian periphery, except for a certain Jewish element (notably Isaac Babel)—but this, too, has been basically Great-Russian in its roots and modes of expression. It is only quite recently that there have been discernible stirrings in the Ukraine (which suffered particularly from the campaign against "bourgeois nationalism"), the Baltic States, the Caucasus, and elsewhere, but it is too early to judge the importance of this centrifugal trend.

Despite the continuity (particularly in formal terms) with pre-revolutionary Russian literature, there are certain features of the literary response to the Soviet experience which are specific to this particular historical setting. The present paper will focus mainly on such distinguishing features. This means looking at Russian literature of the Soviet period for the light it may throw on the thinking of the Russian intelligentsia during this time when it was violently wrenched out of the mainstream of European development and all but physically destroyed. From the contrast between certain typical attitudes of the twenties and moods that have been articulated in literature in the years since Stalin's death, one can draw useful conclusions about the effects of Soviet cultural policy over the last five decades. It is only during these two periods that one can be reasonably certain that ideas expressed in literature were more or less freely arrived at, and not merely the result of intimidation or opportunism.

There is no doubt of the genuineness of the immediate reactions to the October Revolution, and of the attitudes underlying much of the prose and poetry through N.E.P. to the "great turning point" of 1929, and even beyond this into the early thirties. But apart from a slight relaxation during the war, the succeeding years until 1953 saw the development of a literature which offers no insight into the real thoughts or feelings of those writers who still published. There was no way of telling a true conformist from a false conformist, and only after Stalin's death was it possible once again to discern faces behind the masks.

It was not until the early thirties, with the promulgation of the doctrine of "socialist realism," that the Party began to insist that literature and the arts should fulfill a crudely defined political and social function. The ineffectual search in nineteenth-century literature for social ideals and "perfect" human beings to embody them provided antecedents for an aesthetic theory which demanded of writers the portrayal, for avowedly inspirational purposes, of "positive heroes." But the attempt to impose this doctine by external pressure was a total failure. Those responsible for cultural policy in the twenties (including Lenin and Trotsky) were intelligent enough to see this. They realized that the application of mechanical controls and doctrinaire pressures would result only in *false* conformism. Being intellectuals themselves, they understood that the most satisfactory way of controlling and harnessing the intelligentsia would be to allow it to develop with *comparative* latitude some of its own spontaneously generated delusions.

THE LURE OF REVOLUTION

Of course, for many Russian intellectuals the October Revolution was politically sordid. One did not have to be committed to a non-Bolshevik party to see Lenin's seizure of power as a usurpation which could have frightening consequences. Maxim Gorky, as is clear from his famous articles denouncing Lenin in *Novaya Zhizn'*, saw it in this light.[1] If statistics were available, one might discover that a majority of the Russian intellectuals were similarly sceptical of the October Revolution, if not hostile to it.[2] We are interested, however, in the minority whose acceptance of October as some kind of millennial event made it possible for the architects of Bolshevik cultural policy to feel that they could "win over" the intelligentsia, through the medium of art and literature, and incorporate it more or less painlessly, as an ally, in the new scheme of things.

It was soon realized by the Bolshevik leaders (Lenin and Trotsky were specific on this point) that the attempt to create a "proletarian" culture was bound to fail, resulting at best only in the assimilation of a few talented workers and peasants to already existing cultural standards. Bogdanov's *proletkult* was soon condemned and disbanded. The proletariat might in time be able to produce its own writers and artists, just as it would certainly produce engineers and scientists—this was only a matter of education—but in the meantime, there would obviously have to be considerable reliance on "bourgeois specialists" in this field as in others. Hence was born the concept, in art and literature, of the "fellow travelers" whose co-operation, or at least benevolent neutrality, was sought in the first few years after the revolution by guarantees, such as those given in the famous Party resolution of 1925, that there would be no undue interference with the creative process.

Not all Russian writers accepted this compromise and some saw clearly enough that in conditions of half-freedom the intelligentsia would only help to prepare the ground, seemingly of its own free-will, for its own future subjection. But a significant part of the literary intelligentsia in the twenties sought to interpret the Revolution in such a way as to make possible some degree of intellectual and moral accommodation with it. These attempts at rationalization were often (as in the case of Blok and Esenin) short-lived and swiftly ended in disillusionment that brought tragedy in personal terms, but not before they had contributed to the creation of a cultural climate which facilitated the abject surrender of later years. In some measure the literary ferment in the Soviet Union today can be seen as a revolt against attitudes more or less freely arrived at by the fellow-traveling intelligentsia of the twenties.

Some immediate poetic reactions to the October Revolution had already established the archetypes of the fellow-traveling pattern of thought, and there can be no question that they were spontaneous and genuine. Blok's "Twelve" was not written to order, but it gave a kind of higher sanction to the Bolshevik seizure of power by investing it with metaphysical, mystic qualities which put it in a traditional framework of Russian historio-sophic speculation. Blok was consciously paying tribute in his poem to the exalted ideas associated with the noted historian of the Russian intelligentsia, Ivanov-Razumnik,[3] and the "Scyths." This group which also included Andrei Bely and the "peasant" poets Esenin and Kluyev, was brought together on the basis of a common acceptance of the October Revolution. As a "symbolist" Blok had always tended to find cosmic meaning even in the most squalid reality, and he was attracted by an interpretation of the revolutionary events in terms of familiar Russian messianism. The idea of the Russian people as a God-bearer (*narod-bogonosets*) endowed with higher instinctive wisdom before which the intelligentsia must bow, was congenial to Blok as to many other Russian intellectuals who were tormented by their feeling of estrangement from the people.

Ivanov-Razumnik wrote about the "Twelve," in an essay that appeared in 1919, in a way which convincingly relates it to his "Scythian" ideology. He described the October Revolution as, in effect, a sequel to the revolution begun by Christ. Christianity—we are here on familiar Dostoyevskian territory—had gradually been frustrated by the power of the old world, by Rome which had penetrated and taken it over. The role of Russia, whose hour was now at hand, was to renew the gospel of spiritual freedom and to ensure its triumph by translating it on a world scale into terms of political and social freedom:

> Twenty centuries ago there came the good tidings of the spiritual liberation of mankind, but it is clear that apart from the inner freedom proclaimed by Christianity, the world must have *external* freedom, complete political and social liberation. The old world of our times has received the good tidings of universal social revolution just as the old world in the days of Petronius received the good tidings of the spiritual revolution.[4]

In Ivanov-Razumnik's view—also of course a commonplace among a section of the Russian intelligentsia—Russia was uniquely qualified to complete mankind's unfinished revolution (of which October had ushered in the final stage) by virtue of her spiritual maximalism, her capacity for total commitment, her ability to embrace and assimilate the cultural values of the whole world, her *vsechelovechnost'*.

With specific reference to the "Twelve"—and his interpretation was never repudiated by Blok—Ivanov-Razumnik expounded a "symbolic" view of the October Revolution which was breathtaking —but probably no less appealing to some intellectuals—in its audacious universalism. Elaborating on the imagery of the twelve Red

Guards taking pot-shots at the old Russia and led by an invisible Jesus Christ, Ivanov-Razumnik wrote:

> *The Twelve* is a poem about revolutionary Petersburg at the end of 1917 and the beginning of 1918. It is a poem about blood, dirt, crime, and the fall of man, but that is on one level. *On the other level* [italics supplied] it is a poem about the eternal universal truth of the Revolution, about how the new good tidings of the liberation of man come into the world through these blood stained people. For were not the twelve apostles also murderers and sinners?

In reply to this startling question he quotes the fifth chapter of the Acts of the Apostles about how Peter caused Ananias and Sapphira to drop down dead for having hidden part of their property from the Christian commune. The killing of the prostitute in the poem by a Red Guard (also Peter!) because she had been tempted by the material goods offered her by counterrevolutionaries is thus found to be paralleled in the Gospels, and Bolshevik violence against the bourgeoisie is made to appear not to contradict Christian teaching.

From this it is a short step to the insidious idea that the twelve sinful Red Guards (i.e. the Bolsheviks) are the unconscious instruments of a higher truth. They embody the instinctive "God-bearing" rightness of the people and, although in words they reject Christianity ("freedom, freedom, without the cross!"), they are really led by Jesus Christ, because they are completing His revolution. This idea of a higher truth temporarily obscured by the ugliness of every-day reality, the belief that there can be an ultimate, hidden good that is unwittingly served by evil means—at least as expressed in Blok's poem and in Ivanov-Razumnik's exegesis on it—was the most sophisticated of the early intellectual attitudes to the Revolution. It subsisted in more secular forms for a long time. It was quite compatible with the Marxist dialectic, except that the will of God (or "providence") was substituted for the inevitable historical process, and everything that happened in its name could be thought of as ultimately justified.

It is pathetic to see the millennial view of the revolution reflected in the simpler mind of Esenin. He also embraced the theories of the "Scyths" but without dialectical subtlety. With childlike innocence and wholeheartedness, in verse marked by very concrete imagery, he spoke of the revolution in strongly religious language, associating the figure of Christ with the revolution, paraphrasing events in terms of the Passion, and totally misunderstanding the intentions of the Bolsheviks by presenting October as the dawn of a rural utopia in which the power of the accursed machine (identified of course with the

West) would be broken. He seems actually to have believed in the imminent establishment of God's kingdom on earth—he spoke of the revolution as no less than the second coming of Christ, and the beginning counterrevolution as the threat of a new crucifixion. In his poem "Jordan Dove" (June 1918) he proclaimed himself a Bolshevik and drew a picture of a village paradise in which the Virgin Mary was a familiar every-day figure.

This extreme state of self-delusion fostered by the heady sophistries of his intellectual friends was bound to be followed by bitter disenchantment, and it is the disillusioned verse of Esenin, in the few years before his suicide in 1926, that most affected the mood of his contemporaries. His reaction to the disappointment of grotesque hopes was one which only encouraged a feeling of resignation towards the revolutionary *fait accompli.* In 1918, in his long poem "Inonia," he tried to secularize his earlier vision of heaven on earth, violently rejecting Christianity and extolling the cosmic potentialities of man as his own saviour. But this was only a rhetorical flourish which was soon followed by verse in which he dwelt on his sense of being pathetically irrelevant in the new society. In the famous poem "Soviet Russia" (1924) he describes his return to his native village only to find that people are singing "other songs" (those of the brash "proletarian" rhymster Demyan Bedny) and that he is not needed.

Esenin was the first to give effective artistic expression to the idea of the defeated and disillusioned individual who meekly accepts the image of himself as an ineffectual, unwanted alien body who has been "thrown on the rubbish-dump of history." [5] This contagious attitude of surrender to the supposedly inevitable was not quite complete. In one important respect he showed defiance, namely in a refusal to give up his integrity as a poet: "I'll take what comes. / Accept things as they are. / I'm ready to follow in their steps. / To October and May I'll offer up my soul, / But never surrender my beloved lyre." Esenin did not live to see the end of the decade when he would have been expected to give up his lyre too.[6]

It is almost a relief to turn to the only significant Soviet poet, Vladimir Mayakovsky, who really understood and accepted the revolution in the same spirit as its makers. It is true to say that he was the only poet of the Soviet era—Stalin knew what he was doing when he "canonized" him in 1935—who gave original artistic expression, in Marxist and Leninist idiom, to the revolution. He no doubt represented as significant a minority among the Russian intelligentsia of the twenties as those who resignedly accepted their own rejection by the times, or those who claimed to perceive a "higher" reality behind the new scheme of things. Pasternak, his antipode, who was fascinated by him, saw in him an outstanding representative of a traditional Russian type that is fanatically devoted to chaos.

It has been suggested that in *Dr. Zhivago* the strange figure of Klintsov-Pogorevskikh (in the chapter "Farewell to the Past") may have been intended as a portrait of the Mayakovsky type. This provincial intellectual, a deaf mute who has been trained to speak (Mayakovsky once said of himself that an elephant had trod on his ear so that he perceived the world only visually), puts his view very plainly: "What you call disorder is just as normal a state of things as the order you are so keen on. All this destruction—it's the right and proper preliminary stage of a wide constructive plan. Society has not yet disintegrated sufficiently. It must fall to pieces completely, then a genuinely revolutionary government will put the pieces together on a completely new basis." His radical views and the vehemence with which he expounded them remind Zhivago of the nihilists in Dostoevsky, in particular of Peter Verkhovensky.

This type of intellectual, of whom there are enough in all societies, came into their own as Russia disintegrated in war and revolution, and Mayakovsky was their most eloquent spokesman. He had no time for the metaphysics of the "Scyths" and he was specifically anti-Christian. His great epic on the revolution, *Mystery-Bouffe,* performed in 1918 on the first anniversary, was a cheerfully blasphemous paraphrase of the story of the Flood, after which heaven on earth, in which there is no place for Christian humility or forgiveness, is built by proletarian toil: "My heaven is for all except for the poor in spirit, / Who from fasting have swollen up to the size of the moon, / It is easier for a camel to go through the eye of a needle, / Than for such an elephant to come to me, / Let him come, / Who has calmly planted a knife, / Into the enemy's body and walked away with a song! / Come, you who have *not* forgiven! / You shall be the first to enter my earthly kingdom."

Mayakovsky was, at least to outward appearances, the perfect literary ally of the Bolsheviks. He had boundless faith in a crude and schematic rationalism according to which Man could "scientifically" refashion himself and his society, vanquishing nature with machines ("If even [Mount] Kazbek gets in the way, pull it down!"). It is true that the outrageousness of his public performance masked private anguish and that in all the bravado and insolence of both his early and his late verse, there was a note of pain, but the other Mayakovsky rarely got a hearing from the drumbeater of the revolution.

THE FELLOW TRAVELERS

Between the "Scythian" affirmation of the revolution for what it patently was not (shortly before his death in 1921 Blok was to say "It was not these days we summoned") and the Mayakovskian glorification of its literal, surface ideals, there were other, more mundane attitudes amply represented in the prose of the twenties. This prose was for the most part concerned with recent revolutionary history or the contemporary scene, the nature of the drastically changed fabric and texture of Russian society, particularly as these changes affected the behavior and status of the individual. In contrast to later socialist-realist writing it carried conviction because of its undoubted "truth to life," its relative detachment, and its occasional undertones of distaste for the new order. A lot of it tended, like the vatic utterances of some of the poets, to invest the revolution and its aftermath with a kind of "legitimacy" as the expression, when all was said and done, of the *Volksgeist,* as something flowing naturally from Russian history in which a "Bolshevik" (though not a Marxist) current could easily be furnished with the credentials of tradition: the "Russian rebellion merciless and senseless" had good antecedents.

A typical and influential stance in this spirit was that of Boris Pilnyak, the author of the first Soviet novel, *The Naked Year* (1920), in which he depicted the revolution as an unleashing of "dark" and "elemental" (a favorite word of the period) forces. The raw vigor of the "people" was tellingly contrasted with the degeneracy of a moribund "Westernized" society. The Bolsheviks were seen, in a formative image which gained wide currency, as the iron-willed, "energetically functioning men in leather jackets" who appeared, at least in the early stages, to be an emanation of the anarchic, cleansing forces of the revolution, which were inevitably represented, in another characteristic metaphor of the time, as a raging blizzard. Before long (for example in Pilnyak's later novel *Machines and Wolves,* 1923) it became more fashionable in "fellow traveling" literature—this because of increasing awareness of the actual, prosaic role of Leninist party organization—to lay more emphasis on conflict between "elemental" anarchy and the organizing will of the "men in leather jackets."

By the middle twenties, it is no exaggeration to say that Soviet literature was predominantly concerned, in one form or another, with an antagonistic confrontation of forces variously presented as a clash between old and new, town and country, man and machine, anarchy and discipline, even (in Leonov's *Sot*) between engineers and monks.

In this contest, which seemed less and less grandly apocalyptic as the unheroic years of N.E.P. went by, the attitude of most fellow travelers was that of spectators—sometimes benevolently neutral, at other times sceptical or hostile. Common to all the fellow travelers, however, was a feeling, nearly always discernible in their work, that they were witnessing a process which was somehow beyond good and evil, —a clash of implacable historical forces which it was impossible for human beings to influence, except as collective embodiments of them. This acceptance of the idea of society as an arena for the interplay of impersonal "forces," in which individual self-assertion was a futile, romantic gesture, was of more direct advantage to the new regime than the positive affirmation, later exacted from writers, of its ideology and goals. This resignation among the leading writers of the twenties (those, like Zamyatin,[7] who refused to see themselves as impassive witnesses to the Cyclopean struggle found it increasingly difficult to publish) did much to create a public mood in which individual dissent, the clinging to personal idiosyncracy appeared quixotic, irrelevant, comic, and reprehensible.

It is striking that even in novels where the author is plainly sympathetic to him, as in the one artistically outstanding novel of the first decade after the Revolution, Yuri Olesha's *Envy* (1927), the lone, romantic rebel against "history" is a doomed figure, conscious of his own hopelessness and futility, wallowing in his own debasement. Olesha's romantic anti-hero says: "We envy the coming epoch. This is the envy of old age." Furthermore, this last-ditch individualism is identified with *meshchanstvo* (a word always calculated to arouse feelings of guilt among intellectuals)—a petty concern with one's own private life and feelings, a longing to hide in the "musty mattresses of time," to borrow Mayakovsky's phase. The "coming epoch" is presented, through the eyes of the brash "new men," as a bright vista of ever increasing efficiency in the organization of industry and mass-consumption, an era dominated by youthful vigor, collective sport, uninhibited participation in public life—the new harmony of disciplined, purposeful activity crowds out the untidy, amorphous world of private feeling. There will no longer be any such thing as a private act, as Olesha tries to show in a little touch which betrays the residual squeamishness of one fated to live in the transitional period between past and future: his "positive hero," the representative of this future, is a "healthy man, full of the joy of life, who sang in the lavatory in the mornings."

This irony of Olesha's, which only underlines an awareness of defeat on the part of his pathetic "rebels," nevertheless brings out a certain ambiguity in the attitude of the fellow travellers. Throughout the twenties there was often an undertone of doubt as to whether the "new" would really triumph. In Leonov's *Badgers* (1925), for instance, the victory of the leather-jacketed Bolsheviks from the towns seems by no means certain. Breathtaking as it was in its audacity (the actions of "strong men" had then, as always, a fatal attraction for intellectuals) there was something foolhardy about their challenge to peasant Russia, which seemed to know only the two poles of inertia or anarchy. It is never quite clear whether Leonov, whose ambivalence in this respect was fairly typical, was more impressed by the iron will of the men from the towns, or by the capacity of the peasants to withstand their encroachments. The awesome problem of "who—whom?" was still unresolved. Leonov put his doubts (disguising them as the scepticism of one of his peasants) in the form of a parable about the Tsar Kalafat who built a tower "up to heaven" only to find, when it was completed, and he stood on the top to survey the natural world he thought he had vanquished, that he was surrounded by rustling forests as before: his tower had sunk into the ground (Chapter 15 of *Badgers*).

SOCIALIST REALISM

But with the First Five-year Plan and the beginning of collectivization, the possibility of overwhelming the inertia of nature, together with the human masses who had seemed to be just as unyielding, suddenly became real in the eyes of many Russian intellectuals. There is little doubt that Gorki's decision around this time to return to Russia and lend his authority to the Soviet regime was prompted by a genuine feeling that the "revolution from above" might well succeed not only in the construction of an industrial society based on social justice, but also in ending the cultural schism between the people and the intelligentsia.

Dazzled by this glorious vision, a number of Soviet writers abandoned the "wait-and-see" attitude of the N.E.P. period and declared themselves—almost with the millennial fervor of the earliest revolutionary days—for the "splendid surgery" by which not only the material world but human nature itself would now be transformed (for instance, Leonov in *Sot*—1931, and Katayev in *Time, Advance!*—1933). In his Candide-like novel *Hulio Hurenito* (1922), the sardonic Ilya Ehrenburg had prophesied that Communist prisons would not differ greatly from bourgeois ones, and in his *Protochny Street* (1927) had shown the revolution hopelessly bogged down in the mire of N.E.P., but even he was now carried away by the vision of Russian society being hurled into the future—into a new Promethean era in which, among other things, the twilight of a jaded intelligentsia, henceforth redundant except for its technical and professional skills, would be lit up by the garish but warming glow of blast furnaces. The old search for an eternally elusive solution to the "accursed questions" which had traditionally beset the "critically thinking section of society," would be blissfully abandoned and the voice of doubt would be drowned out by the symphony of a revolutionary upsurge unknown in history—men and machines working in harmony, an end to the estrangement of man from man, as well as from his natural environment and the processes and product of his labour.

This attitude on the part of some writers and of a section of the intelligentsia at large was by no means, in the early thirties, merely a response to *force majeure*. It is true that Pilnyak and Zamyatin had been hounded and publicly arraigned in 1929, and that this intimidated rank and file members of the existing literary organizations which were to be "Bolshevized" with as little ceremony as the peasants were to be collectivized.[8] A reign of terror by the "proletarian" writers' association (R.A.P.P.) was openly designed to force literature into specific ideological confines, and life became very difficult for writers who hesitated to make a positive political commitment.

But in a way characteristic of the Stalin period, this campaign of intimidation was followed by a "liberal" breathing space: In April 1932 the Party suddenly disbanded R.A.P.P. and announced its intention to form a "unified" writers' organization which, in an apparent gesture of reconciliation, would be open to all, irrespective of their class antecedents (i.e., whether they had been "proletarians" or "fellow travelers") as long as they were prepared to give their support to the Party and to assent to the literary doctrine of socialist realism: This latter was suddenly sprung on the literary community, without any previous public debate, in May 1932.[9] While this appeared at the time as an attempt to provide a relatively loose organizational and doctrinal framework which would accommodate and give scope to vastly different individualities—ranging from, say, Fadeyev to Pasternak—it became increasingly clear after the fairly easy-going First Writers' Congress held to inaugurate the new Union of Soviet Writers in 1934, that the new arrangement was really meant to homogenize the writers both ideologically and artistically, and to convert them gradually into an obedient adjunct of the Central Committee's propaganda apparatus.

But in the early thirties this was not apparent to everybody. It was a time of confusion in which nobody can be blamed for thinking that the political situation was still fluid and that no irrevocable choices had been made. In any case, some major writers evidently felt that to be yoked, however ignominiously, to what appeared to be a great national enterprise involving the masses, offered at last a release from the particular hell of the Russian intelligentsia—the sense of having been severed from the "people." The sacrifice of one's intellectual and moral independence did not seem too high a price to pay—though in fairness to those Soviet intellectuals who succumbed to this particular temptation, it must be said that it happened in an era when all too many intellectuals in Western societies were easily beguiled into shedding the burden of individual responsibility. The tragedy of the Russian intelligentsia in the thirties was made more poignant by the fact that, after 1929, they had no free choice in the matter, and could only pretend to themselves that they had. It is painful now to read the novels of the late twenties and early thirties in which the hitherto self-evident right to make one's own moral or intellectual judgements was virtually equated with treason to the higher cause of humanity.

The most memorable and subtle work on these lines was Ehrenburg's *Second Day* (1932) whose effect was no doubt at the time all the greater for its having been written in Paris; there could be no question of external constraints on the author. It was also distinguished by a "European" smoothness of style which made it palatable to Western readers and hence positively dazzling to more ingenuous Russian ones. It can still be read as a good summary of most of the delusions of the first post-revolutionary decade. The inevitable biblical parallel suggested already in the title is developed in such a way as to liken the building of socialism to Genesis ("Kuznetsk was like the creation of the world"). The hero—or rather the "anti-hero" in the new topsy-turvy scale of values—is a hereditary intellectual, Volodya Safonov, who, as much as he would like to accept the social and political ideals of October, is by temperament incapable of going against his conscience—the "old disease" which had afflicted his father, a man who got into trouble both before and after the revolution for protesting against injustice. After several attempts to overcome this affliction—he is needless to say envious of those who are able to do so without qualms—Volodya drifts into the despairing state of an outcast whose virtues of mind and character are a source not of strength but of guilt. He becomes a spiritual *émigré.*

Because it is clear that Ehrenburg was thrashing out what he genuinely fancied to be his own dilemma, the portrait of Safonov is full of insight and one gets a vivid idea from this novel of what it was like, in the tightening vise of early Stalinism, to be a lone intellectual clinging to moral and aesthetic standards at variance with those of the "collective." With terrifyingly perverse logic Ehrenburg argued, obviously intent most of all on persuading himself, that the only alternatives before his sensitive and independent minded hero were either to submit to the general will or to become an "enemy," a traitor. The author has him commit suicide, but in the endless variations on this theme in Soviet literature right up to the death of Stalin, he would more likely have found grace by "seeing the light" and making his submission. Alternatively he would be unmasked and destroyed. In retrospect it may be seen that the achievement of socialist realism was not in creating "positive heroes" to serve as inspiring models to the reader (they were far too wooden and contrived), but in playing on a natural feeling of guilt, particularly among intellectuals, and making it appear that there was something shameful about having a mind of one's own. The constant harping on this theme, like all preaching by negative example, was not without effect. Whether or not it increased the production of the blast furnaces, it certainly contributed to the desolation of the spirit by which thinking Russians were even more sorely tried than by physical terror.

THE GENRE OF SILENCE

The promise of the early thirties, which found such persuasive expression in the work of leading fellow-traveler writers such as Ehrenburg, Leonov, Katayev and the now broken Pilnyak (in *The Volga Flows to the Caspian,* 1930), quickly proved to be a mirage. Those who chose, like Isaac Babel, to practice what he called at the Writers' Congress in 1934 the "genre of silence" were the wiser and, oddly enough, had about as much chance of escaping physical extinction as those who, for whatever reason and however abjectly, chose the path of conformity. I have so far laid stress on those writers who "accepted" the revolution and its consequences and were able to find some mode of accommodation with it. In drawing up a balance-sheet of the last fifty years they are clearly crucial to any consideration of the extent to which the cultural policy of the new regime was successful. It could only be successful in so far as it was able to produce true conformists, i.e., people who had really persuaded themselves that submission was right and necessary, and who were able to convey this conviction in artistically effective terms. Only through such spokesmen could literature be expected to play its "educational" role with any authority. But the gradual increase in external constraints failed to achieve anything but a conformity whose genuineness was increasingly in doubt.

This was underlined in the thirties and (except for a short interlude during the war) until Stalin's death by the stubborn silence of Anna Akhmatova and Boris Pasternak, two poets who became symbolic figures, a last source of moral authority for the Soviet intelligentsia. In the worst of times they were most eloquent when they said nothing. There is an astonishing consistency—almost to the point of monotony in the case of Akhmatova—about their lives and their poetic response to the times in which they lived. Neither, unlike Blok, Bely or Esenin, affected to perceive a "higher" meaning in the October Revolution. Akhmatova saw it with prophetic matter-of-factness as the beginning of a long time of troubles in which the life of the poet would be difficult, if not impossible: "Now nobody will want to listen to songs, / The days foretold have come to pass . . . Not long ago, as free as a swallow, / You made your morning flight, / But now you will be a hungry beggar, / Knocking at the door of strangers who will not open up." [10]

Pasternak's attitude toward the revolution was a little more ambiguous, and not easy to read out of his work. Judging by his hero Zhivago's momentary exhilaration at its "splendid surgery," Pasternak was himself perhaps not unaffected for a time by the mood of the left-wing intelligentsia. But this was certainly short-lived and on the evidence of his prose sketch *Without Love* (1918), which prefigures *Zhivago,* he evidently soon decided that the revolutionary zeal of some of his contemporaries was like a state of trance in which they had lost their sense of proportion.[11]

REVALUATION OF ALL VALUES

The trance turned into a nightmare, and when it slowly began to fade after 1953, such central questions in Soviet literature as the place of the individual in society were re-examined in the light of a grim experience which had scarcely been envisaged in the twenties or the early thirties. Only a chosen few of the older surviving writers could stand by what they had written previously, without revising their own past. Akhmatova, for example, had said as much as needed to be said at the height of the nightmare in her *Requiem,* which she lived to see published abroad.[12] Pasternak completed *Dr. Zhivago* not long after Stalin's death and defied the most fearsome of Soviet taboos by deliberately arranging for its publication abroad. The continuing embargo on it inside the country is self-defeating, as is clear from the constant echoes of Pasternakian ideas and beliefs in the work of younger poets.

Of almost equal significance in the post-Stalin period have been those writers, such as Ehrenburg, Leonov, and Katayev, who survived to write work in which the values urged by them in the late twenties and early thirties are drastically reviewed in the light of their subsequent experience. This "defection" has contributed a great deal, in the crude terms of literary politics, to the establishment of conditions in which younger writers, for the most part unknown before Stalin's death, have been able to achieve—fighting every inch of the way—a surprising measure of creative autonomy. What we have witnessed in Russia in the last ten years or so must be historically unique: an inexorable "revaluation of all values" in which a contrite older generation has been an ally of the younger one.

The process of reassessment was begun, fittingly, by Ehrenburg in *The Thaw* (1954) which, despite its jejune manner, must now be regarded as a document of historical importance. The chastened Ehrenburg of the early fifties seems to be replying to the eager fellow-traveling Ehrenburg of the early thirties. If, in the earlier novel, the lone nonconformist had been presented as a socially harmful element who was doomed to be destroyed during the forced march to socialism, in *The Thaw* this judgement is reversed and the reader is made to feel that the only honorable course in a society where public dissent is not tolerated is to hold to one's beliefs (which are here, needless to say, not political, only aesthetic) and wait for better times. The characters in *The Thaw* who are out of sympathy with prevailing artistic standards are quite passive and keep their thoughts to themselves—precisely what Volodya Safonov was condemned for doing. What he might have become, had he "conformed," is conveyed in the portrait of the cynical young artist in *The Thaw,* Volodya Pukhov, who paints socialist-realist canvasses because this is the only way to make a career ("with ideas you will only break your neck"), but hates himself for it and secretly envies another painter who, at the price of being a social outcast, paints as he pleases.

In the few years after publication of *The Thaw* the lone dissident established himself in Soviet literature despite furious opposition from orthodox critics and occasional attempts to reverse the trend by political intimidation (notably in 1957 and 1963). In his *Not by Bread Alone* (1956)—another poor novel which is historically important—Dudintsev went a stage further than Ehrenburg by suggestiong that a person who goes against the current ought to perform an active function in society. He implied that it is the duty of a good citizen—and this goes for "true" Communists in particular—to fight for what they believe to be right. The guardians of official ideology have been peculiarly helpless to prevent the development of this theme which displaced, or made ludicrous, the Stalinist concept of the "positive hero."

But even the Dudintsev kind of hero is now old-fashioned. In recent years a frequent complaint against the young prose writers is that they have ceased to be interested in any kind of hero. Certainly, in many of the stories and novels of Kazakov, Aksyonov, Tendryakov, Voinovich, and others, the exploration of human behaviour and motive tends to revolve less around the "civic" functions of their characters and much more around their socially undirected acts and thoughts or their private moral dilemmas. No amount of fulmination against the "deheroicization" of literature, against preoccupation with small trivial "truths" instead of the "major truth" (which has not been redefined since Stalinist days as consisting in a broadly optimistic view of progress toward "communism") has had any effect.

It is an indirect confession of failure that there is now a tendency to try to make it appear that socialist realism is a much broader and more elastic doctrine than formerly appeared. When it is in decay and can no longer be enforced by terror, a dogmatic system has little choice but to present itself as being in reality more accommodating than it was thought to be. As time goes on, points of view, even large concepts such as cybernetics and sociology, previously denounced as "bourgeois," are being subsumed into the "treasure house of Marxism Leninism." In line with this general trend, socialist realism is gradually being "liberalized" so that at times it appears tolerant of any literary phenomena (this now includes such imports as Kafka and Ionesco) which, in the face of initial opposition, gradually gain currency in the Soviet literary community.[13] Another sign of the new tolerance is the relatively moderate tone of "conservative" literary criticism. Younger prose writers are rebuked for "factography." Not many years ago the charge would have been "naturalism" and "distortion of Soviet reality." The boundary between "critical" and "socialist" realism has become hopelessly blurred, as the facts of life in the *pays réel* have gained admittance to literature. It was impossible to expect even the most complaisant of Soviet writers to draw over-optimistic conclusions about Soviet life in the accounts they were allowed to render after the Twentieth Party Congress in 1956.

The death, from inanition, of the "positive hero," the dislodgment of neat romantic projections by disorderly and disconcerting facts, the tolerance of literary influences formerly denounced as "alien," the uncomfortable (though still controlled) treatment in literature of some of the consequences of the "cult of personality"—all this has eroded the basis of official cultural policy. The result is a comic discrepancy—particularly noticeable in the jubilee year—between the otiose incantations in "authoritative" journals[14] and the actual practice of the literary journals—not only *Novy Mir* but also *Znamya, Moskva, Neva,* and others.[15]

What has really made nonsense of official literary doctrine, however, was the appearance (in one case with the highest approval) of several notable works which question the validity of the Soviet historical experience, *in toto* or in large essential aspects such as collectivization.[16] The best known such work was Solzhenitsyn's *One Day in the Life of Ivan Denisovich* (1963). Of course, Solzhenitsyn's novel would never have been published if Khruschev had not permitted it for tactical reasons in his struggle with his "right wing" opponents. In his usual blundering impetuosity[17] he did not stop to think of the irreversible damage he was inflicting on the very socialist realism he aggressively upheld a little later at the famous Manege art exhibition. Since the novel has the unassailable finality of a true work of art, it cannot be hidden, ignored, or explained away. What makes it peculiarly awkward and unassimilable is that its existence "on the record" as a published work of Soviet literature has forever confused the issue —to put it mildly—of what is "permissible" in print. The piecemeal intrusion into literature of unpleasant detail about the seamy side of the Soviet past and present could always, up to a not easily definable point, be made to appear compatible with a reformed socialist-realism, but Solzhenitsyn destroyed the basis for rough-and-ready theoretical compromise with a neo-realism which, though "critical," could be presented as something helpful to the Party in its never-ending battle with recalcitrant human nature.

Solzhenitsyn is no mere "factographer." The "facts" in *One Day* are not self-contained—they are built into a compact symbolic pattern and prompt ironic reflections on all the cherished features of the Soviet "image." Indeed, the whole "building of socialism" is likened to the setting up of a concentration camp. In the context of the story there is no mistaking the implication of the passage about the prisoners building a new "Socialist Community Development": "But so far it was nothing more than bare fields covered with snowdrifts, and before anything could be done there, holes had to be dug, posts put in, and barbed wire put up—by the prisoners for the prisoners, so they couldn't get out. And then they could start building." Pasternak used exactly the same metaphor in the epilogue of *Dr. Zhivago,* where one of the hero's friends, who had survived the holocaust of the thirties, describes what happened when he was brought with a transport of prisoners to an open field in the middle of a forest: "They told us: 'Here is your camp. Settle down as best you can' . . . We cut down saplings with our bare hands in the frost to build huts. And would you believe it, we gradually built our own camp. We cut down the wood to build our own dungeons, we surrounded ourselves with a stockade, we equipped ourselves with prison-cells and watch-towers —we did it all by ourselves."

Pasternak explicitly took issue with the tragic delusions which had ended for so many Russian intellectuals in the way described by Zhivago's friend, an epitome of the fellow-traveling intellectual of the twenties who, in Zhivago's words, had "broken himself in like a circus horse." It is clear that Pasternak had in mind some of the leading Soviet writers of the twenties when he wrote: "A man who is not free always idealizes his bondage. This is how it was in the Middle Ages and the Jesuits always made play with it. Zhivago could not stand the political mysticism of the Soviet intelligentsia."[18]

The similarity of these two passages, which both make the same symbolic reference to the sense of Soviet history as it appears to the authors (and to many of their generation), shows how incongruous it is to try to maintain a division between the best work in post-Stalin literature published in the Soviet Union and the considerable body of prose and verse that has been published only abroad (apart from Pasternak, one may mention Sinyavsky and Brodsky). Of course very few works published inside the U.S.S.R. have broken through the continuing (but increasingly capricious) constraints on free expression as radically as Solzhenitsyn. Only he has been able to match, in direct utterance, the outspokenness of works so far published only in the West. It is fascinating, however, to see how Soviet writing in recent years has naturally reverted to the celebrated Aesopian techniques of an earlier age. There is almost nothing that cannot be said "between the lines" in the elusive manner which some Soviet writers even seem to prefer, because of the challenge it offers to their ingenuity.[19]

Most of the surviving fellow-travelers have now confronted, however obscurely, their "political mysticism" of the twenties and early thirties. An excellent example, worth giving at length, of how convoluted this can be is the case of Leonid Leonov. In 1963 he published a remarkable parable, *Evgenia Ivanovna,* which was favorably received by conservative critics and caused scarcely a stir among the reading public. The ambiguity that Leonov practiced so successfully for many years under Stalin proved, in this one extraordinary case, to be a fatal impediment to a repentant fellow-traveler trying to settle accounts with his past. There is something tragic-comic in this failure to communicate.

The story is about a Russian woman who at the end of the civil war leaves the country together with her husband. After a few months of destitute *émigré* life in Constantinople, her husband suddenly abandons her and disappears. Some years later, having heard persistent rumors that her first husband is dead, Evgenia Ivanovna marries an English professor of archeology whom she meets by chance in Paris at a moment of total despair, when she is contemplating suicide. The professor takes her on an archeological expedition to the Middle East, and while they are in Turkey, Evgenia Ivanovna suddenly feels acute nostalgia for Russia and urges her new husband to take her there, via the Caucasus, so that she can visit her mother's grave in Rostov. Because of his international standing, the professor, most unusually, is given a visa by the Soviet consul in Turkey to enable him to go to Russia through Georgia. This time is evidently in the middle twenties. The couple are accorded a warm official welcome in Tiflis and are told that the best Intourist guide in the Soviet Union will be attached to them during their stay in Georgia and their subsequent journey to Russia proper. When the guide presents himself he turns out to be Evgenia Ivanovna's first husband, Stratonov.

The purpose of this curiously contrived melodramatic situation is clearly to make it possible for the author to put into the mouth of an utter scoundrel the *sub specie aeternitatis* view of the significance of the October Revolution which had been typical of the fellow travelers in the twenties. Stratonov justifies his return to Russia and his betrayal of his wife in terms of a higher loyalty to Russia's historical destiny which he talks about as follows:

> The great minds of Russia have always prophesied for her a special, heroic—because she is free of European egotism—historical mission . . . It is a matter of the most ancient, universal human longing for peace, goodness and truth, that is, of establishing on earth a higher level of humanity . . . Vast Russia has taken upon herself her predestined task. In essence it is just another way to the stars, but unlike previous ones, which were devious and via heaven, the idea now is to thrust forward by the shortest possible, earthly route . . . I agree that this may require victims, but the inspiration of such eras as this gives those who live in them cataleptic powers of endurance and prolonged insensibility to suffering.

Filled with horror at this encounter with the man who had betrayed her and who has now reappeared suddenly as a kind of harbinger of the "new Russia," and nauseated by his brand of messianic Bolshevism, Evgenia Ivanovna begs her English husband to take her *home* to England—though she has never been there before. She no longer wishes to travel on to Russia.

Thus, in the context of the novel, England seems to embody a type of historical experience and a view of the world antithetic to those now prevalent in Russia. Like the Slavophile Khomyakov before him, Leonov evidently sees in England a pattern of organic social growth which has not been interrupted or violently distorted by "revolutionary" change. As in *Dr. Zhivago,* the betrayal of a woman becomes a symbol for the attempt to transform life in accordance with preconceived notions which, in any case, speedily degenerate into the "ideological" patter of the timeserver.[20]

The younger prose writers, and particularly the poets who have made their mark since 1956, are less obsessed with the Stalinist past, but it weighs too heavily on the national conscience to be ignored by them. Voznesensky, to take the best example, is the author of a historical allegory, *The Skull Ballad,* in which he considers the sense of what happened in 1937 (though he appears to be speaking of Peter the Great) and in which (again an echo of *Dr. Zhivago*) the fate of a woman is the counter-point to preoccupation with reshaping the world. ("Love is so small who cares for love / In times like these men build and set a world on fire.") In general, the writing of the younger generation often betrays a brooding concern with the sense of Russia's destiny. Moreover, in considering the wider problems raised by Soviet history—such as the relationship of means to ends—they clearly find the flexible, "dialectic" ethic of Marxism-Leninism unacceptable, and innumerable articles in recent years rebuking them for "abstract humanism" have had no effect. It is unlikely that Soviet writers could again be induced or forced to ignore the existential dilemmas which troubled the "critical realists."

BACK TO THE ACCURSED QUESTIONS

In his article *What is Socialist Realism,* Sinyavsky has argued that in its heyday, before the onset of its slow decomposition after 1953, socialist realism involved a return to a kind of eighteenth-century classicism for which certainty in the rightness of the Purpose was so strong that the role of literature was mainly to proclaim and propogate it (as Derzhavin and Mayakovsky did) and sing the praises of its apotheosized instruments (Catherine the Great or Stalin). The nineteenth century, on the other hand was a time of scepticism, irony, moral ambiguity, but also of a thirst for faith which is seen in almost all the figures—from Pushkin to Tolstoy—who still dominate the Russian consciousness. In Sinyavsky's view, the perfect image of the nineteenth-century Russian intellectual was Lermontov's Demon ("I wish to make my peace with heaven / I wish to love, I wish to pray. / I wish to believe in the good."). This craving for faith and anguish at one's consignment to a moral limbo was, as Sinyavsky points out, an admirable preparation for a reckless leap into some supposedly liberating commitment. It is only this that can explain the way in which Alexander Blok and other intellectuals in 1917 embraced the revolution with the ardor of religious converts. The more corroded they were by irony and self-doubt, the more prone they were to take the plunge. As Sinyavsky says: "The hunger of the nineteenth century prepared us Russians perhaps, for the way in which we so greedily threw ourselves on the dish cooked by Marx, and swallowed it without bothering to examine its taste or smell, or think about the consequences."

In the freedom of an enquiry not intended for immediate publication inside the country (just as, in his fiction, he has explored the effects of the "cult of personality" in terms of abnormal psychology, an area still largely off limits to Soviet writers), Sinyavsky has spelled out what is implicit in many significant works of post-Stalin literature: that the basic questions, far from being solved by Marx's recipe and its Leninist application, were only temporarily pushed out of sight. The Demon after his fatal love affair with the beautiful Tamara, was thrown back into his old tormented state, his anguished search for faith.

It is difficult to say whether the renewed search for answers to the old "accursed questions" will find any very forceful expression in present-day Soviet literature (only Solzhenitsyn, of the partially published prose writers, shows signs of measuring up to pre-revolutionary standards), or to speculate as to what direction it will take. It is enough for us to note, in general conclusion, that the mere fact of Soviet literature now being dominated by uncertainty about past, present, and future, speaks eloquently of the total failure of Soviet cultural policy. It has failed to harness literature and the arts (except by debasing them) to its aim of the social and moral transformation of man in a new image. It has failed to enlist the support of anyone truly gifted in the younger generation. It has failed even to retain the allegiance of those of the older generation who once thought of service to it, not as bondage, but as a kind of higher spiritual freedom.

Looked at from the point of view of its dominant themes, Soviet literature (at least in some of its best and most genuine representatives) has moved from qualified acceptance of the revolution through a period of meaningless and artistically barren lip-service to it, back to its starting point in traditional Russian literature whose genius was always expressed in its insights into moral and psychological ambivalence. Looked at from the point of view of form, the Soviet experience has been utterly destructive. Early attempts at innovation (e.g., the Serapion brothers, the "Formalist" critics, not to mention the many individual poetic and artistic styles of the twenties) were destroyed and replaced in the late thirties by an empty, bombastic pseudo-popular style which reminded many Russians of the "folksy," nationalist vulgarity of the age of Alexander III. The acolytes of this official style are still numerous and powerful. The Soviet ruling class still insists, for the most part, that literature and art should confirm it in its own crassness and mediocrity, and in the sterility of its social ideals. Perhaps, if it ever becomes more confident of itself, it might, like other ruling classes, cease to regard true aesthetic values as a threat to its power. Only the next fifty years will show.

THE DEMOCRATIC CHALLENGE TO COMMUNISM

Sidney Hook

From almost its very inception in October 1917, we have been hearing about the challenge of the Soviet Union to the West. In the early days the challenge appeared as a revolutionary threat to the stability and survival of the democratic world and its social order. But as the years rolled by, to the surprise of the engineers of the Russian Revolution, the workers of the Western world found that they had more than their "chains" to lose, indeed that the so-called chains of wage slavery gave them greater security and affluence, as well as greater freedom, than that enjoyed by their fellow workers in the Soviet Union. Whereupon the character of the Communist challenge changed. The change gradually developed with the shift in emphasis in the ideology of Soviet communism from international revolutionary messianism to the non-Marxist program of building socialism in one country.

The new challenge of communism was now presented in more positive and persuasive fashion. Soviet society was pictured as a model of social progress, as a community in which the rational ordering of human experience made possible the elimination of wasteful competition and the abolition of the endemic evils of depression, unemployment, hunger, and war. The promise of the socialist planned society was broadcast throughout the world. It was often coupled with the declaration that a new type of man was evolving within a new society whose motivation, ideals, and emotional life would transcend the limits of class societies of the last few millenia to a point that would justify reference to Soviet man as a new species of man.

These glad tidings of the new man in a new society, transmitted by every medium of propaganda, found their deepest resonance not among the workers of the world but primarily among the intellectuals and professional groups of the West. To be sure, this sympathetic answering response was somewhat shadowed by consciousness of the sustained and often raging terror that accompanied the process of human liberation and transformation. But all this was regarded by good people and advanced thinkers as the cost of social progress. The uncounted millions of victims of forced collectivization and periodic purges were explained either as sacrifices on the altar of historical necessity or as a uniquely Russian way of ushering in social change. Thus at the very height of the Moscow Treason Trials and their macabre rituals of public confession and private bloodletting, Beatrice and Sidney Webb published their massive book on *Soviet Communism: A New Civilization* in a second edition from whose title they dropped the question mark which had appeared in the first edition. Refusing a challenge from me to debate in print the evidence, they specifically endorsed the validity of the Moscow Trials, in a postscript, on the amazing ground that it was not impossible that the defendants were guilty, and hailed the new civilization, with its jurisprudential improvements on the Western theory and practice of law, as the wave of the future. About the same time in our own country, referring to the Soviet Union, Lincoln Steffens declared in his declining years that he had seen the future and that it worked.

The future is now and here! Fifty years have passed since the advent of the new society was proclaimed by Lenin in Russia. From the summit of its achievements, the leaders of the Soviet Union have invited their people and the "progressive" peoples of the world to assess and celebrate the accomplishments which they claim mark a "new epoch in world history." The examination of these claims has been made in scores of conferences and institutes throughout the world; this paper, delivered as a luncheon address, concluded one at the Hoover Institution. My remarks are in no way a summary but a personal judgment for which I alone take responsibility—a judgment made on the basis of what I can legitimately call a fifty-year study of the phenomenon.

In assessing the claims made for the Russian Revolution, one cannot but be impressed by their magnitude. The leaders of the Soviet Union claim to have established a socialist classless society, to have abolished the exploitation of man by man, to have introduced a new and higher form of democracy, to have engineered, for the first time in history, profound social changes in the light of a "scientifically grounded program of revolutionary action," to have effected a great liberating cultural revolution, and to have found the one and only key which—if we would only follow them—will unlock the door to world peace, universal prosperity, and universal freedom; in short give us the secular equivalent of the Kingdom of God on Earth.

What can one say in brief compass to these momentous assertions? Let us ignore the promises and turn to the achievements. With respect to the fields of industrialization and allied phenomena, we can acknowledge, even if we discount the exaggerations, the remarkable progress made. This progress is all the more impressive because it was made despite the destructive furies of civil war and military invasion. Let us not begrudge our admiration or be chary of appreciating production figures or look too closely at the statistical techniques by which they are compiled. But we must note at once that the great progress made in the sector of industrial production has not been matched by corresponding increases in the level of consumption—food, clothing, shelter, and the amenities of life. The citizens of the Soviet Union have little power to affect by their choices, political or economic, the relative distribution of capital resources. Further, the productive achievement of the Soviet Union differs in degree but not in kind from the tremendous strides toward industrialization observed in some fifty year intervals of Japanese and German history.

It does not detract from the significance of the Soviet industrial achievement to see it in perspective. The Pyramids are still one of the seven wonders of the world even if they are not as great as the Pharaohs thought they were. Even if all the claims that the Kremlin makes for its industrial achievement were uncontested, there would still remain two questions about it which every reflective person must ask, especially at the solemn moment of stock-taking. The first is: Was the tempo of industrialization and enforced collectivization of agriculture worth the cost in human blood and suffering? The second question is: Were these human costs necessary?

It would be presumptuous for anyone to answer the first question: "Were the results of the fifty-year Russian Revolution worth the human costs?" except the Russian people themselves. They paid the price. Theirs was the glory; theirs was the agony. Our judgment would reflect our moral values, not theirs. How can we tell what the Russian people, as distinct from their rulers, believe about the costs of the Revolution? What do they think when they reflect on the yawning abyss between the program under which the Bolsheviks seized power —"Land to the peasants! Bread to the workers! Peace and freedom for all!"—and present day realities?

There are usually two ways of determining what a people believe —what they say when they are free to say it, and what they do when they are free to do it. If the iron curtains of the world could be raised, one might infer from the movement of people whether they were content with their lot. But Soviet citizens are not only not free to emigrate, they cannot even move about freely within their own country. More important, under existing conditions how can Soviet citizens tell us freely what *they* believe about the costs of the Revolution when every means of expression lies in the hands of the state, and when critical communications, even when published abroad, are a criminal offence? We cannot therefore get a relevant answer to the first question until the Russian people are free to express themselves.

But we can answer the second question: "Were these costs necessary to achieve the desired goals?" A cost is necessary if there are no alternatives to a desired and desirable end. Taken as given, this is a question which can be answered on the basis of evidence, not feeling. Those who consider the events of the Russian Revolution as an indivisible whole and argue that all the actions taken, from the dissolution of the Constituent Assembly, to the enforced industrialization and collectivization, the punishment of peasant recalcitrance in the Ukraine by famine, the Moscow Trials, the blood purges, the deportations to work camps which were death camps for many, the Nazi-Soviet Pact, the resumption of the cold war—that these were all necessary parts of the logic of development—are demonstrably mistaken. There were alternatives. The half-hearted and incomplete process of de-Stalinization is a belated recognition that not all that happened in the darkest years of Stalin's rule was necessary. Rosa Luxemburg showed that under Lenin the dissolution of the Constituent Assembly, the only freely elected body under Communist rule, on the pretext that it was not a representative body, was not required to introduce the reforms demanded. Others have shown that terror was not a means to industrialization but a handicap. The purges of government, army, and Party were not necessary, as one naive, politically innocent American ambassador declared, to eliminate a Fifth Column headed apparently by Lenin's comrades-in-arms. It woefully weakened the readiness of the Soviet Union to resist Hitler's invasion. It is true that Stalin's forced industrialization increased Russia's capacity to withstand the Nazi assault. But it is also true that Stalin's policies, especially his doctrine of "social-fascism" according to which German Social Democracy was the chief enemy of the Germany working class and not German Nazism, helped Hitler come to power, then crush the German democratic, labor, and socialist movement and shortly unleash, with Stalin's benevolent help, the Second World War.

Every statement that an alternative course of action was possible requires detailed support. Some of it has been marshalled in this volume and elsewhere. I am prepared to offer evidence for the rest. These are questions of history that permit only of probable answers which scholars will discuss for many decades. Let us now look away from the questions of the past and turn our face to the present. Whatever the differences that divide us, let us proclaim our hope and willingness to live in permanent peace. Let us remind the Russian leaders of the obvious fact that if words are any clue to intentions, Moscow has far more to fear from Peking than from Washington. Nonetheless, let us ask after half a century, "What is the upshot of the Soviet experience which has been challenging us all these years?" Let us ask, "Wherein lies the challenge that *our* pluralistic open society can make to Soviet society as presently constituted?"

The challenge can be simply put in their own terms. The Soviet Union calls itself a socialist democracy. But how is it possible to have a socialist democracy without having a democracy? How can people be "guaranteed their social and political rights" without enjoying as a *sine qua non* the protection of the Bill of Rights of the so-called bourgeois revolutions of 1776, 1789, and February 1917? Lenin himself once called the Provisional Government the freest in the world. Any reasonable definition of democracy requires that government be based, directly or indirectly, upon the *freely given consent* of the adults governed. But how can consent be free where there is no freedom of speech, press, or assembly—where there is no freedom of art, science, or philosophy to develop autonomously? How can there exist a socialist democracy when people have less freedom of open opposition and dissent than the Bolsheviks themselves enjoyed not only under the democratic Kerensky government but even under the last tsar? How can there be a socialist democracy in a one-party dictatorship which is itself organized dictatorially? How can there be a genuine election where all the candidates are of one party, or must be approved by one party? In one of the few bon-mots which burst from the lips of the exasperated Labour Prime Minister Clement Attlee, when the Communists talked about their elections, he once declared: "An election under Communism is like a horse race with only one horse!"

We can restate the challenge in the idiom of Communist ideology to make it sound more profound: The advent of a socialist classless society was proclaimed in the Soviet Union three decades ago, in the Stalin Constitution of 1936. But according to Leninist doctrine, wherever the state exists there we have a dictatorship of one class over another. Only in a classless society will the state wither away. In the Soviet Union today the existence of the state is proudly hailed in the full panoply of its power. Against and over whom, then, is the state wielding its dictatorship? Who is exploiting whom?

In the Kremlin's little red book, *The Theses of the Central Committee of the C.P.S.U.,* published in 1967 in preparation for the anniversary of the great October Socialist Revolution, we are told: "With the victory of socialism the state of the dictatorship of the proletariat becomes a political organization of the whole people under the leadership of the working class." "As socialism develops the greater becomes the role of the Party." How can there be a proletariat or working class in a classless society? This mystery defies even the logic of dialectics. If the role of the Party becomes greater as socialism develops, what happens to the dictatorship of the proletariat? Does it become transformed into the dictatorship of the Party *over* the proletariat? As if eager to answer this question, the Central Committee declares: "The Communist Party is flesh of the flesh of the working class, of the people who work and create, and it constantly feels their unanimous support. The Party prizes the trust of the people and it has no other interests than those of the people."

Let us disregard the theoretical incoherence and semantic corruption of Communist rhetoric which misleadingly substitutes "leadership" for "dictatorship," "state," for "party," "people" for "class," and simply ask: If the peoples of the Soviet Union "trust" the Communist Party so much, why does the Party fear to give them the opportunity freely to express their support and to manifest that feeling of trust in genuine elections in which there are genuine options for a different point of view? In other words we say to the leaders of the Soviet Union: Why not put your words to the test? For fifty years, during which you exercised a monopoly of power, you have conditioned, purged, punished, trained, educated, and brainwashed the Russian masses—why not risk giving them a chance to show their confidence, trust, and love?

Actually a closer look at the official claims of the Soviet regime to the allegiance of its citizens exposes the hollowness of its democratic professions. For those claims assume that the Communist Party knows better what is in the best interests of the people than the people know themselves. It assumes that it has an historical mission to lead the workers not where they want or wish to go, but where they should go. The Party assumes that it possesses *the* scientific theory—if not absolutely infallible then the least fallible—to guide all of mankind where it should go—no matter at what cost. It refuses to acknowledge the operating maxim of a democracy, to wit, that those who wear the shoes know best where they pinch and have the right and authority to change their political shoes in the light of their own experience. In its arrogant paternalism, the Party assumes that Soviet citizens are like little children or slow witted adults who cannot tell when and where their shoes pinch. They therefore cannot be entrusted with self-government until the never-never era of true communism arrives when all scarcities of goods and services have been abolished, and no evil consequences will result from unwise choices.

It is here that we find the true issue that divides the Western democratic world, with all its evils and imperfections, from the Communist world. It is basically a moral issue, not an economic or religious issue or one of productivity. It is whether the generality of men have a right to choose their own destiny, including the right to choose wrongly, or whether their choices are to be made *for* them by benevolent despots whose despotism is likely to be more enduring than their benevolence. The issue of freedom that divides the two worlds is not one of free enterprise as opposed to collectivized economy. It is not the issue of capitalism or socialism. Neither one nor the other system exists in pure form anywhere in the world. It is rather the *freedom to choose* the system of economic arrangements under which we wish to live, and the right freely to change them in the wake of our experience. Nor is the issue one of religion—belief in one god or many or none. It is rather the freedom to worship or not to worship at any altar. Nor, despite the famous kitchen debate between Nixon and Khrushchev, is the issue one of producing commodities or services, or of who can get to the moon first or to the farther reaches of space. In a technological age, a command economy, in which human beings can be mobilized like so much raw material, may outproduce in some lines a free economy. Some slave societies have been richer than some free societies. But what free man will yield his freedom for comfort?

The challenge, in short, which democracy poses to Soviet communism is not a challenge to catch up with Western affluence or military power or technological efficiency. It is a moral challenge—a challenge to live up to its own claims, and to treat human beings as autonomous creatures with the inherent right to make their basic choices. This right is denied not only to so-called class enemies but to the very groups from which Communists profess to draw the patents of their legitimacy. Despite the double talk about workers' democracy, Soviet workers are denied the rights and privileges possessed by their fellows in democratic Western countries. There are no free and independent trade unions. There is no right to strike. A strike is tantamount to treason against the state. Nor is there an independent judiciary to appraise claims against the state. In any community where there is no right to strike and where there is no independent judiciary, what we have in effect is a system of forced labor.

There is an added moral challenge that is especially poignant after fifty years. Can the government of the Soviet Union tell, and live with, the truth about its own history, even about its early revolutionary history? The names of some of its early leaders still remain unmentioned and unmentionable within its vast borders. Will the regime have the courage, in reciting some of its remarkable triumphs, to disclose the truth about the purges, the genocidal treatment of the peasants who resisted forced collectivization, to unveil the mystery around the gruesome litany of confessions and self-abasement at the Moscow Trials, to open the records of the inferno of the work camps in all their grisly details? Dare it permit Khrushchev's unfinished story before the Twentieth Congress of the Communist Party, still unavailable in the Soviet Union, to be brought to completion?

How strange that to know the truth about much of their own past the people of the Soviet Union must read the accounts of those who live outside the Soviet Union! I do not believe I exaggerate when I say that the Soviet people will be able to find out more about what really happened and how, during some crucial periods of the past, by reading the essays and discussions presented in this and similar volumes than by what they read and hear at the official celebrations. Surely this challenge to permit free inquiry into its own history by its own scholars is really a modest one for the Soviet regime to meet. Its great works of production will appear even more heroic when the hardships, travail, and mistakes that accompanied them are known. Further, does it not proclaim that its attitude toward knowledge is rooted in a scientific outlook? And does not the record show that the greatest triumphs of Soviet science and technology occurred when their autonomy was respected while disasters have resulted in consequence of political intrusion into biology and economics? Why not, then, permit freedom of scientific historical research? Why not make available the materials about those already dead?

What has the Soviet Union to fear—to take one example that can stand for a thousand—from the publication within its borders of Svetlana Alliluyeva's childhood memories of the man who was master of Soviet destiny for twenty-five years? We all know how desperately the Soviet regime has sought to defame and discredit the book of Stalin's daughter—a book that contains no state secrets but reveals the feelings of a simple and courageous human being. It really has nothing to fear from anything that Stalin's daughter can say. What it must fear, because its message is overwhelming, is the significance of her action. If our open society, with all its faults, can inspire and kindle into flame a desire for freedom in the heart of the sheltered offspring of the supreme despot in recent history—who is safe in the Soviet Union from the seduction of the free society? That is what the Soviet regime must really worry about.

I do not wish to leave the impression that Western democratic culture—*our* culture—need fear no challenge from the Soviet Union. Recent events have brought home to us the truth of the Goethean maxim that freedom cannot be a mere legacy handed down to us from the past. It must be won by each generation for itself. The problems on our own doorstep are complex, multiple, and explosive. In solving them we should welcome whatever light, whatever truth, can be found in the Soviet experience. Ultimately, however, it is to our own democratic process we must turn to fulfill our own revolutionary traditions whose vital center is the concept of freely given consent. From this we have developed a political ethos and extended it slowly—alas! sometimes too slowly—to other fields. We who were cradled in revolution need not fear the idea of revolution, provided it avoids despotism, on the one hand, and anarchy on the other. America has been called a sick society and worse, unworthy to be cited as an example to the world. Yet this sick society still feeds a large part of the world and shields an even larger part from aggression. The greatest of our challenges must be to ourselves to take those actions within reason and law that will secure and extend the general welfare and preserve the blessings of liberty for ourselves and all our descendants.

NOTES

Bertram D. Wolfe

1. For a study of the idea of revolution see Hannah Ahrendt, *On Revolution* (New York, 1963).
2. George V. Taylor, "Noncapitalist Wealth and the Origins of the French Revolution," *American Historical Review,* Jan. 1967, pp. 469–96. Cf. Alexander Herzen's vivid image of "the tousled improvisations of revolution."
3. General Cavaignac, Minister of War in the French Provisional Government set up by the uprising of February 1848, put down the uprising of the Paris workingmen in June of the same year. Lenin applied the epithet now to the generals of the army, now to the Kadets, now to Kerensky. Characteristically, he expected his readers to know who Cavaignac was, and since polemics were largely addressed by intellectuals to each other and not to the workers or peasants, his readers, living in the same French dream as he, knew.
4. Versailles had been the headquarters of the Republican government of France which, in 1871, attempted to disarm the National Guard of Paris. Resistance to the disarming was the beginning of the uprising of the Paris Commune.
5. Actually the Paris Commune was an emergency city government, while the Petersburg Soviet of 1905 (imitated in 1917) was an emergency general-strike committee. Marx's final verdict on the Paris Commune, written in a letter to Domela Nieuwenhuis on February 22, 1881, said: "The Commune was merely the rising of a town under exceptional circumstances; the majority of the Commune was in no sense socialist nor could it be. With a small amount of common sense, they could have reached a compromise with Versailles." Lenin read this letter when he was preparing *State and Revolution* but studiously ignored it.
6. The figures and a detailed analysis of the real nature of the Third Estate can be found in Taylor and his sources.
7. Marx's rhetoric was better than the anti-climactic pronouncement of Sieyès, wherefore it went straight into the closing line of the chorus of *The International:* "We have been naught, we shall be all."
8. Lenin, *Sochineniya,* vol. 14, p. 312. References to Lenin's *Collected Works* are to the Fourth Russian Edition unless otherwise noted.
9. On this see the writer's "The Paris Commune: An Ambiguous Revolution," in *Marxism: 100 Years in the Life of a Doctrine* (New York, 1965).
10. On this see *Marxism: 100 Years in the Life of a Doctrine,* pp. 83–101 and 219–29.
11. On this see, "Lenin and Inessa Armand," in *Slavic Review,* Mar. 1963; *Encounter,* Feb. 1964; or in my book of profiles, *Strange Communists I Have Known* (New York, 1965; London, 1966).
12. "O nashei revoliutsii," *Sochineniya,* vol. 33, pp. 436–39.
13. *Marx-Engels Werke,* Vol. VII, pp. 400–401.
14. Or perhaps Marx and Engels thrust out of their consciousness the aware-

ness that the nationalization of all industry and agriculture would necessarily lead to the development of such a bureaucratic "ruling class." On this see Karl A. Wittfogel, *Oriental Despotism* (New Haven, Conn., 1957), Chapter IX.

15. On this see "The Anarchists in the Russian Revolution," by Paul Avrich, *Russian Review,* Oct. 1967, pp. 341–50.
16. *Correspondence of G. V. Plekhanov and P. B. Axelrod,* Vol. I, p. 270.
17. *Sochineniya,* vol. 9, p. 14.
18. *Ibid.,* p. 81.
19. For a more complete treatment of Lenin's vanguard theory see my essay entitled "A Party of a New Type," in M. M. Drachkovitch and B. Lazitch (eds.), *The Comintern: Historical Highlights* (New York, 1966), pp. 20–44.
20. Trotsky had just received an offer of support from a machine gun regiment. He found that "the machine guns were not in working condition and the soldiers had become lazy and were also completely unfit to fight." The quotation is from his remarks at a gathering of various persons active in the October coup, meeting together to match memories and try to pin down the details of the October days as they actually occurred. The meeting took place on November 7, 1920 in Moscow, was recorded stenographically, and printed in *Proletarskaya Revoliutsia,* no. 10 (Moscow, 1922), the cited remark being on p. 66. A French translation is now available in the Fiftieth Anniversary number of *Est & Ouest,* Oct. 1967, with the cited remark on p. 15.
21. V. B. Stankevich, *Vospominaniia 1914–1919 g.* (Berlin, 1920), pp. 70–77. "The well-aimed stray bullets" in a phrase used by Colonel Stankevich in his vivid description of the confused panic among the men who had mutinied and the moment of fear and hesitation among the leaders of political life and even the most popular and radical of the officers. For a more extensive treatment of this subject see my remarks at the fiftieth anniversary discussion of the Russian Revolution held at Harvard University, published under the editorship of Richard Pipes in *Revolutionary Russia* (Cambridge, Mass., 1968), pp. 728–38.
22. Letter to Vera Zasulich, April 23, 1885. Engels wrote it in French, but it has been published so far only in a German translation, in *Werke,* vol. 36, p. 303, and a Russian translation in *Perepiska K. Marksa i F. Engelsa s russkimi politicheskimi deyatelyami* (Moscow, 1947), p. 251. The German translation seems to be from the Russian and not from the original letter.
23. It seems to me that only three regimes in major states can properly be termed totalitarian: the Russia of Lenin and his successors, Hitler's Germany, and Mao Tse-tung's China. Neither Mussolini nor Franco, to mention two regimes frequently called totalitarian, could afford to destroy millions of their population in order to atomize society. Neither tried to make his power coextensive with all the concerns and activities of society. And Mussolini, though he coined the word *totalitarismo* and gave us our first working definition of the term, left extant such institutions as the King, the General Staff, and the Church, which helps to account for his speedy disappearance from power soon after the first reverse in war.
24. For elaboration of these views of Lenin, sources, contexts, and analyses of

their meaning, see my "A Party of a New Type," in *The Comintern: Historical Highlights.*

25. *Sochineniya,* vol. 27, p. 442.
26. When members of his Central Committee insisted that a mass uprising was now impossible because the masses had become passive and indifferent, Lenin did not deny their apathy but explained it: "The absenteeism and indifference of the masses may be explained by the fact that the masses have grown weary of words and resolutions" (minutes of the Central Committee Meeting of Oct. 10/23, 1917). Lenin's coup did not need an uprising of the masses any more than the coups envisaged by Babeuf, Buonarroti, Blanqui, and Tkachev. The flood of words and resolutions that had wearied the masses greatly increased in volume after Lenin took power. This deluge of decrees, he said later, "played a big role as propaganda." (See *Sochineniya,* vol. 29, pp. 185–86, where he speaks of "hundreds" of such unrealizable decrees.) If apathy breeds dictatorship, dictatorship in its turn breeds apathy, a dilemma neither Lenin nor his successors have been able to solve. Today as in Lenin's day the headlines in *Pravda* are largely exhortations to greater "voluntary" activity in fulfilling the will of the leaders and the needs of the state, exhortations to work harder, to produce more, to waste less, to take better care of machines, to improve the quality of the goods, to raise per capita productivity, to be grateful to the Party and the state, to compete in "socialist competition," to fulfill the plan "ahead of time." Even to Party whips this unendingly repetitive exhortation makes dull reading.
27. *Sochineniya,* vol. 27, p. 76.
28. Leon Trotsky, *The History of the Russian Revolution* (Ann Arbor, Mich., 1960), II, 93.
29. From the first work he drafted in his hideout, "Can the Bolsheviks Retain State Power?" *Sochineniya,* vol. 26, pp. 87–88.
30. On the influence of Bukharin's *K teorii imperialisticheskogo gosudarstva* (Toward a Theory of the Imperialist State) upon Lenin, see Sidney Heitman's introduction to the selected works of Bukharin, *Put k sotsializmy v Rossii* (The Path to Socialism in Russia, New York, 1967), pp. 35 and 55; Robert V. Daniels, "The State and Revolution," in *American Slavic and East European Review,* Feb. 1953, pp. 22–43; Sidney Heitman, "The Myth of Bukharin's Anarchism," *The Rocky Mountain Social Science Journal,* April, 1963, pp. 39–53. Bukharin's book was published piecemeal and fragmentarily in various journals in 1916. It received its first complete publication in Moscow in 1925. Lenin makes frequent references to the war-time fragments in letters to Kollontay written during 1916 and 1917 and first published in *Leninskii Sbornik* (Moscow, 1924), II.
31. On Lenin's retooling of his own spirit according to his new blueprint, see my character study of Lenin in Milorad M. Drachkovitch (ed.), *Marxism in the Modern World* (Stanford, Calif. 1965).
32. *Sochineniya,* vol. 25, p. 452.
33. George L. Kline, "Economic Crime and Punishment," *Survey,* Oct. 1965, pp. 67–72.
34. Lenin was obsessed now by the fact that he had seized power in a backward land. All his articles dictated during this last illness returned

again and again to the lack of culture of the Communist administrators and of the masses. In his "On Cooperation" he said: "Complete cooperative organization is impossible without an entire cultural revolution. For us the political and social overturn was proved to be a predecessor of the cultural overturn, that cultural revolution which we nevertheless must now face."

35. *Sochineniya* ("On Cooperation"), vol. 33, pp. 427–31.
36. In a paper presented in 1957 at St. Antony's College, Oxford, "The Durability of Despotism in the Soviet System."
37. Rosa Luxemburg, *The Russian Revolution* (Ann Arbor, 1961), pp. 69–78.
38. *Sochineniya,* vol. 24, p. 423, Speech to the All-Russian Congress of Education Workers, July 31, 1919.
39. *Literaturnaya Gazeta,* Dec. 28, 1957.
40. *Communist Totalitarianism* (Boston, 1961), p. 283.

G. Warren Nutter

1. The major source of data is my own work in progress and already published, for example, *Growth of Industrial Production in the Soviet Union* (Princeton, N. J., 1962) and "The Effects of Economic Growth on Sino-Soviet Strategy," in D. M. Abshire and R. V. Allen (eds.), *National Security: Political, Military, and Economic Strategies in the Decade Ahead* (New York, 1963), pp. 149–68. In general, the figures given in the text are derived from this work, from Tables 1 and 2, from official Soviet statistics, and from studies by other scholars. Only the last source will normally be cited explicitly.
2. M. Florinsky, *Russia: A Short History* (New York, 1964), p. 445.
3. Use of employment to measure output causes an understatement insofar as the productivity of labor has risen in these other sectors, primarily service trades and government. On the other hand, this understatement is counterbalanced, to an unknown degree, by the large growth in employment within the governmental bureaucracy, which should be treated primarily as a cost of running the Soviet system and not as production. Unfortunately, there is no way of estimating the effect of either element taken separately or the net effect of both taken together.
4. See A. Bergson, "National Income," in A. Bergson and S. Kuznets (eds.), *Economic Trends in the Soviet Union* (Cambridge, Mass., 1963), p. 4.
5. See D. G. Johnson, "Agricultural Production," in *ibid.,* p. 216; Diamond, in *New Directions,* p. 328; and N. Kaplan and R. Moorsteen, "Indexes of Soviet Industrial Output," RAND, RM-2495, pp. 179 ff and 272.
6. See Williams, *Freight Transportation,* pp. 98 ff.
7. This estimate is based on the assumption that consumption accounted for 85 per cent of the national product in 1913 compared with 49 per cent in 1964. For the latter, see S. H. Cohn, "Soviet Growth Retardation: Trends in Resource Availability and Efficiency," in *New Directions,* p. 106. The former is based on S. N. Prokopovicz, *Histoire économique de l'URSS* (Paris, 1952), p. 597.
8. A similar conclusion is implied by linking the indexes of per capita consumption of Janet Chapman ("Consumption," in *Economic Trends,* p.

238) and of David W. Bronson and Barbara S. Severin ("Recent Trends in Consumption and Disposable Money Income in the U.S.S.R.," in *New Directions,* p. 521).

9. See G. T. Robinson, *Rural Russia under the Old Regime* (New York, 1949), p. 250; N. Baster, "Working Memorandum on Russian Budget Studies," National Bureau of Economic Research (mimeographed), July 22, 1955, pp. 25 ff; and Chapman, in *Economic Trends,* p. 240.
10. These comments on the origins of planning are based on E. Zaleski, *Planification de la croissance et fluctuations économiques en U.R.S.S.* (Paris, 1962), pp. 26 ff.
11. See F. Lorimer, *The Population of the Soviet Union: History and Prospects* (Geneva: League of Nation, 1946), p. 134.
12. See Chapman, in *Economic Trends,* p. 237.
13. See *Nazi-Soviet Relations, 1939–1941* (Washington, D. C., 1948), p. 133; and W. N. Medlicott, *The Economic Blockade* (London, 1952), I, 667–68.
14. See his *Grenzen der Sowjetmacht* (Würzburg, 1955).
15. Lorimer, *Population of the Soviet Union,* pp. 182 and 188 ff.
16. See W. W. Eason, "The Soviet Population Today," *Foreign Affairs,* July 1959, pp. 2 ff.
17. According to Khrushchev, the armed forces fell from 11.4 million in 1945 to 2.9 million in 1948, or by 75 per cent. The percentage decline in military production seems to have been at least equally large and possibly larger. See Nutter, *Growth of Industrial Production,* pp. 318–28.
18. For an excellent survey of the discussion and resulting reforms, see Eugène Zaleski, *Planning Reforms in the Soviet Union, 1962–1966* (Chapel Hill, N. C., 1967).

Lewis S. Feuer

1. Leon Trotsky, *Literature and Revolution* (New York, 1925), p. 256. Isaac Deutscher, *The Prophet Unarmed: Trotsky 1921–1929* (New York, 1959), p. 197.
2. "For even in the simplest generalisation, in the most elementary general idea there is a certain bit of fantasy. (Vice versa: it would be stupid to deny the role of fantasy, even in the strictest science.)" V. I. Lenin, *Collected Works* (Moscow, 1961), vol. 38, pp. 372–73. Also, V. I. Lenin, *What Is to be Done?* (New York, 1932), pp. 158–59.
3. Leo Wiener, *An Interpretation of the Russian People* (New York, 1951), pp. 1, 7. E. J. Dillon (pseudonym E. B. Lanin), *Russian Characteristics* (London, 1892), p. 99. Also cf. Georg Brandes, *Impressions of Russia* (New York, 1899), pp. 65, 88.
4. E. J. Dillon, *Russia To-Day and Yesterday: An Impartial View of Soviet Russia* (New York, 1930), pp. 34, 35, 55.
5. Maxim Gorky, *Days with Lenin* (New York, 1932), pp. 29, 41, 45.
6. Cf. Lewis S. Feuer, "American Travellers to the Soviet Union 1917–32: The Formation of a Component of New Deal Ideology," *American Quarterly,* XIV (1962), 119–49.
7. J. V. Stalin, *Works* (Moscow, 1955), vol. 13, pp. 40–41. Such a distin-

guished social anthropologist as Clyde Kluckhohn ignored the wastefulness in Stalin's choice among the alternative routes to industrialization: "Does anyone seriously think that the industrialization of Russia would have proceeded so rapidly had not Russia been under the sway of Marxist ideas?" *Mirror for Man* (reprint, New York, 1965), p. 62.

8. Louis Fischer, "Communist Puritans," in *Our Changing Morality,* ed. Freda Kirchwey (New York, 1924), p. 210.
9. Leon Trotsky, *Problems of Life* (reprinted, Ceylon, 1962), p. 37.
10. "For the Bolshevik Revolution brought out with unmistakable vividness the repressed hostile feeling, compounded of envy, hatred and mistrust, with which Russia's illiterate and semi-illiterate masses regarded the small propertied and educated class"—William Henry Chamberlin, *The Russian Revolution 1917–1921* (New York, 1935), I, 356. Bertrand Russell, *Bolshevism: Practice and Theory* (New York, 1920), pp. 35–37; Also, *Portraits from Memory* (New York, 1956), pp. 34–38.
11. Leon Trotsky, *My Life* (reprinted, New York, 1960), pp. 512–13. Max Eastman, *Leon Trotsky: The Portrait of a Youth* (New York, 1925), pp. 167–68.
12. Gorky, *Days with Lenin,* p. 48.
13. Trotsky, *My Life,* p. 351.
14. N. K. Krupskaya, *On Education* (Moscow, 1957), p. 206; also Krupskaya, *Reminiscences of Lenin* (Moscow, 1959), pp. 41, 71, 269. A. I. Ulyanova-Yelizarova in *Reminiscences of Lenin by His Relatives* (Moscow, 1956), p. 43. Gorky, *Days with Lenin,* p. 52.
15. Cf. Raymond Bauer, *The New Man in Soviet Psychology* (Cambridge, Mass., 1952), p. 111.
16. *Ammianus Marcellinus,* tr. John C. Rolfe (London, 1935–39), I, 121–23.
17. Leon Trotsky, *Literature and Revolution,* pp. 42–43, 220. Isaac Deutscher, *The Prophet Unarmed,* p. 179. Leon Trotsky, *The Testament of Lenin* (reprinted, New York, 1946), p. 10.
18. People's Commissariat of Justice of the U.S.S.R., *Report of Court Proceedings in the Case of the Anti-Soviet Bloc of Rights and Trotskyites* (Moscow, 1938), p. 777.
19. Zbigniew K. Brzezinski, *The Permanent Purge* (Cambridge, Mass., 1956), p. 89. Markoosha Fischer, *Reunion in Moscow* (New York, 1962), p. 142.
20. Leo Kamenev, "Preface to Machiavelli," reprinted, *New Left Review,* no. 15 (May–June 1962), pp. 40–41. I. Ehrenburg, "People, Years, Life," *Novy mir,* April 1965; translation in *Current Digest of the Soviet Press* (hereafter *CDSP*), vol. XVII, no. 23, p. 9.
21. I. Ehrenburg, "People, Years, Life," *Novy mir,* Feb. 1965; *CDSP,* vol. XVII, no. 23, p. 5.
22. Peter Kropotkin, *Memoirs of a Revolutionist* (reprinted, Boston, 1930), p. 297.
23. I. Ehrenburg, "People, Years, Life," *Novy mir,* April, 1965; *CDSP,* vol. XVII, no. 23, p. 9.
24. J. Stalin, *Defects in Party Work and Measures for Liquidating Trotskyite and Other Double-Dealers* (Moscow, 1937), p. 41.
25. V. I. Lenin, *The State and Revolution* (New York, 1932), p. 44.
26. "Problems of Leisure Recreation," *Komsomolskaya Pravda,* June 16, 1965; *CDSP,* vol. XVII, no. 31, p. 14.

27. Y. Polyanichko, "Thirteen Days Around the Clock at Meetings," *Molodoi Kommunist,* Feb. 1965; *CDSP,* vol. XVII, no. 15, pp. 7–9.
28. Frederick C. Barghoorn, *Soviet Russian Nationalism* (New York, 1956), p. 270.
29. Ernst Henry, "Reflections on the Future," *Literaturnaya Gazeta,* Jan. 1, 1968; *CDSP,* vol. XX, no. 1, pp. 6–7.
30. V. Perevedentsev, "Concerning Demographic Ignorance and the Problem of the Birth Rate," *Literaturnaya Gazeta,* Aug. 13, 1966; *CDSP,* vol. XVIII, no. 32, p. 8. Farnsworth Fowle, "Population Rise of Soviet Slows," *New York Times,* Mar. 12, 1967. A. Kharchev, *Marriage and Family Relations in the U.S.S.R.* (Moscow, 1965), 1965, p. 25.
31. "G. A. Smirnov, the Andreyev chairman, remarks bitterly that in all his years as a collective farm chairman he has never married off a milkmaid." Aleksandr Yanov, "The Kostroma Experiment," *Literaturnaya Gazeta,* no. 52, December 27, 1967, p. 10; *CDSP,* vol. XX, no. 2, p. 11. Yu. V. Arutyunyan, "The Social Structure of the Rural Population of the U.S.S.R.," *Voprosy filosofii,* no. 5, May, 1965; *CDSP,* vol. XVIII, no. 25, p. 20. *Statistical Abstract of the United States,* Washington, 1966, p. 15.
32. V. Perevedentsev, *Literaturnaya Gazeta,* Aug. 13, 1966; quoted in "Demographic Problems in the USSR," *Radio Liberty Dispatches,* Sep. 23, 1966.
33. Peter Juviler, "Soviet Families," *Survey,* July, 1960, p. 59. I. Mindlin, "The Old in the New," *Novy mir,* Dec. 1964, pp. 260–62; *CDSP,* vol. XVII, no. 8, p. 9.
34. N. Bukharin, *Culture in Two Worlds* (New York, 1934), pp. 18–19. Bukharin was perhaps the first Soviet thinker to cite passages from Marx's *Economic-Philosophic Manuscripts* to formulate his ethical standpoint thirty years before young Soviet critics rediscovered "alienation." His tribute to Pasternak was as one "far removed from the peculiar technicism of the period." Stalinist critics naturally held Bukharin's friendliness against Pasternak. Cf. Nikolai Bukharin, in A. Zhdanov, *et al., Problems of Soviet Literature* (New York, 1935), pp. 233, 246. "Judgment on Pasternak," *Survey,* July, 1966, p. 152.
35. N. Abalkin, "Tradition and Fashion," *Pravda,* Aug. 22, 1965; *CDSP,* vol. XVII, no. 34, pp. 10–11.
36. On the Bolshevized personality's assault on the law of diminishing returns, cf. John W. Boldyreff, "The Law of Diminishing Fertility of the Soil, from the Point of View of some of the Russian Economists of Today," *Journal of Farm Economics,* July, 1931, pp. 470–85.
37. In the social sciences, "as a rule, the value of someone's work is determined by its thickness, that is, by the number of pages. This quantitative approach is the source of many shortcomings . . ." B. Mochalov, "Party Works in Institutions of Higher Education," *Kommunist,* no. 10, July, 1966, pp. 34–42; *CDSP,* vol. XVIII, Sept. 28, 1966.
38. "Strength and Weakness of a Young Science," *Literaturnaya Gazeta,* Aug. 6, 1966; *CDSP,* vol. XVIII, no. 32, pp. 11–12.
39. "Necessity or Fashion? Sociological Methods in Y. C. L. Work," *Komsomolskaya Pravda,* Oct. 28, 1966; *CDSP,* vol. XVIII, no. 44, p. 14.
40. *Literaturnaya Gazeta,* Aug. 6, 1966.
41. "In Search of Scientific Work Methods in the Young Communist League," *Komsomolskaya Pravda,* May 11, 1967; *CDSP,* vol. XIX, no. 19, p. 17. Cf.

the complaint of an assembly brigade worker against a researcher from a sociological laboratory, "I Need No Other Joy," *Izvestia,* May 5, 1967; *CDSP,* vol. XIX, no. 18, 1967, p. 21.

42. Em. Kazakevich, "Enemies," *Izvestia,* April 21, 1962; *CDSP,* vol. XIV, no. 16, pp. 18–21. Also *New York Times,* April 26, 1962.
43. "White Doctor," *Izvestia,* Sep. 9, 1965; *CDSP,* vol. XVII, no. 36, pp. 14–15.
44. V. Pomerantsev, "The Writer's Diary: On Sincerity in Literature," *Novy mir,* Dec. 1953; *CDSP,* vol. VI, no. 5, pp. 3–9, and no. 6, pp. 3–7. Vitaly Vasilevsky, "From False Positions," *Literaturnaya Gazeta,* Jan. 30, 1954; *CDSP,* vol. VI, no. 6, pp. 8–9.
45. Ilya Ehrenburg, "In Greece," *Literaturnaya Gazeta,* May 9, 1967; *CDSP,* vol. XIX, no. 19, p. 16.
46. *New York Times,* April 22, 1967.
47. V. Tikunov, "No Visa for 'The Black Mask'," *Izvestia,* May 28, 1965; *CDSP,* vol. XVII, no. 21, p. 14.
48. Mihajlo Mihajlov, *Moscow Summer* (New York, 1965), p. 22.
49. Maya Zlobena, "The Surprises in Somerset Maugham," *Novy mir,* 1961, no. 9; translated in *The Soviet Review,* June 1962, pp. 4, 6.
50. L. Zhukhovitsky, "Boredom and Free Time," *Literaturnaya Gazeta,* Jan. 4, 1967, p. 7; *CDSP,* vol. XIX, no. 7, pp. 12–13. Also cf. V. Patrushev, "Studying the Time Budgets of Working People," *Vestnik Statistiki,* 1961, no. 11; E. V. Beliaev, *et al.,* "Workers' Time-Budget Research: A Method of Concrete Sociological Investigation," *Vestnik Leningradskogo Universiteta, Seriya Ekonomiki, Filosofii i Prava,* 1961, no. 4; G. Prudenskii, "Time Budgets and Leisure Activities," *Kommunist,* 1960, no. 15; all in *Soviet Sociology,* summer 1962, pp. 37, 43, 47.
51. "Poll of Izvestia Readers," *Nedelya,* March 11, 1967; *CDSP,* vol. XIX, no. 16, p. 27.
52. Yu. Lukin, "Merely a Semblance of Truth," *Pravda,* Aug. 11, 1967; *CDSP,* vol. XVII, no. 32, p. 32.
53. *On Trial: The Soviet State versus "Abram Tertz" and "Nikolai Arzhak,"* tr. and ed. Max Hayward (New York, 1966), pp. 98, 143.
54. Walter Duranty, *Duranty Reports Russia* (New York, 1934), p. 45.
55. Leon Trotsky, *Problems of Life,* p. 30.
56. "Don't Engage in Cap-Tossing! Notes of an Atheist Lecturer," *Komsomolskaya Pravda,* May 29, 1965; *CDSP,* vol. XVII, no. 22, p. 15.
57. Alexander Solzhenitsyn, *One Day in the Life of Ivan Denisovich,* tr. Max Hayward and Ronald Hingley (New York, 1963), pp. 49, 28, 98, 198. Also, cf. Iu. Karakin, "An Episode in the Current Battle of Ideas," *Novy mir,* 1964, no. 9; translated in *Soviet Sociology,* vol. V, no. 1, p. 48.
58. Abram Tertz, "Thought Unaware," tr. Andrew Field and Robert Szulkin, *The New Leader,* July 19, 1965, p. 20.
59. Lev Ozerov, the critic, discussed the views on immortality of the poet Ilya Selvinsky in *Literaturnaya Rossiya,* Aug. 12, 1966; cf. *Radio Liberty Dispatches,* Nov. 30, 1966.
60. Victor Orlov, "The Words I Told You Were the Wrong Ones," *Literaturnaya Gazeta,* Dec. 13, 1966; *CDSP,* vol. XIX, no. 9, pp. 24–25.
61. L. N. Mitrokhin, "Education in Atheism and Methodology of Studying the Survival of Religious Beliefs," *Voprosy filosofii* (1962), no. 3; translated in *Soviet Sociology,* summer 1962, p. 27.

62. D. M. Aptekman, "The Vitality of the Baptismal Ceremony Under Modern Social Conditions: An Empirical Study," *Voprosy filosofii* (1965), no. 3; translated in *Soviet Sociology,* ed. Alex Simirenko (Chicago, 1966), pp. 376–77. Bohden R. Bociurkiw, "Religion and Soviet Society," *Survey,* July 1966, pp. 63, 70.
63. A. Luk and V. Tardov, "The Patient and His Relatives," *Literaturnaya Gazeta,* Dec. 8, 1966; *CDSP,* vol. XVIII, no. 50, pp. 8–9. Cf. *The New York Times,* Dec. 9, 1967, for a description of a private clinic at Arbat St., one of nine in Moscow.
64. Vera Karbovskaya, *Literaturnaya Gazeta,* Oct. 12, 1965; reported in *Radio Liberty Dispatches,* Oct. 29, 1965.
65. "Invitation to Debate," *Yunost',* Jan. 1967; *CDSP,* vol. XIX, no. 16, pp. 15–16.

John N. Hazard

1. See Evgenii B. Pashukanis, quoted by the author in his introduction to *Soviet Legal Philosophy,* Hugh W. Babb, trans. (Cambridge, Mass., 1951), p. xvii.
2. See V. I. Lenin, "Concerning a Caricature of Marxism and Concerning 'Imperialist' Economism," *Sochineniia* (4th ed., Moscow, 1949), vol. 23, p. 36.
3. See John C. H. Wu, "Law," *The Catholic Encyclopedia,* Sixth Section, Supplement II (1955) column 1.
4. [1917–18] I *Sobranie uzakonenii i rasporiazhenii rabochego i krest'ianskogo pravitel'stva RSFSR,* no. 4, item 50 (cited hereafter as *Sob. Uzak. RSFSR*).
5. *Ibid.,* Art. 8.
6. Statute on court organization in the RSFSR, [1922] I *Sob. Uzak. RSFSR,* no. 69, item 902.
7. Ia. Berman, "K voprosu ob ugolovnom kodekse sotsialisticheskogo gosudarstva," *Proletarskaia revoliutsiia i pravo,* Feb.–April 1919, p. 24.
8. [1917–18] I *Sob. Uzak. RSFSR,* no. 28, item 366.
9. For his memoirs, see I. N. Steinberg, *In the Workshop of the Revolution* (New York, 1953). His name is spelled in the text in direct transliteration from the Russian, and not as adopted in New York for his memoirs.
10. July 20, 1918 [1917–18] I *Sob. Uzak. RSFSR,* no. 52, item 589.
11. *Ibid.,* no. 85, item 889.
12. People's Court Act, Secs. 7 and 8.
13. July 23, 1918 [1917–18] I *Sob. Uzak. RSFSR,* no. 53, item 597.
14. Oct. (undated) 1918 *ibid.,* no. 76–77, item 818.
15. Dec. (undated) 1918 *ibid.,* no. 87–88, item 905.
16. See P. I. Stuchka, *Narodny sud v voprosakh i otvetakh* (Moscow, 1918).
17. See D. I. Kurskii, "O edinom narodnom sude," *Proletarskaia revoliutsiia i pravo,* Jan. 1919, pp. 16–19.
18. See D. I. Kurskii, "Novoe ugolovnoe pravo," *Proletarskaia revoliutsiia i pravo,* Feb.–April 1919, p. 24.
19. Part V. For English translation, see William E. Rappard *et al, Source Book on European Governments* (New York, 1937), pp. 19–20.

20. February 17, 1919 [1919] I *Sob. Uzak. RSFSR,* no. 12, item 130.
21. February 4, 1919 *ibid.,* no. 13, item 131.
22. April 3, 1919 *ibid.,* no. 13, item 133.
23. *Ibid.,* no. 66, item 590.
24. [1922] *Ibid.,* no. 15, item 153.
25. "Circular No. 1," Published only as a separate flyer; not in official collections.
26. For a review of the debate, see Ia. Berman, *Ocherki po istorii sudoustroistva RSFSR s predisloviem N. V. Krylenko* (Moscow, 1924) p. 37.
27. Oct. 21, 1920 [1920] I *Sob. Uzak. RSFSR,* no. 83, item 407.
28. Instruction of November 6, 1920, *ibid.,* no. 100, item 542.
29. *Sobranie uzakonenii i rasporiazhenii rabochego i krest'ianskogo pravitel'stva: sistematicheskii sbornik vazhneishikh dekretov 1917–1920* (Moscow, 1920).
30. See Berman, *Ocherki . . . ,* p. 45.
31. See D. I. Kurskii, *Izbrannye stat'i i rechi* (Moscow, 1948) pp. 69–80.
32. [1922] I *Sob. Uzak. RSFSR,* no. 69, item 902.
33. For the debates, see RSFSR, *IV sessia VTsIK, biulleten',* no. 1, pp. 24 ff.
34. Judiciary Act RSFSR, Part III.
35. U.S.S.R. Constitution of 1923, Chapter VII, and Supreme Court Act of November 23, 1923 [1923] *Vestnik Tsentralnogo Ispol'nitelnogo Komiteta, Soveta Narodnykh Komiissarov i Soveta Truda i Oborona,* no. 10, item 311, revised by Order of July 14, 1924 [1924] I *Sobranie zakonov i rasporiazhenii raboche-krest'ianskogo pravitel'stva SSSR,* no. 2, item 25 (cited hereafter as *Sob. Zak. SSSR*).
36. Statute on the Institutions of Advocacy, May 26, 1922 [1922] I *Sob. Uzak. RSFSR,* no. 36, item 425.
37. For Lenin's letter to the Politburo, see *Sochineniia* (4th ed., Moscow, 1951), vol. 33, p. 326.
38. [1922] I *Sob. Uzak. RSFSR,* no. 36, item 424.
39. November 23, 1923, Supreme Court Statute, Part VII [1924] *ibid.,* no. 29–30, item 278.
40. *Ezhenedel'nik sovetskoi iustitsii,* Jan. 29, 1922, p. 6.
41. June 1, 1922 [1922] I *Sob. Uzak. RSFSR,* no. 15, item 153, art. 10.
42. October 31, 1922 [1922] I *Sob. Uzak. RSFSR,* no. 71, item 904.
43. See N. V. Krylenko, *Sudoustroistvo RSFSR: Lektsii po teorii i istorii sudoustroistva* (Moscow, 1923) pp. 159–60.
44. "The General Theory of Law and Marxism," translated in Babb, *Soviet Legal Philosophy,* pp. 111–25.
45. See N. V. Krylenko, "K proektu novogo UPK," *Ezhenedel'nik sovetskoi iustitsii,* Dec. 5, 1927, p. 1457. Also *Proekt novogo ugolovnogo kodeksa RSFSR so vstupitel'noi stat'ei N. V. Krylenko* (Moscow, 1930), Also Gosudarstvennyi Institut po Izucheniiu Prestupnosti i Prestupnika, *Proekt osnovnykh nachal ugolovnogo kodeksa RSFSR* (Moscow, 1930).
46. The issue is reviewed in Whitmore Gray, "Soviet Tort Law: The New Principles Annotated," in Wayne R. LaFave ed., *Law in the Soviet Society* (Urbana, Ill., 1965), pp. 183–84.
47. See N. N. Agarkov, "Problemy zloupotrebleniia prav v Sovetskom grazhdanskom prave," *Izvestiia Akademii Nauk SSSR, otdelenie ekonomiki i prava,* vol. 6 (1946), p. 424.

48. The history of criminal law with special reference to "guilt" is summarized in Harold J. Berman, *Soviet Criminal Law and Procedure: The RSFSR Codes, Introduction and Analysis* (Cambridge, Mass., 1966), pp. 24–35.
49. This paragraph is translated in Babb, *Soviet Legal Philosophy,* p. 235.
50. [1932] I *Sob. Zak. SSSR,* no. 62, item 360.
51. This policy has been analyzed by Barrington Moore Jr., *Terror and Progress—USSR: Some Sources of Change and Stability in the Soviet Dictatorship* (Cambridge, Mass., 1954).
52. July 10, 1934 [1934] I *Sob. Zak., SSSR,* no. 36, item 283 and [1935] *ibid.,* no. 11, item 84.
53. December 1, 1934 [1934] *ibid.,* no. 64, item 459.
54. [1937] *ibid.,* no. 61, item 266.
55. Written by P. Yudin, it is translated in Babb, *Soviet Legal Philosophy,* pp. 281–301.
56. Pashukanis' and Krylenko's names were cleared of treason by a published announcement that they had perished and had committed no crime. See the account of N. P. Platonov, *Sovetskoe Gosudarstvo i Pravo,* no. 9 (1960), p. 130.
57. See A. Y. Vyshinsky, "Fundamental Tasks of Soviet Law," 1938; English translation in Babb, *Soviet Legal Philosophy,* pp. 303–341.
58. For the history of this event and the secrecy with which it was cloaked, see Harold J. Berman, "Law Reform in the Soviet Union," *American Slavic and East European Review,* vol. 15 (1956), pp. 183–85.
59. May 24, 1955 [1955] *Vedomosti Verkhovnogo Soveta SSSR,* no. 9, item 222.
60. [1959] *ibid.,* no. 1 (933), item 6. For English translation, see *Fundamentals of Soviet Criminal Legislation, the Judicial System and Criminal Court Procedure: Official Texts and Commentaries* (Moscow, 1960). A detailed analysis of the measure of the reforms appears in Berman, *Soviet Criminal Law and Procedure.* This work is relied upon heavily in discussing the details of the changes.
61. *Sovetskoe Gosudarstvo i Pravo,* no. 11 (1962), pp. 3–14.
62. *Ibid.,* no. 4 (1963), pp. 60–71.
63. Leading article, *Sotsialisticheskaia Zakonnost',* no. 4 (1965), p. 2.
64. See G. Z. Anashkin, "The Role of Law-Consciousness and Public Opinion in Settling Law Punishment," *Sovetskoe Gosudarstvo i Pravo,* no. 1 (1967), p. 42. English translation in *Current Digest of the Soviet Press,* March 22, 1967, p. 8.
65. See G. M. Minkovskii, "Some Causes of Juvenile Delinquency in the U.S.S.R. and Measures to Prevent It," *Sovetskoe Gosudarstvo i Pravo,* no. 5 (1966), p. 84. English translation in *Current Digest of the Soviet Press,* Aug. 17, 1966, p. 9.
66. See A. Sapeyer, "A Difficult Subject," *Literaturnaia Gazeta,* July 2, 1966, p. 2. English translation in *Current Digest of the Soviet Press,* Aug. 3, 1966, p. 10.
67. See A. Gertsenzon, "Biology Has Nothing to Do with It," *Izvestiia,* January 26, 1967, p. 4. English translation in *Current Digest of the Soviet Press,* February 15, 1967, p. 27.
68. See D. N. Ushakov, *Tolkovyi Slovar' Russkogo Iazyka* (Moscow, 1940), vol. 4, p. 1393.

69. April 27, 1918 [1918] I *Sob. Uzak. RSFSR,* no. 34, item 456.
70. May 21, 1919 [1919] *ibid.,* no. 20, item 242.
71. February 15, 1926 [1926] *ibid.,* no. 10; item 73.
72. March 14, 1945, *Sbornik Zakonov SSSR 1945–1946* (Moscow, 1947) p. 163.
73. Fundamental Principles of Civil Legislation (1961), carried into the Civil Code of the R.S.F.S.R. at Part VII. For English translation, see Whitmore Gray and Raymond Stults, *Civil Code of the Russian Soviet Federated Socialist Republic* (Ann Arbor, Mich., 1965).
74. Civil Code, R.S.F.S.R., arts. 106, 107 and 304. The tariff established by order of the Council of Ministers of the R.S.F.S.R. of August 9, 1963 is published in E. A. Fleishits, *Nauchno-Prakticheskii Kommentarii k G. K. RSFSR* (Moscow, 1966), pp. 354–55.
75. Civil Code, R.S.F.S.R., arts. 238 and 239. Also Criminal Code R.S.F.S.R., art. 154. Notaries complain that they have no way of discovering falsity of statements since they are passive registrars. See "Notariat—the Prevention of Violations of Law," *Sotsialisticheskaia Zakonnost'* no. 6 (1965), p. 40.
76. Decree of July 6, 1964 [1964] *Sobranie postanovlenii i rasporiazhenii pravitel'stva RSFSR,* no. 12, item 12.
77. Decree of November 20, 1948 [1948] *Sobranie postanovlenii i raspori-azhenii pravitel'stva SSSR,* no. 7, item 89.
78. Decree of June 26, 1940 [1940] *Vedomosti Verkhovnogo Soveta SSSR,* no. 20.
79. July 3, 1961 [1961] *Vedomosti Verkhovnogo Soveta RSFSR,* no. 26, item 371. English translation in *Current Digest of the Soviet Press,* September 13, 1961, p. 8.
80. October 23, 1963. English translation in *Current Digest of the Soviet Press,* December 18, 1963, p. 9. See also report in *Sotsialisticheskaia Zakonnost',* no. 8 (1966), p. 90.
81. For a summary of the various decrees, see R. Beerman, "The Parasite Law," *Soviet Studies,* vol. 13 (1961), p. 191. Also L. Lipson, "The Future Belongs to—Parasites?" *Problems of Communism,* no. 3 (May–June 1963), p. 1.
82. See V. Semenov and V. Iakushev, "Narodnyi Universitet Iuridicheskogo Soznaniia," *Sovetskaia Iustitsiia,* no. 4 (1960), p. 15.
83. Law of September 20, 1965 [1965] *Vedomosti Verkhovnogo Soveta RSFSR,* no. 38 (364), p. 737.
84. See "Ilichev Speech Indicts Chinese Social Sciences," *Current Digest of the Soviet Press,* September 23, 1964, p. 14.
85. No study has caught this feature so well as George Feifer's *Justice in Moscow* (New York, 1964).

Ivo J. Lederer

1. Leon Trotsky, *My Life* (New York, 1960), p. 341.
2. The first Bolshevik negotiating experience came between late December 1917 and March 1918 in connection with the Brest-Litovsk Peace. Here Trotsky showed a flair for unconventional, revolutionary diplomacy and a talent for disruptive tactics and for coining new slogans such as "no war,

no peace" to the bewilderment (but not frustration) of the Germans. Chicherin turned out to be no less inventive though somewhat less flamboyant. See Theodore H. Von Laue, "Soviet Diplomacy: G. V. Chicherin, People's Commissar for Foreign Affairs, 1918–1930," in Gordon A. Craig and Felix Gilbert (eds.), *The Diplomats, 1919–1939* (Princeton, 1953), pp. 234–81.

3. Alexander Dallin, "The Use of International Movements," in Ivo J. Lederer (ed.), *Russian Foreign Policy: Essays in Historical Perspective* (New Haven and London, 1962), p. 322.
4. *Ibid.*, p. 323.
5. "Resolution on the Report of D. Z. Manuilsky, Adopted August 20, 1935," *Resolutions, Seventh Congress of the Communist International* (New York, 1935), p. 56.
6. Vernon V. Aspaturian, "Moscow's Foreign Policy," *Survey* (October 1967), p. 43.
7. See Lenin, *Sochineniia* (Moscow, 1950), XXIX, 133.
8. Lenin, " 'Left-Wing' Communism, an Infantile Disorder" (April 27, 1920), *Selected Works* (New York, 1943), X, 116.
9. See Charles W. Thayer, *Diplomat* (New York, 1959), pp. 49–63.
10. A. J. Vyshinsky and S. A. Lozovsky, *Diplomaticheskii Slovar'* (Moscow, 1948), I, 591–92.
11. I. V. Stalin, *Sochineniia* (Moscow, 1946), II, 277.
12. Western diplomacy, in turn, has since World War II exhibited considerable capacity to adapt itself to Soviet tactics.
13. Lenin, *Sochineniia* (Moscow, 1950), XXIX, 133; and " 'Left-Wing' Communism, an Infantile Disorder," *Selected Works,* X, 112.
14. For details see Werner T. Angress, *Stillborn Revolution* (Princeton, 1963), pp. 42–74; and Lionel Kochan, *Russia and the Weimar Republic* (Cambridge, Mass., 1954), pp. 26–29.
15. Lenin also overestimated the significance of the Hungarian Communist regime of Bela Kun in 1919. So did the Hungarians. See Alfred D. Low, "The Soviet Hungarian Republic and the Paris Peace Conference," *Transactions of the American Philosophical Society* (volume 53, Part 10, 1963), pp. 39–40.
16. The lure of the Russian market was cleverly used by the Soviet leaders who, however, almost never made political concessions on their part in the interests of trade.
17. In Xenia Joukoff Eudin and Harold H. Fisher, *Soviet Russia and the West, 1920–1927: A Documentary Survey* (Stanford, 1957), pp. 93–94.
18. Two years earlier, Chicherin had argued that the period of "offensive revolutionary policy" must be replaced by a period of "retreat and maneuver." See G. V. Chicherin, *Vneshnaia Politika Sovetskoi za dva goda* (Moscow, 1920). For descriptions and analyses of Soviet diplomacy and Rapallo see Louis Fischer, *The Soviets in World Affairs, 1917–1929* (Princeton, N. J., 1951), I, *passim.;* F. L. Carsten, "The Reichswehr and the Red Army 1920–1933," *Survey* (October 1962), pp. 115–32; G. V. Chicherin, *Stat'i i Rechi* (Moscow, 1961), pp. 224–31; S. Iu. Vygodskii, *et al., Istoriya Diplomatii* (Moscow, 1965), III, 271–94.
19. The Soviet government has of course always denied any link with the Comintern.

20. For an analysis of the position of the Foreign Commissariat in the 1930s, see Robert M. Slusser, "The Role of the Foreign Ministry," in Lederer (ed.), *Russian Foreign Policy,* pp. 216–30.
21. In 1928, however, the Shakty Trial of several German citizens had strained relations with Germany and was viewed with alarm elsewhere. In the Far East, there were tensions with China over the Chinese-Eastern Railway, and the Japanese seizure of Manchuria in 1931 precipitated clashes and strained relations between Moscow and Tokyo throughout the 1930s.
22. In December 1941 Soviet officials proposed establishing spheres of influence to Anthony Eden during his visit in Moscow. This caused much concern in the United States. "One of the greatest preoccupations of the President and me during the first half of 1942," wrote Cordell Hull, "was Russia's suddenly revealed territorial aims in Europe, coupled with her determination to induce the Western Allies to guarantee them in advance." *The Memoirs of Cordell Hull* (New York, 1948), II, 1165.
23. It might also be noted that during 1944–47 the Western powers made no effective effort to intervene to prevent the communization of Eastern Europe, and the later policy of containment, in effect, recognized de facto Soviet control in the area.
24. As Charles Yost noted, "Neither at Yalta nor elsewhere did the United States and Britain turn over Eastern Europe to the Soviets, other than agreeing to cede to Russia that part of Poland east of the Curzon Line, northern East Prussia, and Bessarabia and Northern Bukovina. On the contrary, they exerted the most strenuous, even though on the whole unavailing, efforts to prevent Soviet domination of the area." *The Insecurity of Nations* (New York, 1968), p. 91.
25. In Soviet terms coexistence is a process of dynamic though not military struggle. A Soviet statement on the subject in 1956 put it thus: "One of the perfidious suggestions, which the foes of peaceful co-existence make, consists in proposing 'to end' the ideological struggle . . . there is not and cannot be anything in common between the question of relations between states with different social systems and that of the ideological struggle. Peaceful co-existence between the bourgeois and the Communist ideologies, a compromise or an armistice between them, are impossible." "Leninskii printsip mirnogo sosushchestvovaniia gosudarstv razlichnykh sotsial'nykh sistem," *Voprosy Ekonomiki,* April 1956, p. 16.
26. In Khrushchev's words: ". . . there are only two ways: either peaceful co-existence or the most destructive war in history. There is no third way." *Pravda,* February 15, 1956.
27. By all accounts it was Stalin who played the decisive role in the North Korean invasion of South Korea in June 1950, following by a year the evacuation of American troops and by some months Dean Acheson's speech which seemed to place Korea outside the perimeter of American "national interests."

Jean Laloy

1. Bertram D. Wolfe, *Marxism: One Hundred Years in the Life of a Doctrine* (New York, 1965), pp. 83–101.

2. Isaac Deutscher, *The Prophet Armed* (London, 1954), p. 238.
3. J. Y. Calvez, *Droit international et souveraineté en URSS* (Paris, 1953), p. 51.
4. "Speech at 8th Congress of Soviets," 21 December 1920, *Sochineniya* (5th Edition, Moscow, 1963), vol. 42, pp. 104, 106.
5. G. von Rauch, *Geschichte des bolschewistischen Russlands* (Cologne, 1957), p. 202.
6. *Pravda,* June 25, 1967.

Raymond L. Garthoff

1. See Raymond L. Garthoff, *Soviet Military Policy: A Historical Analysis* (New York, 1966), especially Chapters 1, 4, and 10, for a fuller examination of this subject.
2. Louis Fischer, *The Soviets in World Affairs* (Princeton, 1951), I, 194, cited from the original order in the archives of the Peoples' Commissariat of War in Moscow.
3. Edward H. Carr, *The Bolshevik Revolution, 1917–1923* (New York, 1953), III, 153.
4. *Ibid.,* pp. 165–215. For Lenin's admission, see Clara Zetkin, *Reminiscences of Lenin* (New York, 1934), pp. 18–19.
5. See Chiang Kai-shek, *Soviet Russia in China* (New York, 1957), p. 22.
6. Carr, *Bolshevik Revolution,* III, 297–303; Georg von Rauch, *A History of Soviet Russia* (New York, 1957), p. 122; and Richard Pipes, *The Formation of the Soviet Union: Communism and Nationalism, 1917–1923* (Cambridge, Mass., 1964), pp. 193–241.
7. Nasrollah S. Fatemi, *Diplomatic History of Persia, 1917–1923* (New York, 1952), pp. 191–243; and Ivar Spector, *The Soviet Union and the Muslim World* (Seattle, 1959), pp. 86–95.
8. Carr, *Bolshevik Revolution,* III, 511–23; David Dallin, *Soviet Russia and the Far East* (London, 1949), pp. 80–86; and Kh. Choibalsan, *Kratkii ocherk istorii mongol'skoi narodnoi revoliutsii* (A Brief History of the Mongolian People's Revolution—Moscow, 1952), pp. 62–74.
9. See D. D. Fedotoff White, *The Growth of the Red Army,* (Princeton, 1944), pp. 127–57; Robert V. Daniels, "The Kronstadt Revolt of 1921: A Study in the Dynamics of Revolution," *American Slavic and East European Review,* X (December 1951), pp. 241 ff.
10. S. Singleton, "The Tambov Revolt (1920–1921)," *Slavic Review,* XXV (September 1966), 497–512.
11. A. I. Cherepanov, *Pervye boi krasnoi armii* (The First Battles of the Red Army—Moscow, 1961), p. 4.
12. For an example of the standard myth, see *ibid.,* pp. 10–43. For the recent argument over debunking the myth, see V. Kardin, "Legends and Facts," *Novy mir* (New World), February 1966, pp. 238–39; A. Krivitsky, "Facts and Legends," *Literaturnaya gazeta* (The Literary Gazette), March 19, 1966, p. 3; and F. Petrov, Marshal K. K. Rokossovsky, Admiral I. Baikov, and Colonel General of Artillery N. Khlebnikov, "The Legendary Cannot Be Erased," *Krasnaya zvezda* (Red Star), April 21, 1966, p. 4.

13. See White, *Growth of the Red Army,* pp. 41–42, citing Soviet sources.
14. A. S. Bubnov et al. (eds.), *Grazhdanskaya voina* (The Civil War—Moscow, 1928), II, 95.
15. For a few of the many works on the Russian Civil War, see: *Istoriya grazhdanskoi voiny SSSR* (History of the Civil War in the USSR—Moscow, 1957–60); G. G. Alkhverdov et al., *Kratkaya istoriya grazhdanskoi voiny v SSSR* (A Short History of the Civil War in the USSR—Moscow, 1960); G. V. Kuzmin, *Grazhdanskaya voina i voennaya interventsiya v SSSR* (The Civil War and the Military Intervention in the USSR—Moscow, 1958); *Sovetskaya strana v period grazhdanskoi voiny, 1918–1920: bibliograficheskii ukazatel' dokumental'nykh publikatsii* (The Soviet Land in the Civil War, 1918–1920: A Bibliography . . .—Moscow, 1961); General A. I. Denikin, *Ocherki Russkoi smuty* (Notes on the Russian Turmoil—Paris, 1921); William H. Chamberlin, *The Russian Revolution, 1917–1921* (New York, 1935 and 1952); George Stewart, *The White Armies of Russia* (New York, 1933); David Footman, *The Civil War in Russia* (New York, 1962); and James Bunyan, *Intervention, Civil War, and Communism in Russia, April–December, 1918* (Baltimore, 1936).
16. See Colonel I. Kardashov, *Internatsional'nyi dolg vooruzhennykh sil SSSR* (The International Duty of the Armed Forces of the USSR—Moscow, 1960), pp. 53–59, for a listing of such units, and for a detailed review see *Internatsionalisty v boyakh za vlast' sovetov* (Internationalists in the Battles for the Soviet Power—Moscow, 1965), 395 pp.
17. See M. N. Tukhachevsky, *Voina klassov* (The War of the Classes—Moscow, 1921), pp. 139–40.
18. See *O Sovetskoi voennoi nauke* (On Soviet Military Science—Moscow, 1960), p. 198, for these strength figures.
19. See Gustav Hilger and Alfred Meyer, *The Incompatible Allies: A Memoir History of German-Soviet Relations, 1918–1941* (New York, 1953), pp. 187–208; Carr, *Bolshevik Revolution,* III, 305–76, 435–39; and Gerald Freund, *The Unholy Alliance* (London, 1957), pp. 92–126, 201–12.
20. Franz Borkenau, *The Communist International* (London, 1938), p. 243; Rauch, *History of Russia,* p. 194; E. H. Carr, *The Interregnum, 1923–1924* (New York, 1954), pp. 201–26; and Walter G. Krivitsky, *In Stalin's Secret Service* (New York, 1940), pp. 40–47.
21. J. V. Stalin, *Sochineniya* (Collected Works, vol. 7, Moscow, 1947), p. 14.
22. For good brief accounts of the Soviet-Finnish War, see John Erickson, *The Soviet High Command, 1918–1941* (New York, 1962), pp. 542–52; and J. Malcolm Mackintosh, *Juggernaut: The Russian Armed Forces, 1918–1966* (New York, 1967), pp. 111–36. See also Vaino Tanner, *The Winter War: Finland Against Russia, 1939–40* (Stanford, 1957), and K. G. Mannerheim, *Memoirs* (New York, 1954).
23. See the chapter by O. Edmund Clubb in R. Garthoff, ed., *Sino-Soviet Military Relations* (New York, 1966), pp. 20–24. See also J. E. McSherry, *Stalin, Hitler, and Europe* (Cleveland and New York, 1968——), I, 15–22; the most detailed account of the 1938 fighting is a manuscript, as yet unpublished, by Alvin D. Coox which is based on Japanese documents and interviews.
24. Fischer, *Soviets in World Affairs,* I, 390–93.

25. Lt. Col. James C. Bowden in Garthoff, ed., *Sino-Soviet Military Relations,* pp. 44–54.
26. Fischer, *Soviets in World Affairs,* II, 650, 800–801; David Dallin, *The Rise of Russia in Asia* (New Haven, 1949), pp. 210–30; Chiang Kai-shek, *Soviet Russia in China,* p. 58; Peter S. H. Tang, *Russia and Soviet Policy in Manchuria and Outer Mongolia, 1911–1931* (Durham, N. C., 1959), pp. 208–34; Clubb and Bowden in Garthoff, ed., *Sino-Soviet Military Relations,* pp. 25–27, 40–43.
27. Krivitsky, *In Stalin's Secret Service,* pp. 82–115. See also Hugh Thomas, *The Spanish Civil War* (New York, 1961), *passim;* David C. Cattell, *Communism and the Spanish Civil War* (Berkeley, 1955), *passim;* Cattell, *Soviet Diplomacy and the Spanish Civil War* (Berkeley, 1957), *passim;* and Verle B. Johnston, *Legions of Babel: The International Brigades in the Spanish Civil War* (University Park, Pa., and London, 1967).
28. Bowden in Garthoff, ed., *Sino-Soviet Military Relations,* pp. 54–56; U. S. Department of State, *Foreign Relations of the United States, 1937* (Washington, D. C., continuing series), III, 635–36, 827–28.
29. For good comprehensive studies of the development of the Red Army in the 1920's and 1930's, see Fedotoff White, *The Growth of the Red Army;* Erickson, *The Soviet High Command;* and Mackintosh, *Juggernaut; passim.*
30. These figures are given in Colonel N. Pyatnitsky, *Krasnaya armiya SSSR* (The Red Army of the USSR—Paris, 1932), II, 116. An official Soviet source (N. Yefimov, in *Grazhdanskaya voina,* II, 106) notes that officers with prerevolutionary military education represented 30 per cent of the total in 1923 and 15 per cent in 1926.
31. Bubnov, et al., *Grazhdanskaya voina,* II, 97–98.
32. S. Nikitin-Zubrovsky, in *Voina i revoliutsiya* (War and Revolution), September, 1929, pp. 111–14.
33. N. Yefimov, in *Grazhdanskaya voina,* II, 108, cites the official figure for 1924; the figure for 1928 is an estimate by Erich Wollenberg, *The Red Army* (London, 1938), pp. 72–73.
34. From *Grazhdanskaya voina,* II, 105–9.
35. Compiled by the author from data in the Soviet Air Forces' journal *Vestnik vozdushnogo flota* (Herald of the Air Fleet). In these and other official figures any bias would have inflated the figures for the prestigious worker or peasant categories.
36. Pyatnitsky, *Krasnaya armiya,* I, p. 21, gives the 1931 and 1933 figures; the 1939 figure was given by Marshal K. Ye. Voroshilov, *Rech' na XVIII s'yezde VKP(b)* (Speech to the 18th Congress of the CPSU [b]—Moscow, 1939), p. 12.
37. See Erickson, *Soviet High Command,* pp. 449–509.
38. Voroshilov, *Rech',* p. 32.
39. See R. Garthoff, *Soviet Military Doctrine* (Glencoe, Ill., 1953), *passim,* for a detailed review and analysis of Soviet military doctrine from 1917 to 1953.
40. N. G. Kuznetsov, "Before the War," *International Affairs,* December, 1966, p. 95.
41. See the official *Istoriya velikoi otechestvennoi voiny Sovetskogo Soiuza*

(History of the Great Fatherland War of the Soviet Union—Moscow, 1960–65); Alexander Werth, *Russia at War, 1941–1945* (New York, 1964); Alan Clark, *Barbarossa: The Russian-German Conflict, 1941–1945* (New York, 1965); Paul Carell, *Hitler Moves East: 1941–1943* (Boston, 1965); Mackintosh, *Juggernaut,* pp. 137–268; and for the crucial 1941 campaigns, Erickson, *Soviet High Command,* pp. 565–668, and Garthoff, *Soviet Military Doctrine,* pp. 423–38.

42. See Garthoff, *Soviet Military Policy,* pp. 134–37 and 143–44, and Garthoff, *Sino-Soviet Military Relations,* pp. 57–67.
43. The figure on personnel strength in 1945 was disclosed by N. S. Khrushchev, *Pravda,* January 15, 1960; the figure for divisions is based on American and German intelligence information in 1945.
44. Garthoff, *Sino-Soviet Military Relations,* pp. 70–81.
45. See James H. Billington, in C. Black and T. Thornton, eds., *Communism and Revolution* (Princeton, 1964), pp. 127–29.
46. N. S. Khrushchev, *Pravda,* January 15, 1960.
47. *Ibid.*
48. Garthoff, *Soviet Military Doctrine, passim.*
49. See R. Garthoff, *Soviet Strategy in the Nuclear Age* (New York, 1958 and 1962), pp. 18–26; and H. S. Dinerstein, *War and the Soviet Union* (New York, 1959), pp. 91–163.
50. See Garthoff, *Soviet Military Policy,* pp. 162–72.
51. See Garthoff, *Soviet Strategy in the Nuclear Age,* especially pp. 61–266, and Garthoff, *The Soviet Image of Future War* (Washington, 1959), *passim.*
52. Zhukov's speech in Leningrad reported by Moscow Radio, July 16, 1957; see also *Krasnaya zvezda,* July 5, 1967.
53. See Garthoff, *Soviet Military Policy,* p. 39. Marshal A. Grechko gave the most recent figures over Moscow Radio on February 22, 1967.
54. On political-military relations in recent years, see Roman Kolkowicz, *The Soviet Military and the Communist Party* (Princeton, 1967), *passim;* Thomas W. Wolfe, *Soviet Strategy at the Crossroads* (Cambridge, 1964), pp. 91–109 *et passim;* Garthoff, *Soviet Military Policy,* pp. 42–62; and R. Garthoff, in A. Dallin and A. Westin, eds., *Politics in the Soviet Union: Seven Cases* (New York, 1966), pp. 243–73.
55. See Wolfe, *Soviet Strategy at the Crossroads,* especially pp. 18–37, 79–171, 225–30; Garthoff, *Soviet Strategy in the Nuclear Age,* especially pp. 241–66; Garthoff, in *Politics in the Soviet Union,* pp. 243–73; and for the key Soviet review of doctrine, see Marshal Vasily D. Sokolovsky, ed., *Military Strategy: Soviet Doctrine and Concepts* (New York, 1963).
56. See Garthoff, *Soviet Military Policy,* pp. 115–19.
57. *Ibid.,* pp. 120–23; and Arnold Horelick, "The Cuban Missile Crisis: An Analysis of Soviet Calculations and Behavior," *World Politics,* April 1964, pp. 363–89.
58. See Garthoff, *Sino-Soviet Military Relations,* pp. 87–113, 183–192.
59. Theses of the Central Committee of the C.P.S.U. "On the Fiftieth Anniversary of the Great October Socialist Revolution," as broadcast over Moscow Radio, June 25, 1967.
60. The first quotation is from M. Suslov, Report to the C.P.S.U. C.C. Plenum on February 14, 1964, "On the CPSU Struggle for Cohesion of the

International Communist Movement," as broadcast over Moscow Radio, April 3, 1964; the second is from N. G. Yegorychev, *Pravda,* April 23, 1966 (Yegorychev has since fallen from favor, but this Lenin Day address was a cleared statement by the leadership). See also the discussion, and other sources cited, in Garthoff, *Soviet Military Policy,* pp. 191–206.

61. P. Fedoseyev, "Materialist Understanding of History and the 'Theory of Violence,' " *Kommunist,* no. 7, May, 1964, p. 62. See also the discussion in Garthoff, *Soviet Military Policy,* pp. 191–206.
62. See Admiral of the Fleet S. G. Gorshkov, "The Development of Soviet Naval Science," *Morskoi sbornik* (Naval Journal), February 1967, p. 3, for these statements, and p. 18 for a similar statement on the effect of this mission on the composition of the fleet.

Max Hayward

1. For example, on November 10th, 1917: "Lenin is, of course, a man of exceptional force. . . . He has all the qualities of a leader, including the indispensable amoral quality and an aristocratic merciless attitude to the lives of common people. . . . Life in its real complexity is unknown to Lenin. He does not know the masses of the people. He has never lived among them. Only from books he learned how to raise this mass on to its haunches, and how most effectively to rouse its instincts to a fury. . . . He is working like a chemist in his laboratory—with this difference—that the chemist employs dead matter to gain results valuable for life, whereas Lenin works on living material and is leading the revolution to disaster." Quoted by Richard Hare, *Maxim Gorky: Romantic Realist and Conservative Revolutionary* (London, 1962).
2. In December 1917, the newly appointed cultural "commissar" Lunacharski invited more than 120 writers and artists to a conference in Petrograd; only five appeared including Blok, Mayakovsky, and Meyerhold. See Yu. Elagin, *Tyomny Genii* (New York, 1955), p. 209.
3. Ivanov-Razumnik was a Social Revolutionary whose direct influence on Blok and Esenin was considerable. He was arrested by the Cheka in 1919, after the assassination of Count Mirbach, ostensibly by the left S.R.'s, and spent a good part of the following two decades in jail. See R. V. Ivanov-Razumnik, *Memoirs* (London, 1965).
4. *Alexander Blok, Andrei Bely: Sbornik Statei* (Petrograd, 1919). The essay quoted here is dated April 1918.
5. Esenin's importance as a symbolic figure is brilliantly defined by Georgi Ivanov in *Peterburgskie Zimy* (New York, 1952), Chapter 18.
6. It is the "resigned" verse of Esenin which gained the widest currency, but there are lesser known works in which he gave vent to a rebellious mood. He wrote an unfinished play in blank verse, *The Country of Scoundrels* (1922–23); in which the Revolution appears almost as a foreign plot against the Russian people. The hero is the anarchist leader Makhno (thinly disguised as Nomakh). The Bolshevik villains are Chekistov (a German from Weimar whose ambition is to turn all Russia's churches into lavatories) and a Chinese sleuth. The play has a combative "counter-

revolutionary" flavour about it. It is astonishing that it got through the censorship in the early twenties, and still more that it was republished in the latest Soviet edition of Esenin's works.

7. Evgeni Zamyatin is best known as the author of the novel *We,* an anti-utopian nightmare, in which—evidently as the ultimate consequence of the trend he saw in Soviet life of the early twenties—he prophesies the extinction of the free personality. In his literary essays, published in Russia before his emigration in 1931, he spoke of the need for heresy and of its social utility: "Heretics are the only remedy for the entropy of human thought. . . . Heretics are necessary to health. If there are no heretics, they have to be invented" (*Literature, Revolution and Entropy,* 1924). His play on the Spanish Inquisition, *The Fires of St. Dominic* (1922), was an obvious cautionary tale for his times.
8. For a detailed account of this affair, see my article "Pilnyak and Zamyatin: Two Tragedies of the Twenties," *Survey,* April–June, 1961.
9. The first use of the term "socialist realism" was almost casual. It appeared in a leading article entitled "Down to Work!" in *Literary Gazette* of May 29, 1932: "Truthfulness in the depiction of the Revolution—this is the demand we have the right to put to all Soviet writers without exception. . . . The masses demand from the artist sincerity, truthfulness, revolutionary *socialist realism* in portraying the proletarian revolution." The literary scholar Valerii Kirpotin has recently revealed (in *Questions of Literature,* May 1967) that he was the author of this lead article. As secretary of the Organizational Committee of the Union of Soviet Writers, he also drafted, together with Fadeyev and Pavel Yudin, the Union's statutes (*ustav*) which included a clause requiring members to be guided by socialist realism. Pavel Yudin, the "philosopher" who later edited the Cominform journal in Belgrade and became Soviet Ambassador to Peking in 1953, again figured as an expert in literary matters in 1966 when he wrote a report for the prosecution at the trial of Sinyavsky and Daniel. In it he testified that the work of the latter showed him to be a "consummate and convinced anti-Semite." See *On Trial: The Soviet State versus "Abram Tertz" and "Nikolai Arzhak"* (revised and enlarged edition, New York, 1967), p. 190.
10. This poem, dated by the author 1917, was first published in February 1918. Akhmatova had a true prophetic quality, as one sees in the last four lines (not yet published in the Soviet Union) of her poem "Voronezh," written in 1936 after a visit to Mandelshtam who was in exile there: "In the banished poet's room / terror and the muse watch by turn, / And a night is coming / that has no dawn."
11. As Sinyavsky shows in his introduction to Pasternak's verse (Moscow, 1965), Pasternak's relative immunity to the blandishments of "historical" reality was rooted in his conception (set out in his article *The Black Chalice,* 1916) that poetry and history are separate universes which exist side by side, the one in eternity, the other only in time. This idea is expressed in his famous line defining the poet as "eternity's hostage captive to time" (*vechnosti zalozhnik u vremeni v plenu*).
12. It will be impossible to give a balanced account of the thirties and forties until more of these "delayed reports" come to light. They will certainly be an important corrective to the present dreary picture. Lydia Chukovskaya's *Deserted House,* recently published in the West, is a courageous pendant in

prose to *Requiem.* It is a hopeful sign that Mikhail Bulgakov's great comic philosophical novel *The Master and Margarita* (completed just before the author's death in 1940) has at last been published (with cuts) in Moscow.

13. This, of course, particularly applies to the past. So far it is chiefly a matter of grudging tolerance. But this does not extend to allowing (or rather not preventing) the selective publication of such hitherto "submerged" figures as Marina Tsvetayeva and Osip Mandelshtam. Even more symptomatic is the offhanded mention, in lists of Soviet "achievements" in literature and art, of work by people whose lives were spent—and sometimes lost—in tragic conflict with socialist realism. *Literary Gazette* of November 1, 1967 has a panoramic "jubilee" drawing of Soviet writers over the last fifty years in which Akhmatova, Pasternak, and Tsvetayeva are shown in the company of such as Aleksei Surkov and Vsevolod Kochetov.
14. An almost random example, from an article by V. Ozerov in *Kommunist,* August, 1967: "Honorable is the mission of the artists, called on to show the strength and beauty of the institutions of socialism, which are developing a new communist morality. . . . In the last few years moral-ethical [*sic!*] themes are being elaborated by Soviet literature very intensively." This is followed by the inevitable, grotesquely understated rider: "However, their correct solution is hindered by moods of abstract humanism which have made themselves felt in certain books, plays and films."
15. One reason for the spread of "liberalism" from *Novy Mir* to other "central" journals is the need to compete commercially: editors take political risks in order to boost circulation. An interesting development in the past few years has been the "liberal" editorial policy of two Russian-language literary journals in non-Russian republics: *Literaturnaya Gruzia* in Georgia and *Prostor* in Kazakhstan, both of which on occasion give "literary asylum" to Moscow writers.
16. A lot of writing on the Kolkhoz theme, almost by the nature of the subject, must lead Soviet readers to the conclusion that collectivization was a fearful mistake. This can even be so if the author's intention was the opposite (e.g., Ivan Stadnyuk's *People are not Angels*). One remarkable but curiously neglected novel on collectivizatiion is S. Zalygin's *On the Irtysh* (*Novy Mir,* February 1964).
17. A similar intervention, about a year later, resulted in the publication of Tvardovsky's *Vasili Tyorkin in the Other World,* a mordant satire on ideological humbug in general. Perhaps there were moments when Khrushchev himself saw through it all.
18. For a discussion of *Dr. Zhivago* and the Soviet intelligentsia of the twenties, see my article in *Survey,* April–June 1958.
19. It is clear that there is now an elaborate game between censors, editors, and authors. It is unlikely that the former are deceived by the sometimes blatantly "Aesopian" techniques used to "put across" dissident ideas. One suspects that, as in liberal periods under the tsars, some censors are by no means unsympathetic to the censored. But the first rule of the game is that authors should adopt some disguise—even if it is as intentionally obvious as the masks of classical drama—so that the censor can also "cover" himself if called to account. The jubilee year has been notable for direct and indirect attacks on the censorship. Solzhenitsyn sent a strong denunciation of it (dated May 16) to participants at the Fourth Writers' Congress,

which, however, took good care not to discuss this or any other controversial issues.

20. There is a good portrait of the sort of timeserver who began to thrive in the thirties in the latest work by a repentant fellow-traveler: Valentin Katayev's *Holy Well* (*Novy Mir,* 1966). The figure of a "modern version of Bulgarin," the "human woodpecker" Prokhindeikin, almost seems intended to represent the author's alter ego of former years, as in the following description of him: "Like a shadow he never left me but followed a step behind. This most rare cross between a man and a woodpecker, a heavily built swine, a real animal, a buffoon, a timeserver, an archracketeer, an informer, a bootlicker, an extortioner and a bribetaker —a monstrous product of those far-off days. Yet I remembered him as a slim, hard-up young man, with a tiny spark in his breast." Katayev also tries to convey something of the unspeakable indignities to which he and the other writers of his generation were subjected if, like Zhivago's friend, they had "broken themselves in." In the *Holy Well* writers who had committed themselves in the thirties to socialist realism are symbolized by a talking cat which has been trained by its Georgian owner to mouth human words. For a brilliant examination of the fellow traveling ethos, see the article by B. Sarnov on Katayev's latest work in *Questions of Literature,* Jan. 1968.